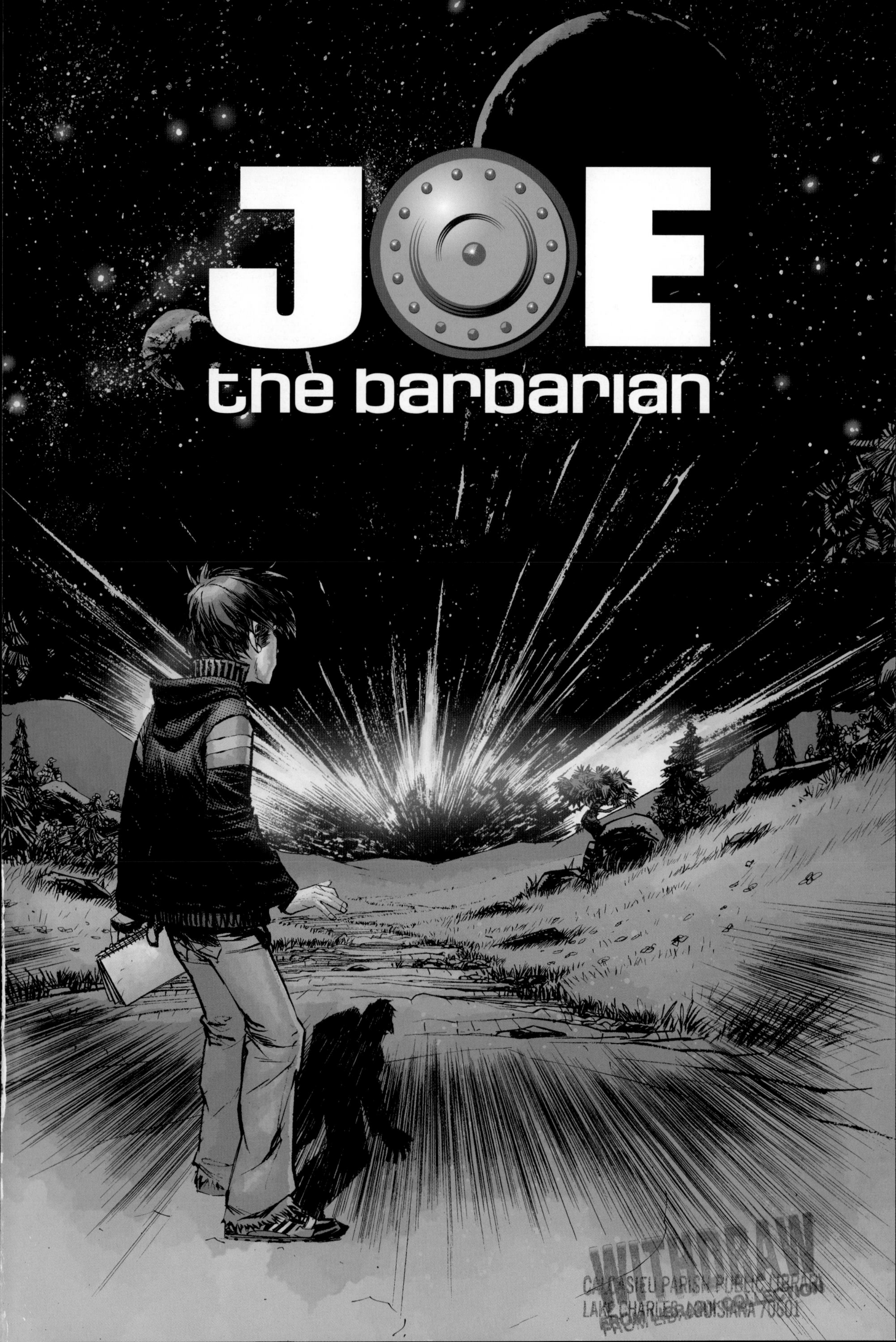
JOE
the barbarian

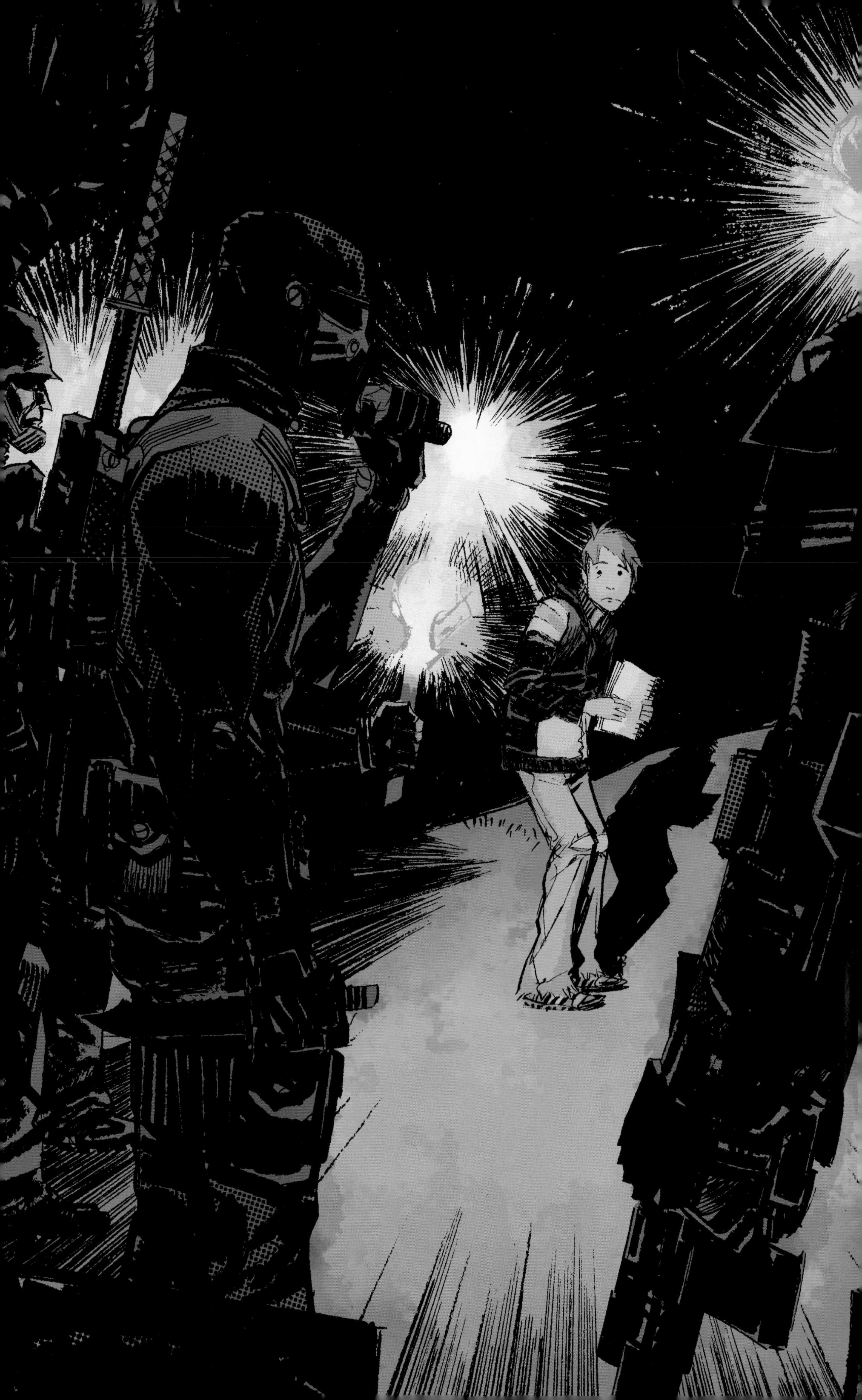

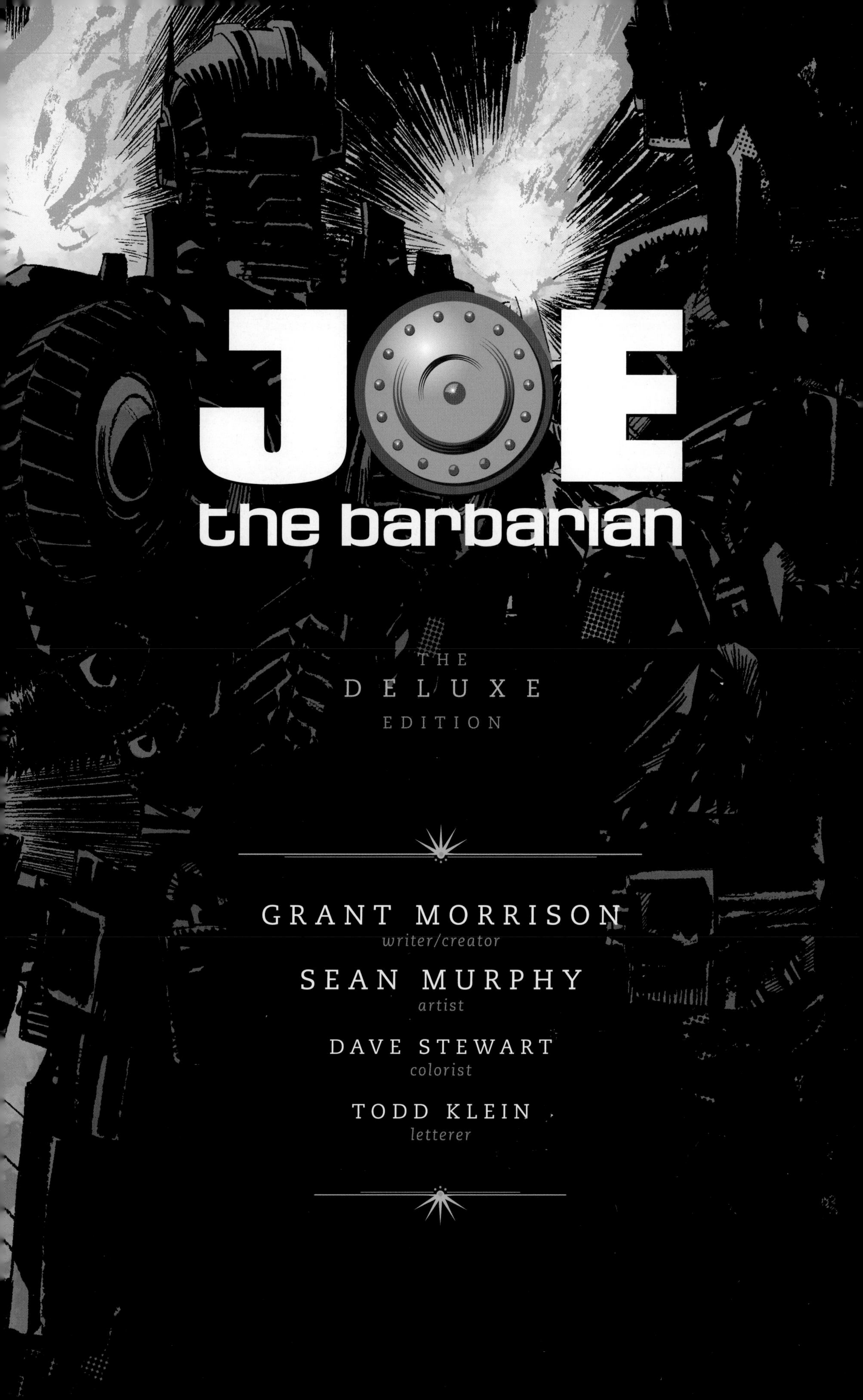

# JOE the barbarian

THE DELUXE EDITION


GRANT MORRISON
*writer/creator*

SEAN MURPHY
*artist*

DAVE STEWART
*colorist*

TODD KLEIN
*letterer*

Karen Berger
*Senior VP – Executive Editor, Vertigo and Editor – Original Series*

Pornsak Pichetshote
*Associate Editor – Original Series*

Ian Sattler
*Director – Editorial, Special Projects and Archival Editions*

Scott Nybakken
*Editor*

Robbin Brosterman
*Design Director – Books*

Brainchild Studios/NYC
*Publication Design*

Bob Harras
*VP – Editor in Chief*

Diane Nelson
*President*

Dan DiDio and Jim Lee
*Co-Publishers*

Geoff Johns
*Chief Creative Officer*

John Rood
*Executive VP – Sales, Marketing and Business Development*

Amy Genkins
*Senior VP – Business and Legal Affairs*

Nairi Gardiner
*Senior VP – Finance*

Jeff Boison
*VP – Publishing Operations*

Mark Chiarello
*VP – Art Direction and Design*

John Cunningham
*VP – Marketing*

Terri Cunningham
*VP – Talent Relations and Services*

Alison Gill
*Senior VP – Manufacturing and Operations*

David Hyde
*VP – Publicity*

Hank Kanalz
*Senior VP – Digital*

Jay Kogan
*VP – Business and Legal Affairs, Publishing*

Jack Mahan
*VP – Business Affairs, Talent*

Nick Napolitano
*VP – Manufacturing Administration*

Sue Pohja
*VP – Book Sales*

Courtney Simmons
*Senior VP – Publicity*

Bob Wayne
*Senior VP – Sales*

**JOE THE BARBARIAN: THE DELUXE EDITION**





DC Comics, 1700 Broadway, New York, NY 10019
A Warner Bros. Entertainment Company
Printed in the USA. 9/23/11. First printing.
ISBN: 978-1-4102-2971-9

SUSTAINABLE FORESTRY INITIATIVE
Certified Chain of Custody
Promoting Sustainable Forest Management

Fiber used in this product line meets the sourcing requirements of the SFI program. www.sfiprogram.org SGS-SFI/COC-US10/81072

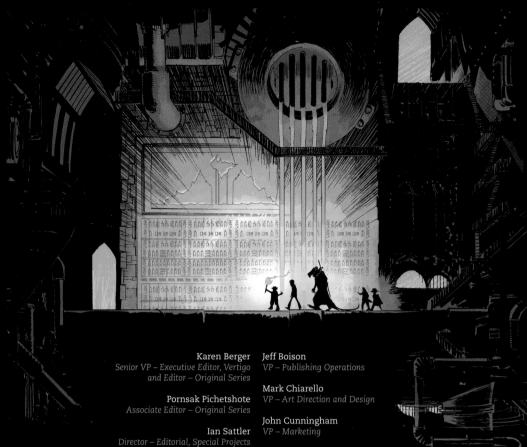

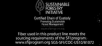

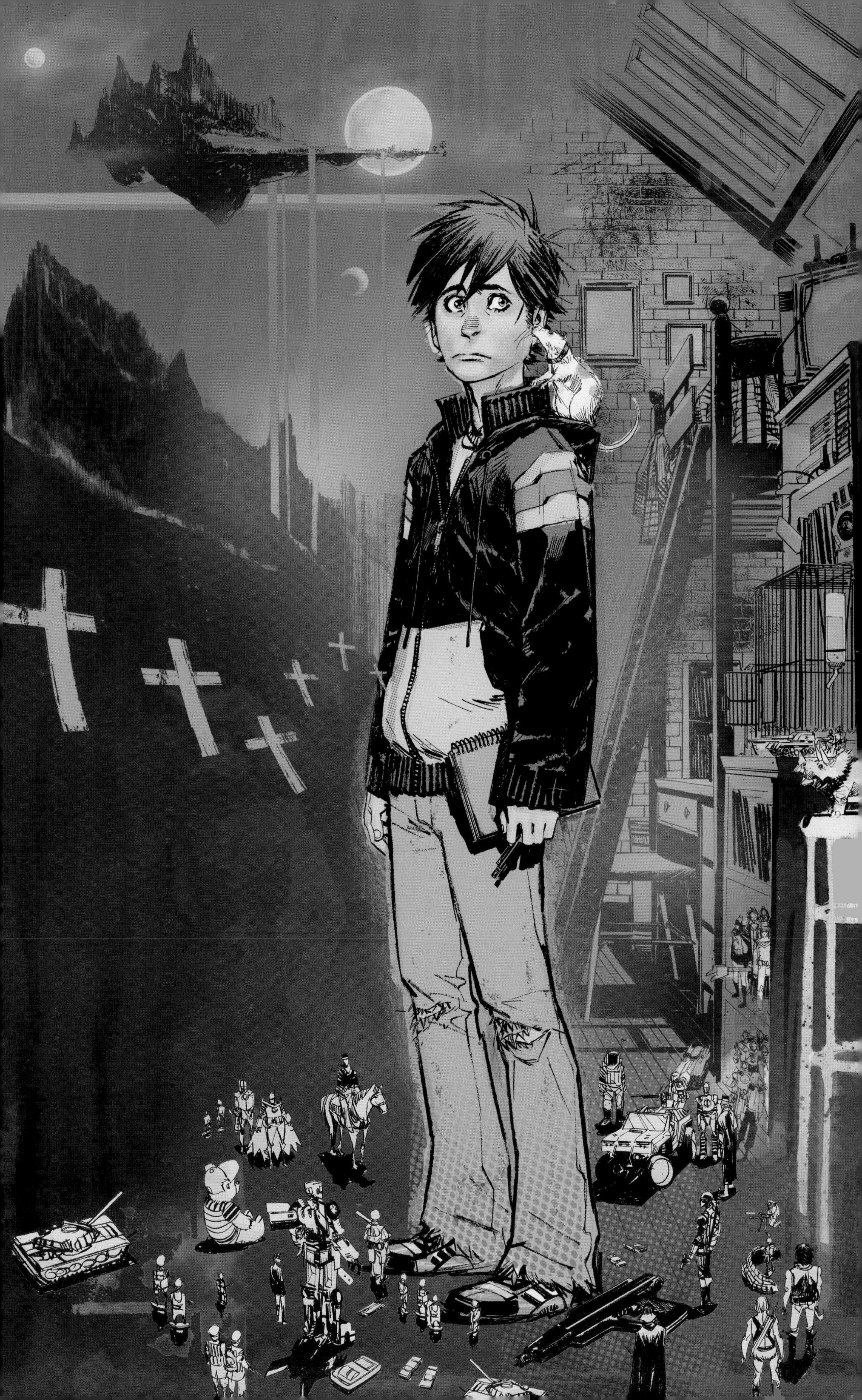

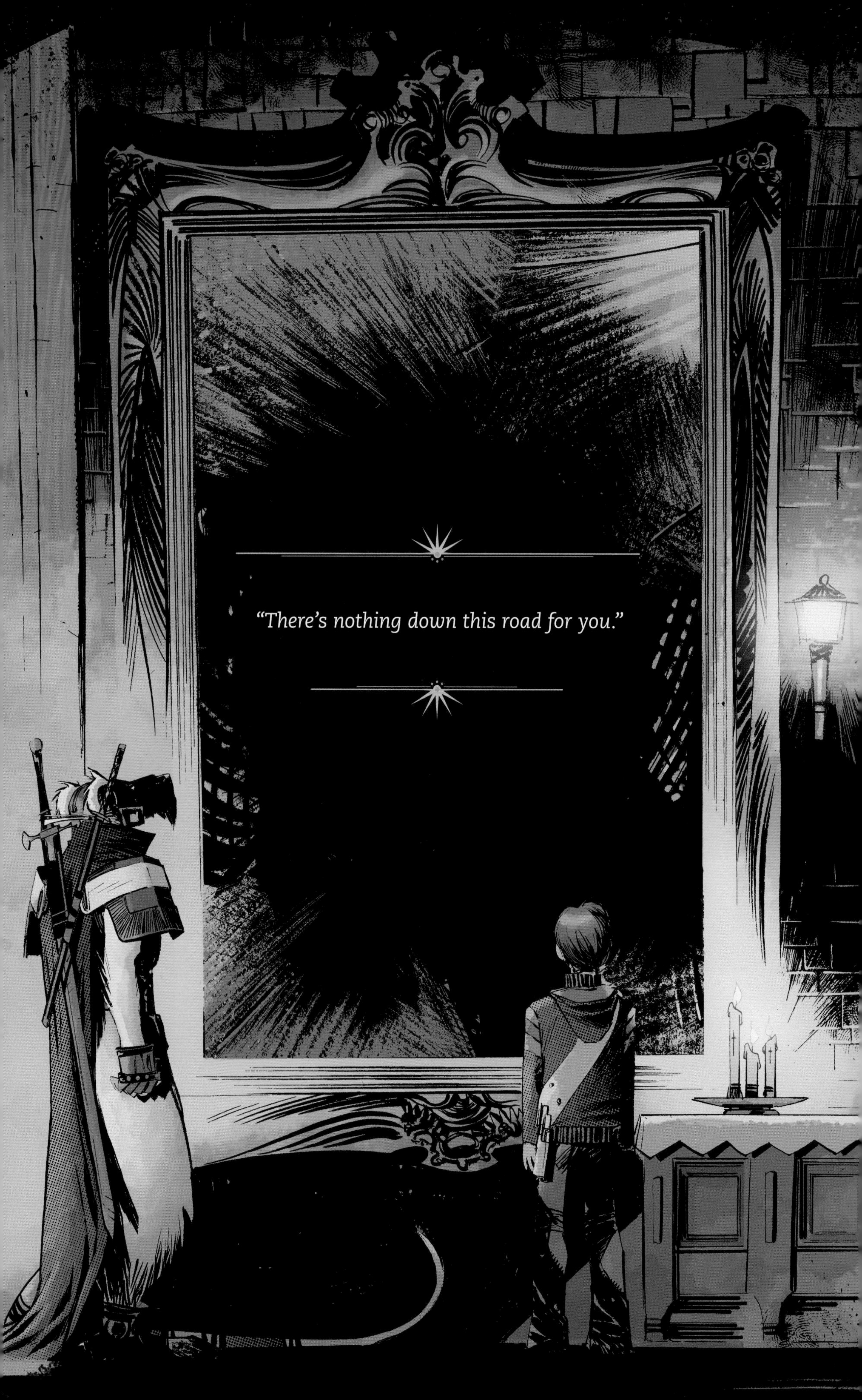
*"There's nothing down this road for you."*

# chapter 1: hypo

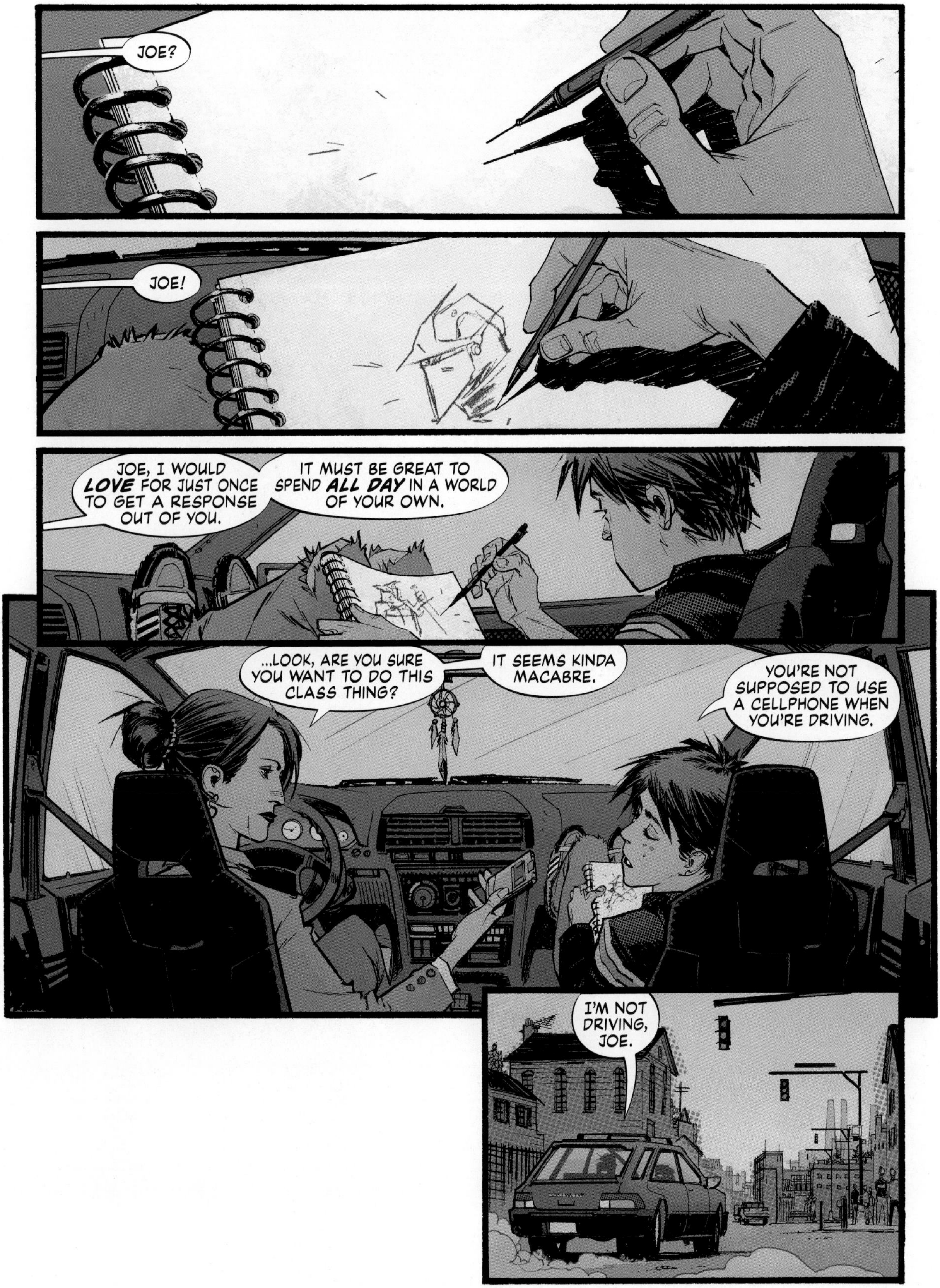
JOE?
JOE!
JOE, I WOULD LOVE FOR JUST ONCE TO GET A RESPONSE OUT OF YOU.
IT MUST BE GREAT TO SPEND ALL DAY IN A WORLD OF YOUR OWN.
...LOOK, ARE YOU SURE YOU WANT TO DO THIS CLASS THING?
IT SEEMS KINDA MACABRE.
YOU'RE NOT SUPPOSED TO USE A CELLPHONE WHEN YOU'RE DRIVING.
I'M NOT DRIVING, JOE.

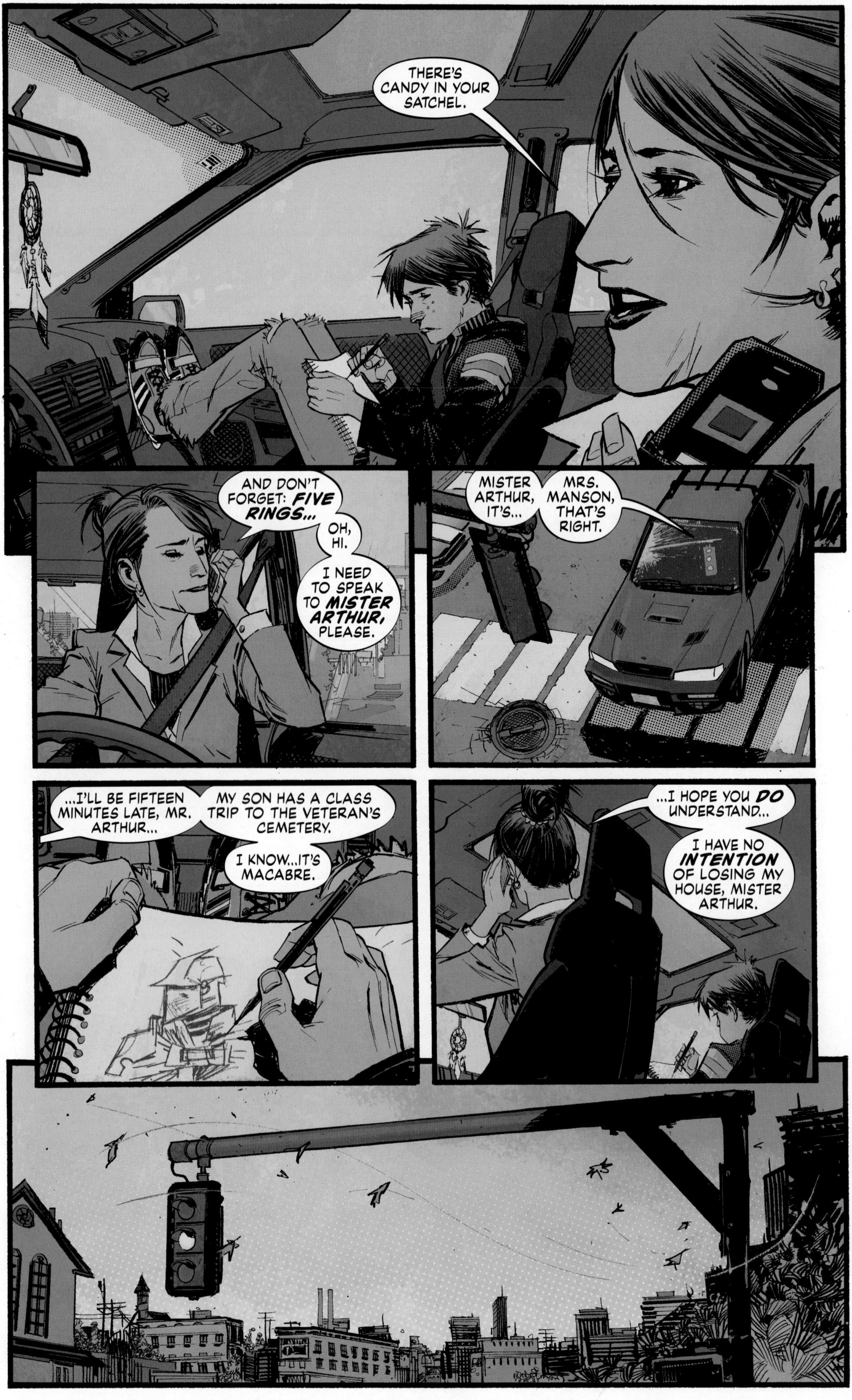
THERE'S CANDY IN YOUR SATCHEL.
AND DON'T FORGET: FIVE RINGS...
OH, HI.
I NEED TO SPEAK TO MISTER ARTHUR, PLEASE.
MISTER ARTHUR, IT'S...
MRS. MANSON, THAT'S RIGHT.
...I'LL BE FIFTEEN MINUTES LATE, MR. ARTHUR...
MY SON HAS A CLASS TRIP TO THE VETERAN'S CEMETERY.
I KNOW...IT'S MACABRE.
...I HOPE YOU DO UNDERSTAND...
I HAVE NO INTENTION OF LOSING MY HOUSE, MISTER ARTHUR.

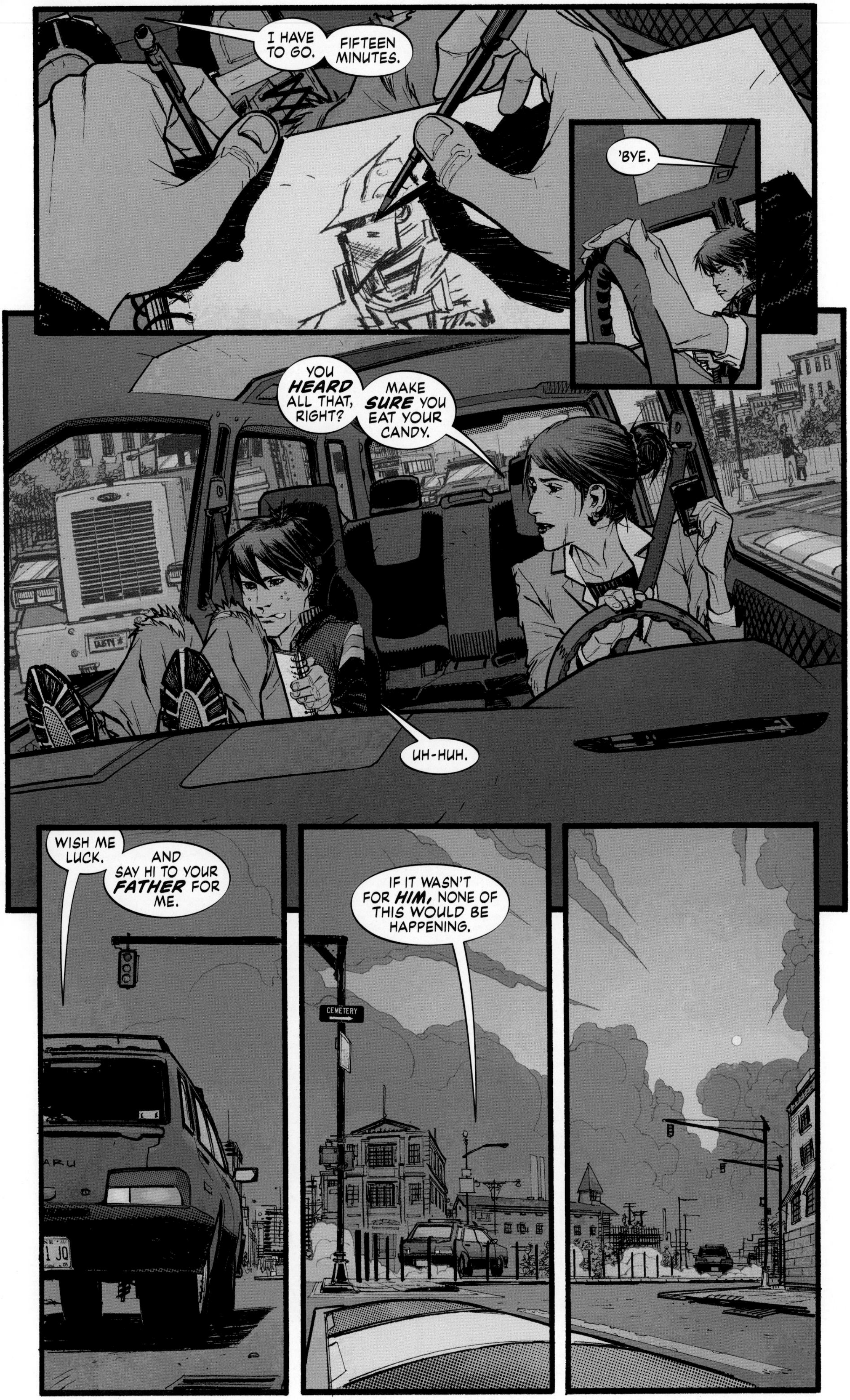
I HAVE TO GO.
FIFTEEN MINUTES.
'BYE.
YOU HEARD ALL THAT, RIGHT?
MAKE SURE YOU EAT YOUR CANDY.
UH-HUH.
WISH ME LUCK.
AND SAY HI TO YOUR FATHER FOR ME.
IF IT WASN'T FOR HIM, NONE OF THIS WOULD BE HAPPENING.
CEMETERY

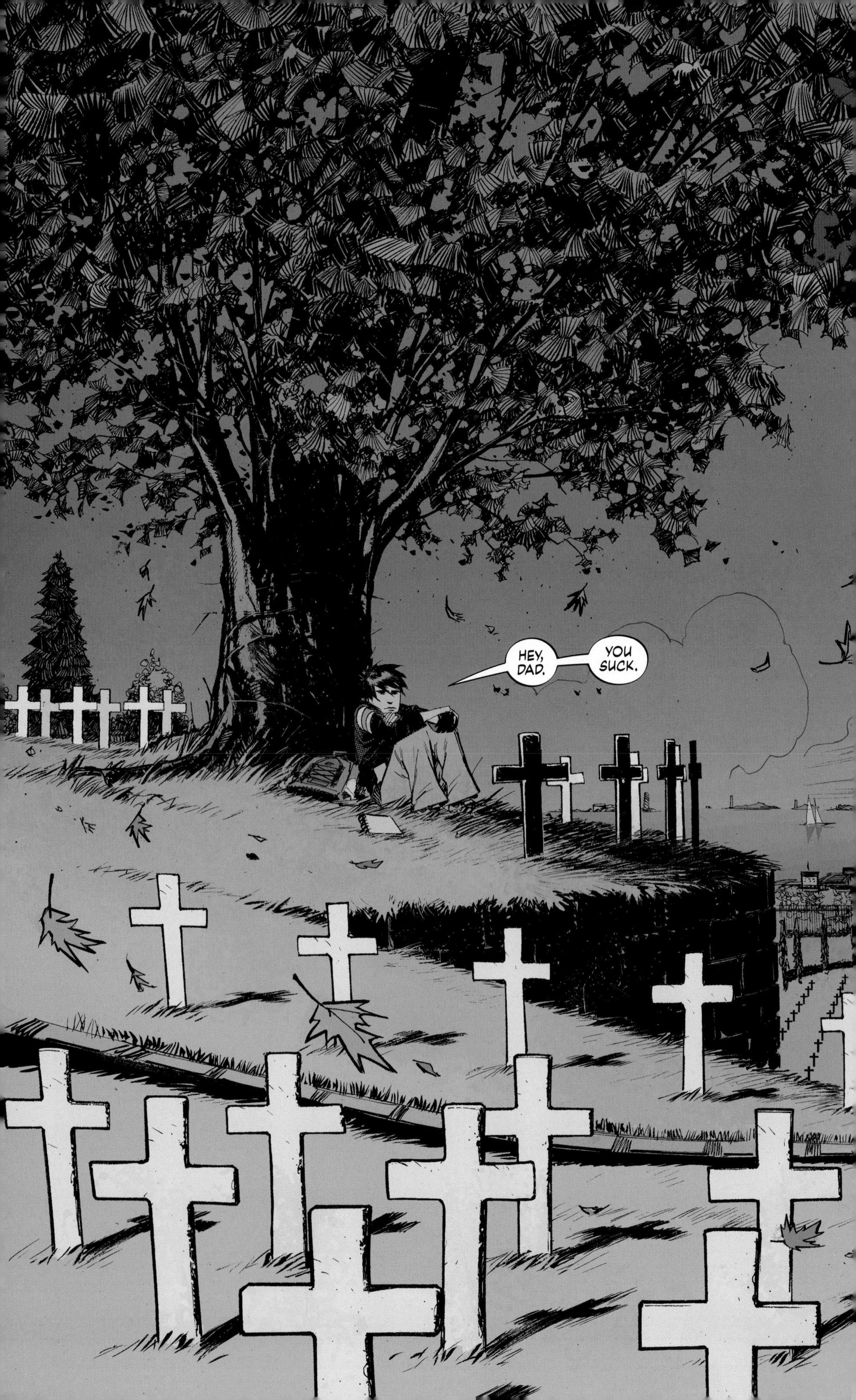
HEY, DAD.
YOU SUCK.

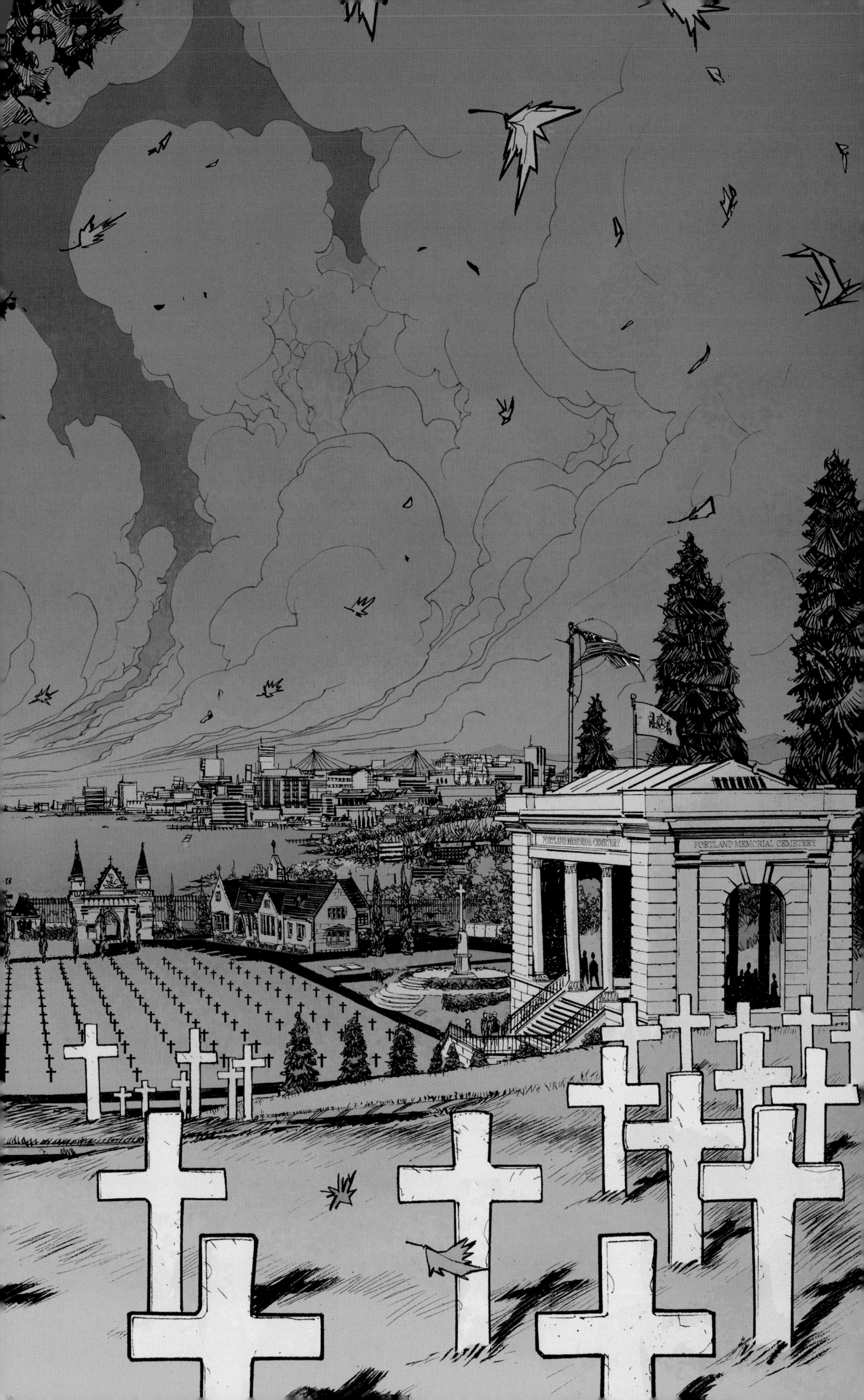
PORTLAND MEMORIAL CEMETERY
PORTLAND MEMORIAL CEMETERY

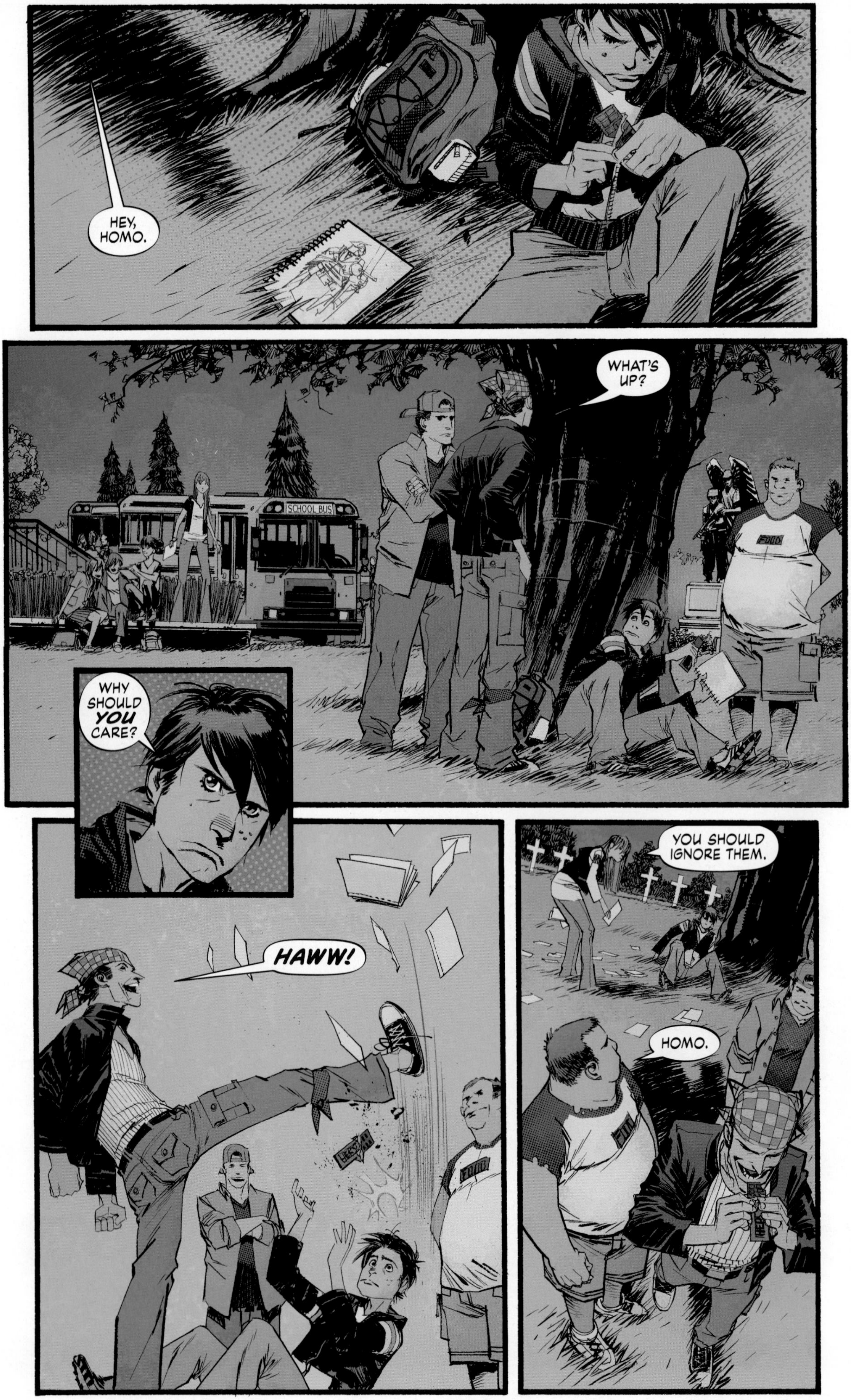
HEY, HOMO.
WHAT'S UP?
WHY SHOULD *YOU* CARE?
HAWW!
YOU SHOULD IGNORE THEM.
HOMO.

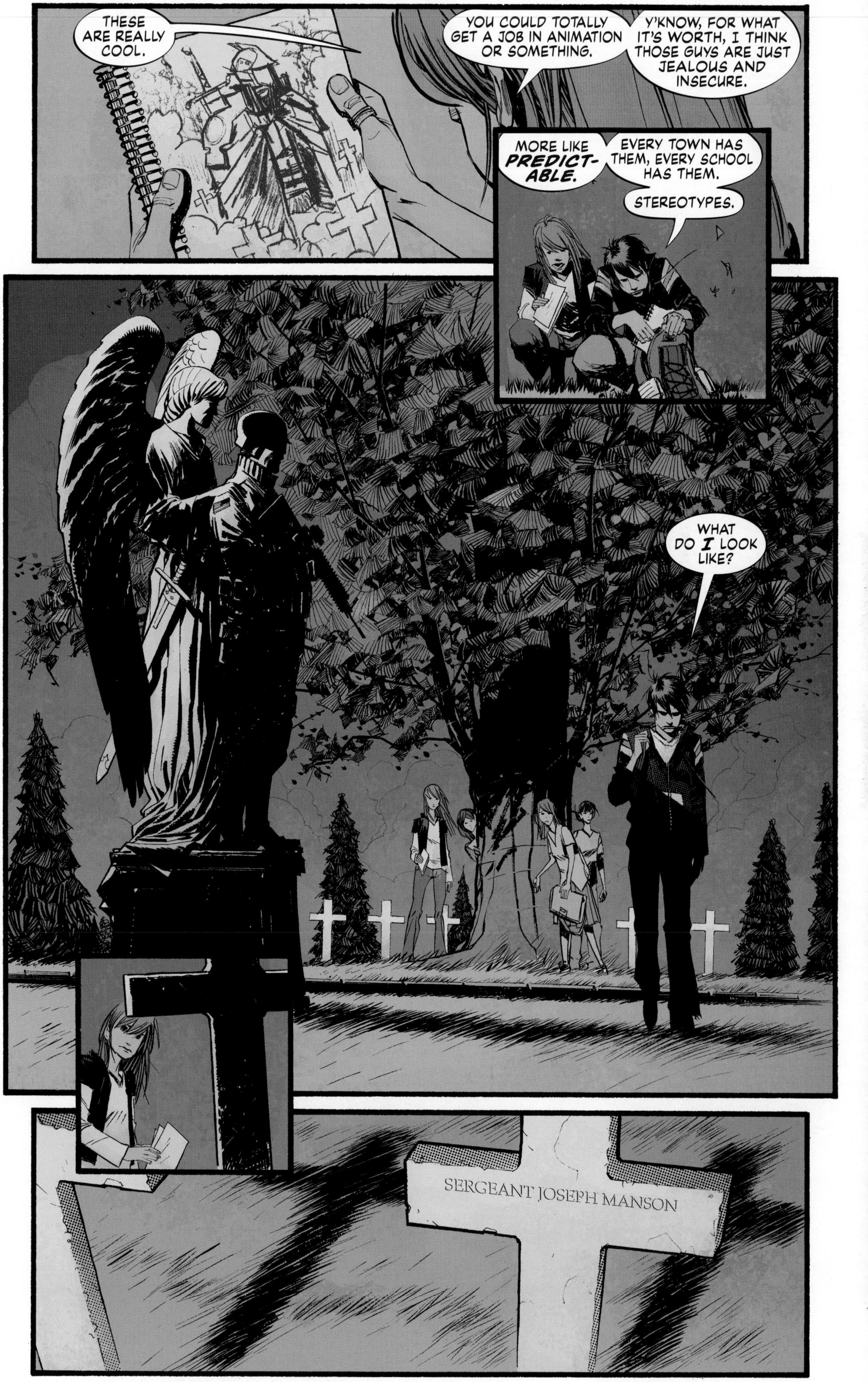
THESE ARE REALLY COOL.
YOU COULD TOTALLY GET A JOB IN ANIMATION OR SOMETHING.
Y'KNOW, FOR WHAT IT'S WORTH, I THINK THOSE GUYS ARE JUST JEALOUS AND INSECURE.
MORE LIKE *PREDICTABLE.*
EVERY TOWN HAS THEM, EVERY SCHOOL HAS THEM.
STEREOTYPES.
WHAT DO *I* LOOK LIKE?
SERGEANT JOSEPH MANSON

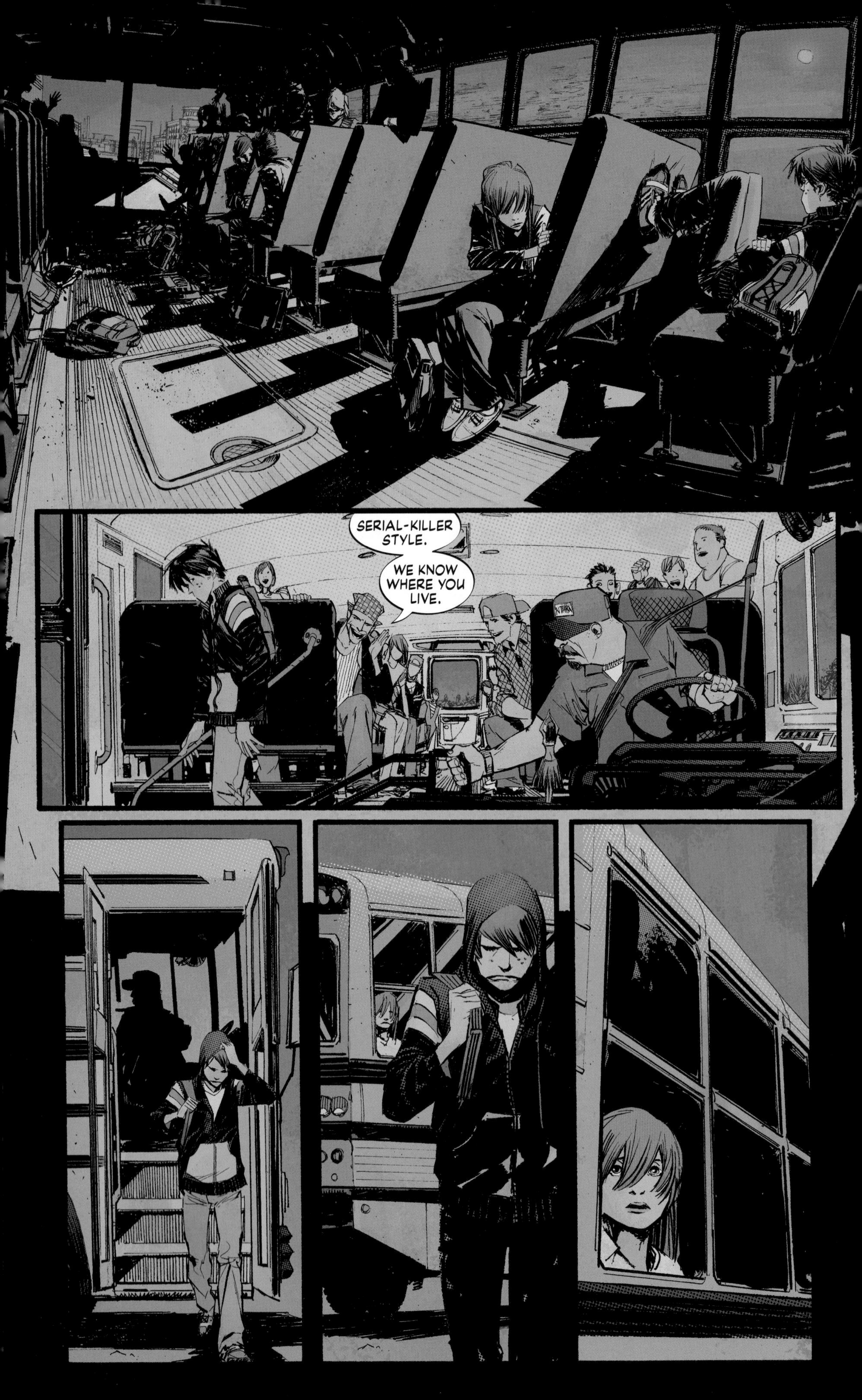
SERIAL-KILLER STYLE.
WE KNOW WHERE YOU LIVE.

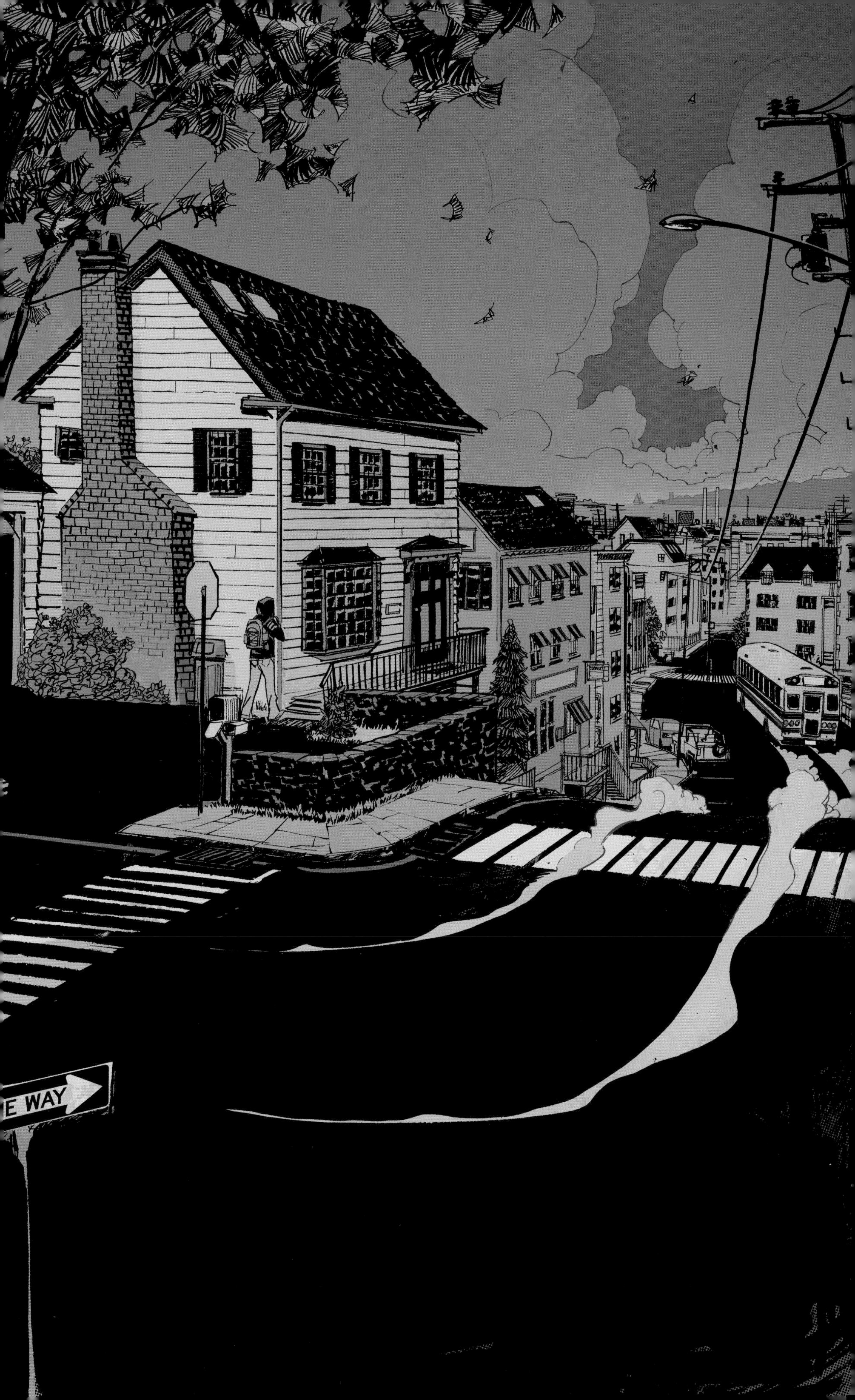
E WAY

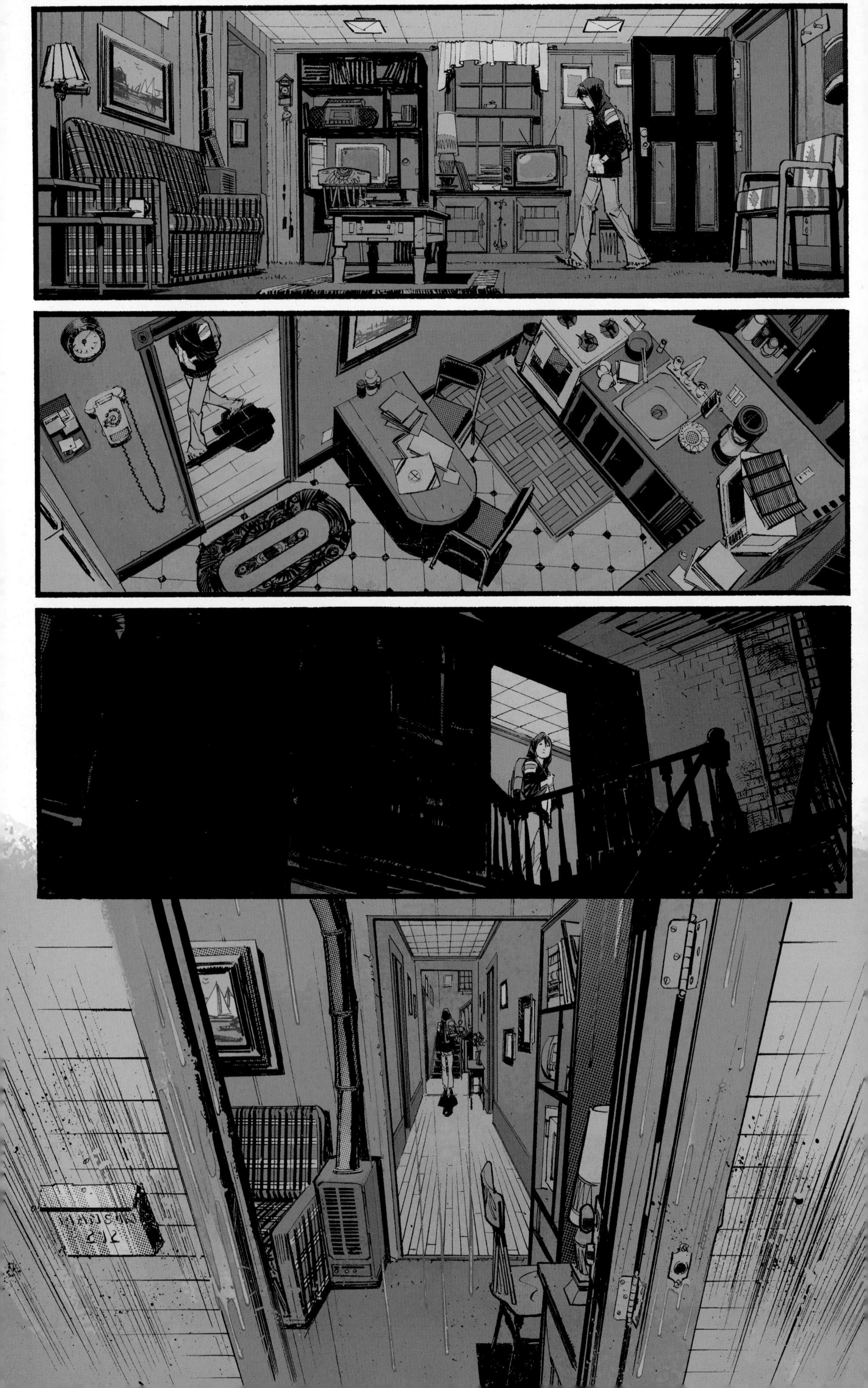

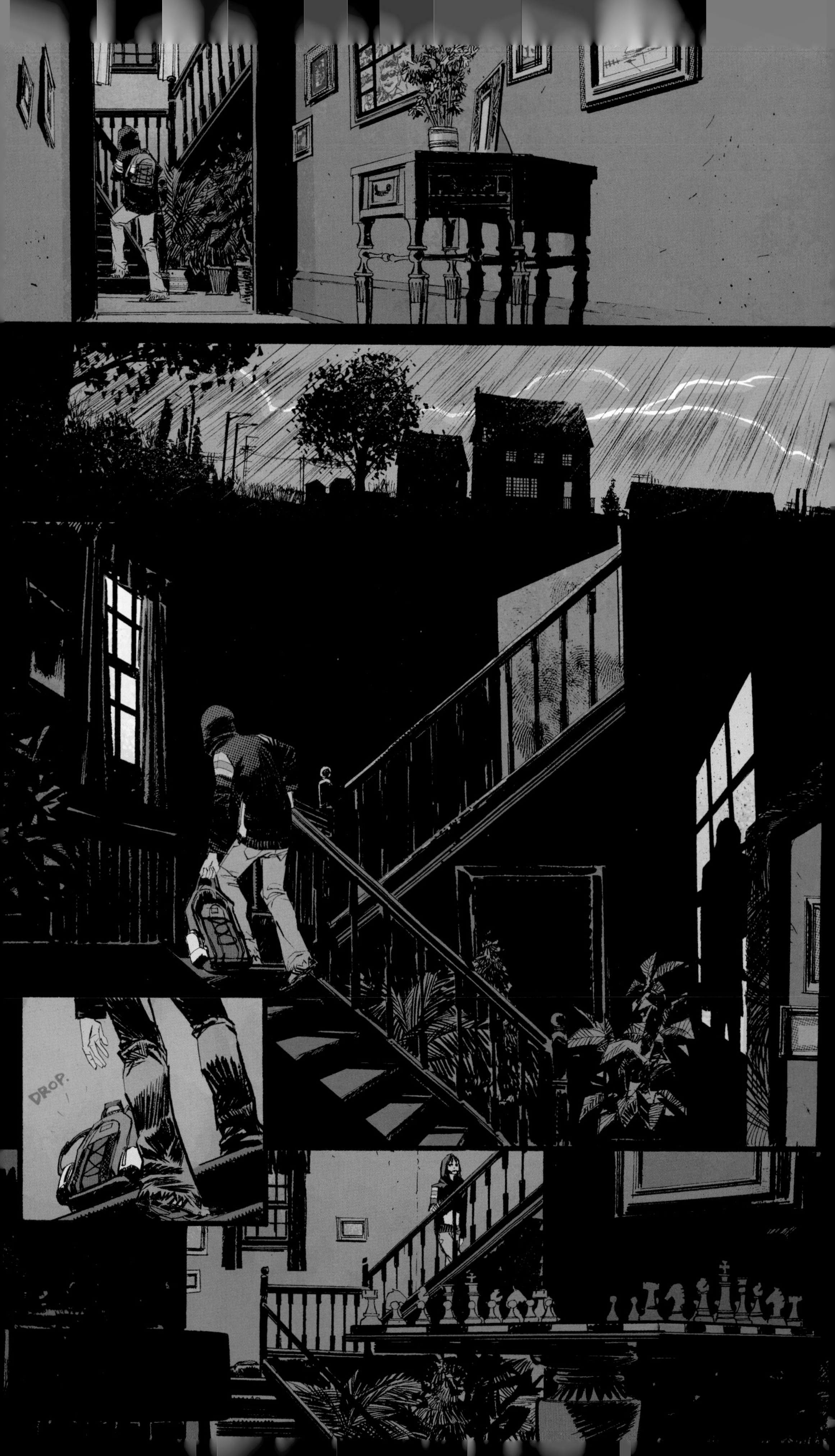
DROP.

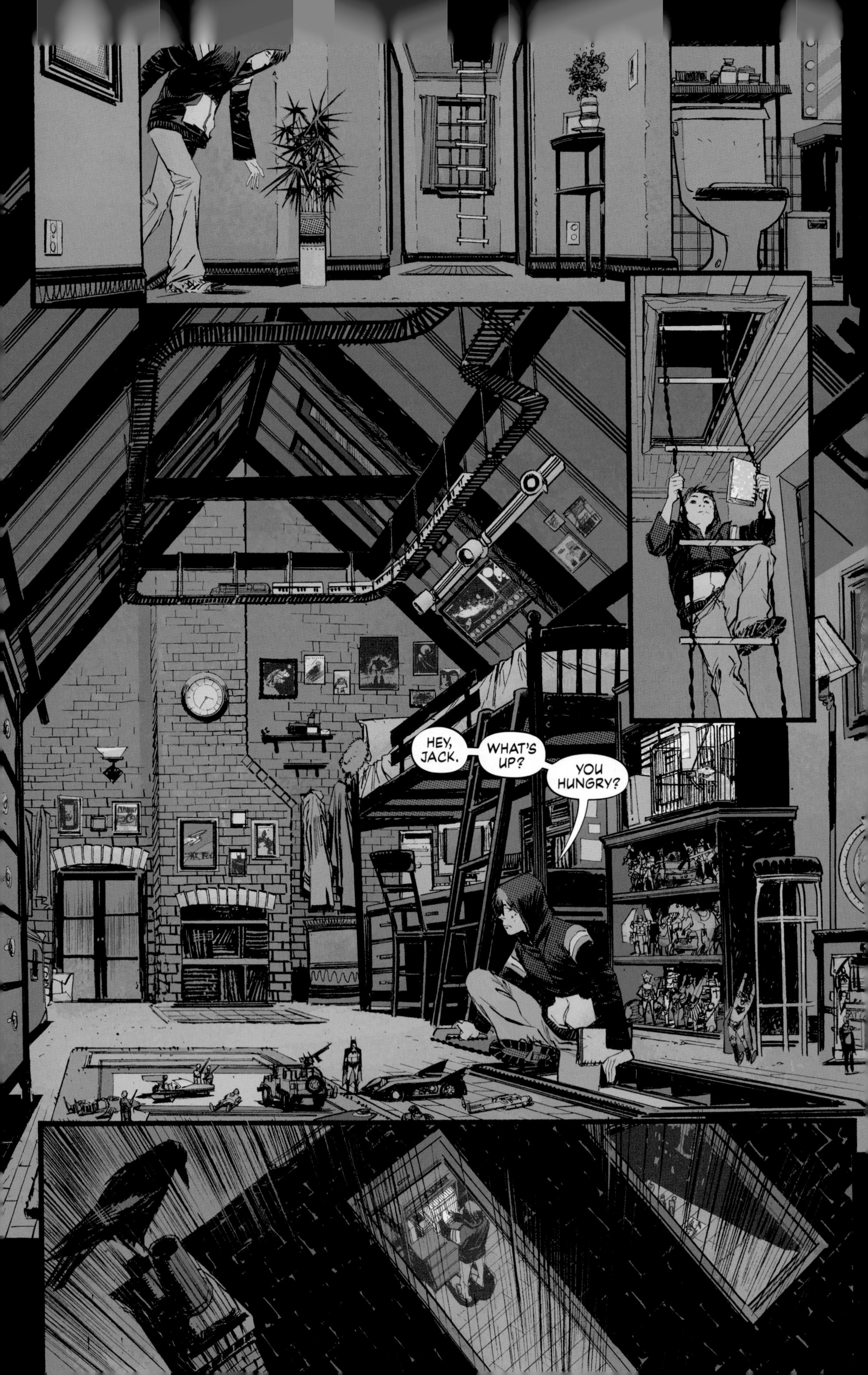
HEY, JACK.
WHAT'S UP?
YOU HUNGRY?

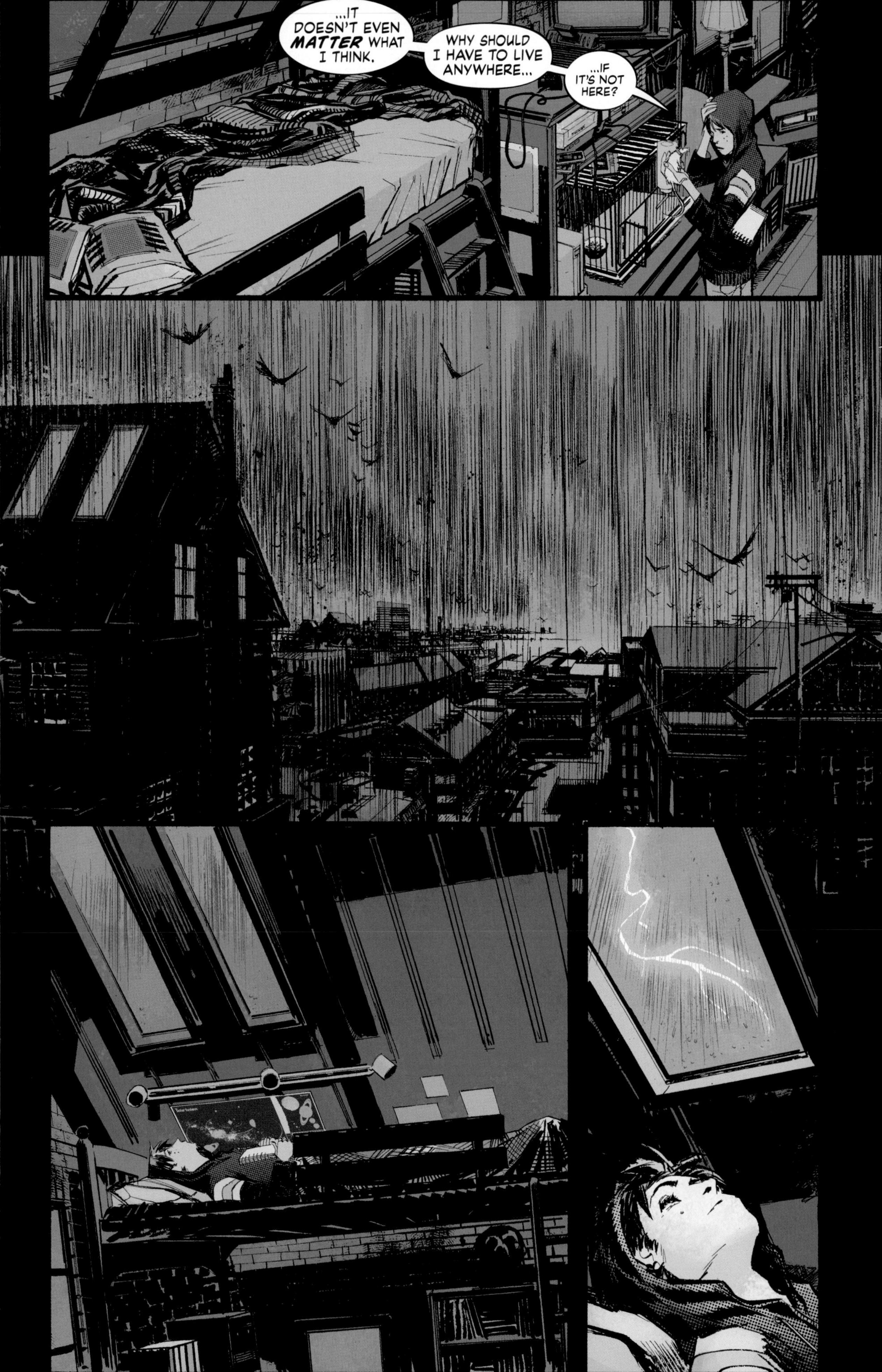
...IT DOESN'T EVEN MATTER WHAT I THINK.
WHY SHOULD I HAVE TO LIVE ANYWHERE...
...IF IT'S NOT HERE?

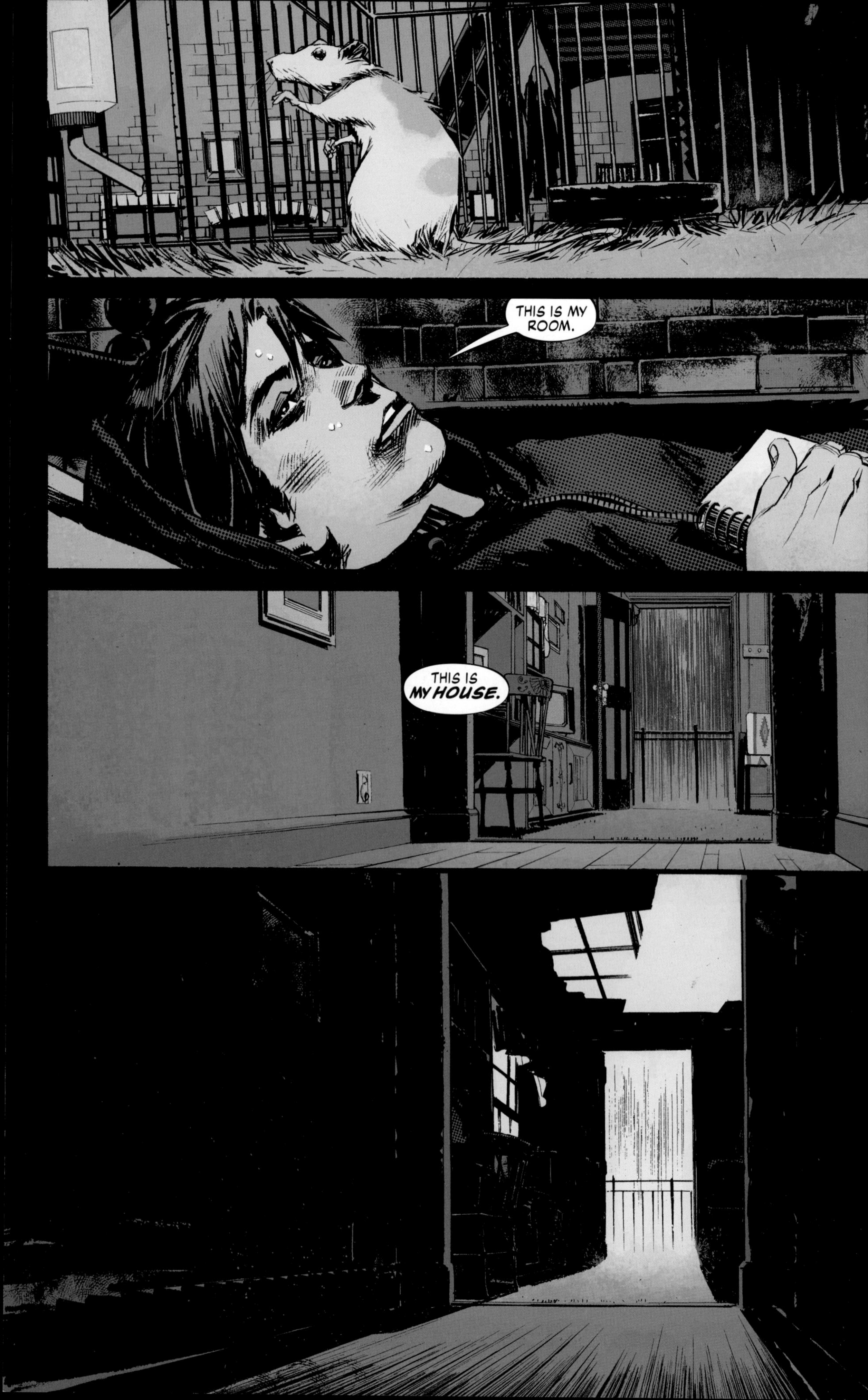
THIS IS MY ROOM.
THIS IS MY HOUSE.

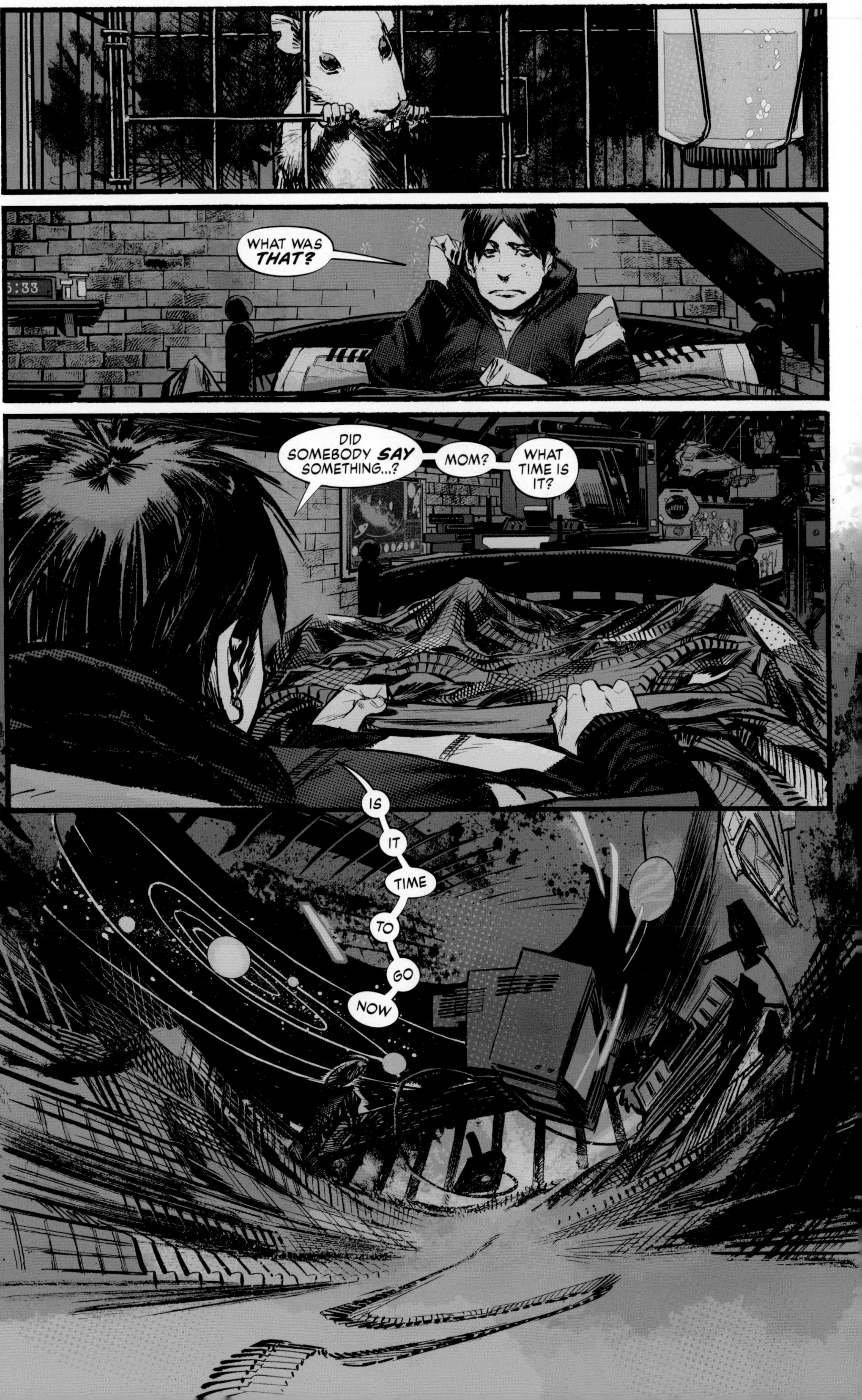
WHAT WAS *THAT?*
DID SOMEBODY *SAY* SOMETHING...?
MOM?
WHAT TIME IS IT?
IS IT TIME TO GO NOW

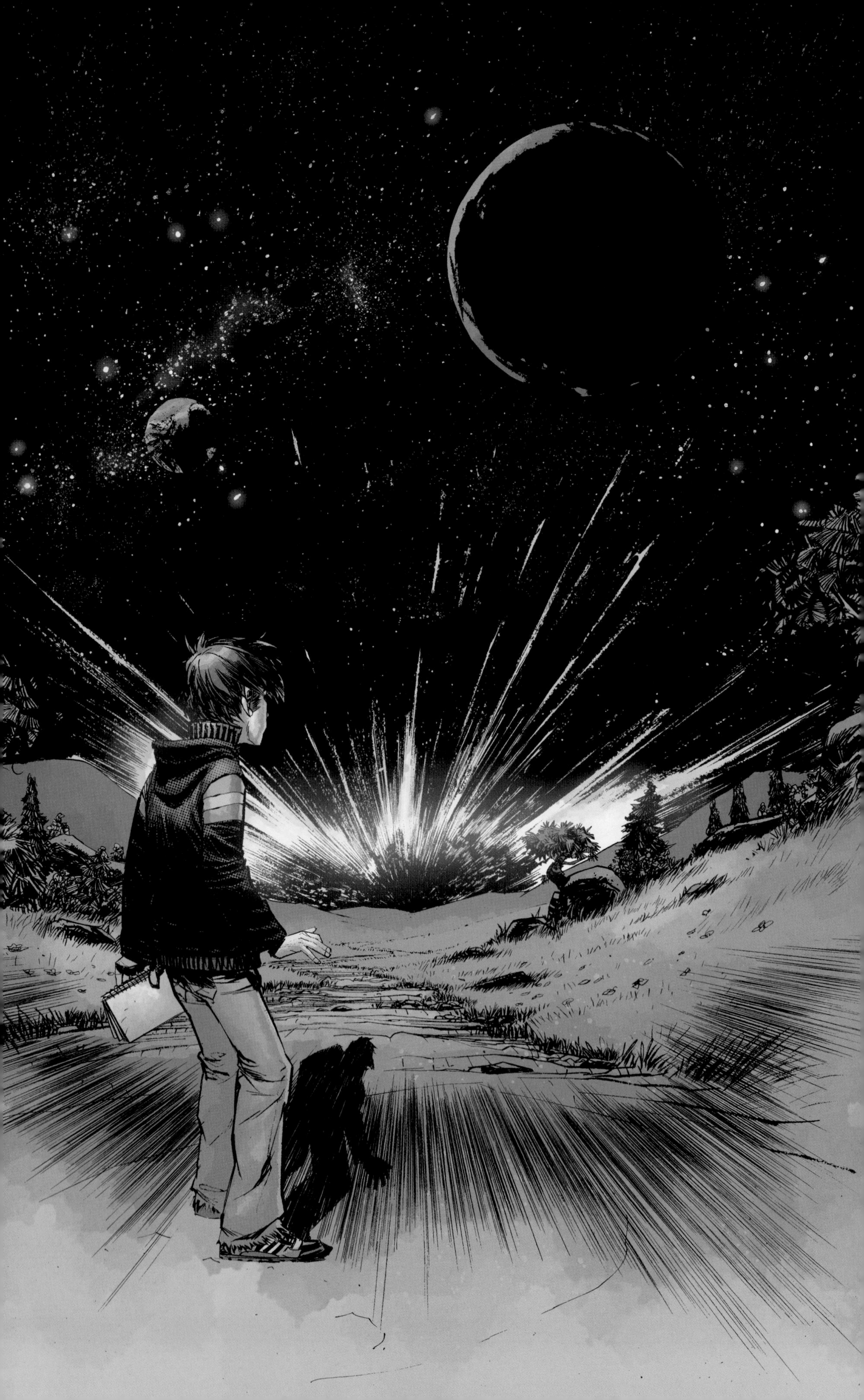

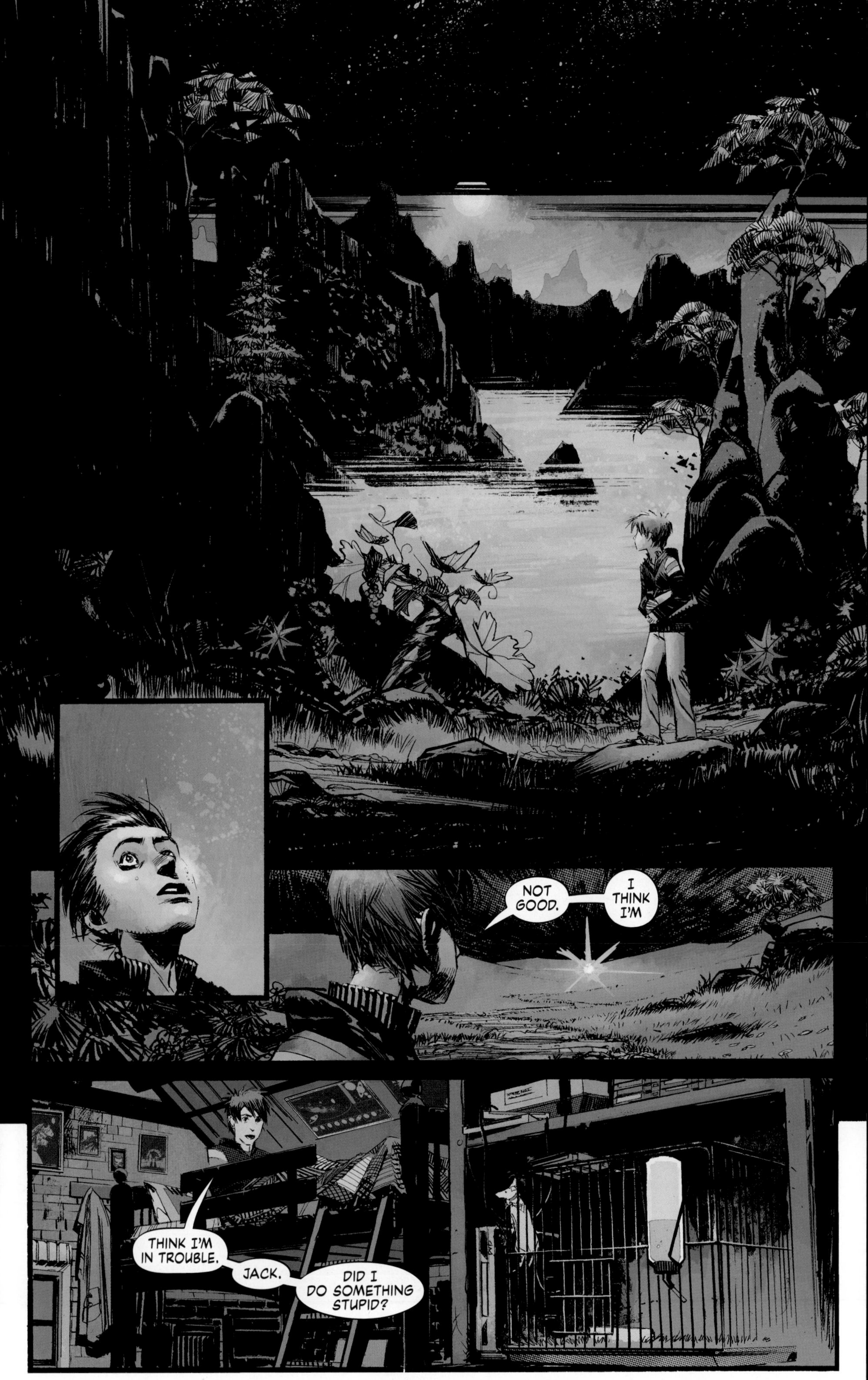
NOT GOOD.
I THINK I'M
THINK I'M IN TROUBLE.
JACK.
DID I DO SOMETHING STUPID?

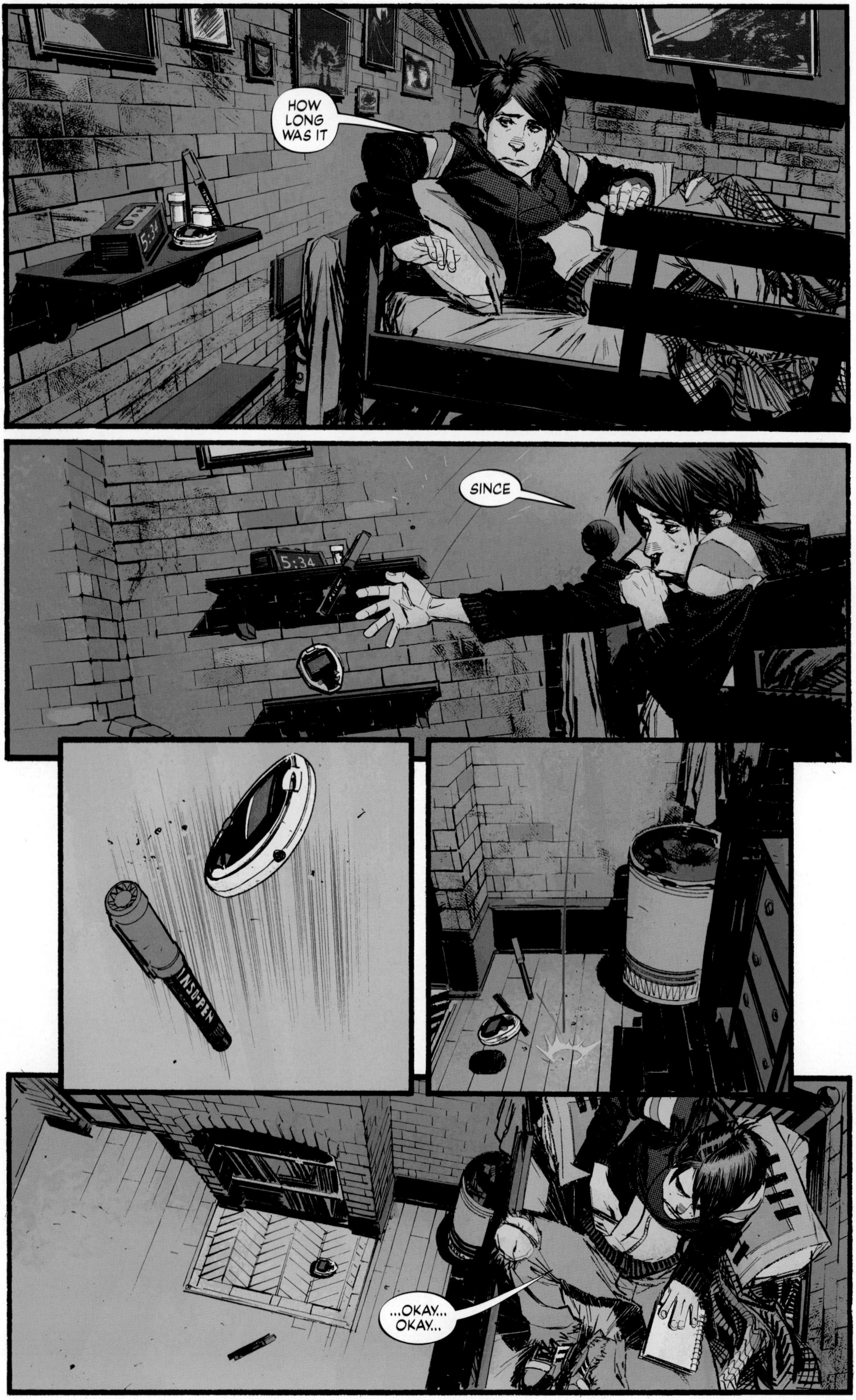
HOW LONG WAS IT
SINCE
...OKAY... OKAY...

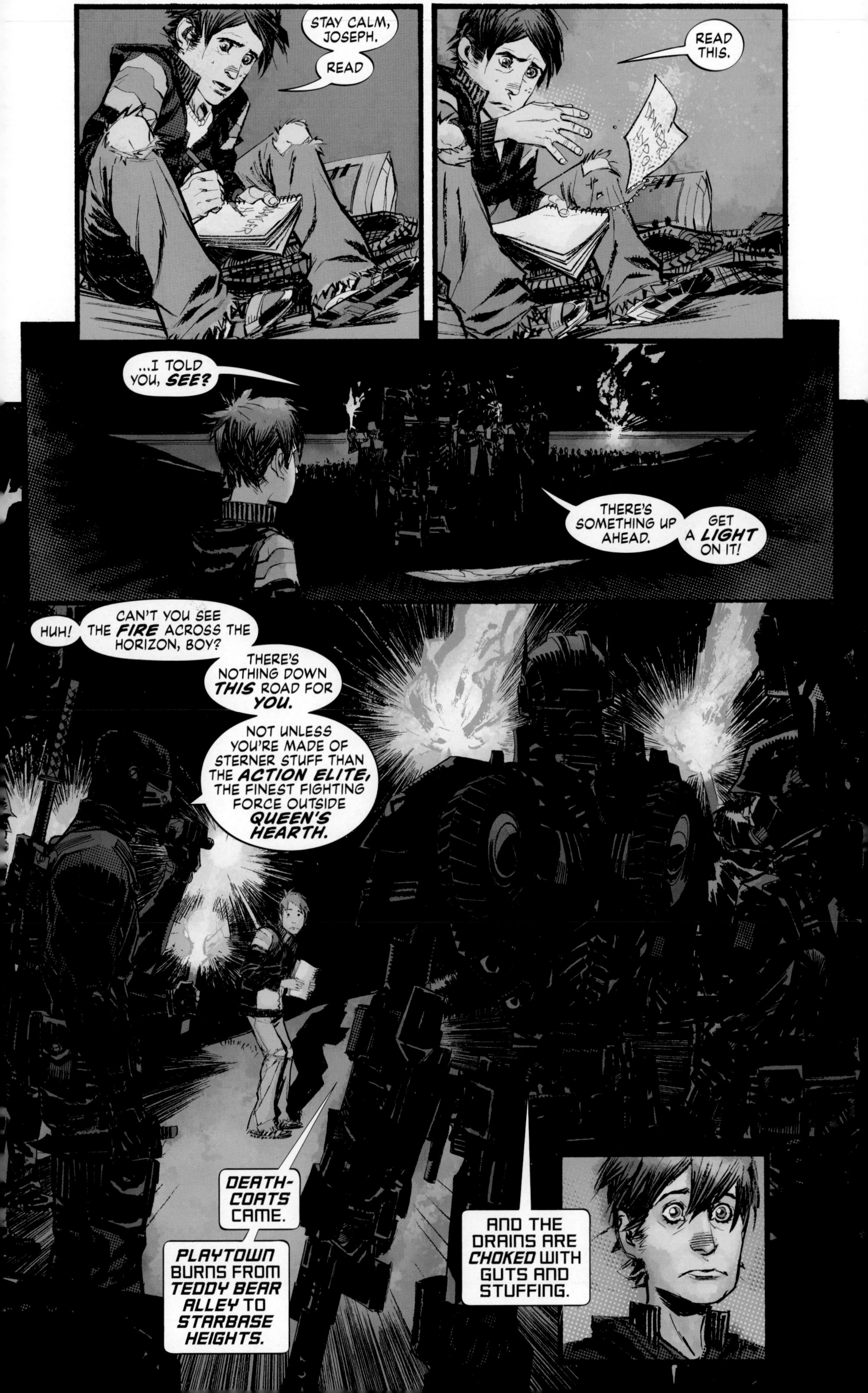

STAY CALM, JOSEPH.
READ
READ THIS.
DANGER HYPO
...I TOLD YOU, SEE?
THERE'S SOMETHING UP AHEAD.
GET A LIGHT ON IT!
HUH!
CAN'T YOU SEE THE FIRE ACROSS THE HORIZON, BOY?
THERE'S NOTHING DOWN THIS ROAD FOR YOU.
NOT UNLESS YOU'RE MADE OF STERNER STUFF THAN THE ACTION ELITE, THE FINEST FIGHTING FORCE OUTSIDE QUEEN'S HEARTH.
DEATH-COATS CAME.
PLAYTOWN BURNS FROM TEDDY BEAR ALLEY TO STARBASE HEIGHTS.
AND THE DRAINS ARE CHOKED WITH GUTS AND STUFFING.

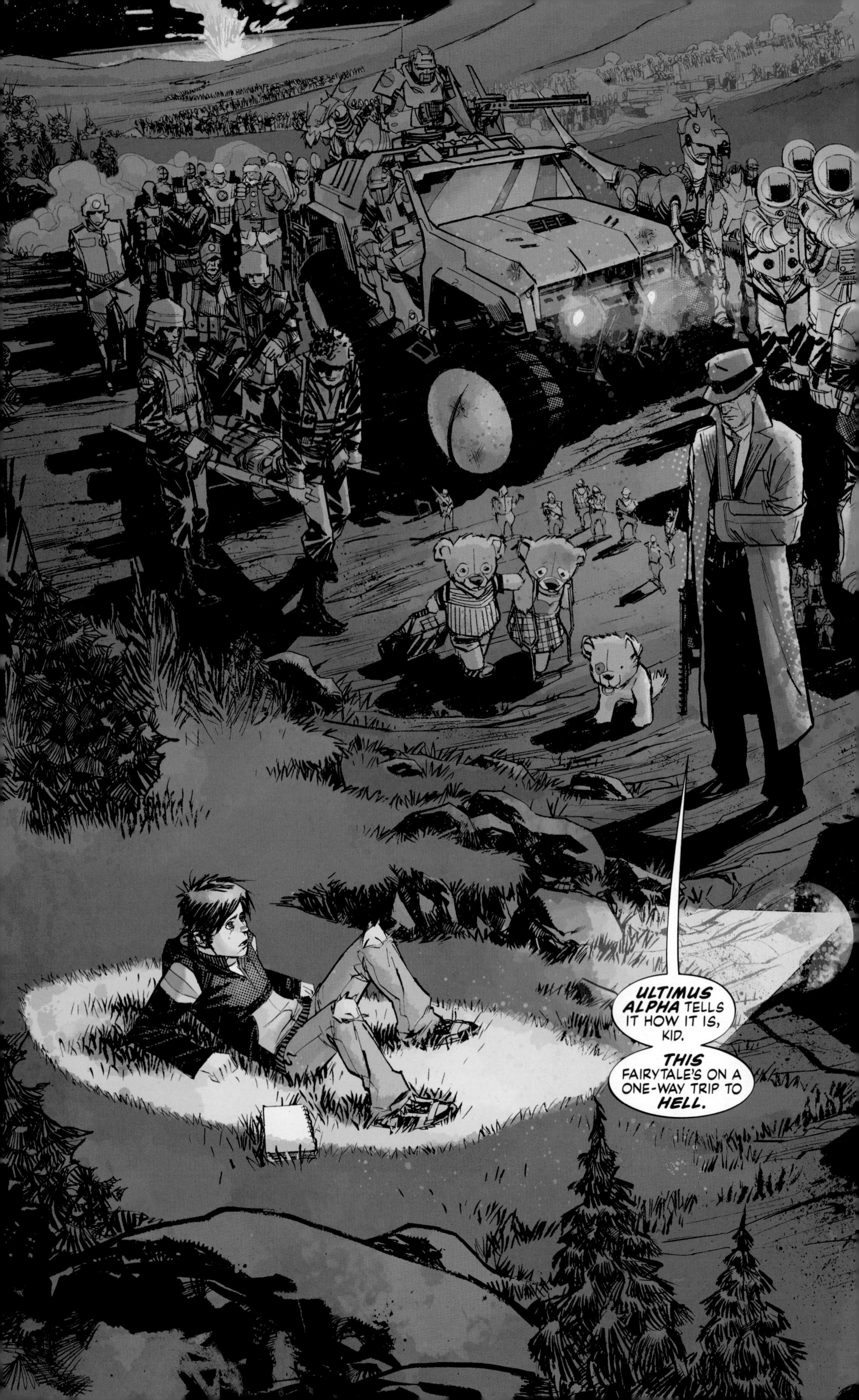

ULTIMUS ALPHA TELLS IT HOW IT IS, KID.
THIS FAIRYTALE'S ON A ONE-WAY TRIP TO HELL.

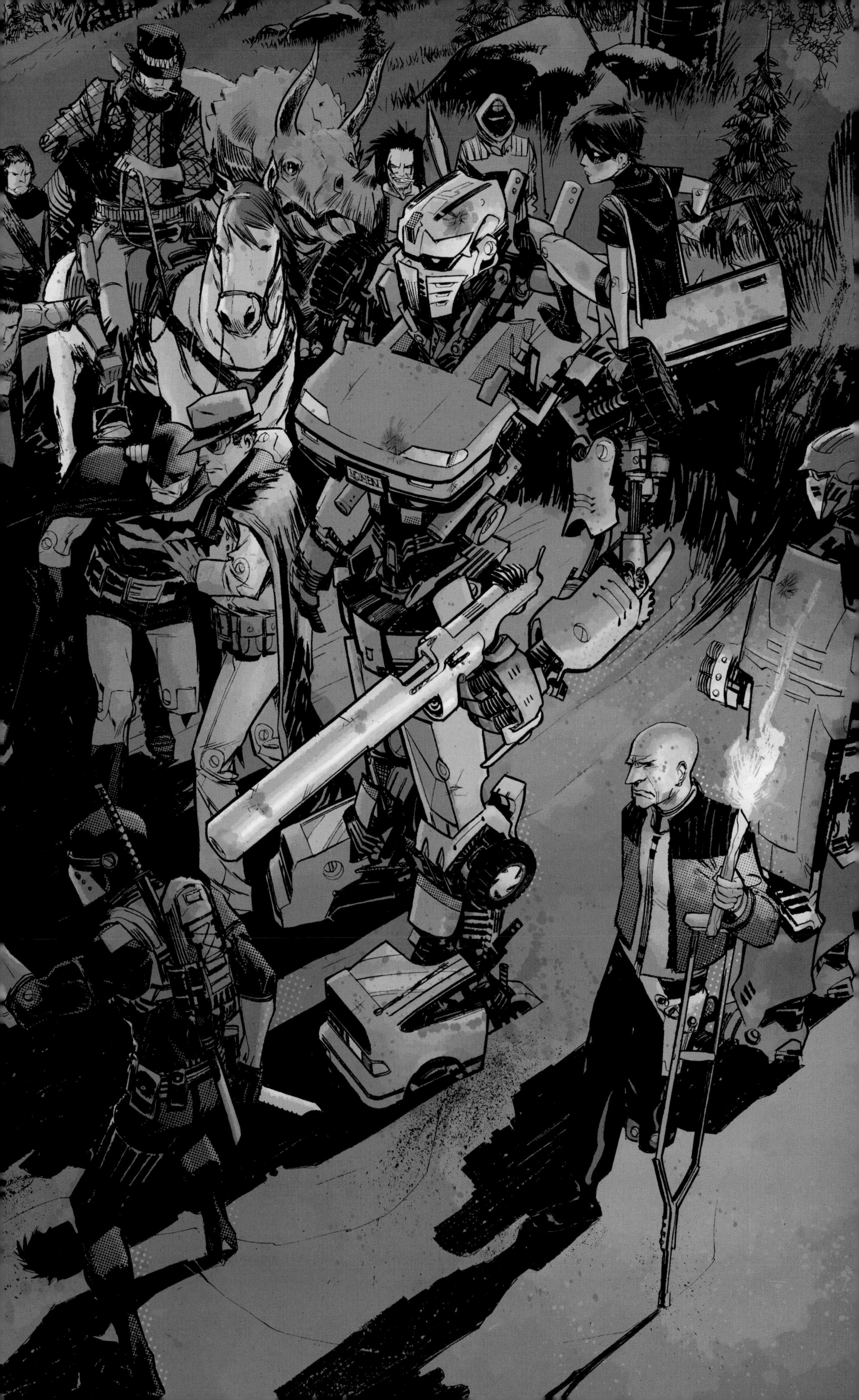

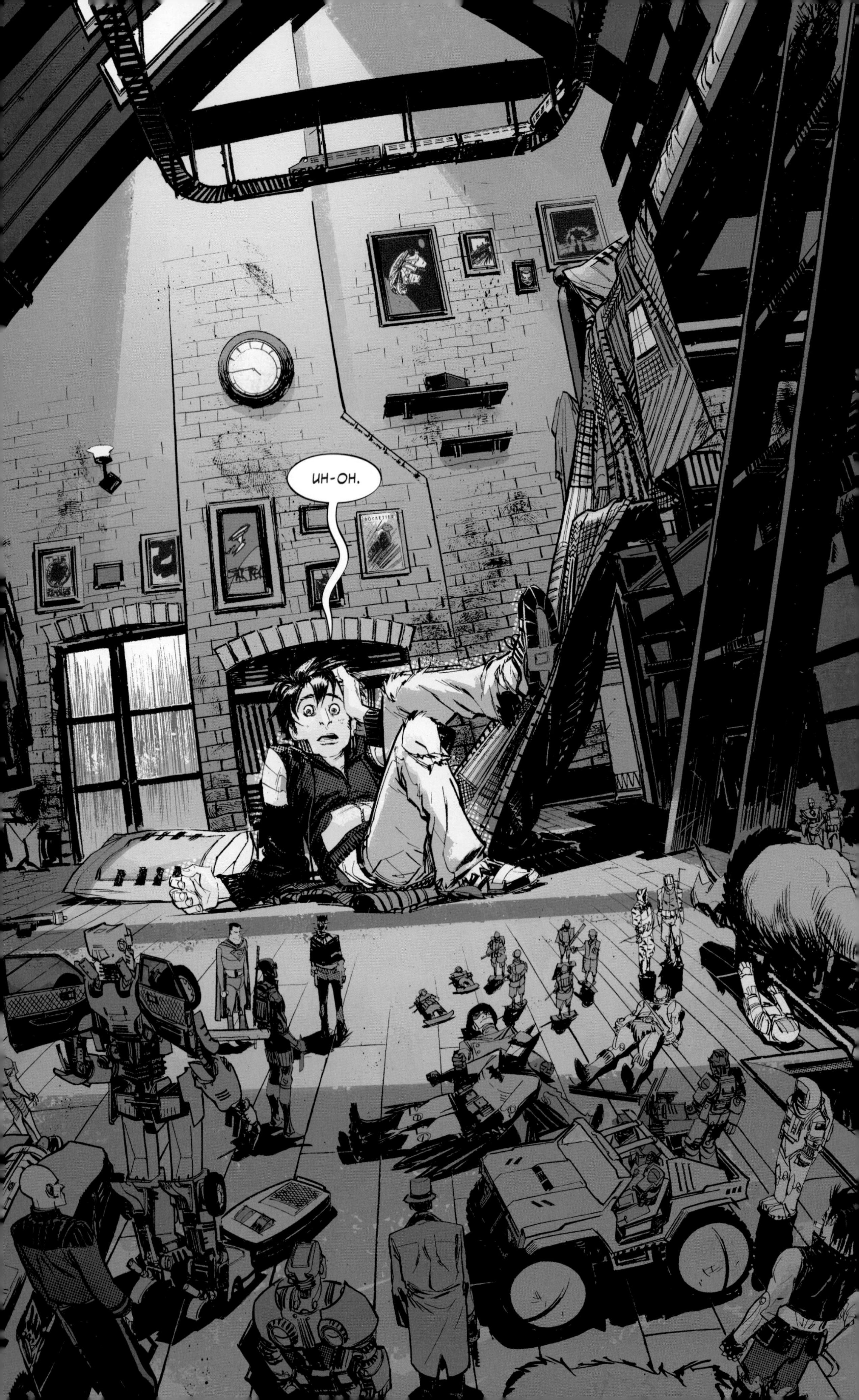
UH-OH.

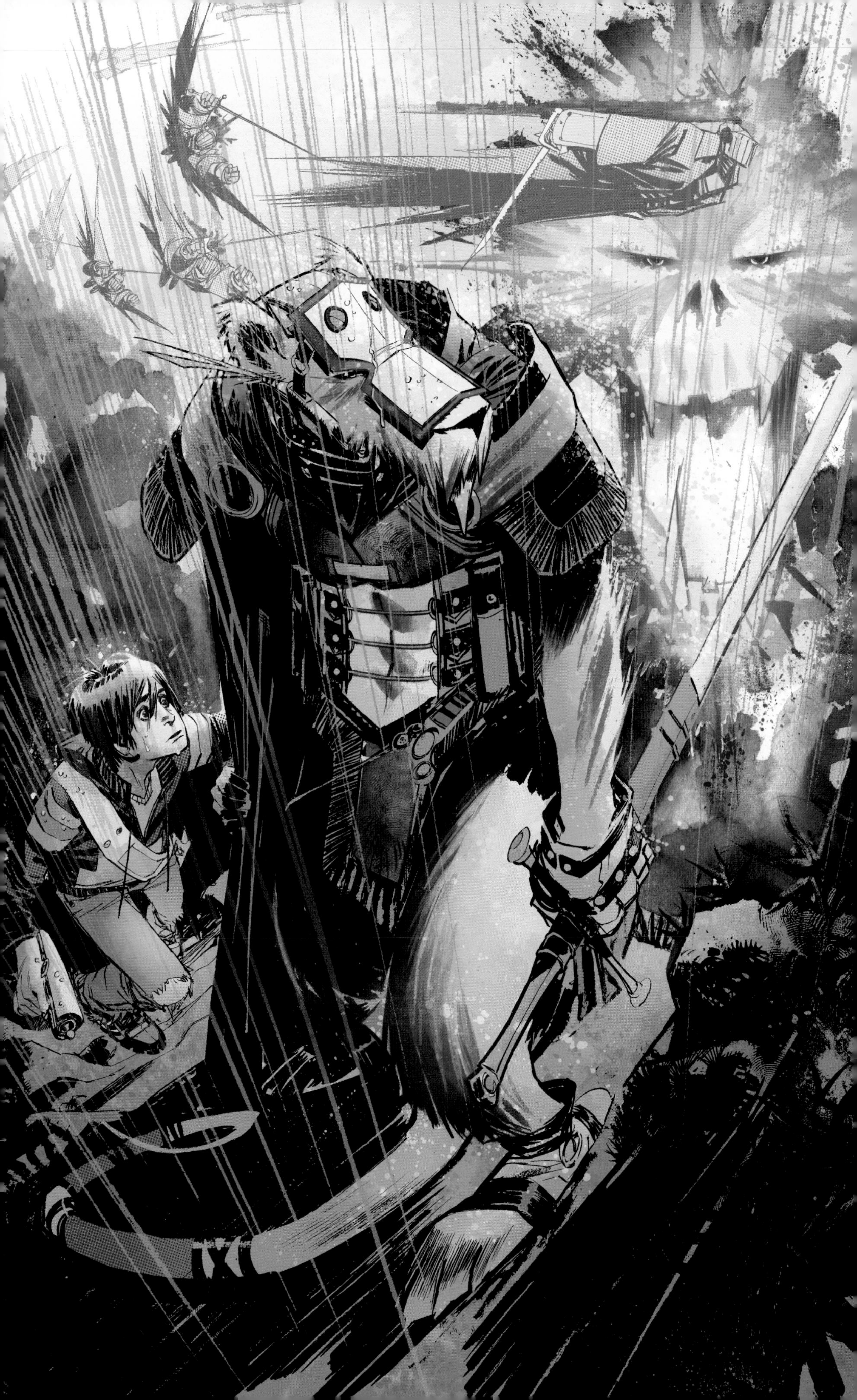

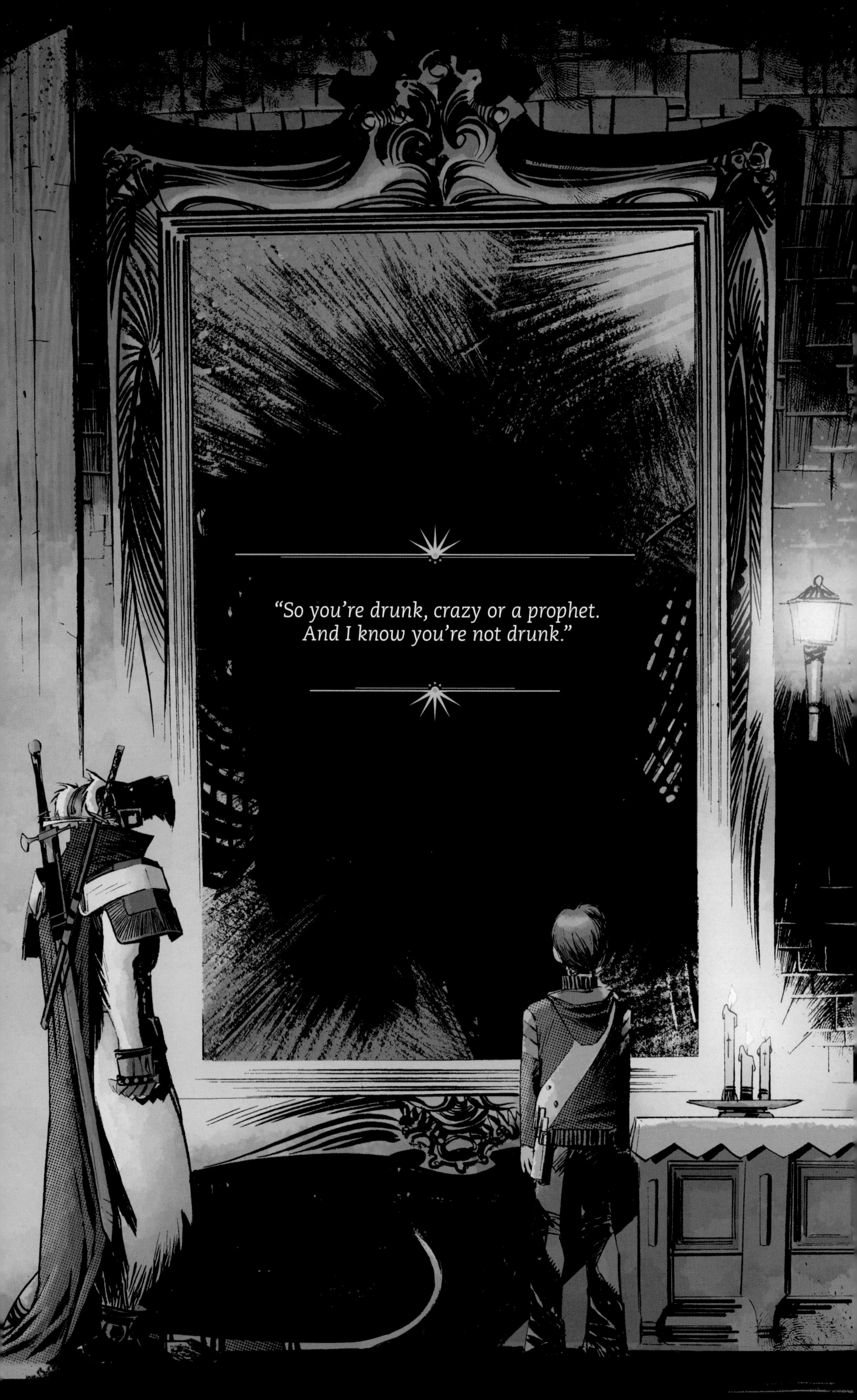
"So you're drunk, crazy or a prophet.
And I know you're not drunk."

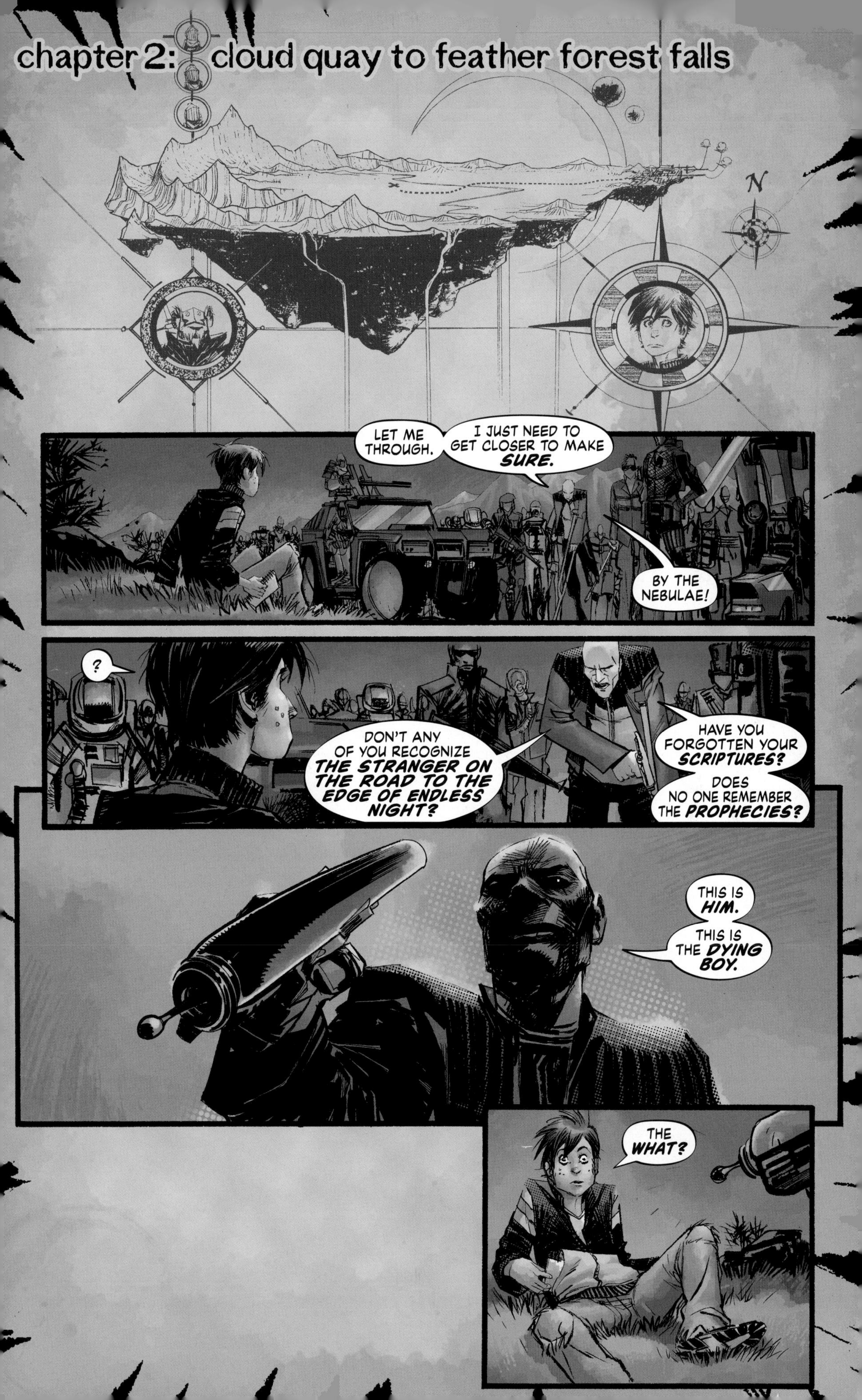
chapter 2: cloud quay to feather forest falls
LET ME THROUGH.
I JUST NEED TO GET CLOSER TO MAKE SURE.
BY THE NEBULAE!
?
DON'T ANY OF YOU RECOGNIZE THE STRANGER ON THE ROAD TO THE EDGE OF ENDLESS NIGHT?
HAVE YOU FORGOTTEN YOUR SCRIPTURES?
DOES NO ONE REMEMBER THE PROPHECIES?
THIS IS HIM.
THIS IS THE DYING BOY.
THE WHAT?

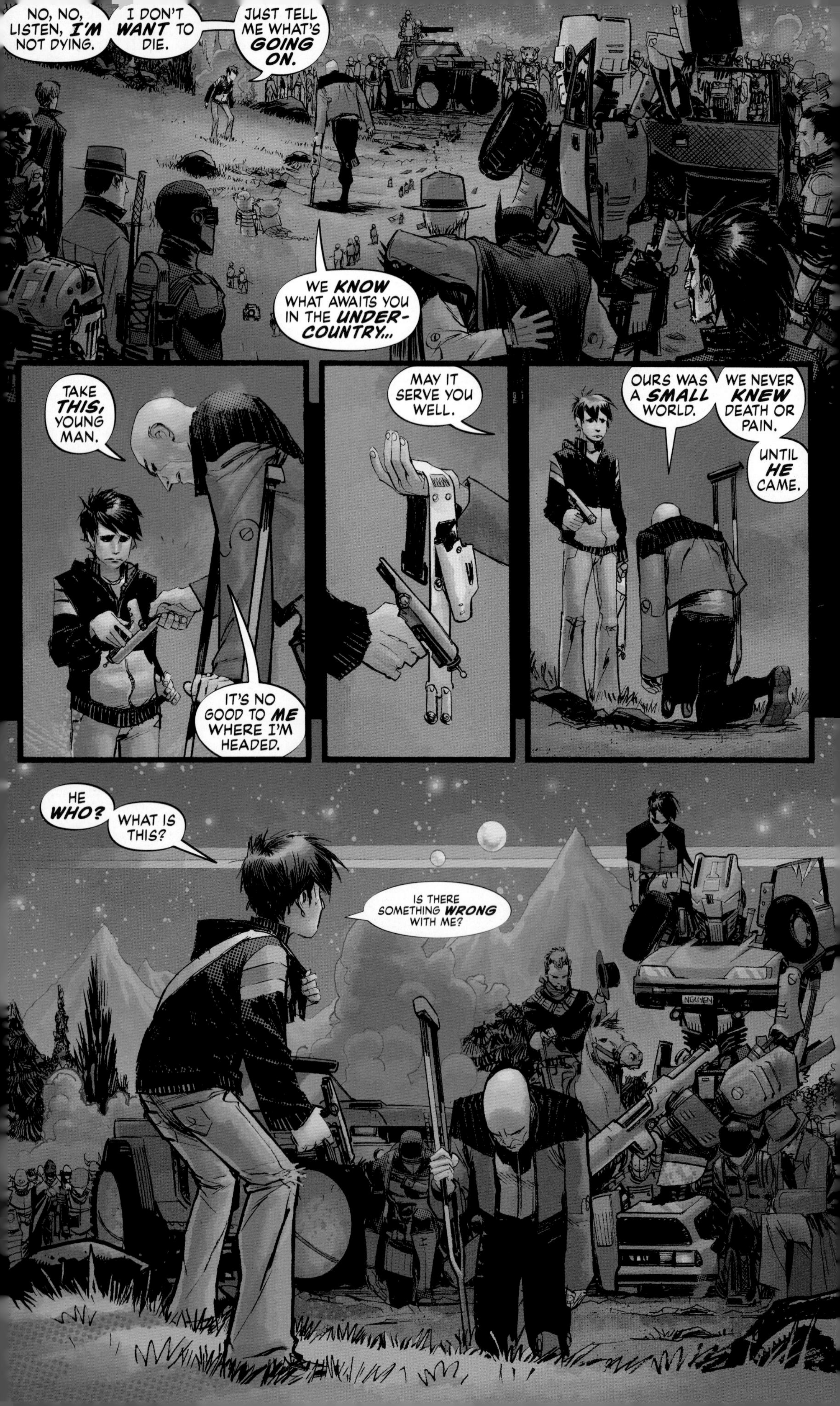

NO, NO, LISTEN, I'M NOT DYING.
I DON'T WANT TO DIE.
JUST TELL ME WHAT'S GOING ON.
WE KNOW WHAT AWAITS YOU IN THE UNDER-COUNTRY...
TAKE THIS, YOUNG MAN.
IT'S NO GOOD TO ME WHERE I'M HEADED.
MAY IT SERVE YOU WELL.
OURS WAS A SMALL WORLD.
WE NEVER KNEW DEATH OR PAIN.
UNTIL HE CAME.
HE WHO?
WHAT IS THIS?
IS THERE SOMETHING WRONG WITH ME?
NGUYEN

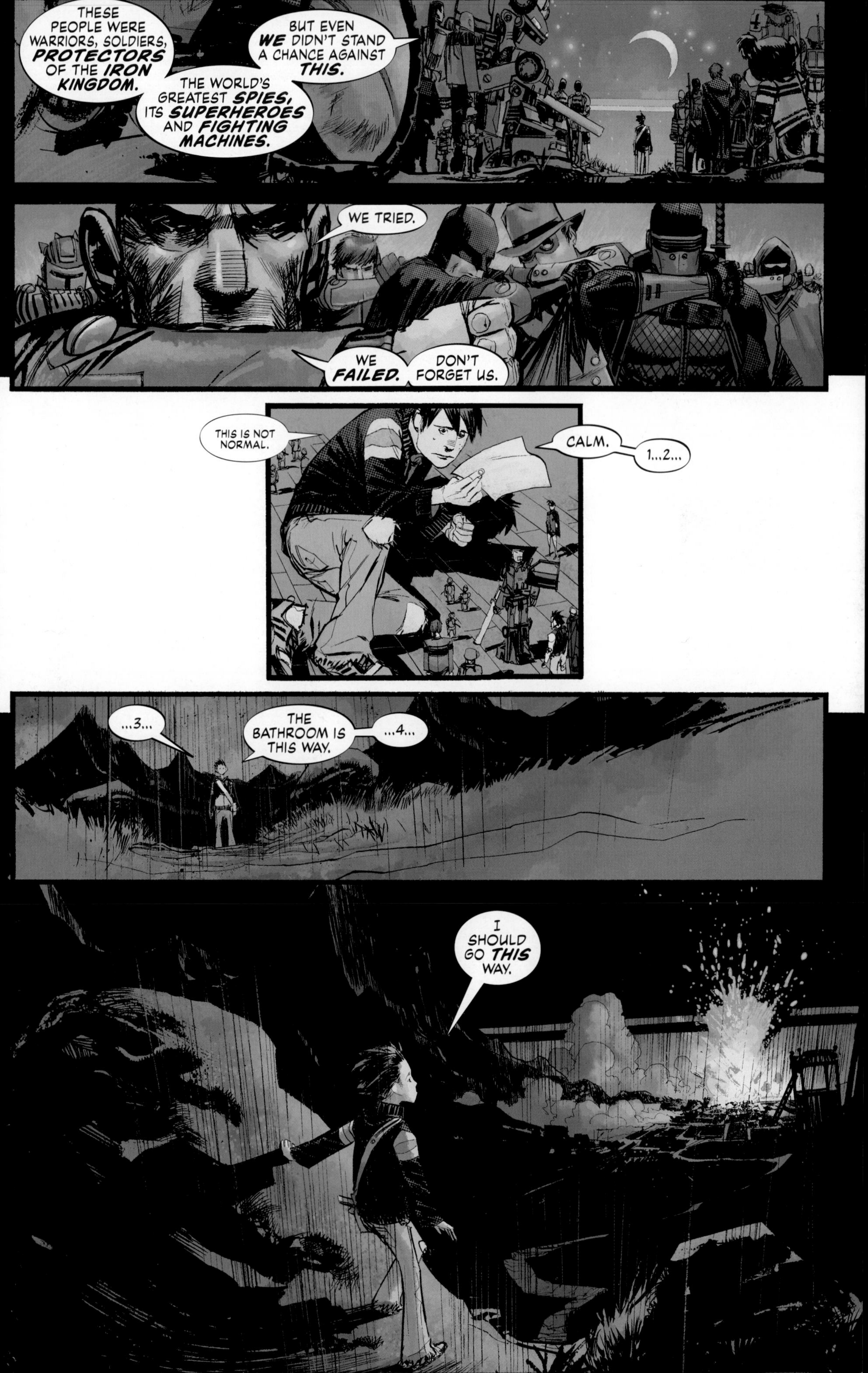
THESE PEOPLE WERE WARRIORS, SOLDIERS, PROTECTORS OF THE IRON KINGDOM.
THE WORLD'S GREATEST SPIES, ITS SUPERHEROES AND FIGHTING MACHINES.
BUT EVEN WE DIDN'T STAND A CHANCE AGAINST THIS.
WE TRIED.
WE FAILED.
DON'T FORGET US.
THIS IS NOT NORMAL.
CALM.
1...2...
...3...
THE BATHROOM IS THIS WAY.
...4...
I SHOULD GO THIS WAY.

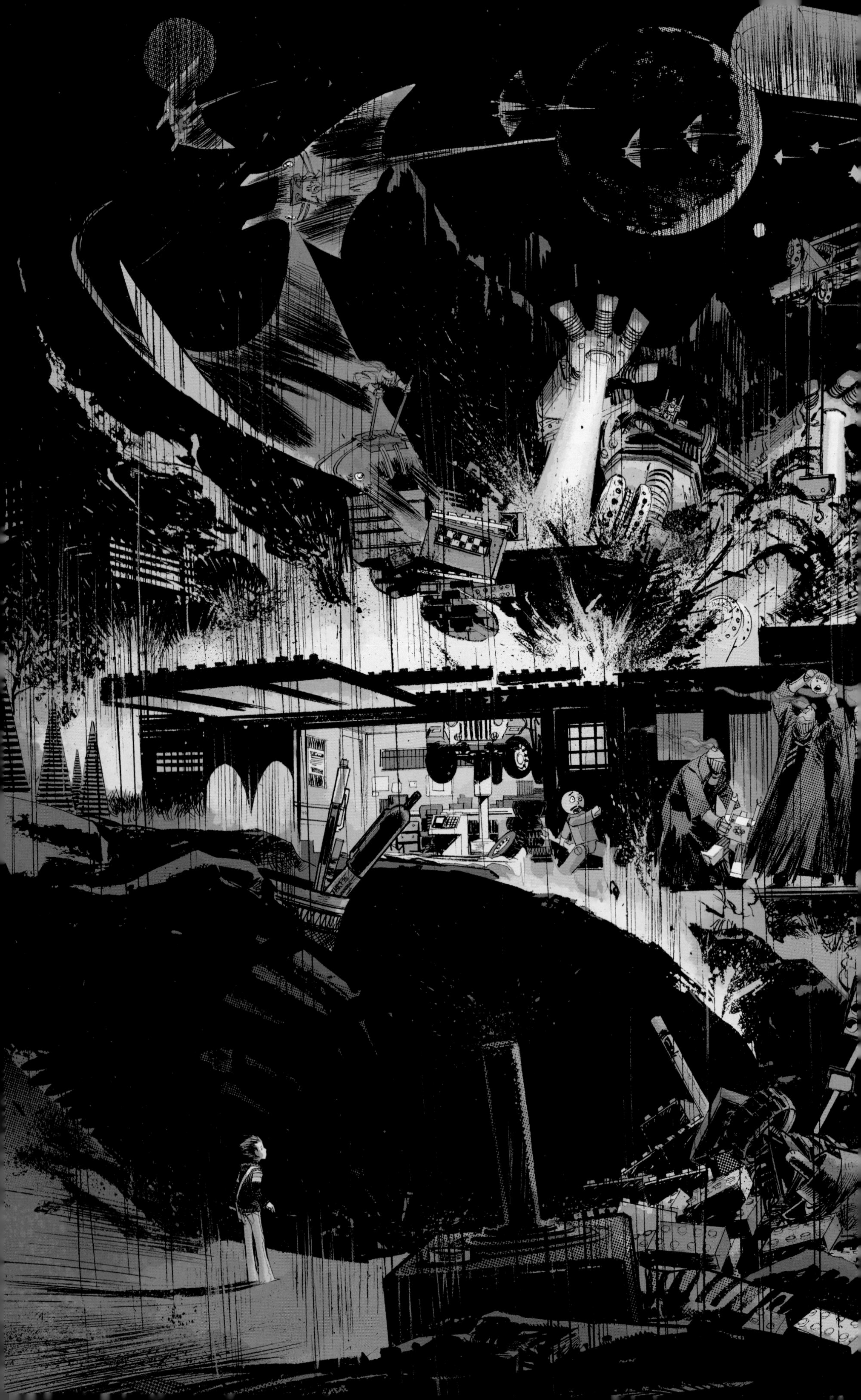

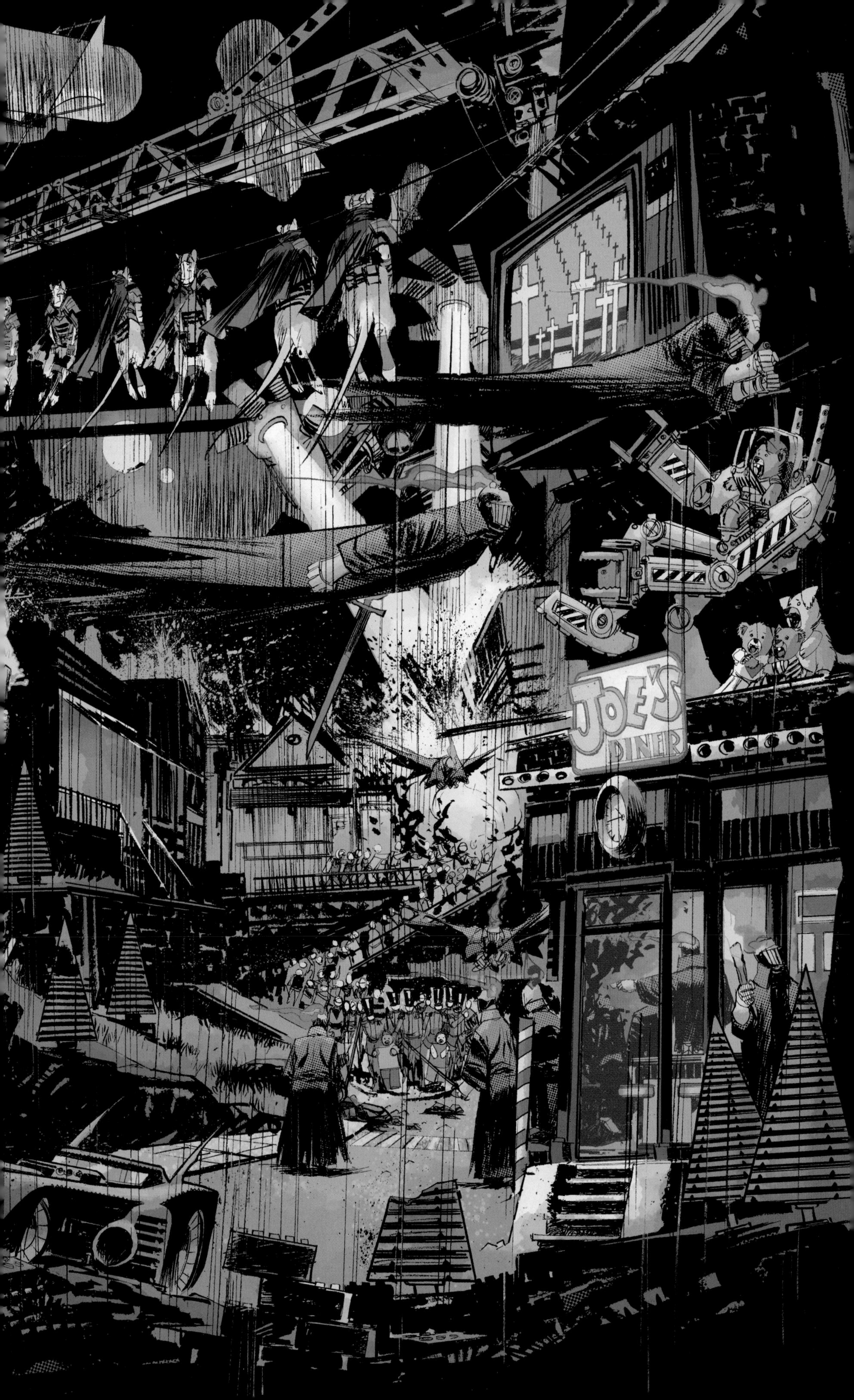
JOE'S
DINER

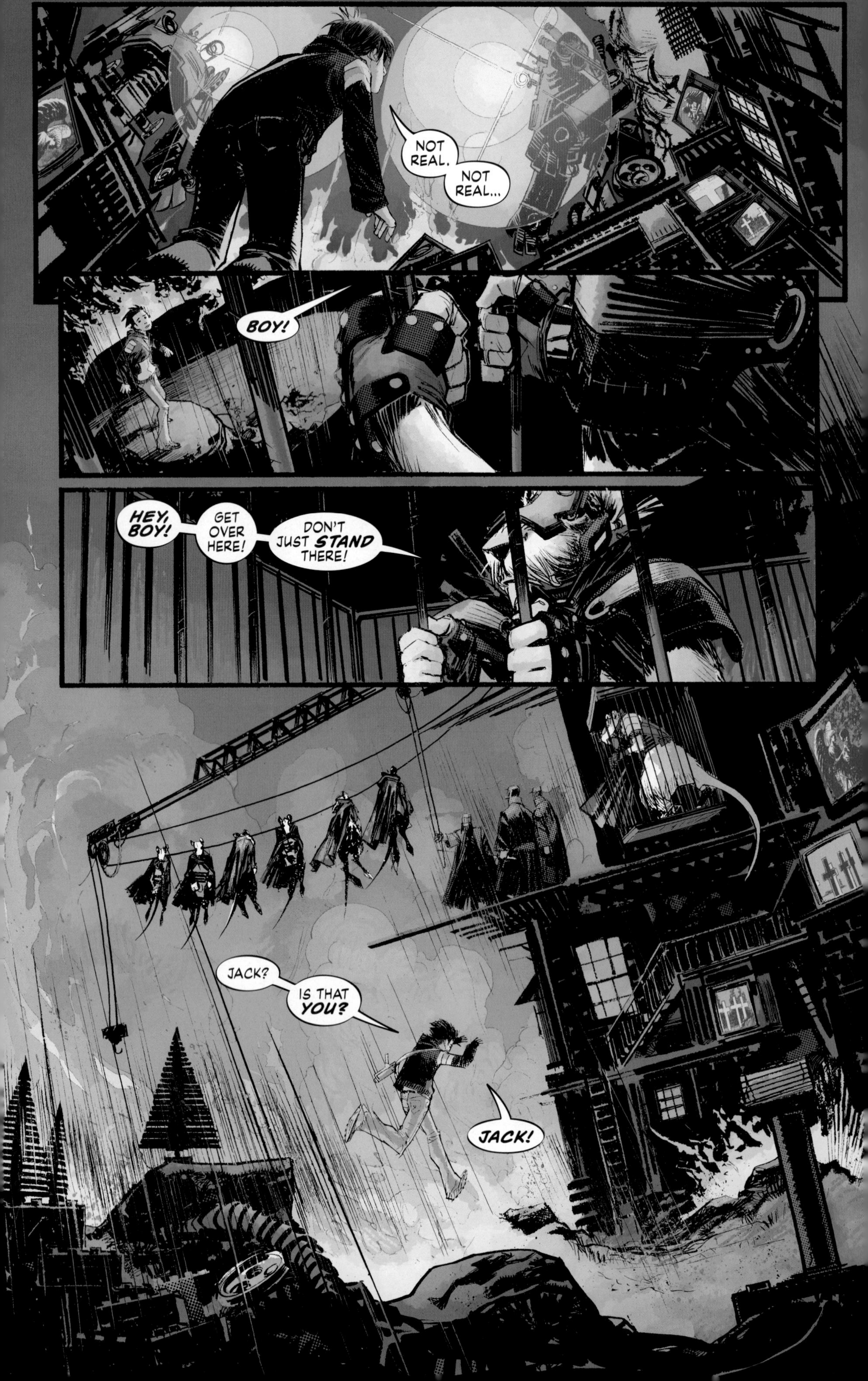
NOT REAL.
NOT REAL...
BOY!
HEY, BOY!
GET OVER HERE!
DON'T JUST STAND THERE!
JACK?
IS THAT YOU?
JACK!

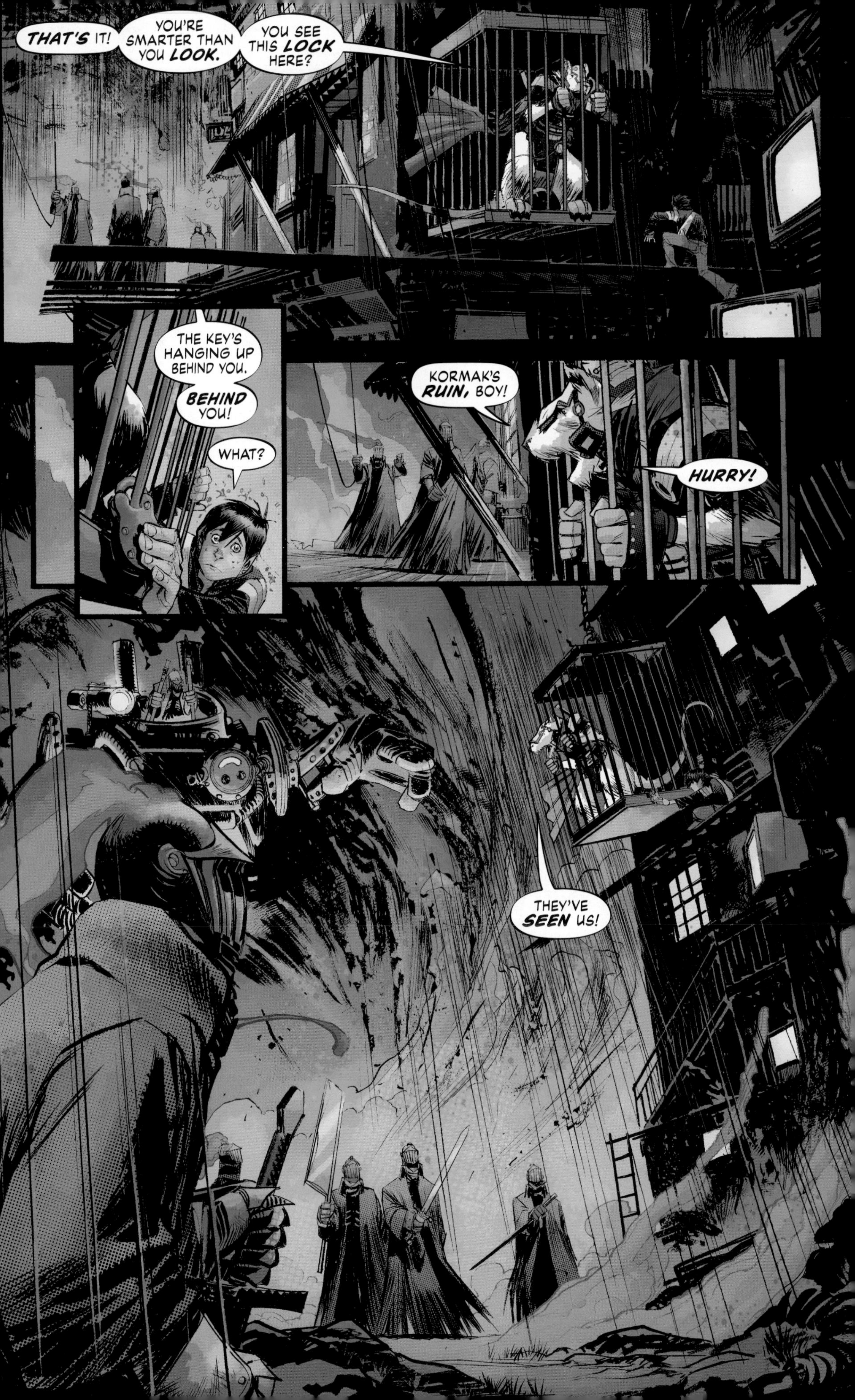
THAT'S IT!
YOU'RE SMARTER THAN YOU LOOK.
YOU SEE THIS LOCK HERE?
THE KEY'S HANGING UP BEHIND YOU. BEHIND YOU!
WHAT?
KORMAK'S RUIN, BOY!
HURRY!
THEY'VE SEEN US!

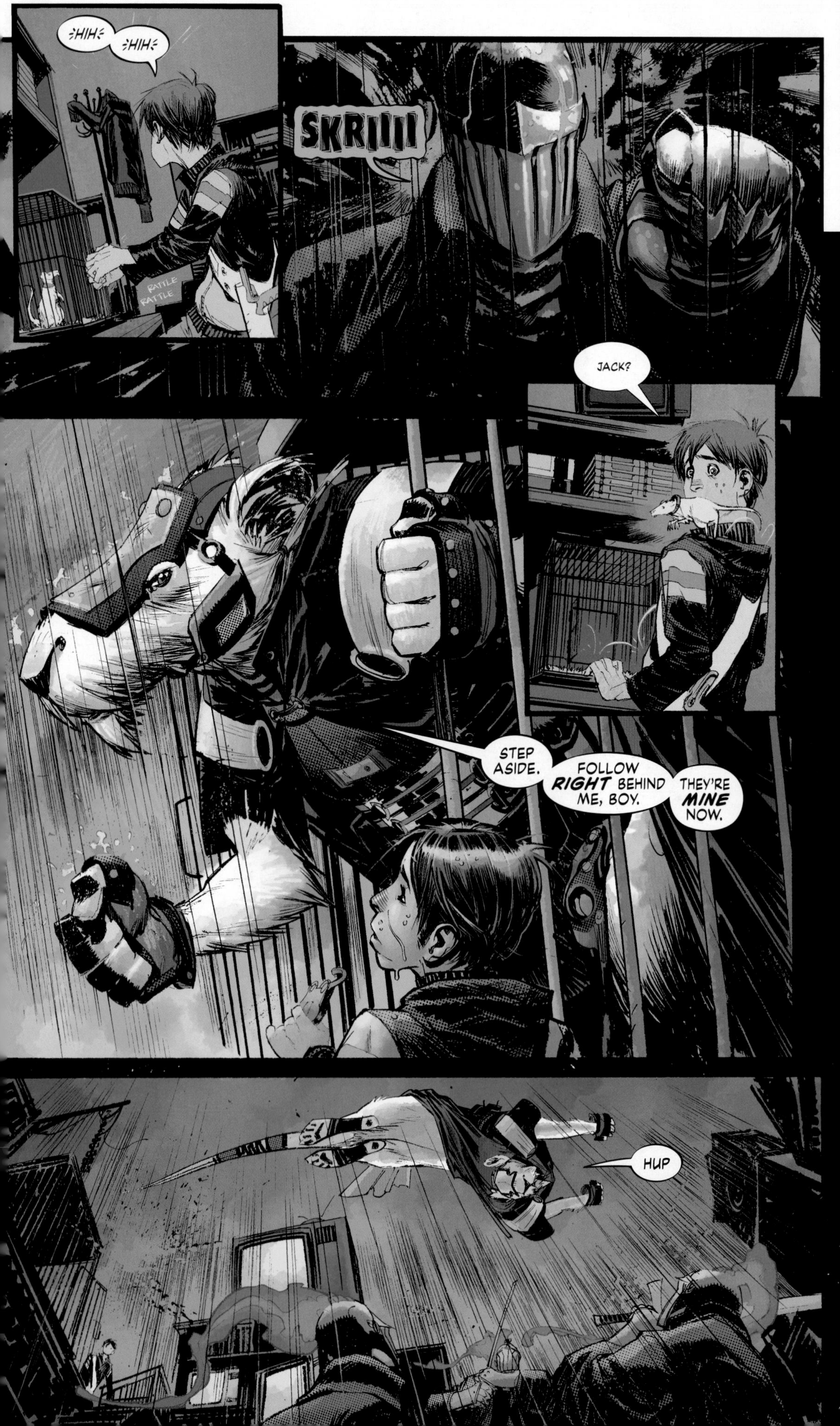

HIH
HIH
RATTLE RATTLE
SKRIIII
JACK?
STEP ASIDE.
FOLLOW RIGHT BEHIND ME, BOY.
THEY'RE MINE NOW.
HUP

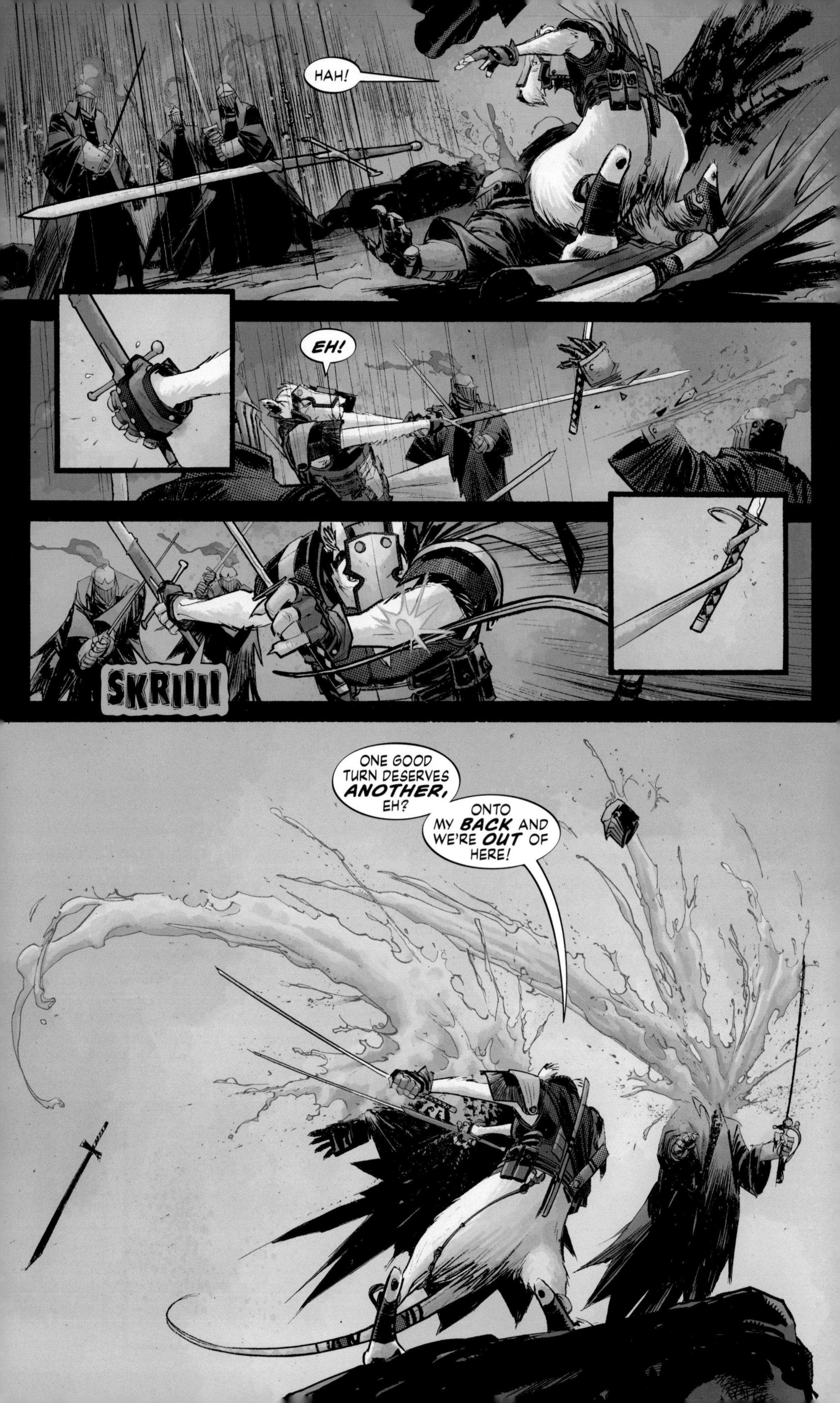

HAH!
EH!
SKRIIII
ONE GOOD TURN DESERVES ANOTHER, EH?
ONTO MY BACK AND WE'RE OUT OF HERE!

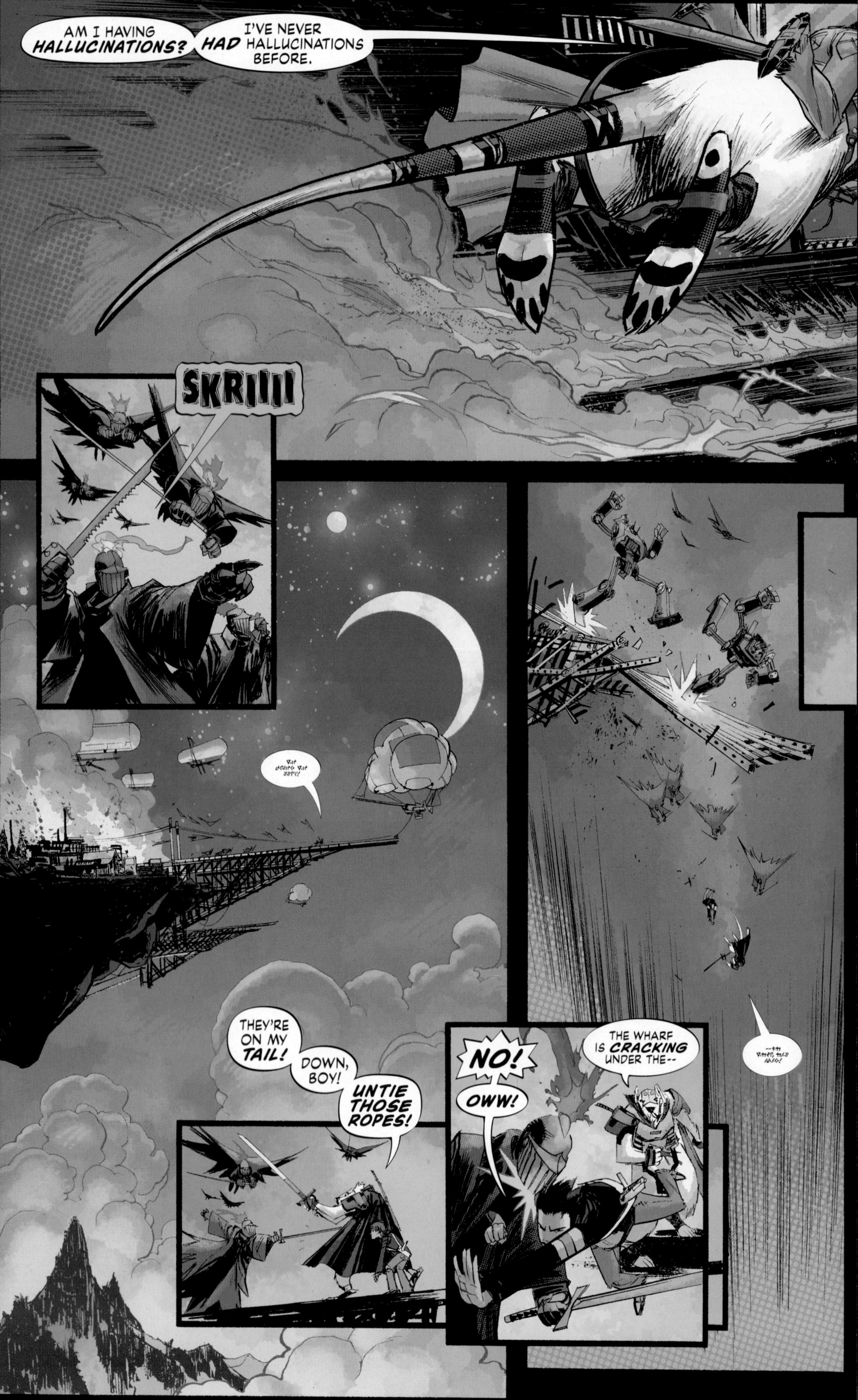
AM I HAVING HALLUCINATIONS?
I'VE NEVER HAD HALLUCINATIONS BEFORE.
SKRIIII
THEY'RE ON MY TAIL!
DOWN, BOY!
UNTIE THOSE ROPES!
NO!
OWW!
THE WHARF IS CRACKING UNDER THE--

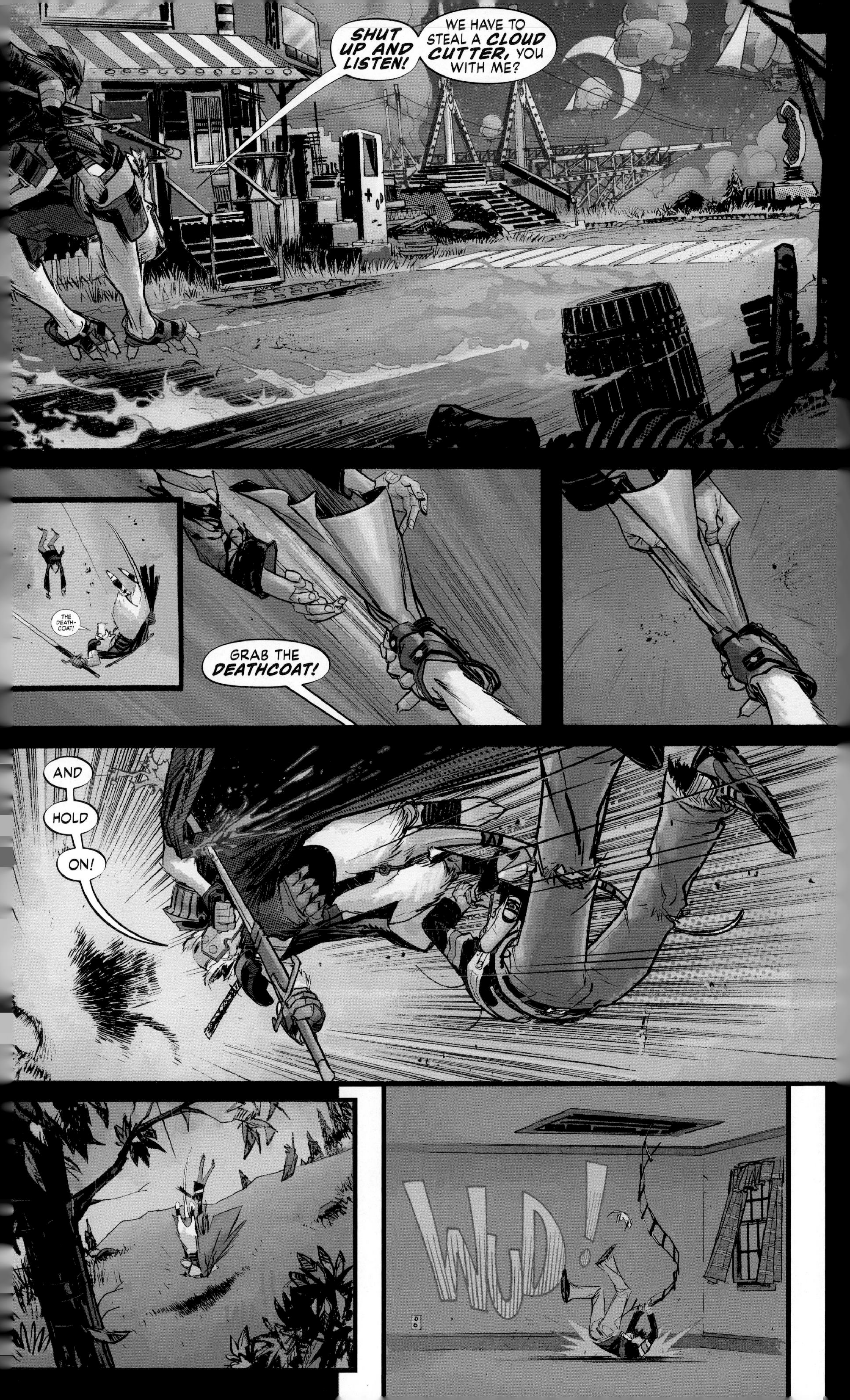
SHUT UP AND LISTEN!
WE HAVE TO STEAL A CLOUD CUTTER, YOU WITH ME?
THE DEATH-COAT!
GRAB THE DEATHCOAT!
AND
HOLD
ON!
WUD!

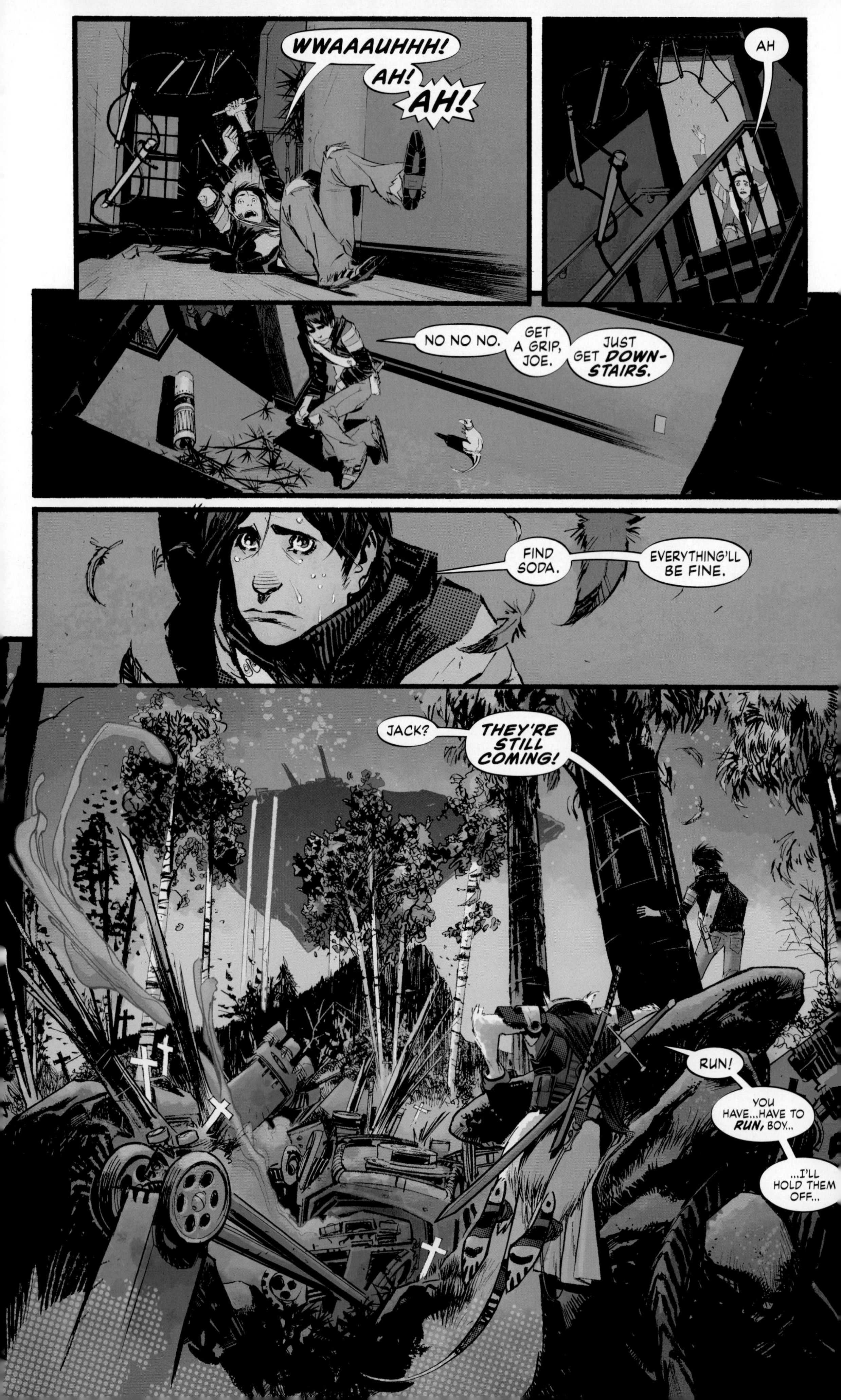

WWAAAUHHH!
AH!
AH!
AH
NO NO NO.
GET A GRIP, JOE.
JUST GET DOWN-STAIRS.
FIND SODA.
EVERYTHING'LL BE FINE.
JACK?
THEY'RE STILL COMING!
RUN!
YOU HAVE...HAVE TO RUN, BOY...
...I'LL HOLD THEM OFF...

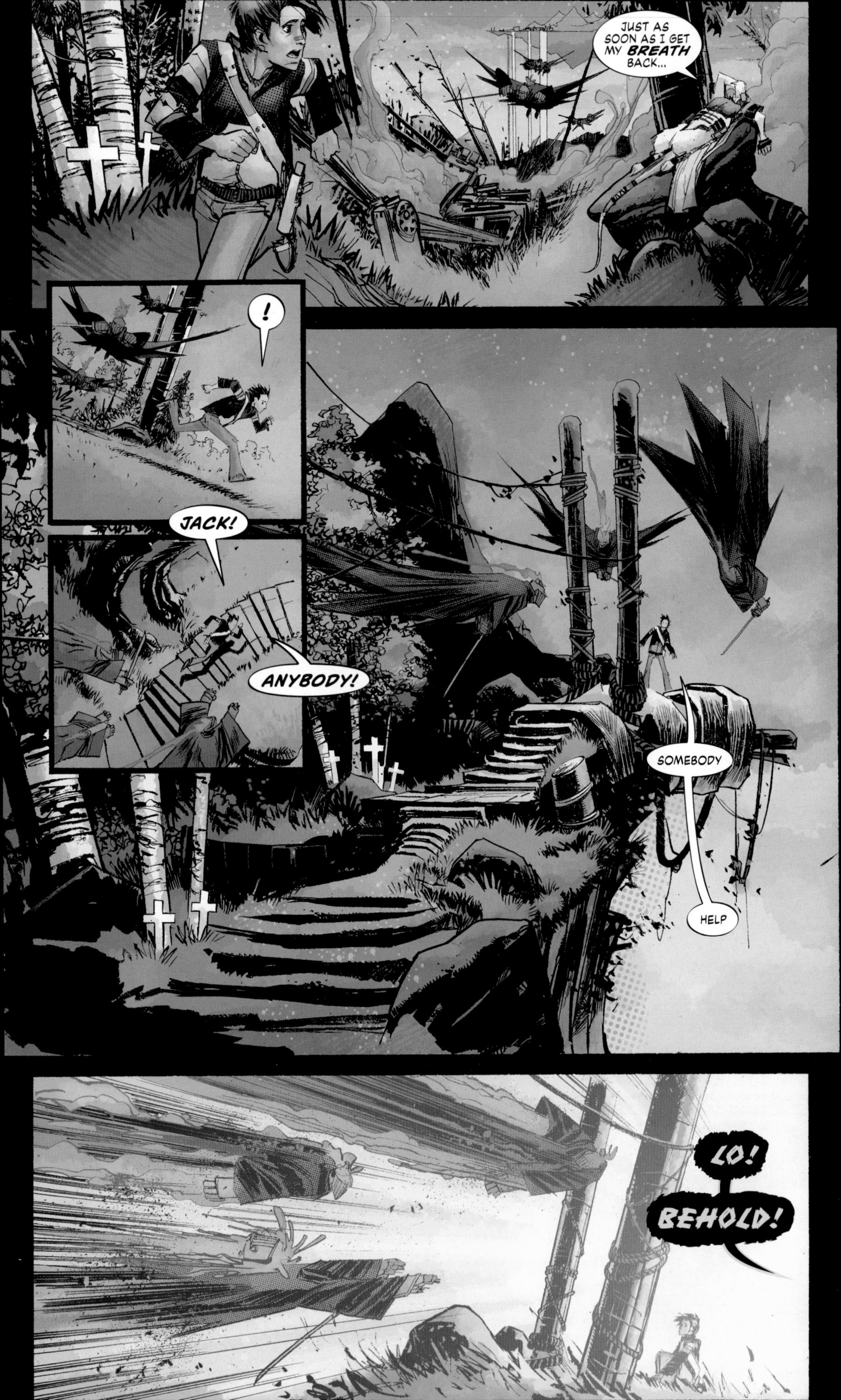
JUST AS SOON AS I GET MY BREATH BACK...
!
JACK!
ANYBODY!
SOMEBODY
HELP
LO!
BEHOLD!

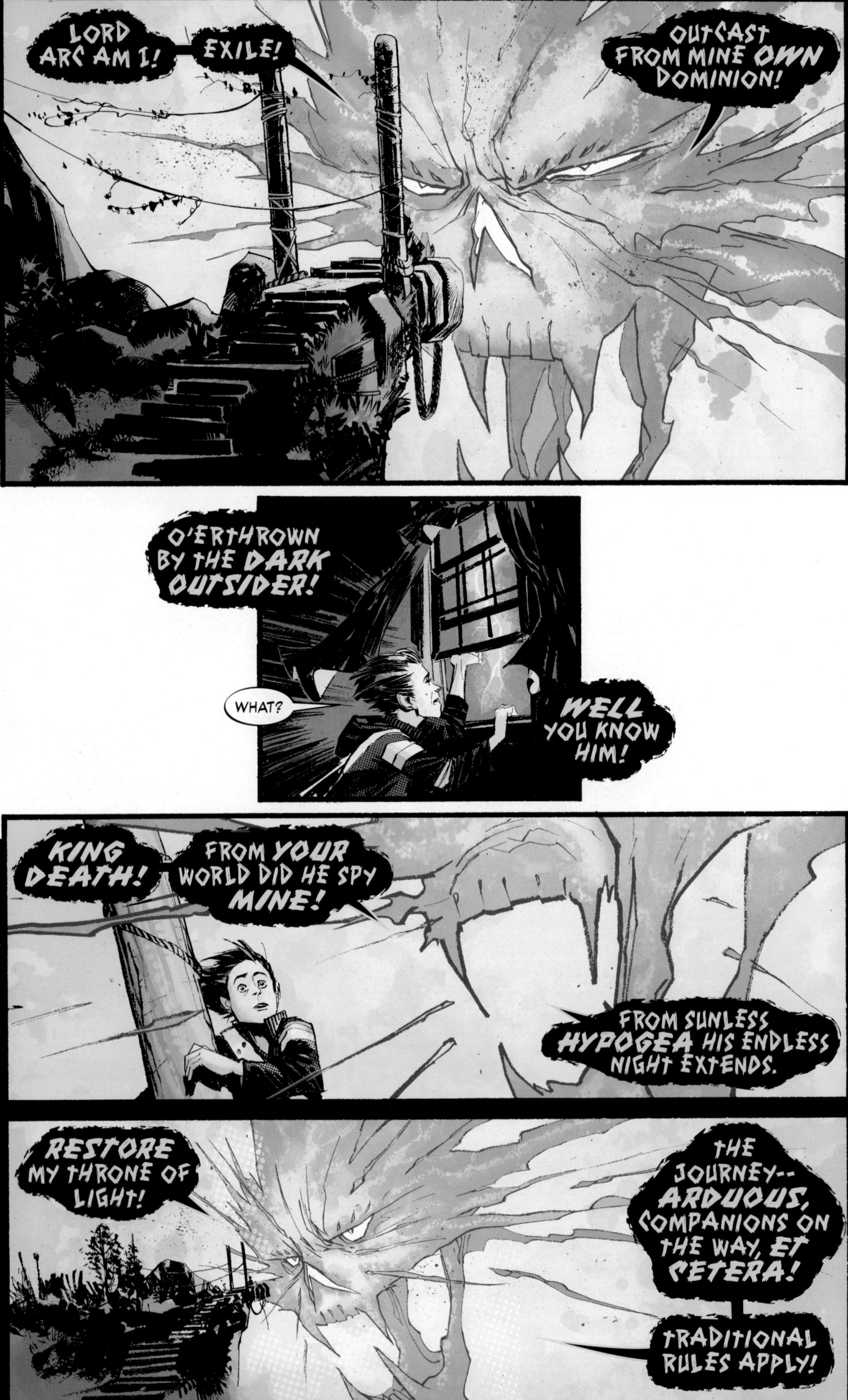
LORD ARC AM I!
EXILE!
OUTCAST FROM MINE OWN DOMINION!
O'ERTHROWN BY THE DARK OUTSIDER!
WHAT?
WELL YOU KNOW HIM!
KING DEATH!
FROM YOUR WORLD DID HE SPY MINE!
FROM SUNLESS HYPOGEA HIS ENDLESS NIGHT EXTENDS.
RESTORE MY THRONE OF LIGHT!
THE JOURNEY-- ARDUOUS, COMPANIONS ON THE WAY, ET CETERA!
TRADITIONAL RULES APPLY!

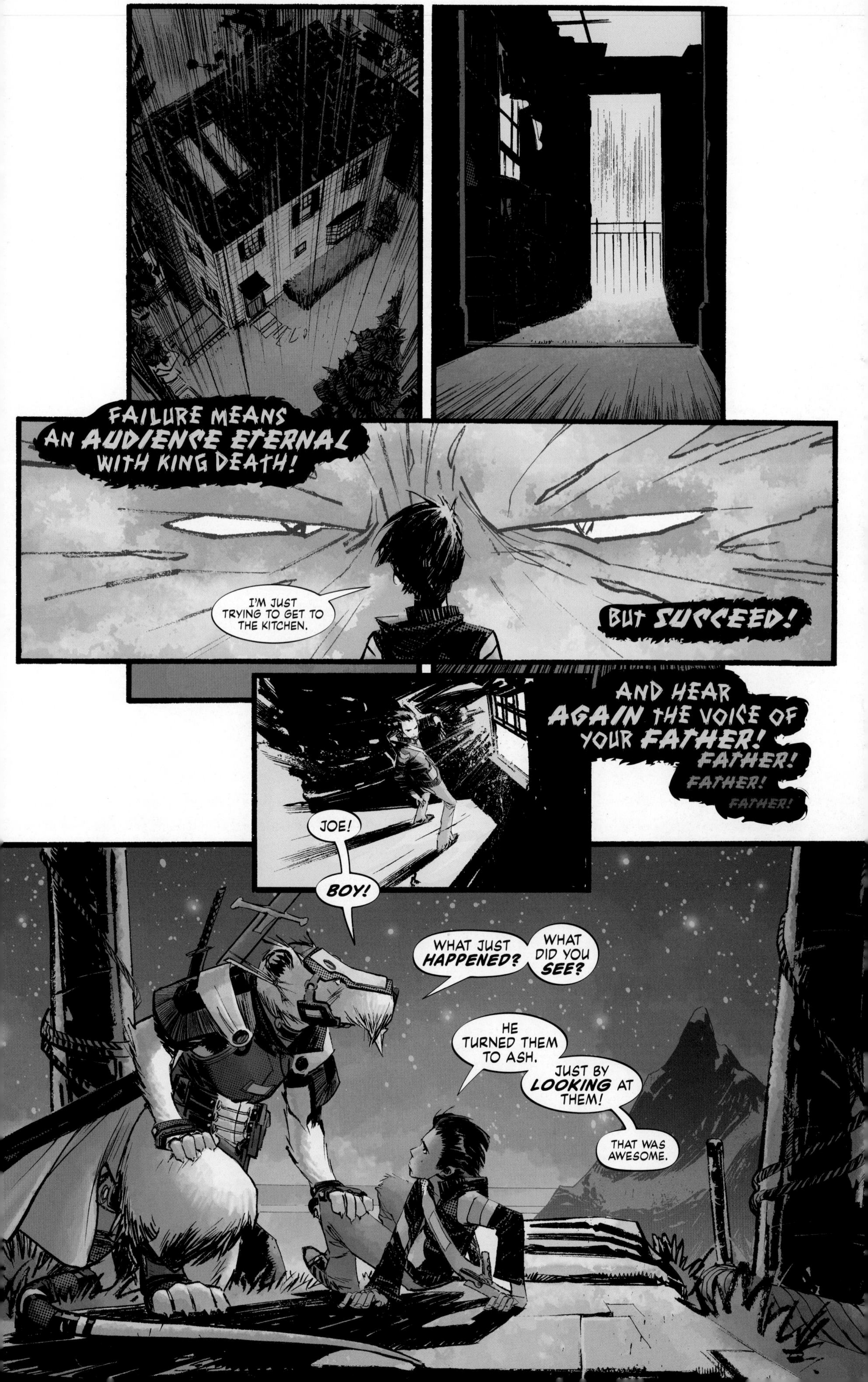
FAILURE MEANS AN AUDIENCE ETERNAL WITH KING DEATH!
I'M JUST TRYING TO GET TO THE KITCHEN.
BUT SUCCEED!
AND HEAR AGAIN THE VOICE OF YOUR FATHER!
FATHER!
FATHER!
FATHER!
JOE!
BOY!
WHAT JUST HAPPENED?
WHAT DID YOU SEE?
HE TURNED THEM TO ASH.
JUST BY LOOKING AT THEM!
THAT WAS AWESOME.

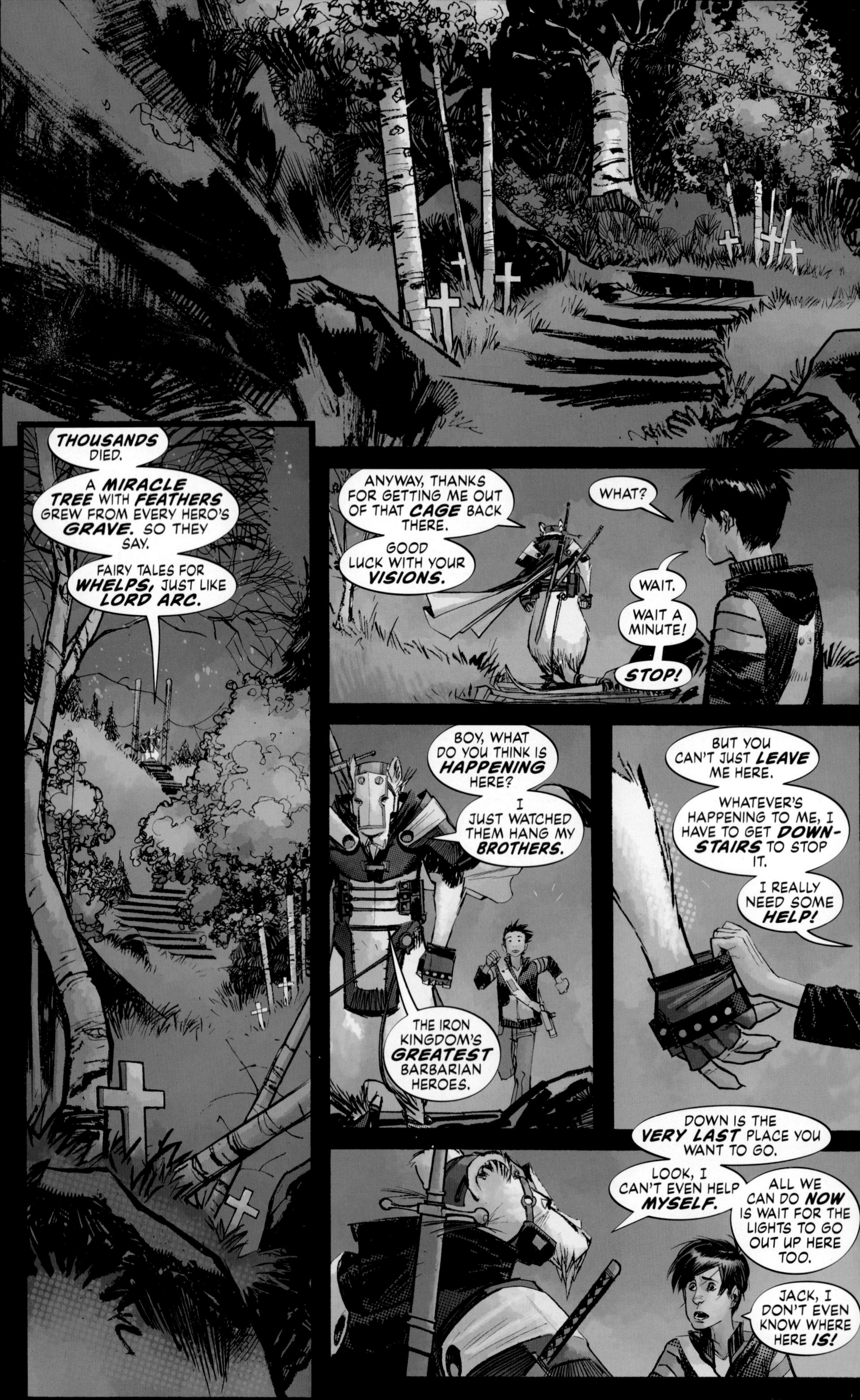
THOUSANDS DIED.
A MIRACLE TREE WITH FEATHERS GREW FROM EVERY HERO'S GRAVE. SO THEY SAY.
FAIRY TALES FOR WHELPS, JUST LIKE LORD ARC.
ANYWAY, THANKS FOR GETTING ME OUT OF THAT CAGE BACK THERE.
GOOD LUCK WITH YOUR VISIONS.
WHAT?
WAIT.
WAIT A MINUTE!
STOP!
BOY, WHAT DO YOU THINK IS HAPPENING HERE?
I JUST WATCHED THEM HANG MY BROTHERS.
THE IRON KINGDOM'S GREATEST BARBARIAN HEROES.
BUT YOU CAN'T JUST LEAVE ME HERE.
WHATEVER'S HAPPENING TO ME, I HAVE TO GET DOWN-STAIRS TO STOP IT.
I REALLY NEED SOME HELP!
DOWN IS THE VERY LAST PLACE YOU WANT TO GO.
LOOK, I CAN'T EVEN HELP MYSELF.
ALL WE CAN DO NOW IS WAIT FOR THE LIGHTS TO GO OUT UP HERE TOO.
JACK, I DON'T EVEN KNOW WHERE HERE IS!

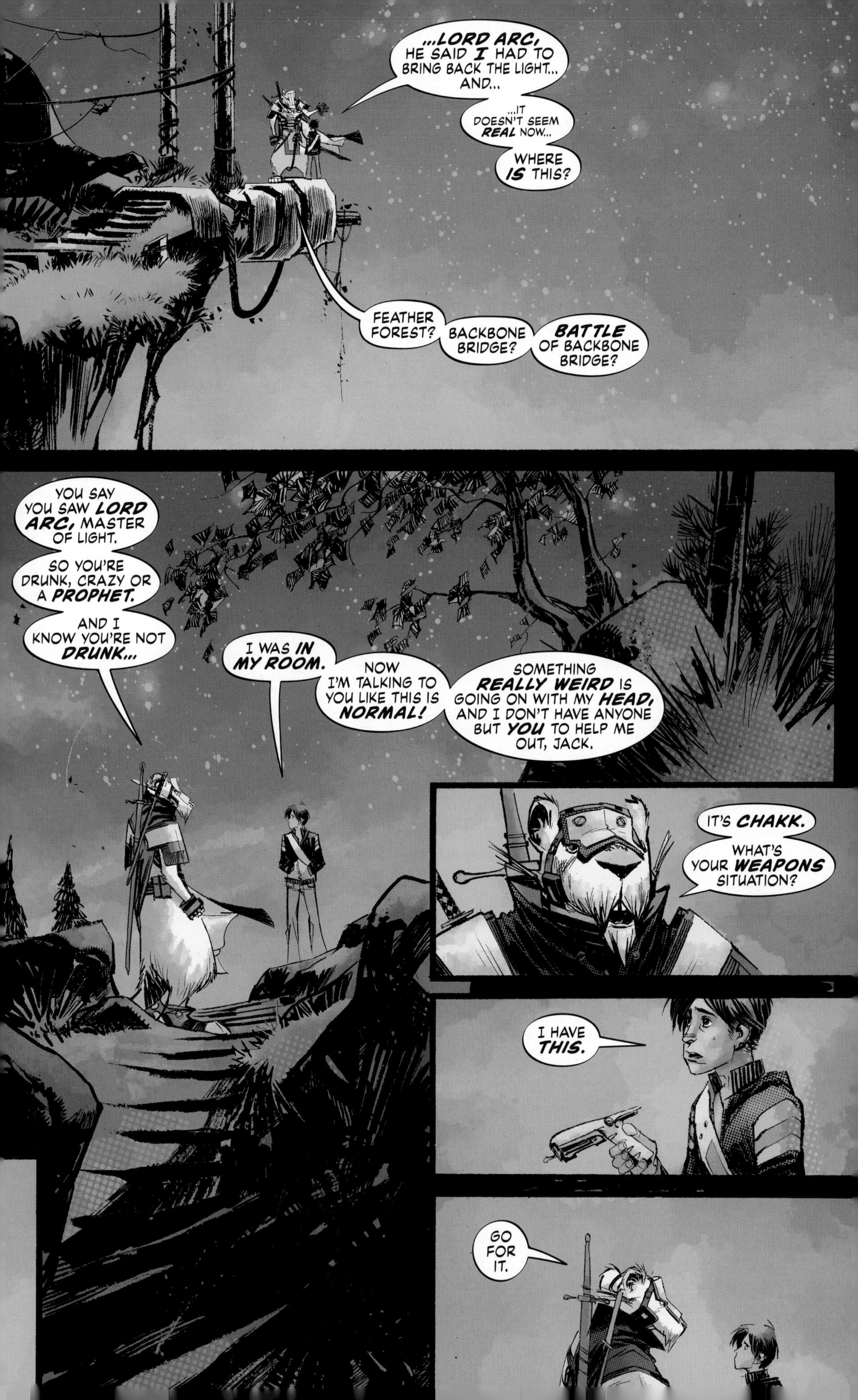
...LORD ARC, HE SAID I HAD TO BRING BACK THE LIGHT... AND...
...IT DOESN'T SEEM REAL NOW...
WHERE IS THIS?
FEATHER FOREST?
BACKBONE BRIDGE?
BATTLE OF BACKBONE BRIDGE?
YOU SAY YOU SAW LORD ARC, MASTER OF LIGHT.
SO YOU'RE DRUNK, CRAZY OR A PROPHET.
AND I KNOW YOU'RE NOT DRUNK...
I WAS IN MY ROOM.
NOW I'M TALKING TO YOU LIKE THIS IS NORMAL!
SOMETHING REALLY WEIRD IS GOING ON WITH MY HEAD, AND I DON'T HAVE ANYONE BUT YOU TO HELP ME OUT, JACK.
IT'S CHAKK.
WHAT'S YOUR WEAPONS SITUATION?
I HAVE THIS.
GO FOR IT.

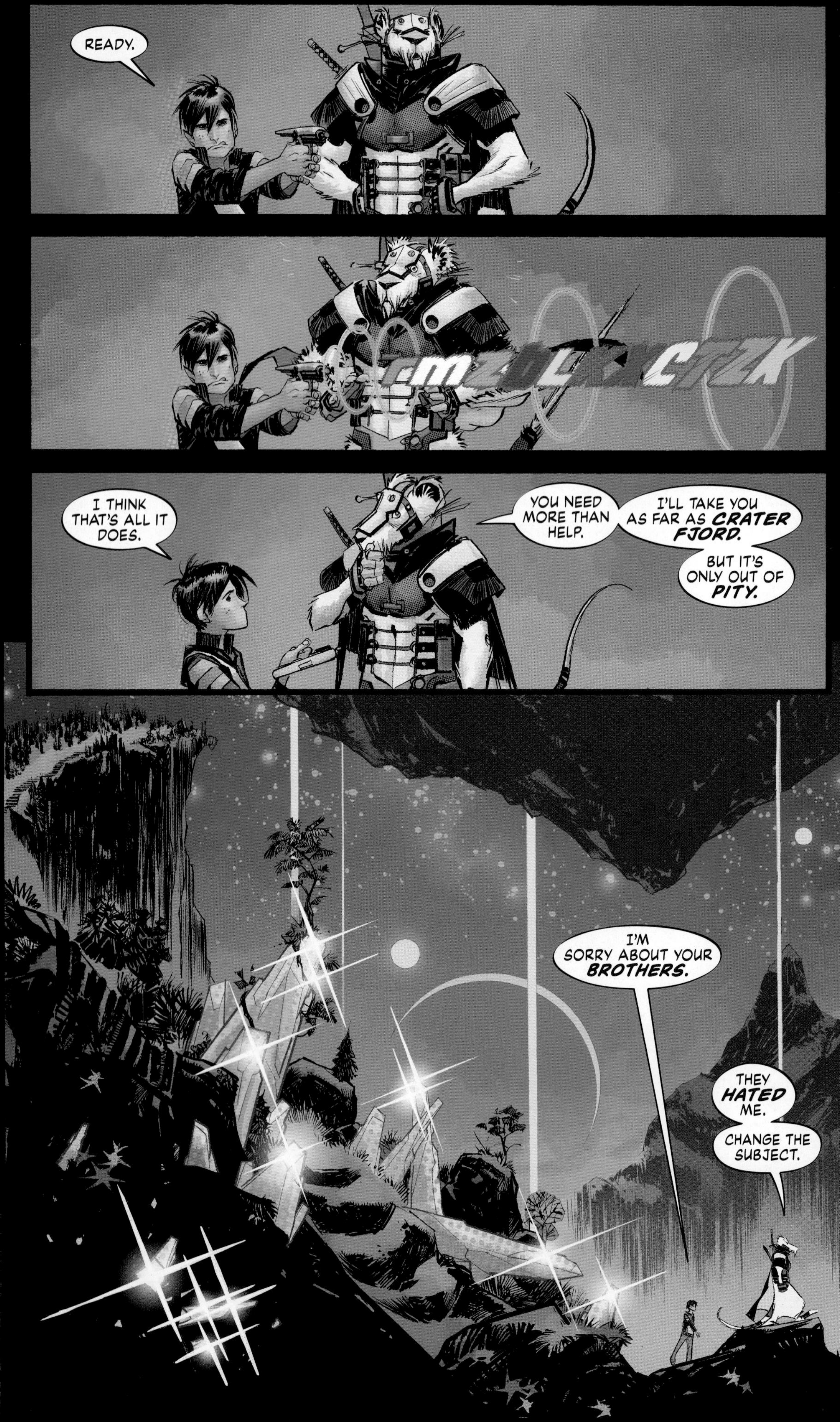
READY.
CMZDLKXCTZK
I THINK THAT'S ALL IT DOES.
YOU NEED MORE THAN HELP.
I'LL TAKE YOU AS FAR AS **CRATER FJORD.**
BUT IT'S ONLY OUT OF **PITY.**
I'M SORRY ABOUT YOUR **BROTHERS.**
THEY **HATED** ME.
CHANGE THE SUBJECT.

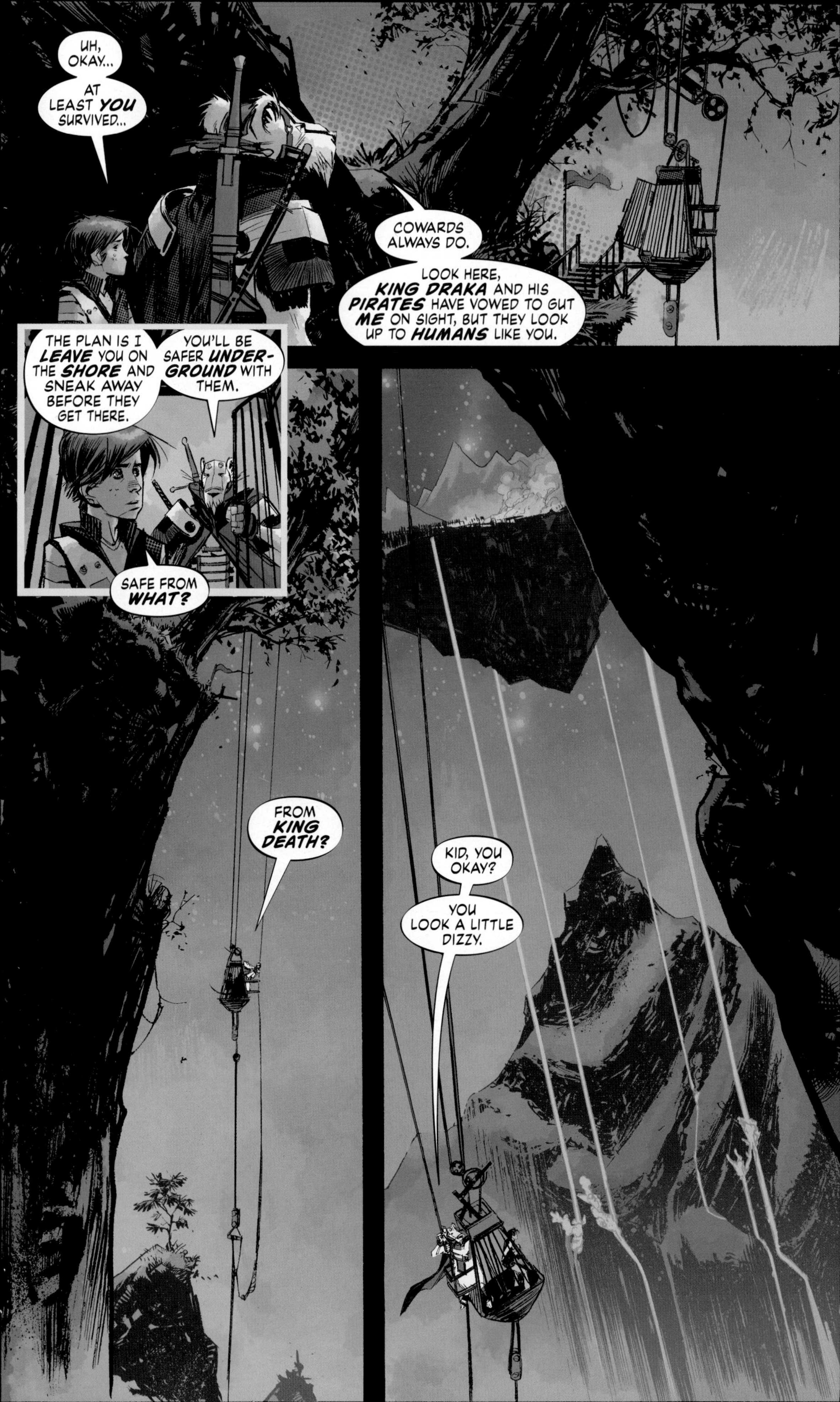
UH, OKAY... AT LEAST YOU SURVIVED...
COWARDS ALWAYS DO.
LOOK HERE, KING DRAKA AND HIS PIRATES HAVE VOWED TO GUT ME ON SIGHT, BUT THEY LOOK UP TO HUMANS LIKE YOU.
THE PLAN IS I LEAVE YOU ON THE SHORE AND SNEAK AWAY BEFORE THEY GET THERE.
YOU'LL BE SAFER UNDER-GROUND WITH THEM.
SAFE FROM WHAT?
FROM KING DEATH?
KID, YOU OKAY?
YOU LOOK A LITTLE DIZZY.

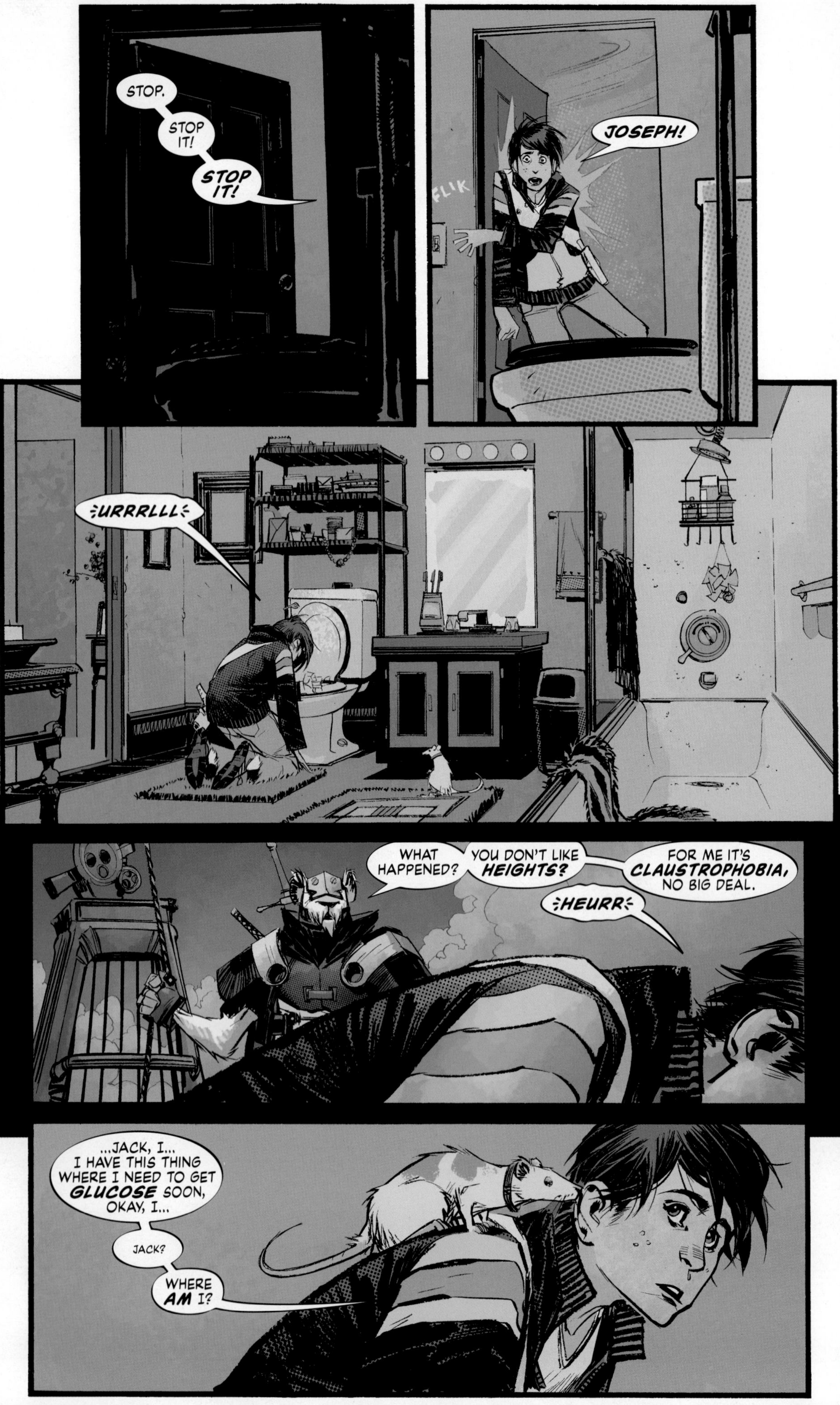
STOP.
STOP IT!
STOP IT!
JOSEPH!
FLIK
URRRLLL
WHAT HAPPENED?
YOU DON'T LIKE HEIGHTS?
FOR ME IT'S CLAUSTROPHOBIA, NO BIG DEAL.
HEURR
...JACK, I... I HAVE THIS THING WHERE I NEED TO GET GLUCOSE SOON, OKAY, I...
JACK?
WHERE AM I?

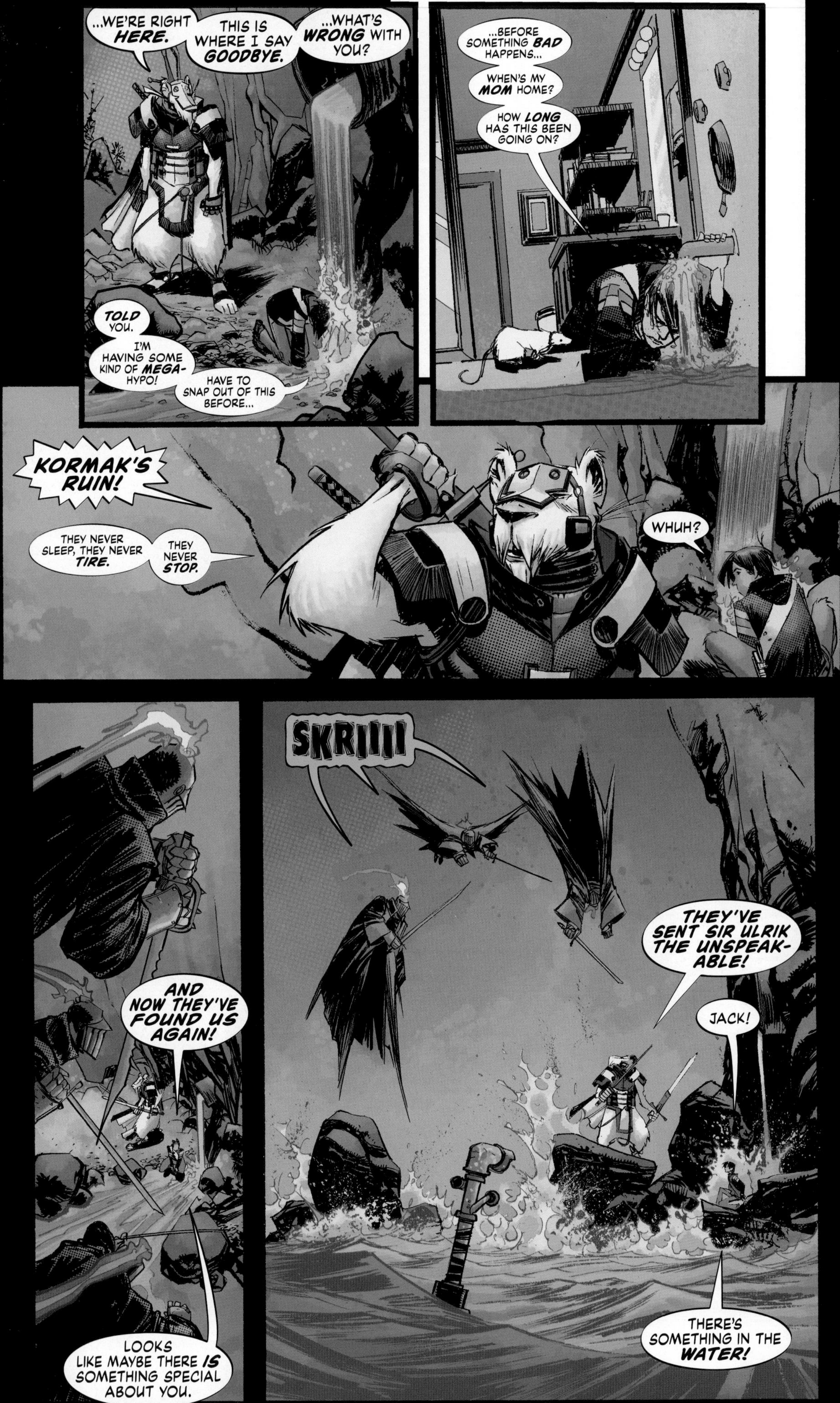
...WE'RE RIGHT HERE.
THIS IS WHERE I SAY GOODBYE.
...WHAT'S WRONG WITH YOU?
TOLD YOU.
I'M HAVING SOME KIND OF MEGA-HYPO!
HAVE TO SNAP OUT OF THIS BEFORE...
...BEFORE SOMETHING BAD HAPPENS...
WHEN'S MY MOM HOME?
HOW LONG HAS THIS BEEN GOING ON?
KORMAK'S RUIN!
THEY NEVER SLEEP, THEY NEVER TIRE.
THEY NEVER STOP.
WHUH?
AND NOW THEY'VE FOUND US AGAIN!
LOOKS LIKE MAYBE THERE IS SOMETHING SPECIAL ABOUT YOU.
SKRIIII
THEY'VE SENT SIR ULRIK THE UNSPEAK-ABLE!
JACK!
THERE'S SOMETHING IN THE WATER!

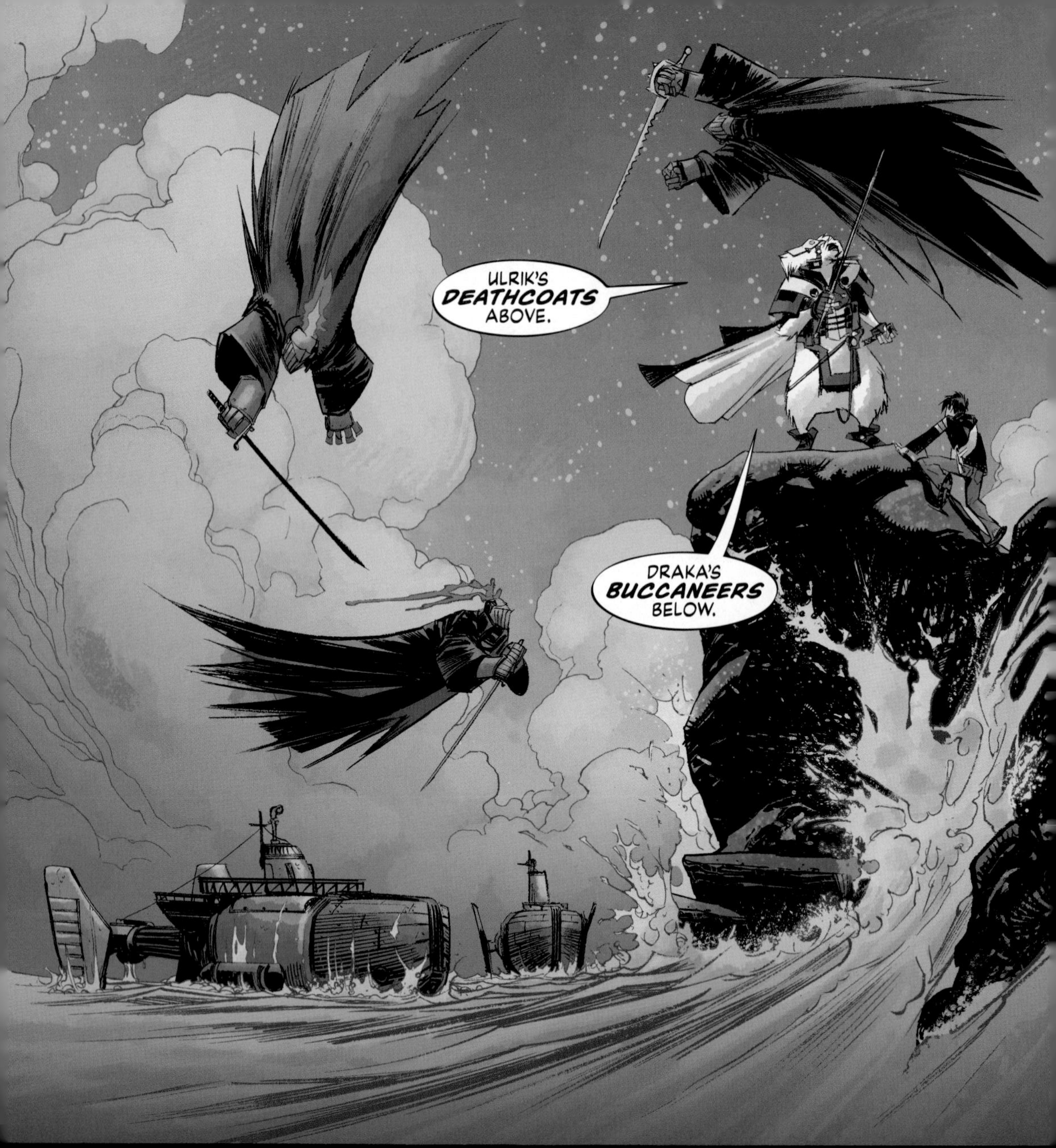
ULRIK'S DEATHCOATS ABOVE.
DRAKA'S BUCCANEERS BELOW.
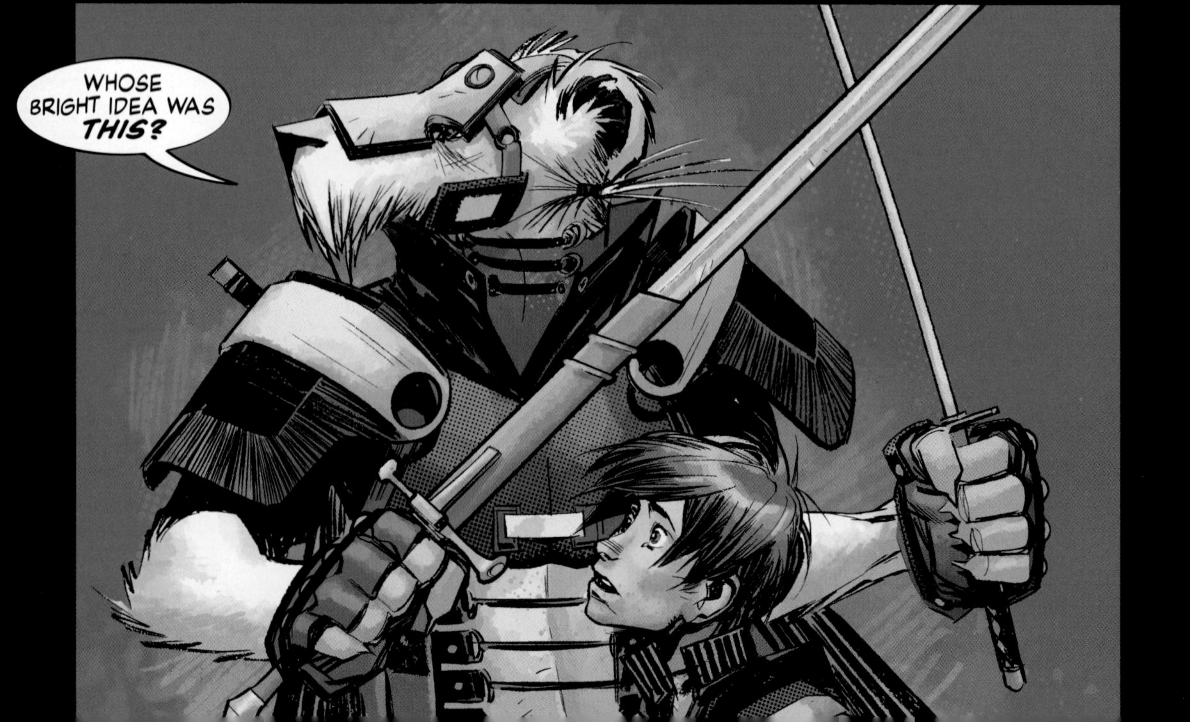
WHOSE BRIGHT IDEA WAS THIS?

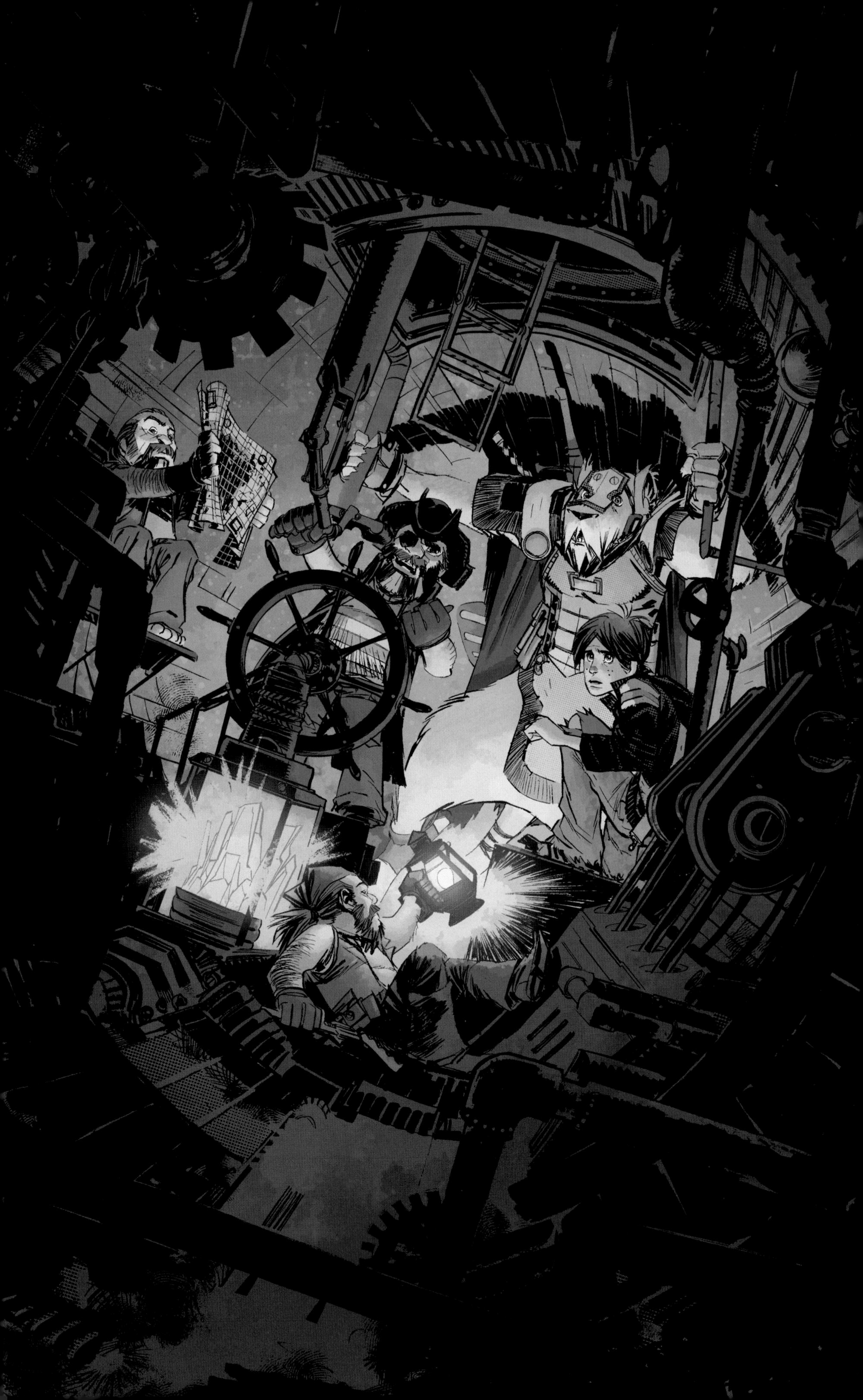

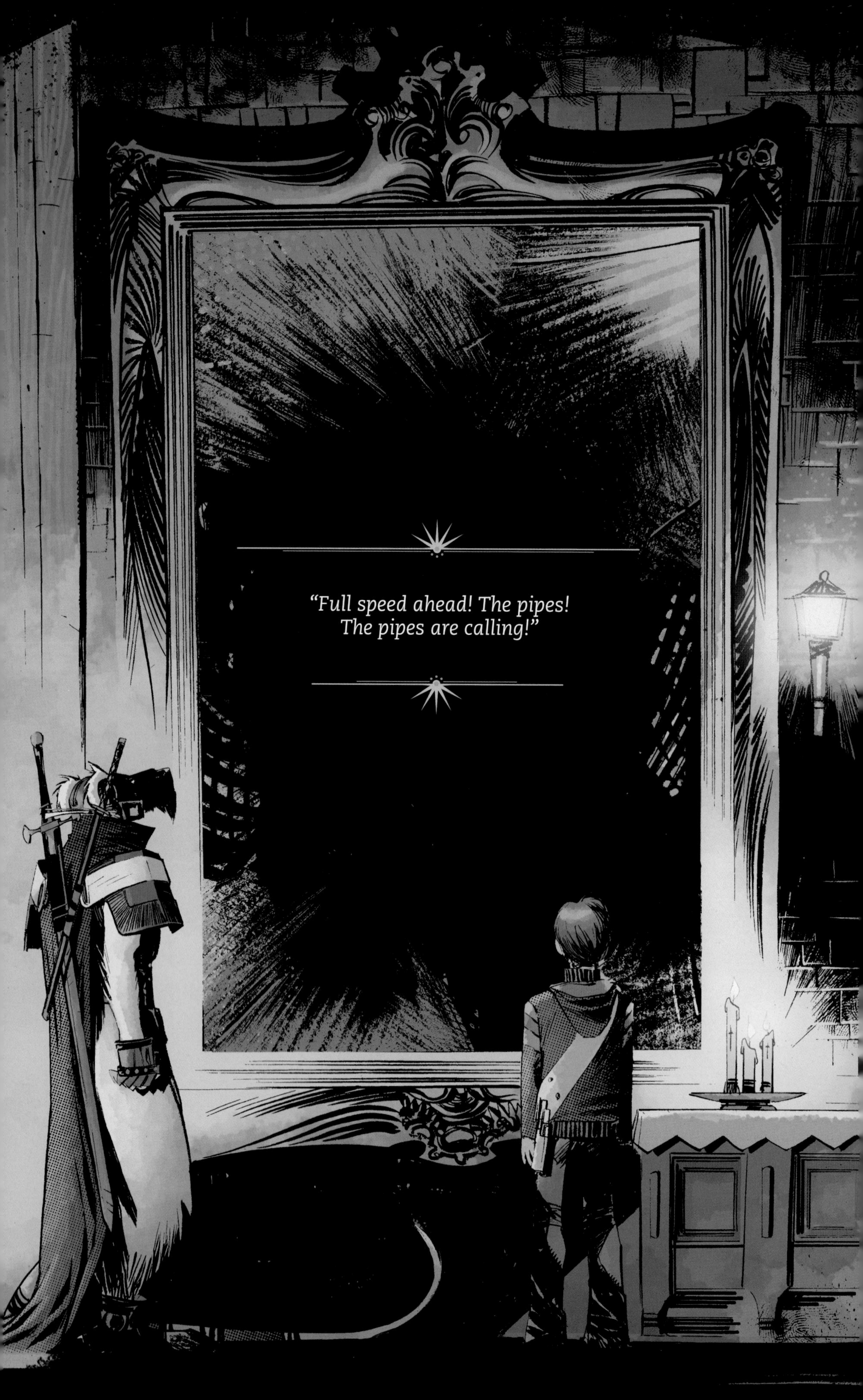
"Full speed ahead! The pipes! The pipes are calling!"

# chapter 3: the dying boy

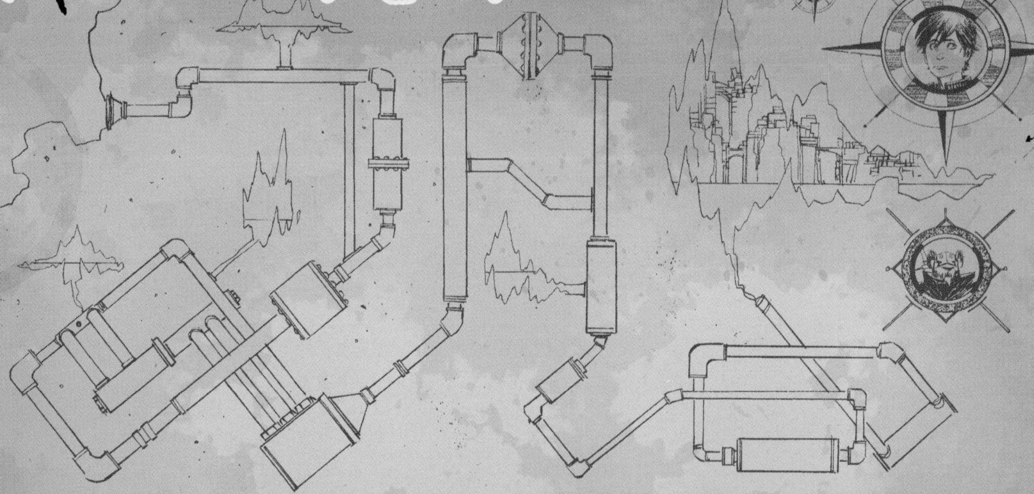

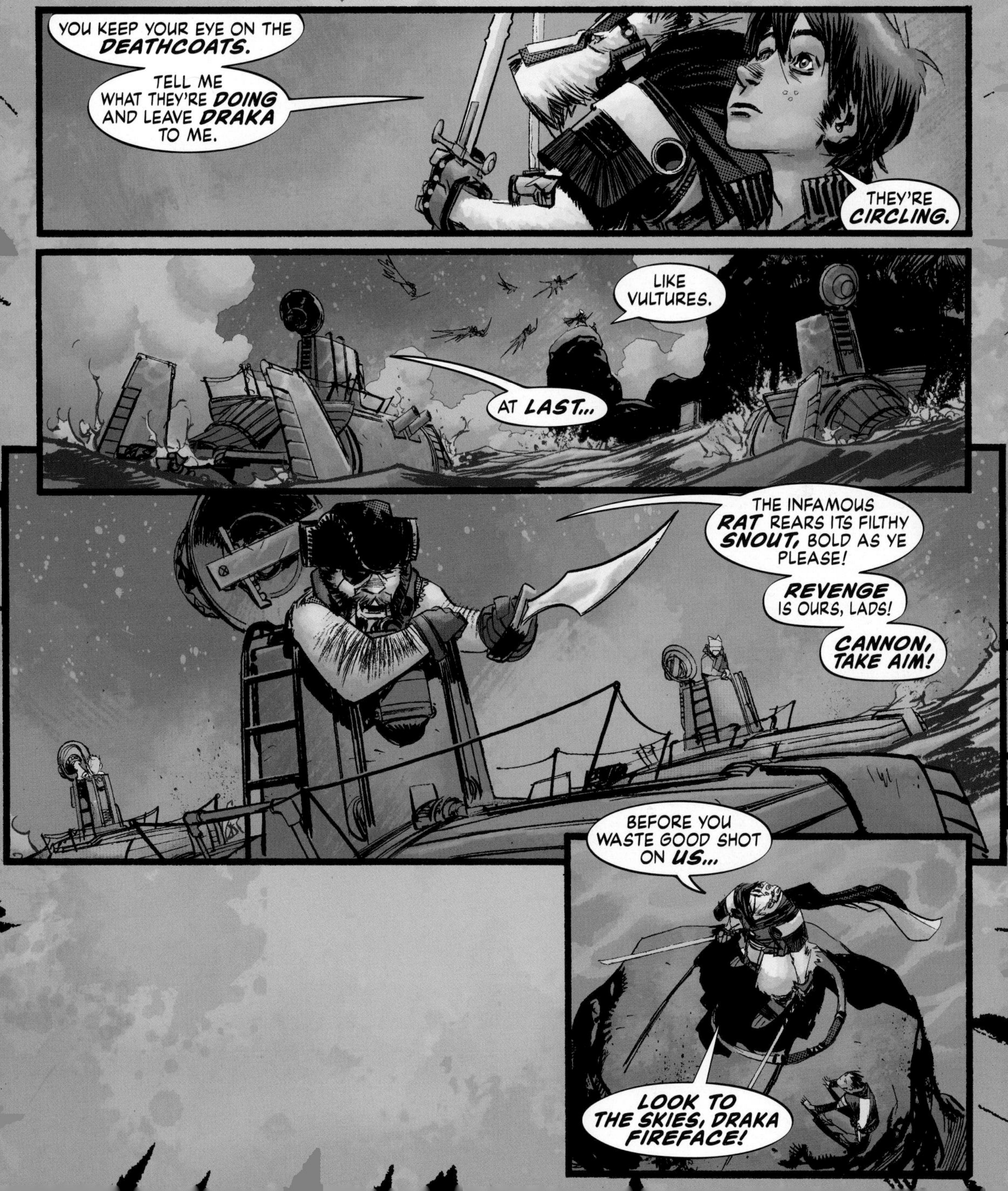

YOU KEEP YOUR EYE ON THE DEATHCOATS.
TELL ME WHAT THEY'RE DOING AND LEAVE DRAKA TO ME.
THEY'RE CIRCLING.
LIKE VULTURES.
AT LAST...
THE INFAMOUS RAT REARS ITS FILTHY SNOUT, BOLD AS YE PLEASE!
REVENGE IS OURS, LADS!
CANNON, TAKE AIM!
BEFORE YOU WASTE GOOD SHOT ON US...
LOOK TO THE SKIES, DRAKA FIREFACE!

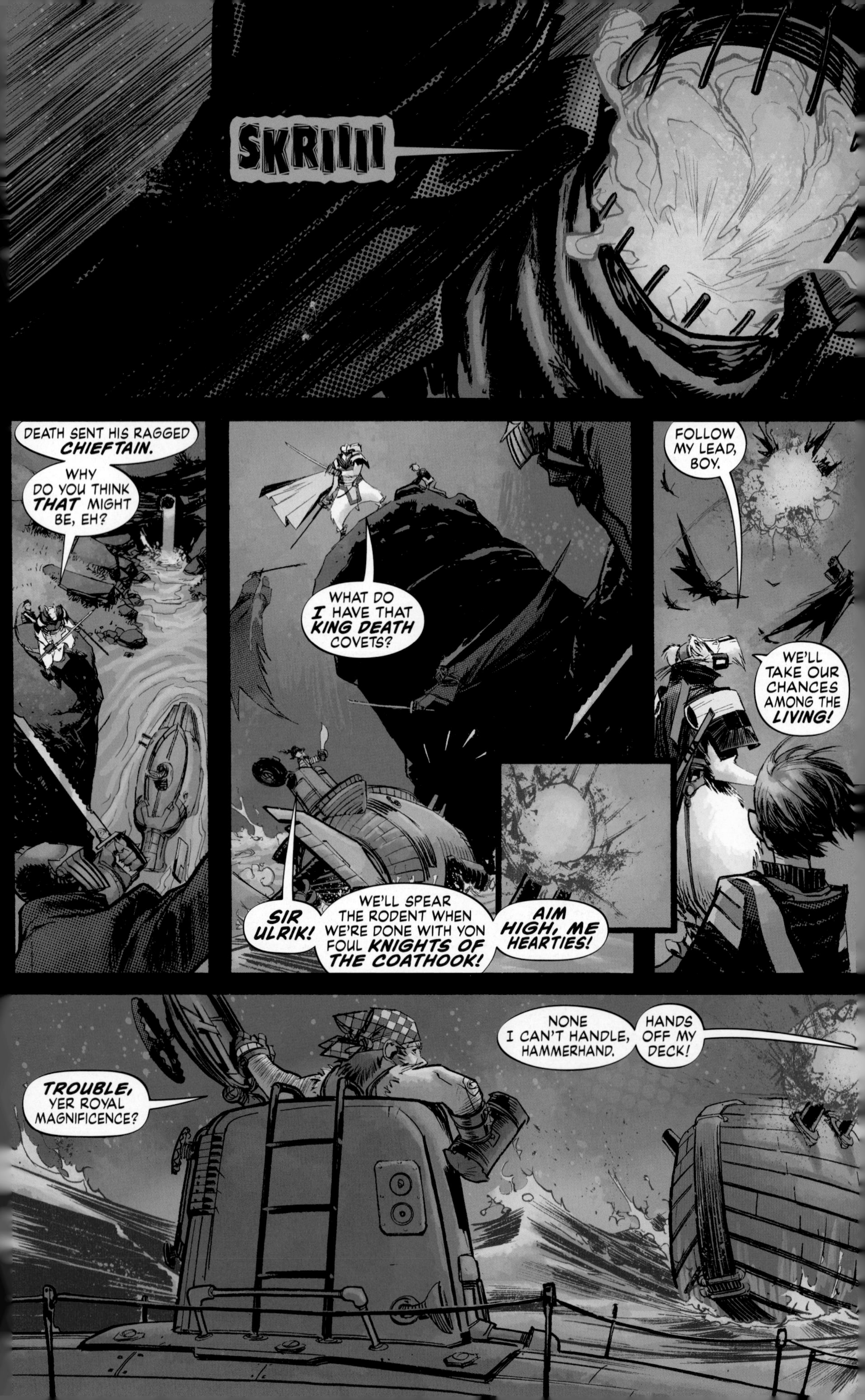
SKRIIII
DEATH SENT HIS RAGGED CHIEFTAIN.
WHY DO YOU THINK THAT MIGHT BE, EH?
WHAT DO I HAVE THAT KING DEATH COVETS?
SIR ULRIK!
WE'LL SPEAR THE RODENT WHEN WE'RE DONE WITH YON FOUL KNIGHTS OF THE COATHOOK!
AIM HIGH, ME HEARTIES!
FOLLOW MY LEAD, BOY.
WE'LL TAKE OUR CHANCES AMONG THE LIVING!
TROUBLE, YER ROYAL MAGNIFICENCE?
NONE I CAN'T HANDLE, HAMMERHAND.
HANDS OFF MY DECK!

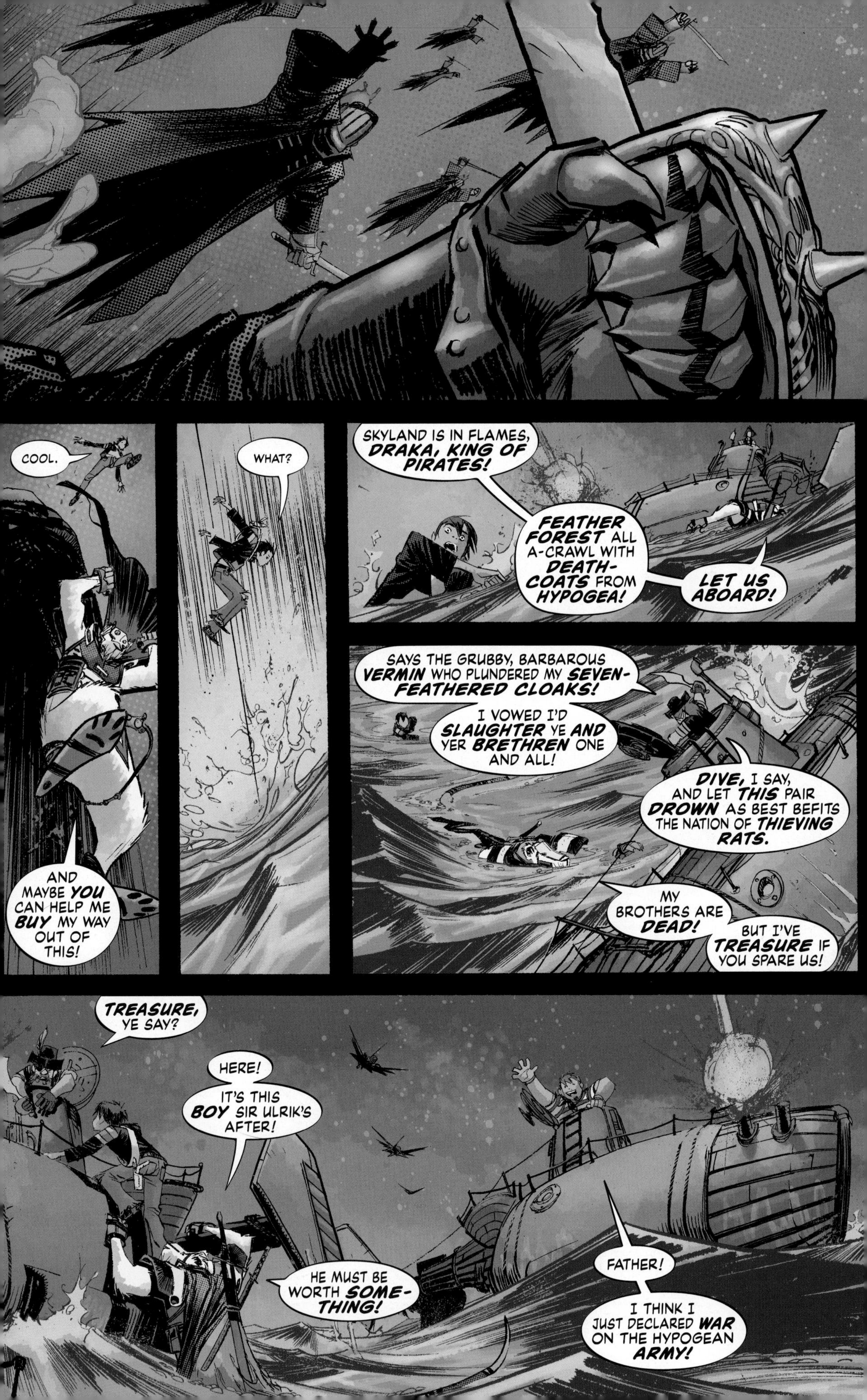
COOL.
AND MAYBE YOU CAN HELP ME BUY MY WAY OUT OF THIS!
WHAT?
SKYLAND IS IN FLAMES, DRAKA, KING OF PIRATES!
FEATHER FOREST ALL A-CRAWL WITH DEATH-COATS FROM HYPOGEA!
LET US ABOARD!
SAYS THE GRUBBY, BARBAROUS VERMIN WHO PLUNDERED MY SEVEN-FEATHERED CLOAKS!
I VOWED I'D SLAUGHTER YE AND YER BRETHREN ONE AND ALL!
DIVE, I SAY, AND LET THIS PAIR DROWN AS BEST BEFITS THE NATION OF THIEVING RATS.
MY BROTHERS ARE DEAD!
BUT I'VE TREASURE IF YOU SPARE US!
TREASURE, YE SAY?
HERE!
IT'S THIS BOY SIR ULRIK'S AFTER!
HE MUST BE WORTH SOME-THING!
FATHER!
I THINK I JUST DECLARED WAR ON THE HYPOGEAN ARMY!

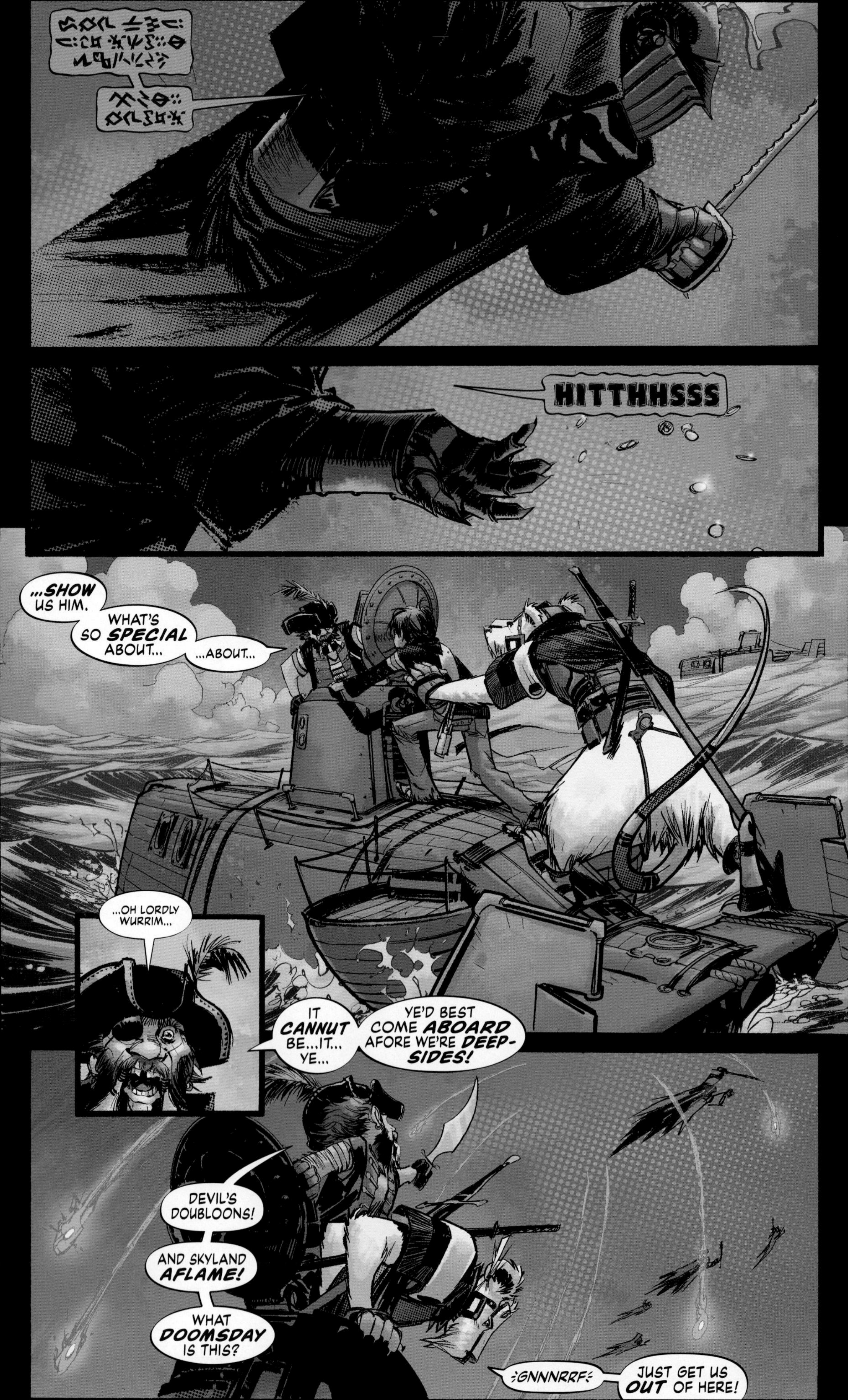
HITTHHSSS
...SHOW US HIM.
WHAT'S SO SPECIAL ABOUT...
...ABOUT...
...OH LORDLY WURRIM...
IT CANNUT BE...IT... YE...
YE'D BEST COME ABOARD AFORE WE'RE DEEP-SIDES!
DEVIL'S DOUBLOONS!
AND SKYLAND AFLAME!
WHAT DOOMSDAY IS THIS?
GNNNRRF
JUST GET US OUT OF HERE!

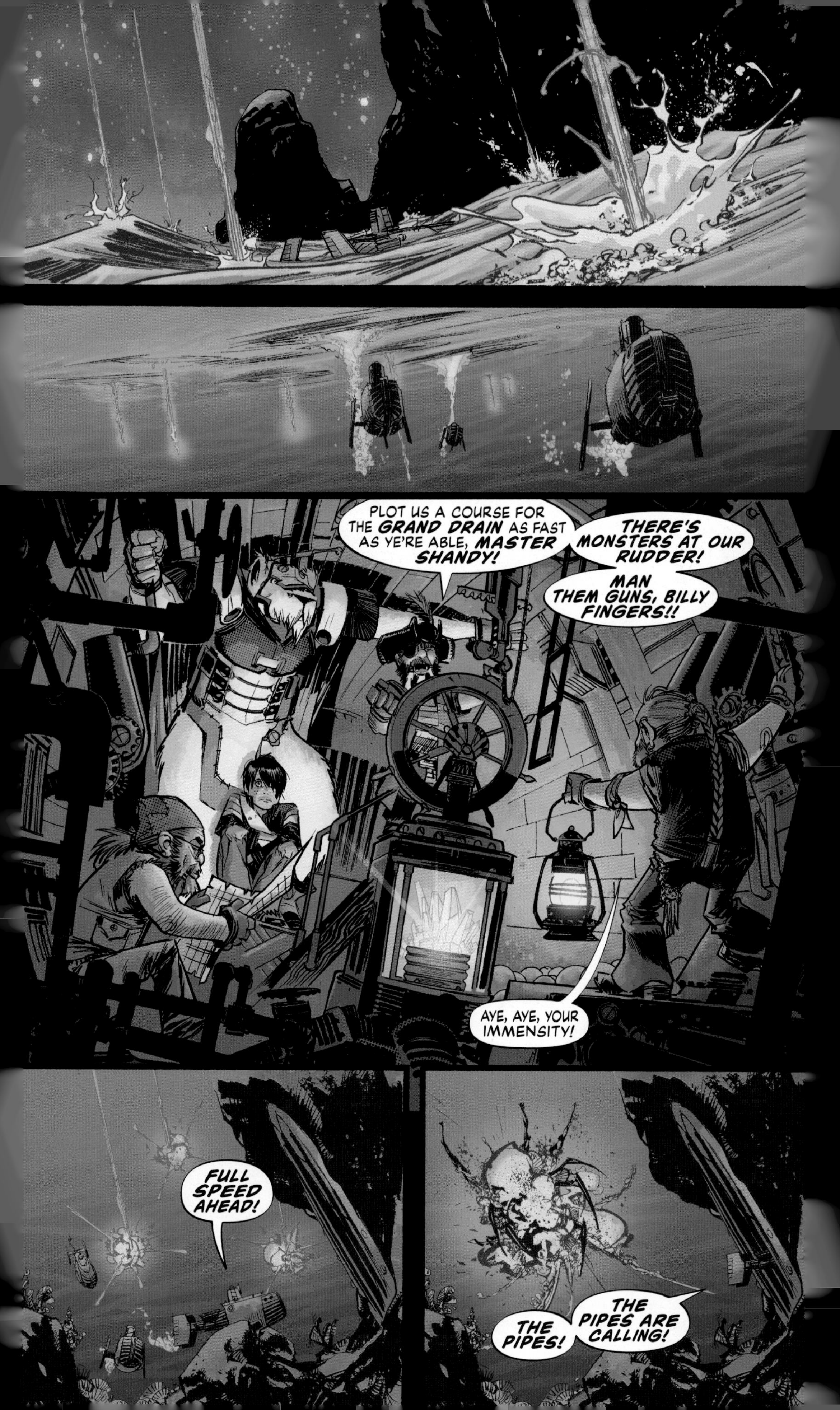
PLOT US A COURSE FOR THE GRAND DRAIN AS FAST AS YE'RE ABLE, MASTER SHANDY!
THERE'S MONSTERS AT OUR RUDDER!
MAN THEM GUNS, BILLY FINGERS!!
AYE, AYE, YOUR IMMENSITY!
FULL SPEED AHEAD!
THE PIPES!
THE PIPES ARE CALLING!

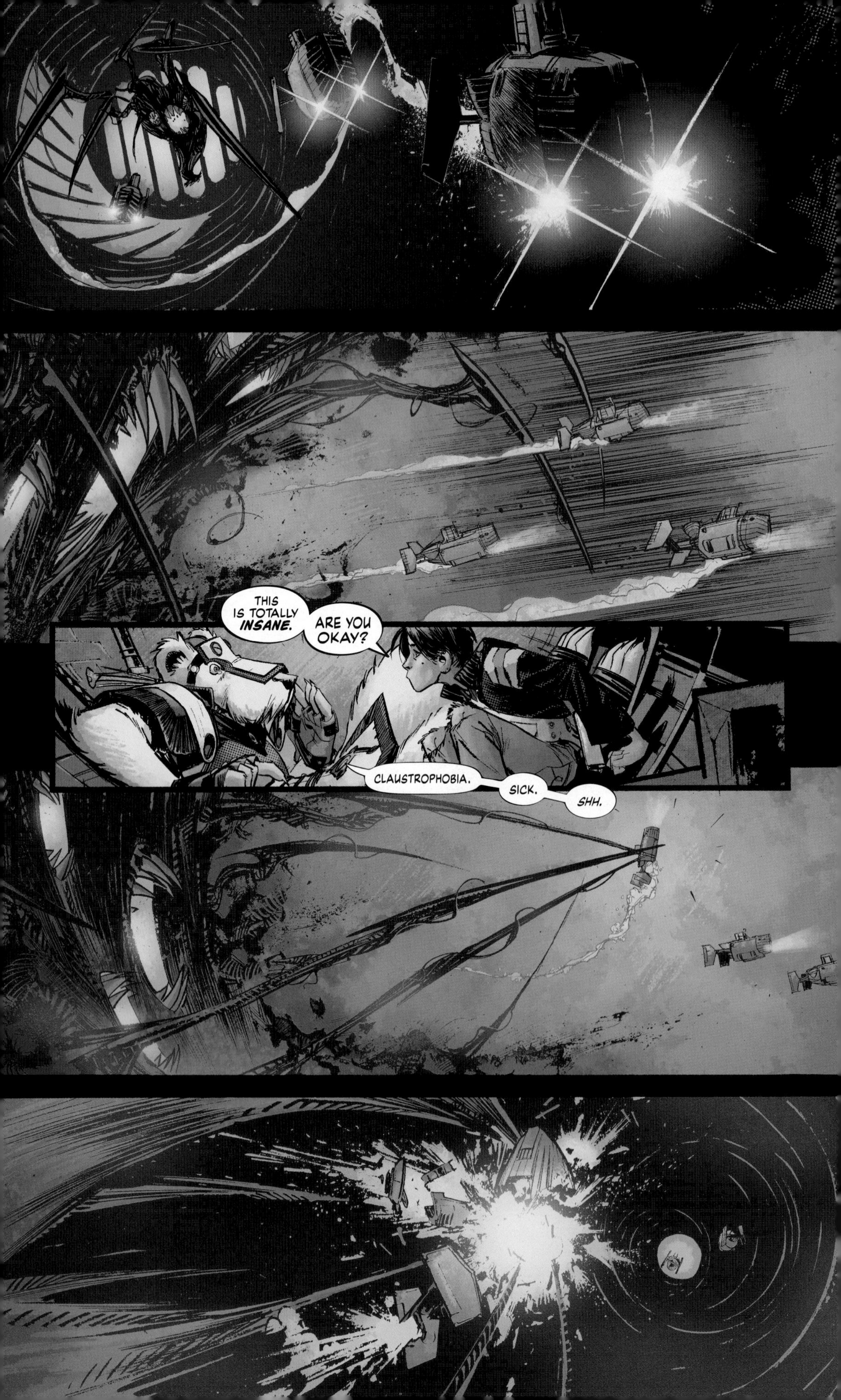
THIS IS TOTALLY INSANE.
ARE YOU OKAY?
CLAUSTROPHOBIA.
SICK.
SHH.

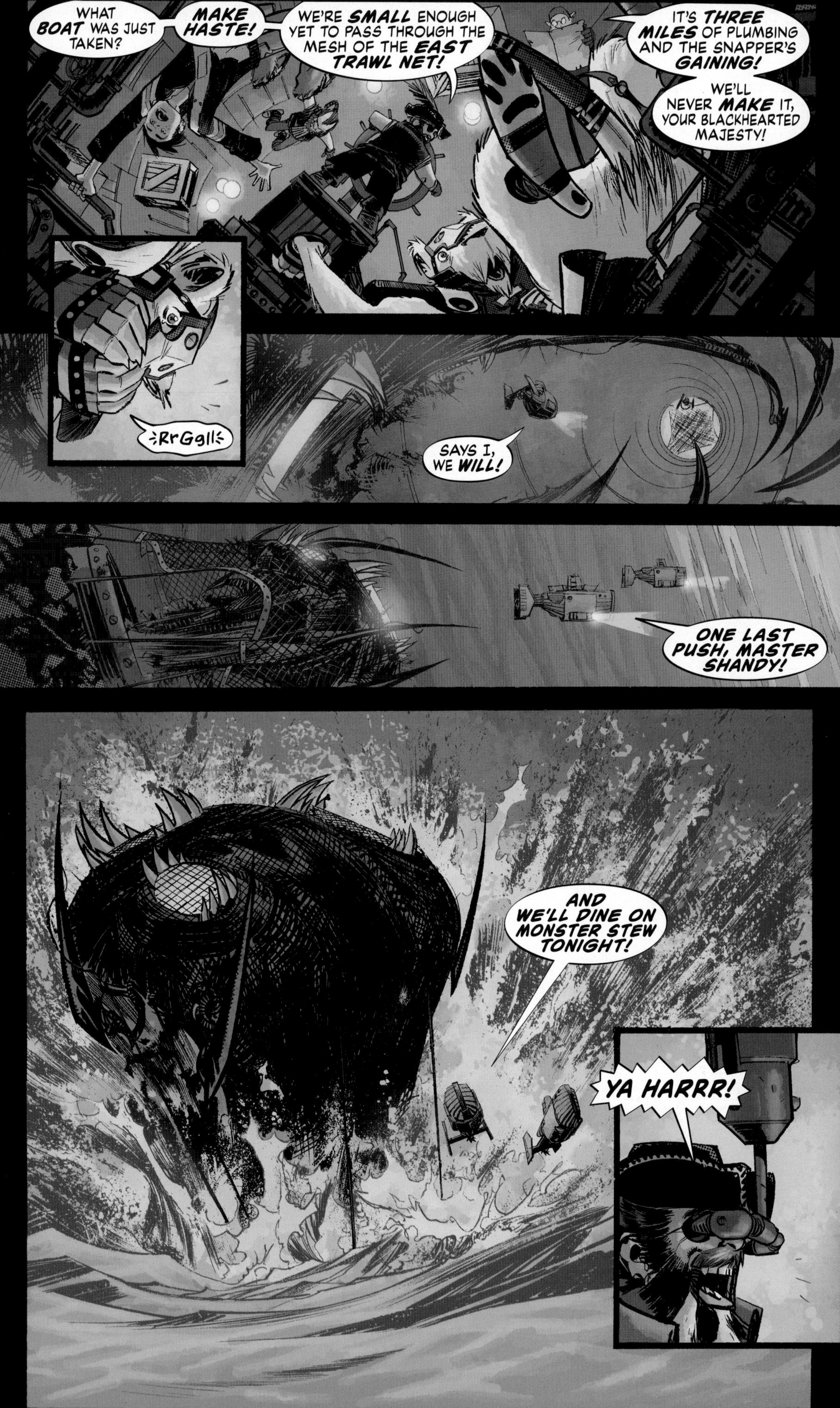
WHAT BOAT WAS JUST TAKEN?
MAKE HASTE!
WE'RE SMALL ENOUGH YET TO PASS THROUGH THE MESH OF THE EAST TRAWL NET!
IT'S THREE MILES OF PLUMBING AND THE SNAPPER'S GAINING!
WE'LL NEVER MAKE IT, YOUR BLACKHEARTED MAJESTY!
RrGgll
SAYS I, WE WILL!
ONE LAST PUSH, MASTER SHANDY!
AND WE'LL DINE ON MONSTER STEW TONIGHT!
YA HARRR!

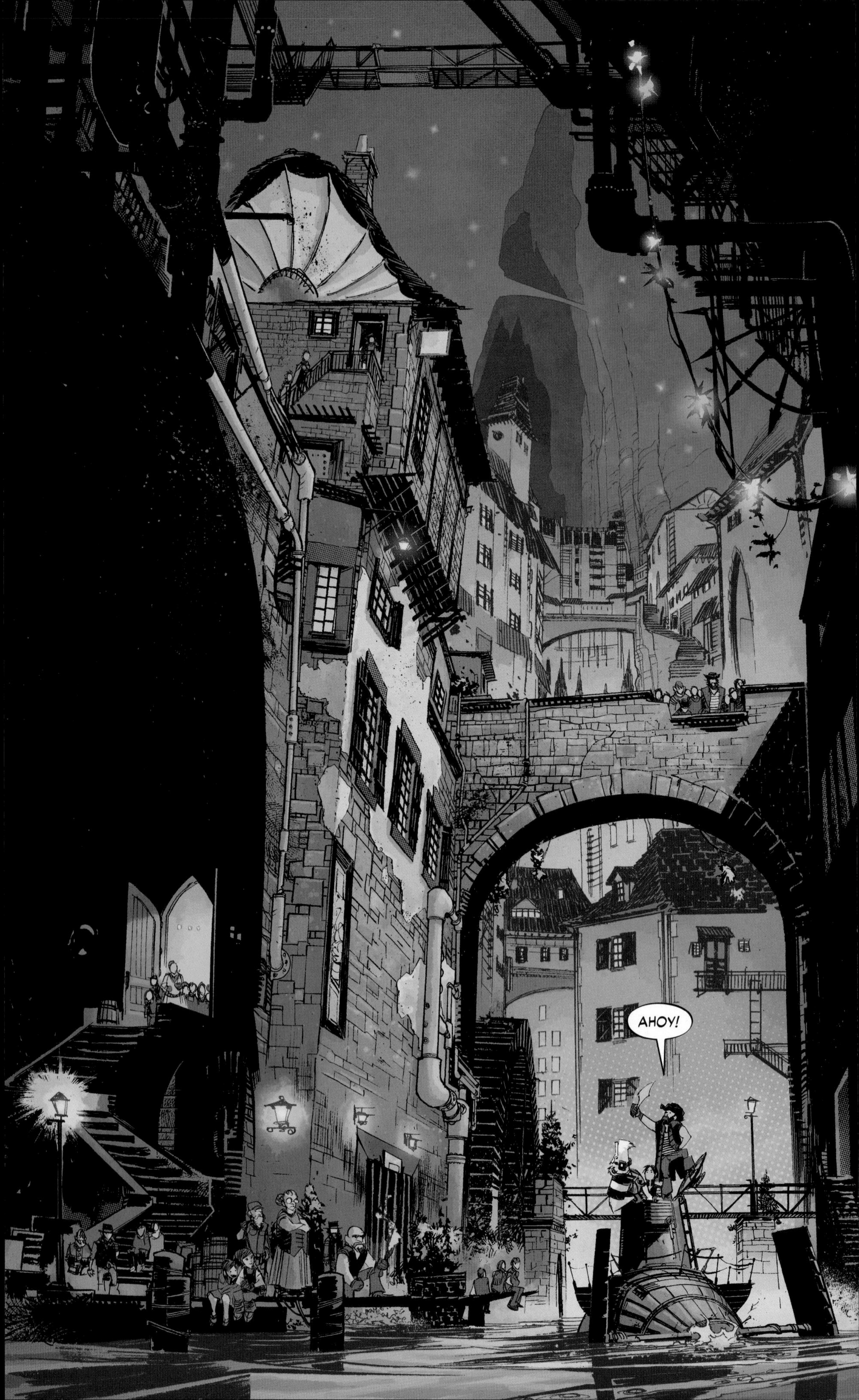
AHOY!

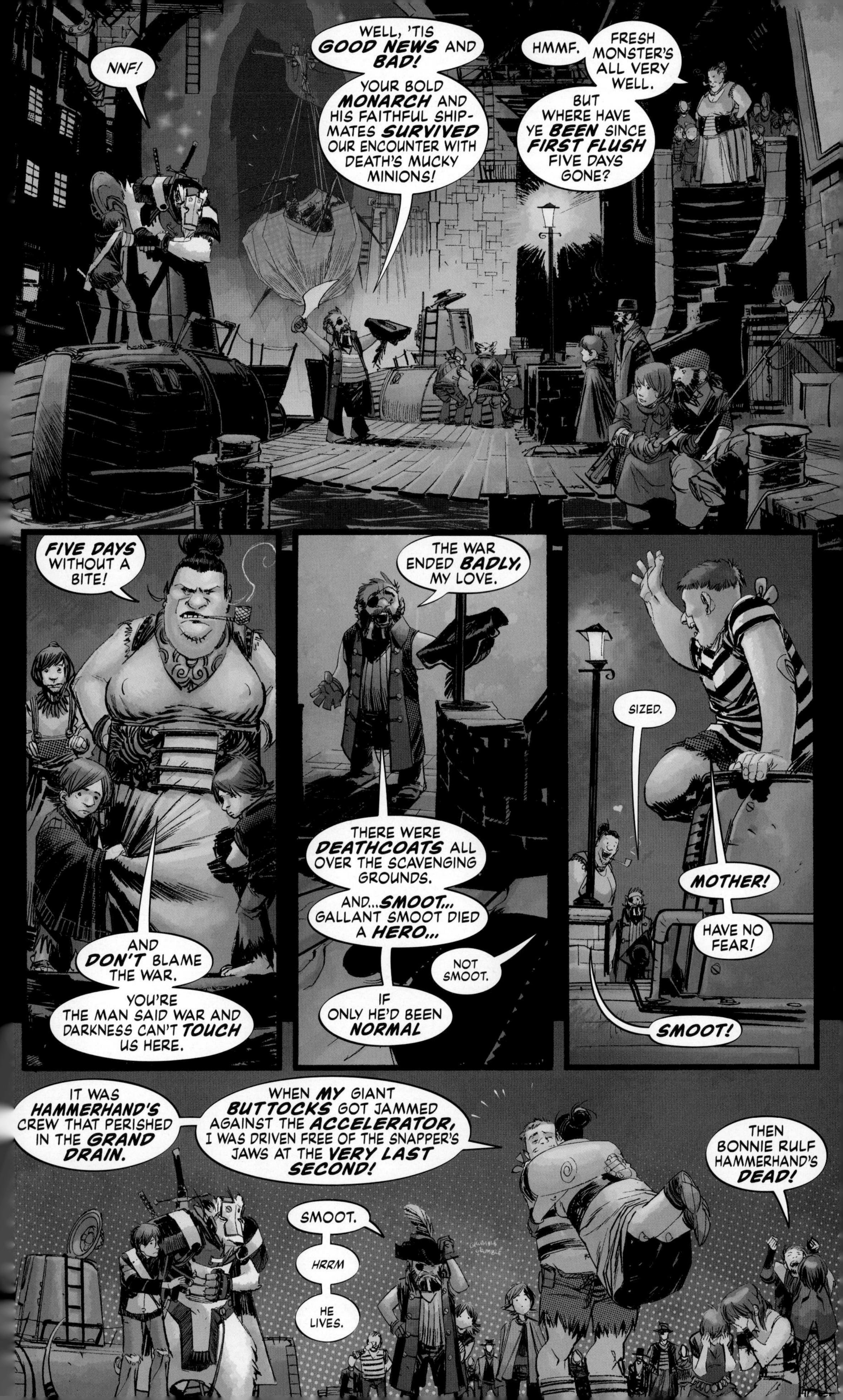
NNF!
WELL, 'TIS GOOD NEWS AND BAD!
YOUR BOLD MONARCH AND HIS FAITHFUL SHIP-MATES SURVIVED OUR ENCOUNTER WITH DEATH'S MUCKY MINIONS!
HMMF.
FRESH MONSTER'S ALL VERY WELL.
BUT WHERE HAVE YE BEEN SINCE FIRST FLUSH FIVE DAYS GONE?
FIVE DAYS WITHOUT A BITE!
AND DON'T BLAME THE WAR.
YOU'RE THE MAN SAID WAR AND DARKNESS CAN'T TOUCH US HERE.
THE WAR ENDED BADLY, MY LOVE.
THERE WERE DEATHCOATS ALL OVER THE SCAVENGING GROUNDS.
AND...SMOOT... GALLANT SMOOT DIED A HERO...
NOT SMOOT.
IF ONLY HE'D BEEN NORMAL
SIZED.
MOTHER!
HAVE NO FEAR!
SMOOT!
IT WAS HAMMERHAND'S CREW THAT PERISHED IN THE GRAND DRAIN.
WHEN MY GIANT BUTTOCKS GOT JAMMED AGAINST THE ACCELERATOR, I WAS DRIVEN FREE OF THE SNAPPER'S JAWS AT THE VERY LAST SECOND!
SMOOT.
HRRM
HE LIVES.
GRUMBLE GRUMBLE
THEN BONNIE RULF HAMMERHAND'S DEAD!

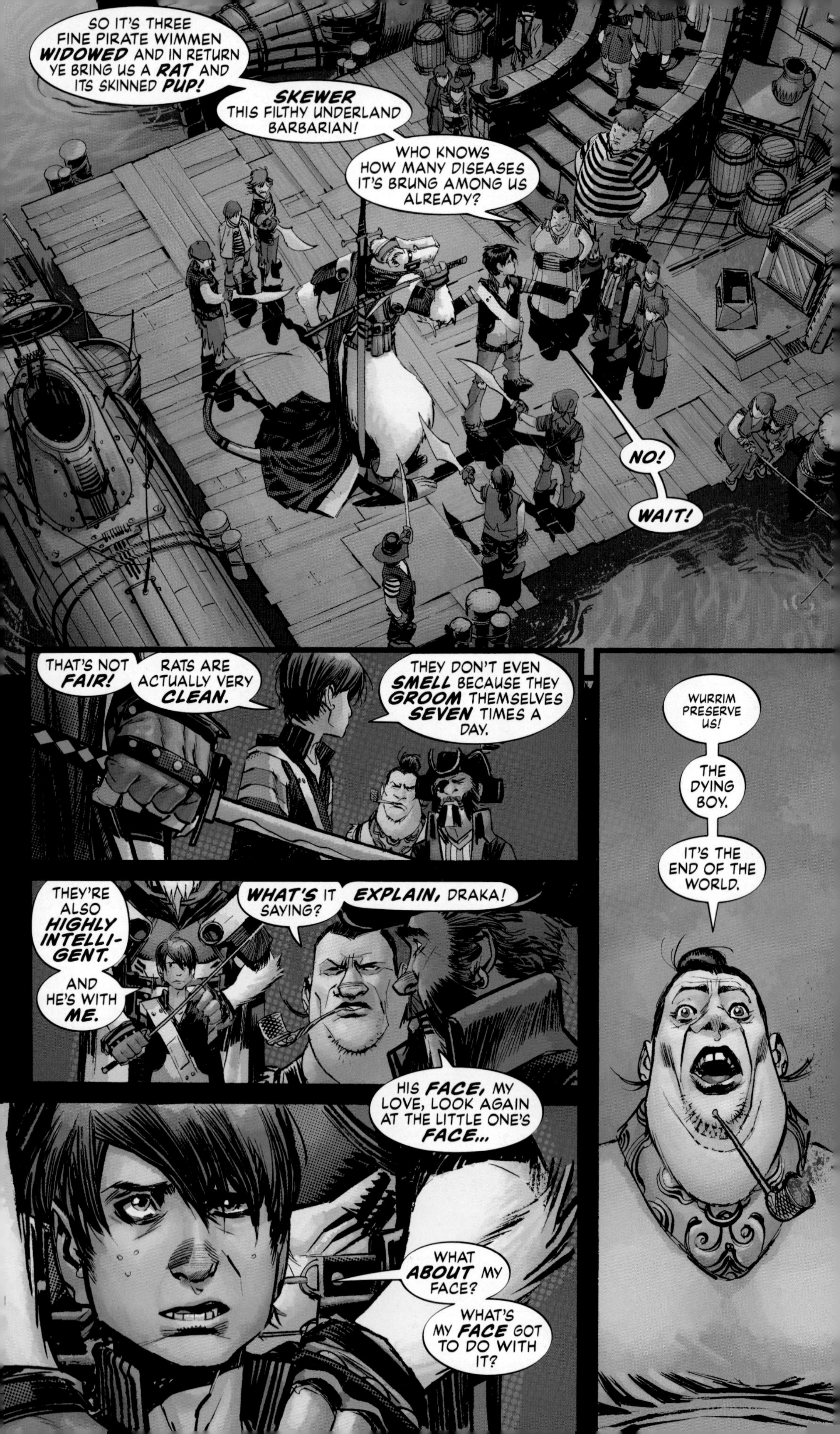
SO IT'S THREE FINE PIRATE WIMMEN WIDOWED AND IN RETURN YE BRING US A RAT AND ITS SKINNED PUP!
SKEWER THIS FILTHY UNDERLAND BARBARIAN!
WHO KNOWS HOW MANY DISEASES IT'S BRUNG AMONG US ALREADY?
NO!
WAIT!
THAT'S NOT FAIR!
RATS ARE ACTUALLY VERY CLEAN.
THEY DON'T EVEN SMELL BECAUSE THEY GROOM THEMSELVES SEVEN TIMES A DAY.
THEY'RE ALSO HIGHLY INTELLI-GENT.
AND HE'S WITH ME.
WHAT'S IT SAYING?
EXPLAIN, DRAKA!
HIS FACE, MY LOVE, LOOK AGAIN AT THE LITTLE ONE'S FACE...
WHAT ABOUT MY FACE?
WHAT'S MY FACE GOT TO DO WITH IT?
WURRIM PRESERVE US!
THE DYING BOY.
IT'S THE END OF THE WORLD.

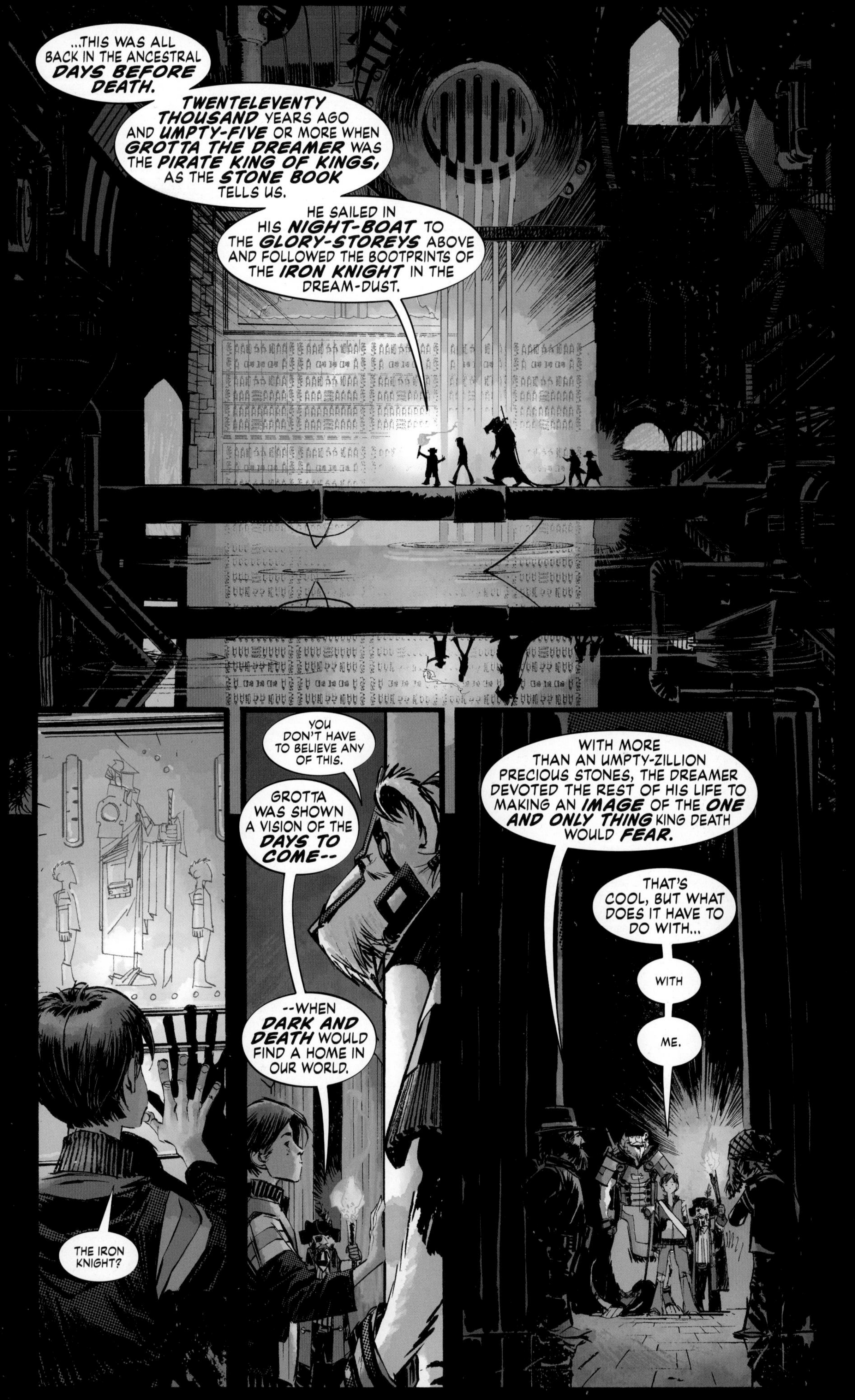

...THIS WAS ALL BACK IN THE ANCESTRAL DAYS BEFORE DEATH.
TWENTELEVENTY THOUSAND YEARS AGO AND UMPTY-FIVE OR MORE WHEN GROTTA THE DREAMER WAS THE PIRATE KING OF KINGS, AS THE STONE BOOK TELLS US.
HE SAILED IN HIS NIGHT-BOAT TO THE GLORY-STOREYS ABOVE AND FOLLOWED THE BOOTPRINTS OF THE IRON KNIGHT IN THE DREAM-DUST.
THE IRON KNIGHT?
YOU DON'T HAVE TO BELIEVE ANY OF THIS.
GROTTA WAS SHOWN A VISION OF THE DAYS TO COME--
--WHEN DARK AND DEATH WOULD FIND A HOME IN OUR WORLD.
WITH MORE THAN AN UMPTY-ZILLION PRECIOUS STONES, THE DREAMER DEVOTED THE REST OF HIS LIFE TO MAKING AN IMAGE OF THE ONE AND ONLY THING KING DEATH WOULD FEAR.
THAT'S COOL, BUT WHAT DOES IT HAVE TO DO WITH...
WITH
ME.

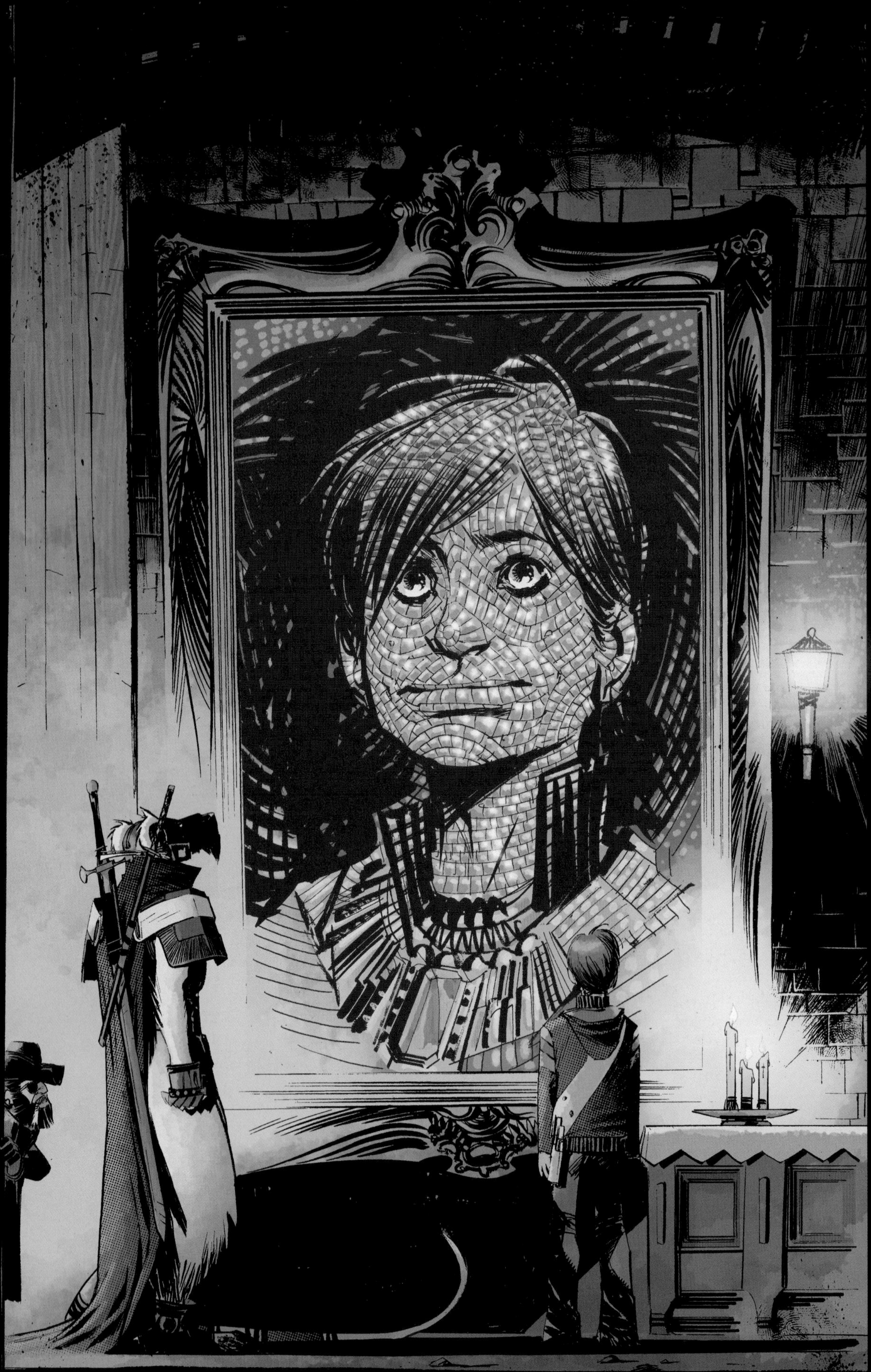

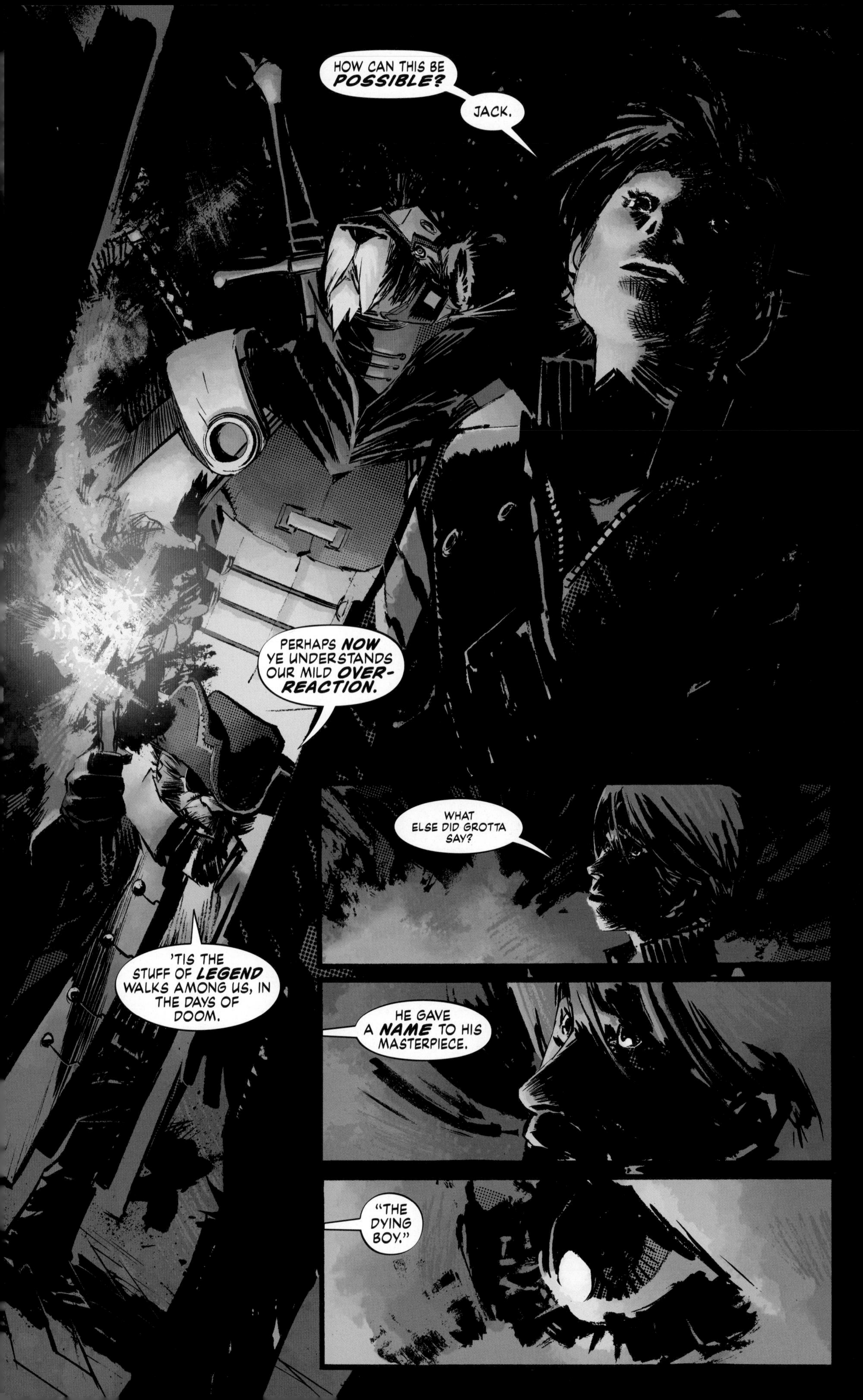
HOW CAN THIS BE **POSSIBLE?**
JACK.
PERHAPS **NOW** YE UNDERSTANDS OUR MILD **OVER-REACTION.**
'TIS THE STUFF OF **LEGEND** WALKS AMONG US, IN THE DAYS OF DOOM.
WHAT ELSE DID GROTTA SAY?
HE GAVE A **NAME** TO HIS MASTERPIECE.
"THE DYING BOY."

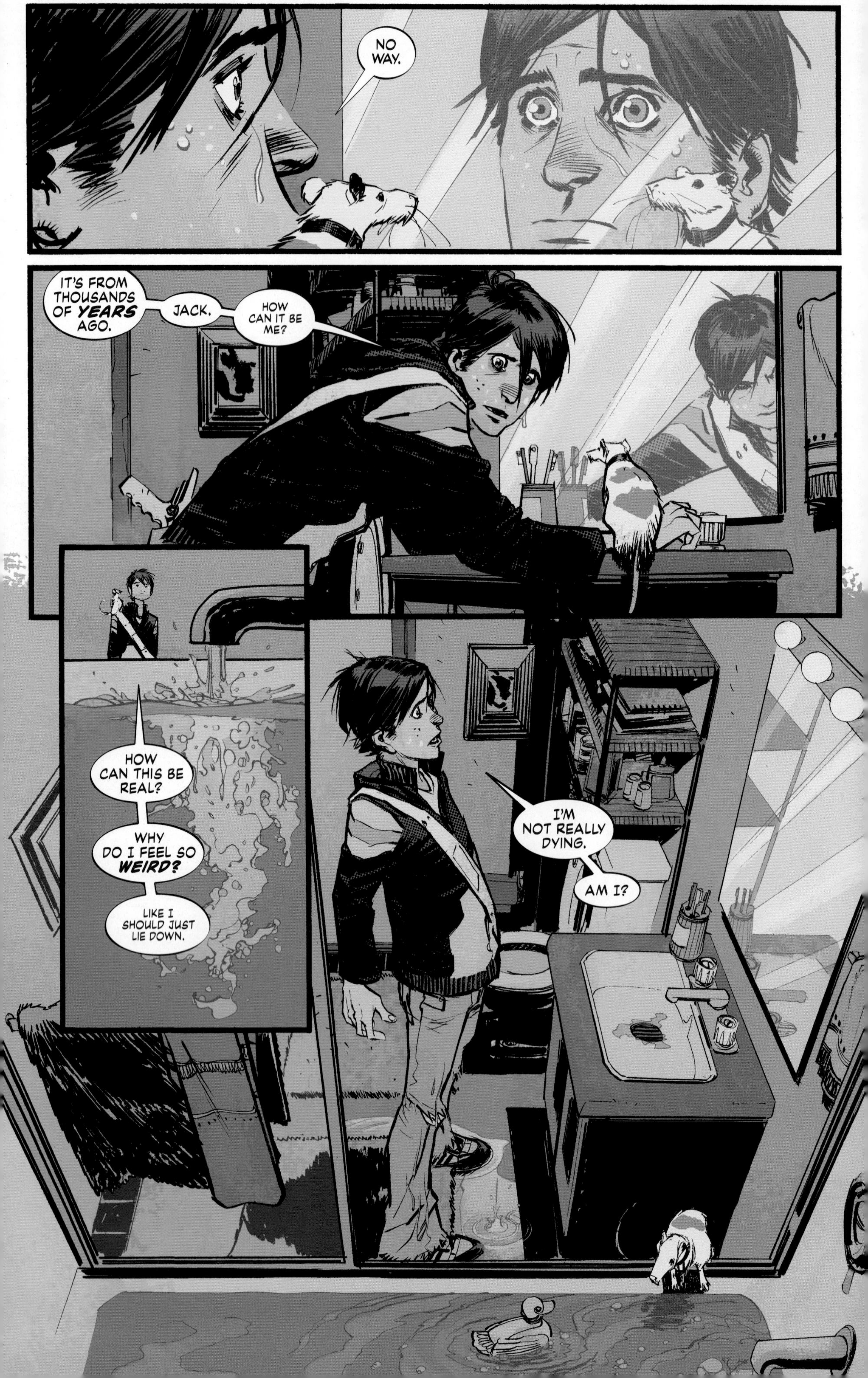
NO WAY.
IT'S FROM THOUSANDS OF **YEARS** AGO.
JACK.
HOW CAN IT BE ME?
HOW CAN THIS BE REAL?
WHY DO I FEEL SO **WEIRD?**
LIKE I SHOULD JUST LIE DOWN.
I'M NOT REALLY DYING.
AM I?

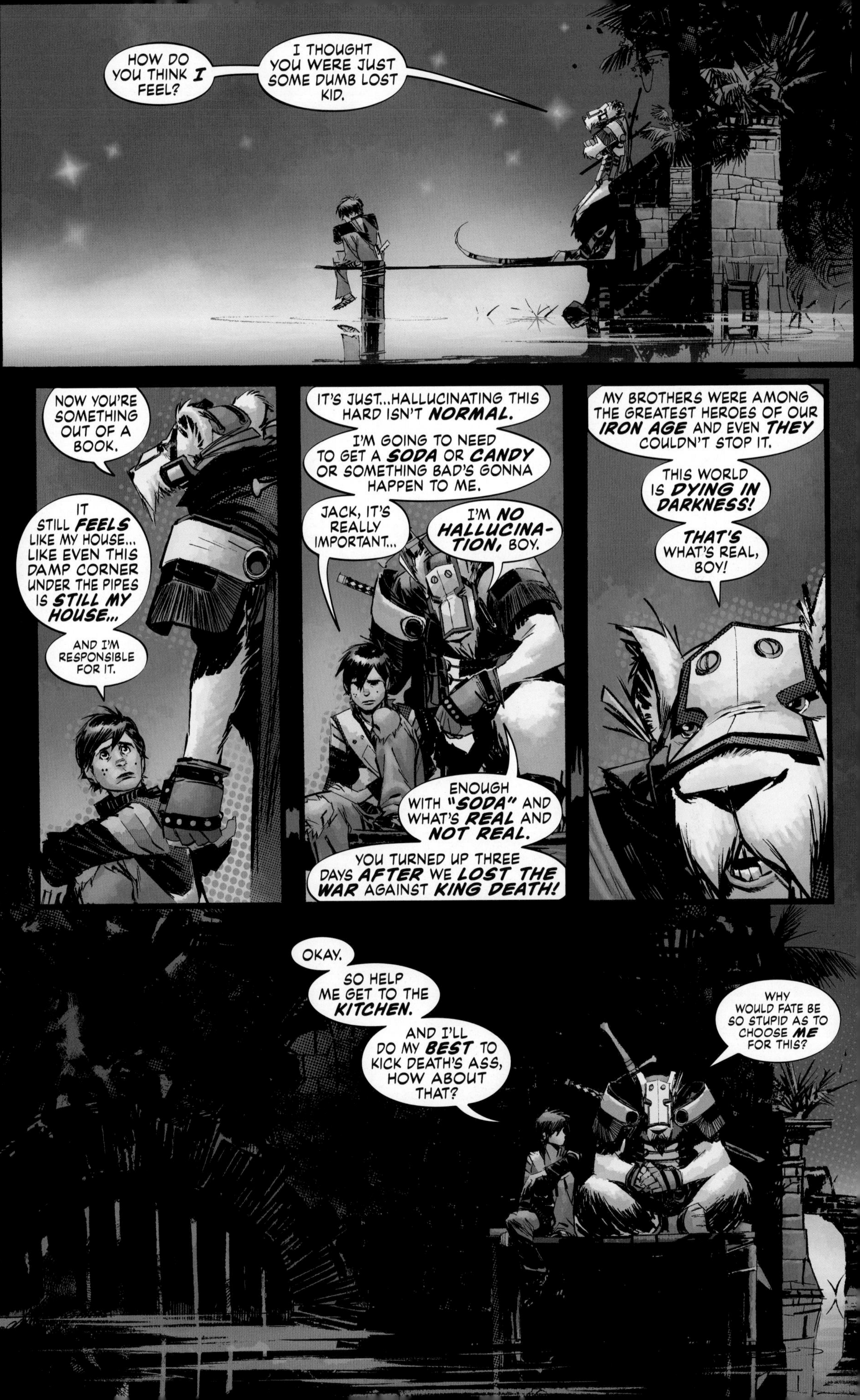
HOW DO YOU THINK *I* FEEL?
I THOUGHT YOU WERE JUST SOME DUMB LOST KID.
NOW YOU'RE SOMETHING OUT OF A BOOK.
IT STILL *FEELS* LIKE MY HOUSE... LIKE EVEN THIS DAMP CORNER UNDER THE PIPES IS *STILL MY HOUSE...*
AND I'M RESPONSIBLE FOR IT.
IT'S JUST...HALLUCINATING THIS HARD ISN'T *NORMAL.*
I'M GOING TO NEED TO GET A *SODA* OR *CANDY* OR SOMETHING BAD'S GONNA HAPPEN TO ME.
JACK, IT'S REALLY IMPORTANT...
I'M *NO HALLUCINATION,* BOY.
ENOUGH WITH *"SODA"* AND WHAT'S *REAL* AND *NOT REAL.*
YOU TURNED UP THREE DAYS *AFTER* WE *LOST THE WAR* AGAINST *KING DEATH!*
MY BROTHERS WERE AMONG THE GREATEST HEROES OF OUR *IRON AGE* AND EVEN *THEY* COULDN'T STOP IT.
THIS WORLD IS *DYING IN DARKNESS!*
*THAT'S* WHAT'S REAL, BOY!
OKAY.
SO HELP ME GET TO THE *KITCHEN.*
AND I'LL DO MY *BEST* TO KICK DEATH'S ASS, HOW ABOUT THAT?
WHY WOULD FATE BE SO STUPID AS TO CHOOSE *ME* FOR THIS?

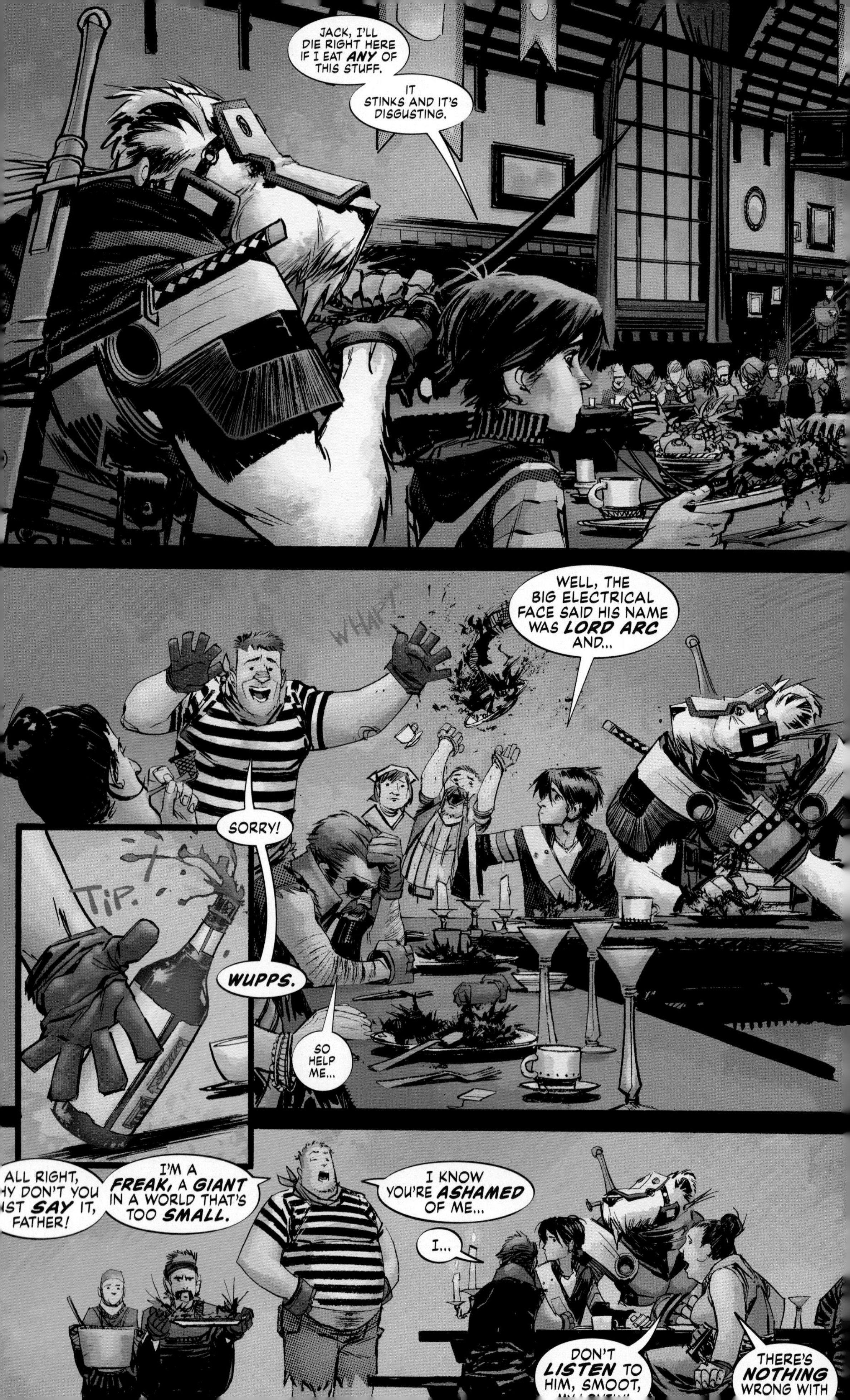
JACK, I'LL DIE RIGHT HERE IF I EAT ANY OF THIS STUFF.
IT STINKS AND IT'S DISGUSTING.
WHAP!
WELL, THE BIG ELECTRICAL FACE SAID HIS NAME WAS LORD ARC AND...
SORRY!
WUPPS.
TIP.
SO HELP ME...
I'M A FREAK, A GIANT IN A WORLD THAT'S TOO SMALL.
I KNOW YOU'RE ASHAMED OF ME...
I...
DON'T LISTEN TO HIM, SMOOT,
THERE'S NOTHING WRONG WITH

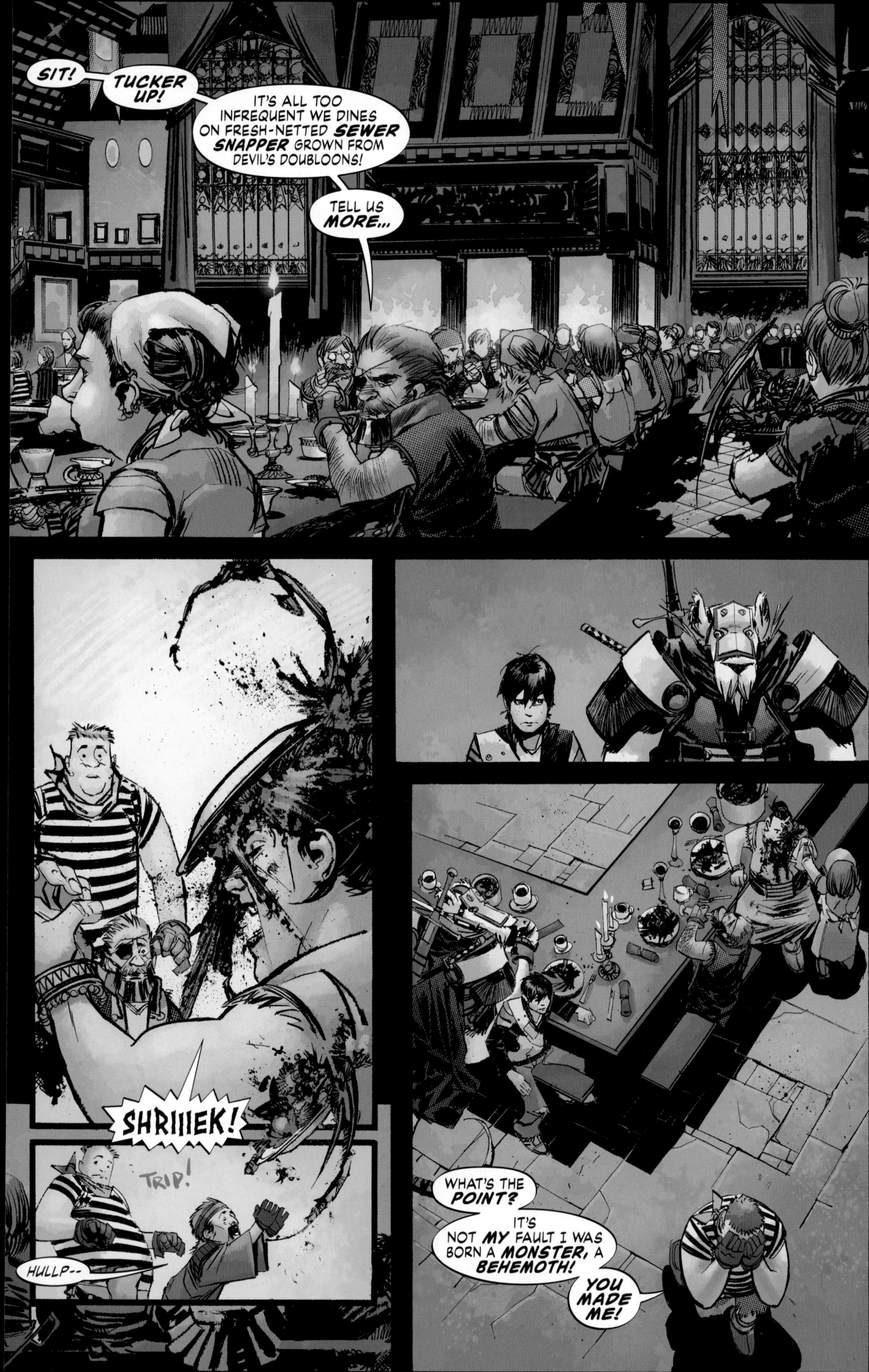
SIT!
TUCKER UP!
IT'S ALL TOO INFREQUENT WE DINES ON FRESH-NETTED SEWER SNAPPER GROWN FROM DEVIL'S DOUBLOONS!
TELL US MORE...
SHRIIIEK!
TRIP!
HULLP--
WHAT'S THE POINT?
IT'S NOT MY FAULT I WAS BORN A MONSTER, A BEHEMOTH!
YOU MADE ME!

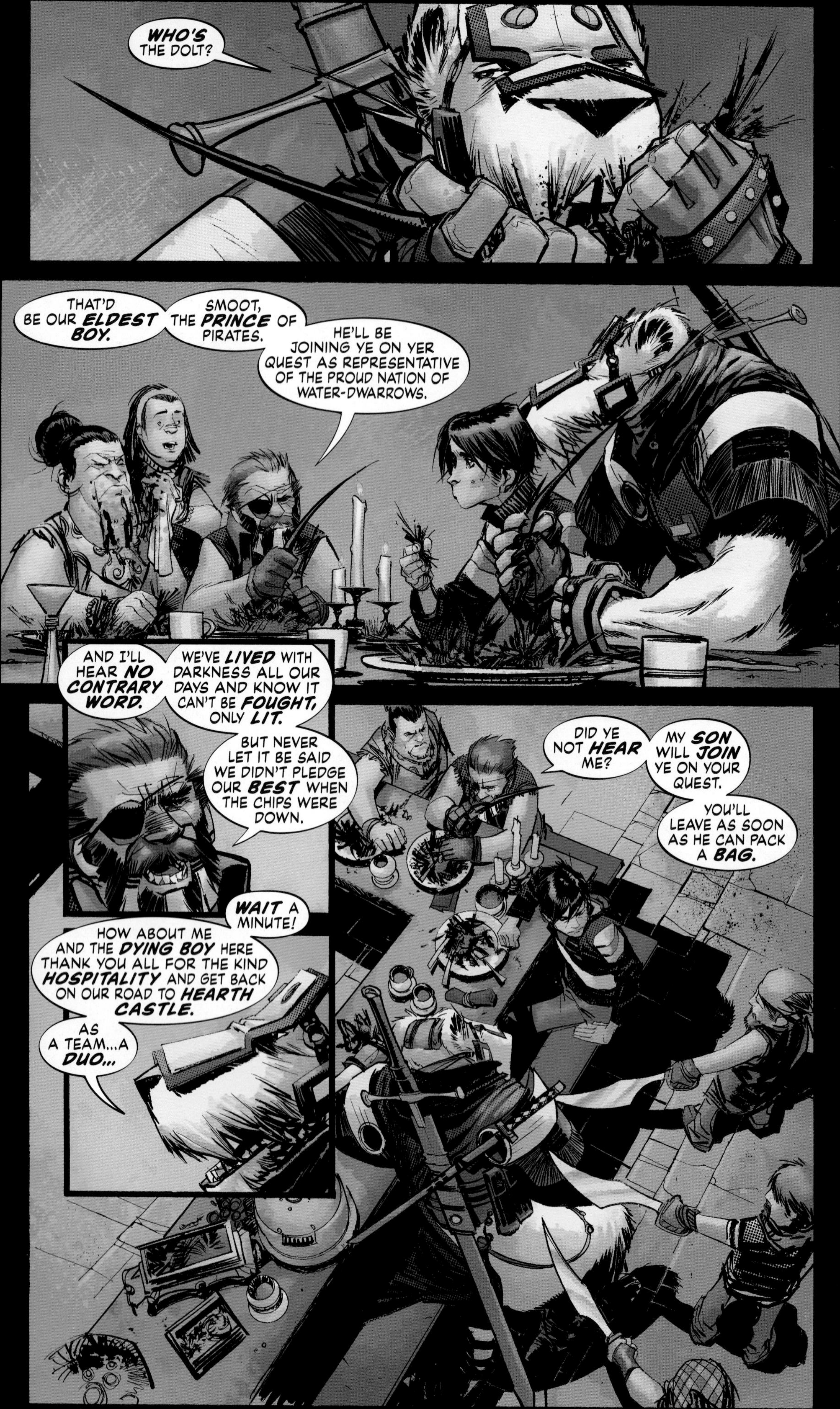
WHO'S THE DOLT?
THAT'D BE OUR ELDEST BOY.
SMOOT, THE PRINCE OF PIRATES.
HE'LL BE JOINING YE ON YER QUEST AS REPRESENTATIVE OF THE PROUD NATION OF WATER-DWARROWS.
AND I'LL HEAR NO CONTRARY WORD.
WE'VE LIVED WITH DARKNESS ALL OUR DAYS AND KNOW IT CAN'T BE FOUGHT, ONLY LIT.
BUT NEVER LET IT BE SAID WE DIDN'T PLEDGE OUR BEST WHEN THE CHIPS WERE DOWN.
DID YE NOT HEAR ME?
MY SON WILL JOIN YE ON YOUR QUEST.
YOU'LL LEAVE AS SOON AS HE CAN PACK A BAG.
WAIT A MINUTE!
HOW ABOUT ME AND THE DYING BOY HERE THANK YOU ALL FOR THE KIND HOSPITALITY AND GET BACK ON OUR ROAD TO HEARTH CASTLE.
AS A TEAM...A DUO...

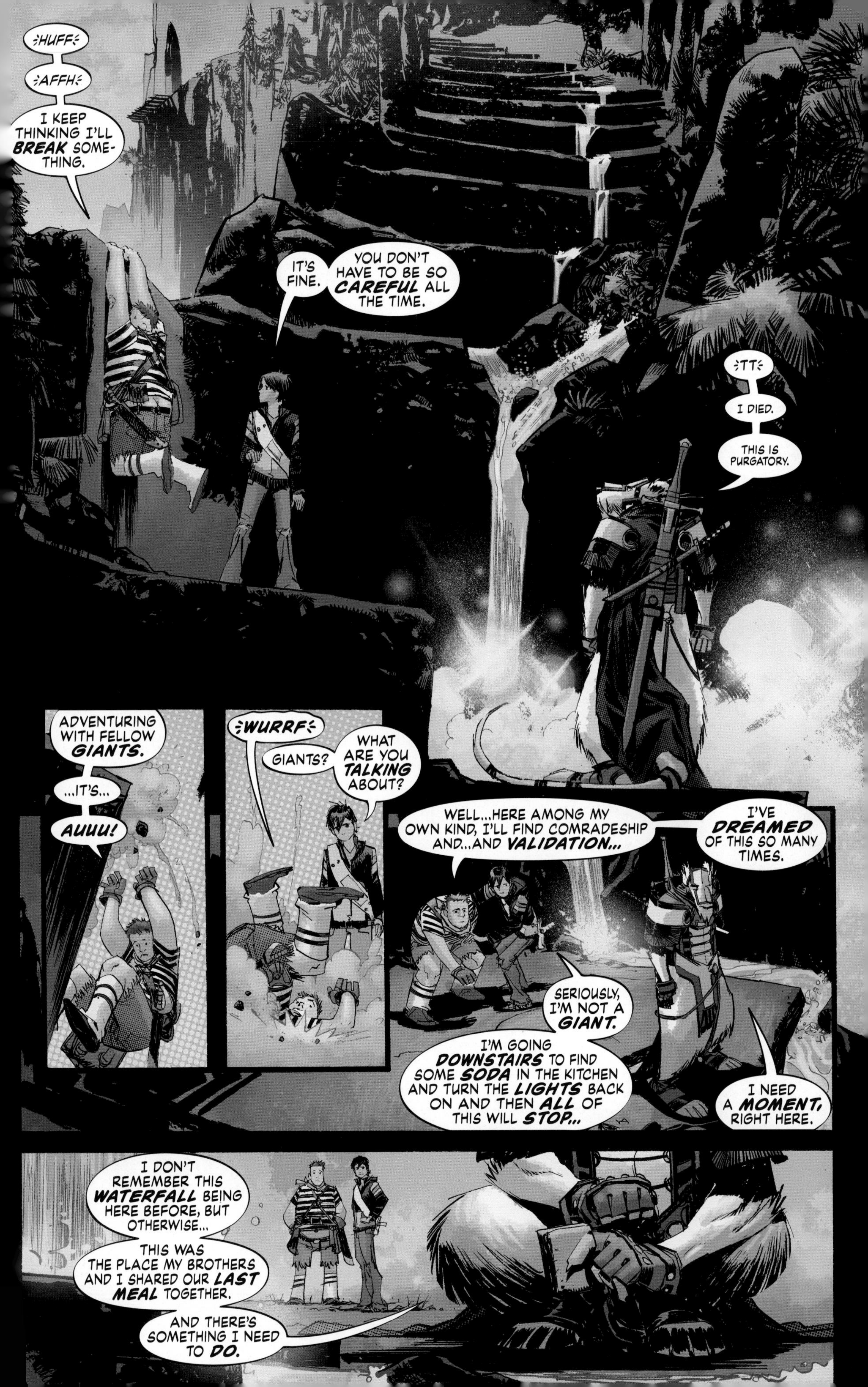
HUFF
AFFH
I KEEP THINKING I'LL BREAK SOMETHING.
IT'S FINE.
YOU DON'T HAVE TO BE SO CAREFUL ALL THE TIME.
TT
I DIED.
THIS IS PURGATORY.
ADVENTURING WITH FELLOW GIANTS.
...IT'S...
AUUU!
WURRF
GIANTS?
WHAT ARE YOU TALKING ABOUT?
WELL...HERE AMONG MY OWN KIND, I'LL FIND COMRADESHIP AND...AND VALIDATION...
I'VE DREAMED OF THIS SO MANY TIMES.
SERIOUSLY, I'M NOT A GIANT.
I'M GOING DOWNSTAIRS TO FIND SOME SODA IN THE KITCHEN AND TURN THE LIGHTS BACK ON AND THEN ALL OF THIS WILL STOP...
I NEED A MOMENT, RIGHT HERE.
I DON'T REMEMBER THIS WATERFALL BEING HERE BEFORE, BUT OTHERWISE...
THIS WAS THE PLACE MY BROTHERS AND I SHARED OUR LAST MEAL TOGETHER.
AND THERE'S SOMETHING I NEED TO DO.

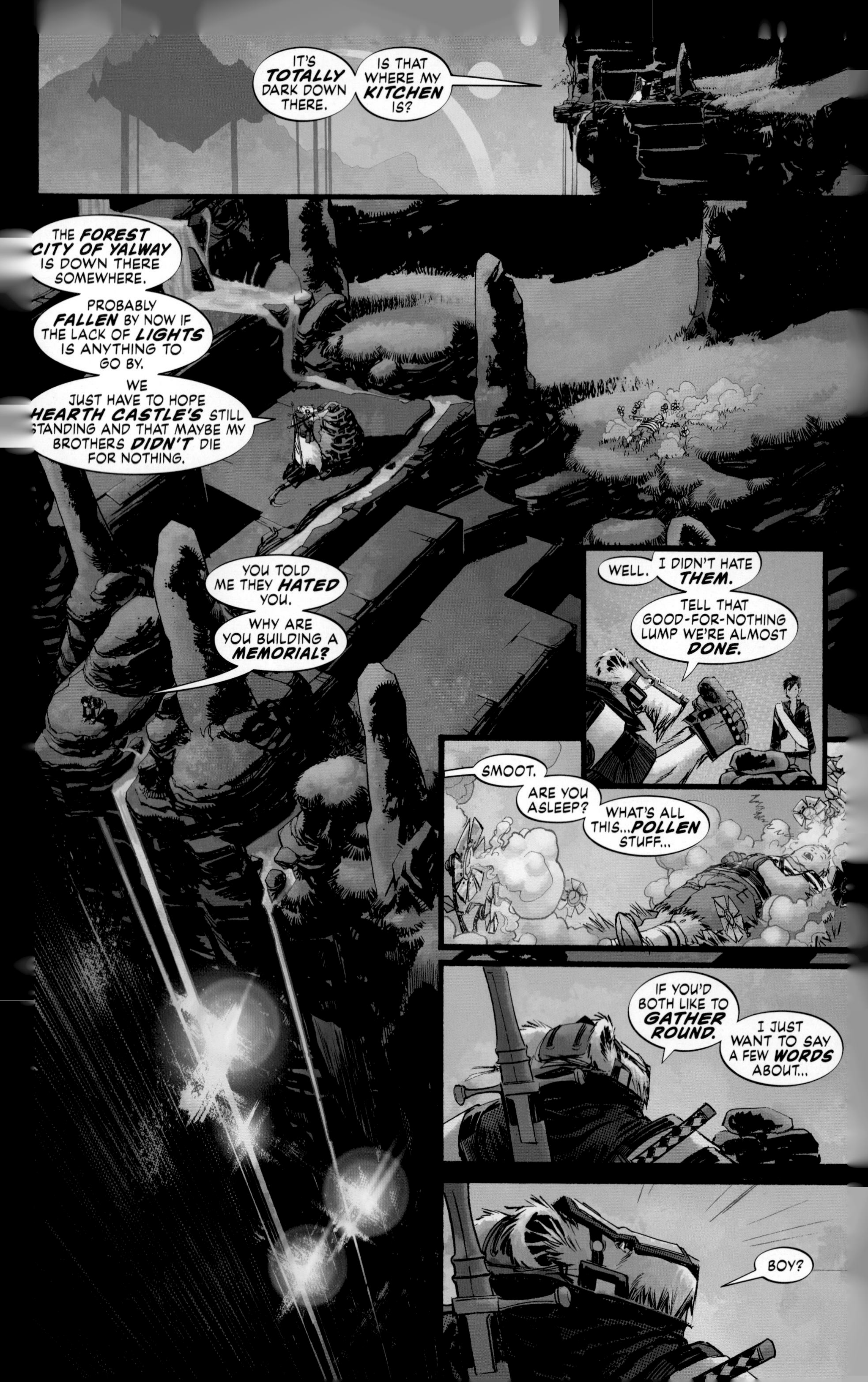
IT'S TOTALLY DARK DOWN THERE.
IS THAT WHERE MY KITCHEN IS?
THE FOREST CITY OF YALWAY IS DOWN THERE SOMEWHERE.
PROBABLY FALLEN BY NOW IF THE LACK OF LIGHTS IS ANYTHING TO GO BY.
WE JUST HAVE TO HOPE HEARTH CASTLE'S STILL STANDING AND THAT MAYBE MY BROTHERS DIDN'T DIE FOR NOTHING.
YOU TOLD ME THEY HATED YOU.
WHY ARE YOU BUILDING A MEMORIAL?
WELL.
I DIDN'T HATE THEM.
TELL THAT GOOD-FOR-NOTHING LUMP WE'RE ALMOST DONE.
SMOOT.
ARE YOU ASLEEP?
WHAT'S ALL THIS...POLLEN STUFF...
IF YOU'D BOTH LIKE TO GATHER ROUND.
I JUST WANT TO SAY A FEW WORDS ABOUT...
BOY?

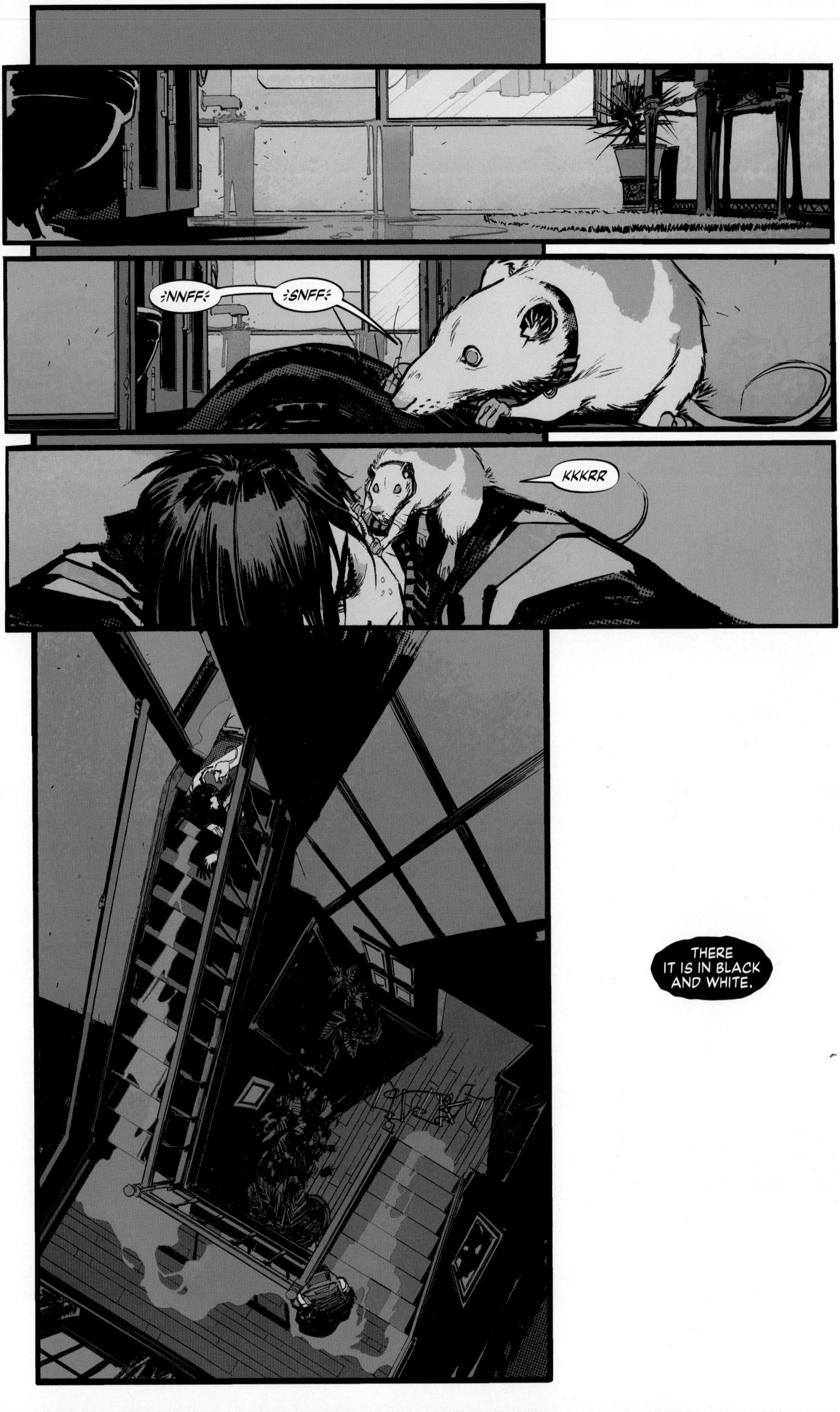

NNFF
SNFF
KKKRR
THERE IT IS IN BLACK AND WHITE.

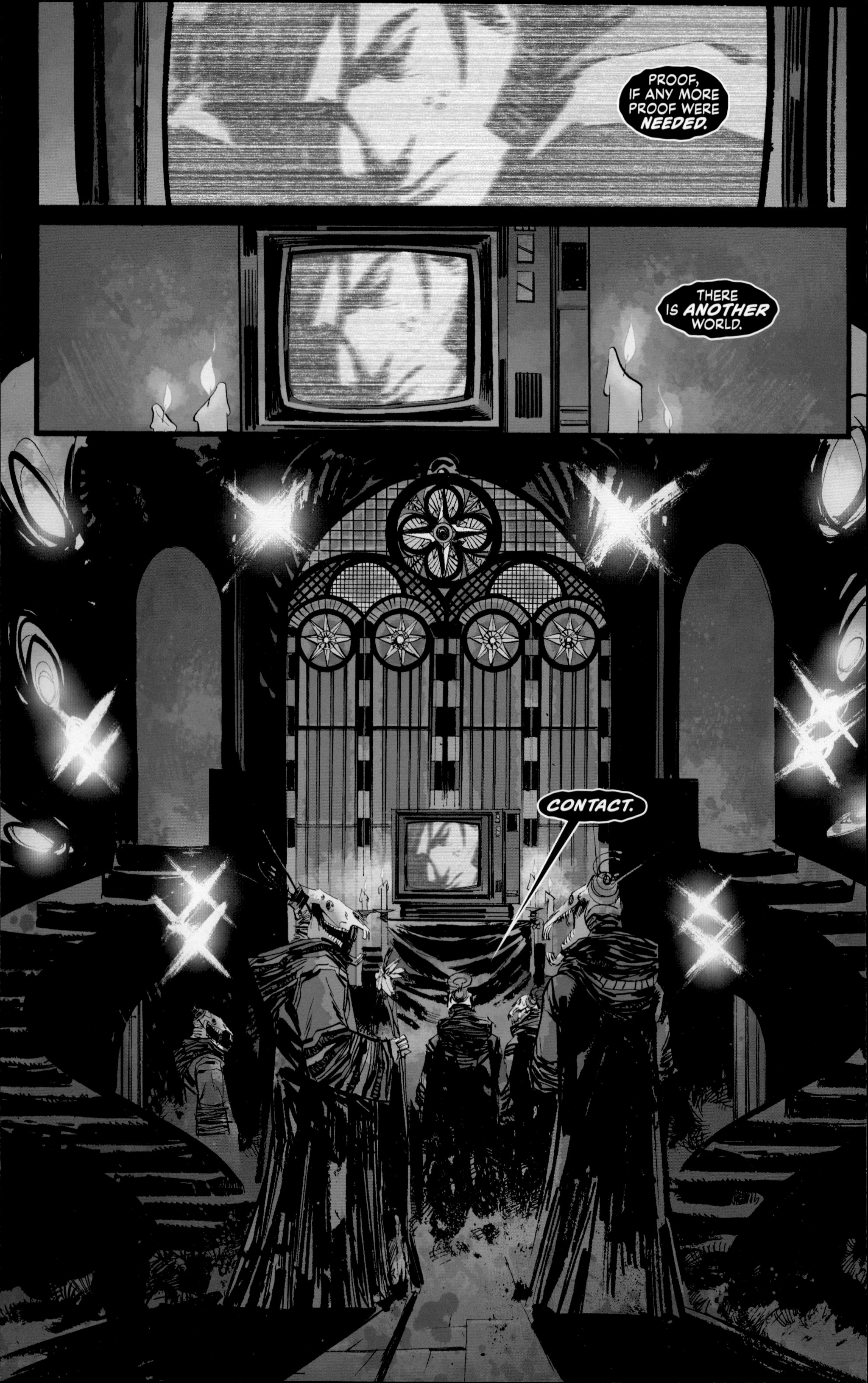
PROOF, IF ANY MORE PROOF WERE NEEDED.
THERE IS ANOTHER WORLD.
CONTACT.

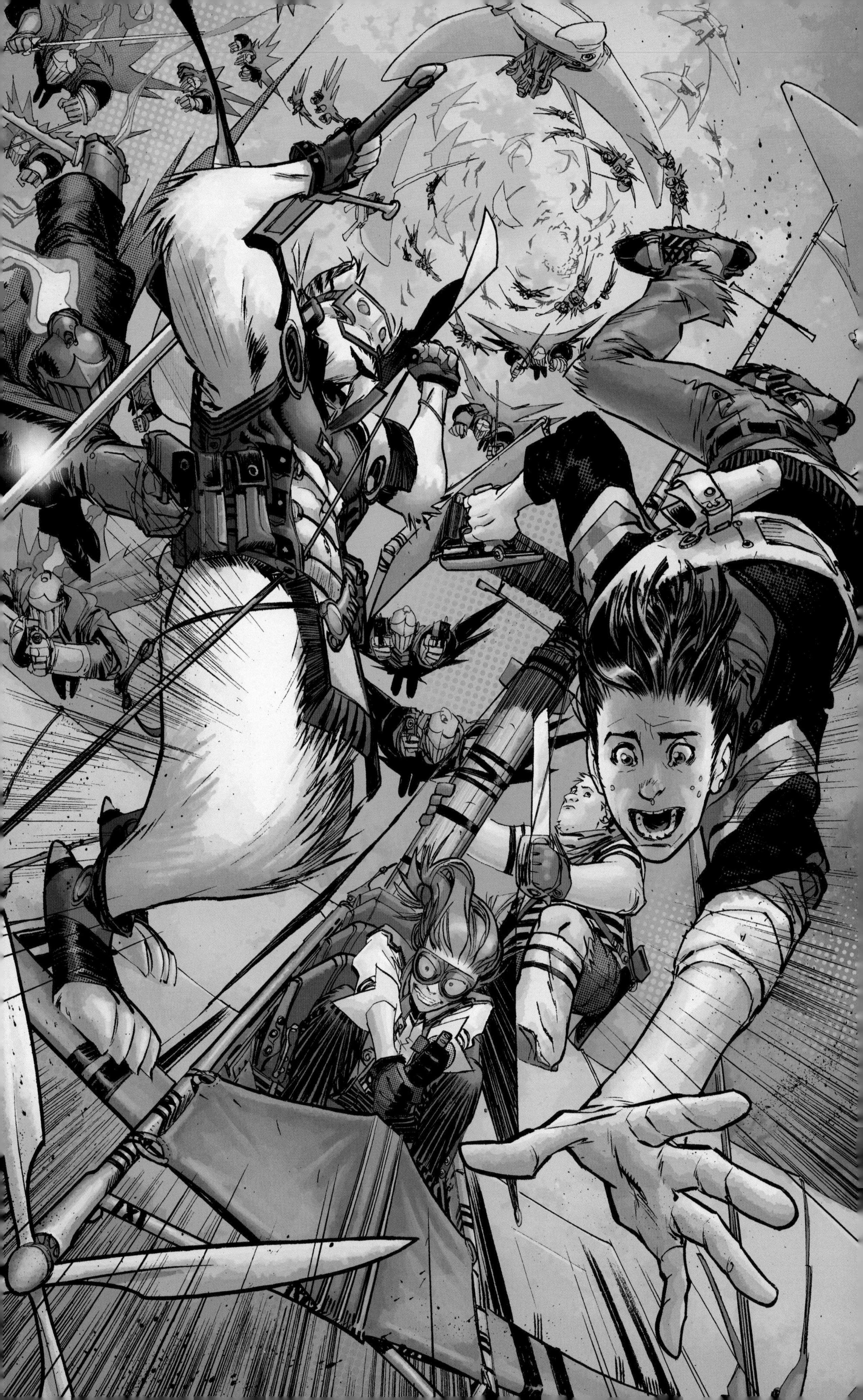

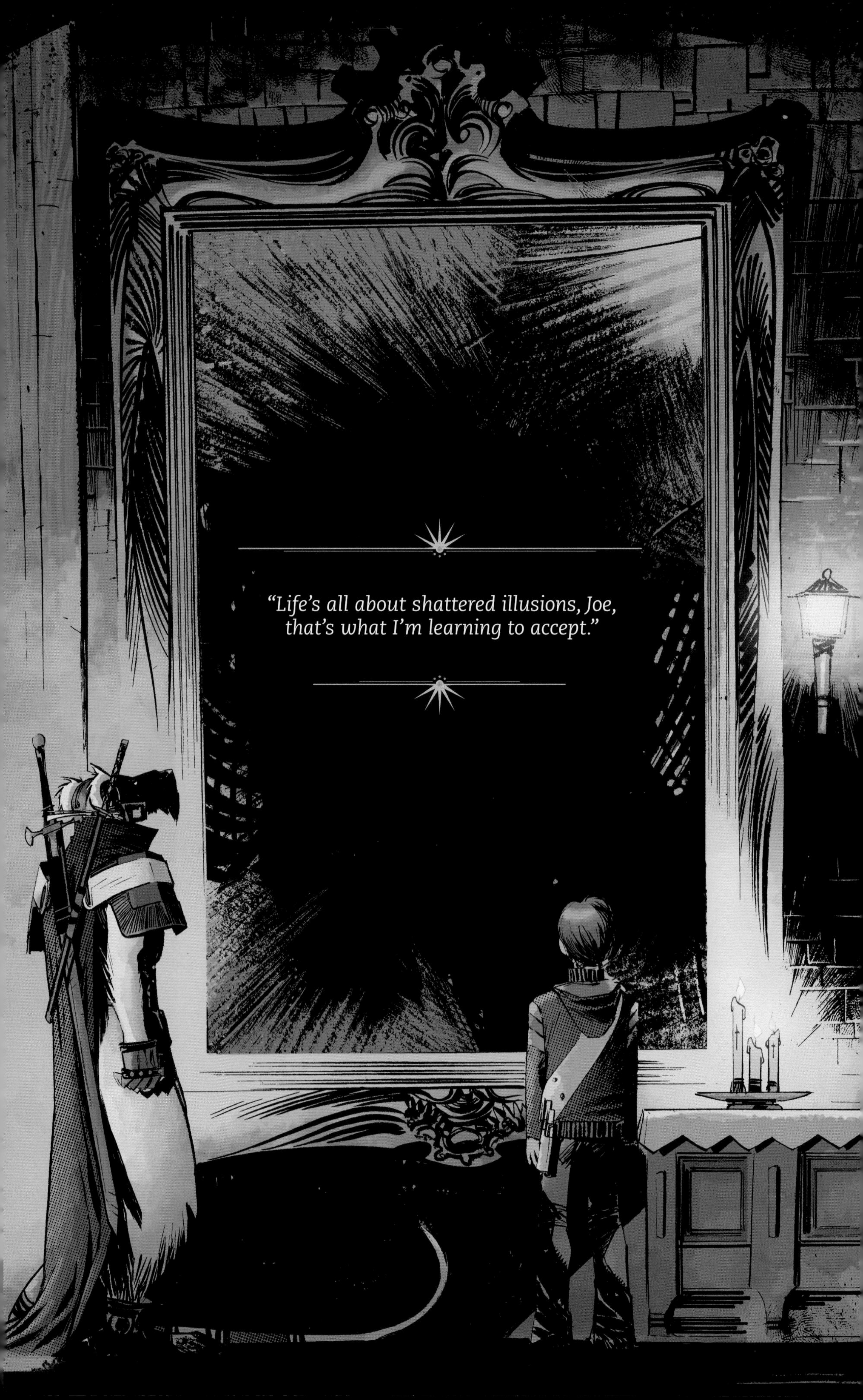
"Life's all about shattered illusions, Joe,
that's what I'm learning to accept."

# chapter 4: inventoria

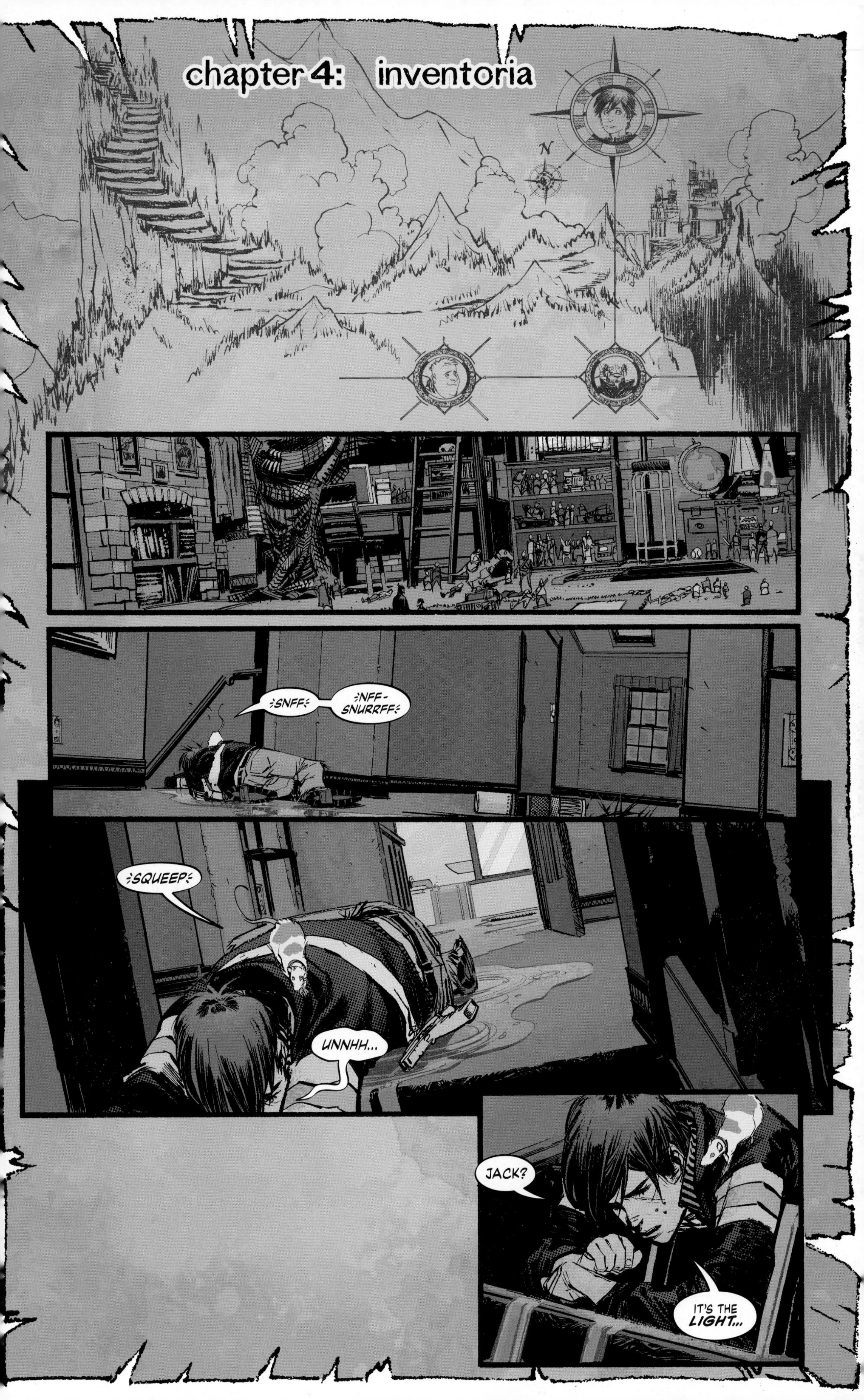

SNFF
NFF-SNURRFF
SQUEEP
UNNHH...
JACK?
IT'S THE LIGHT...

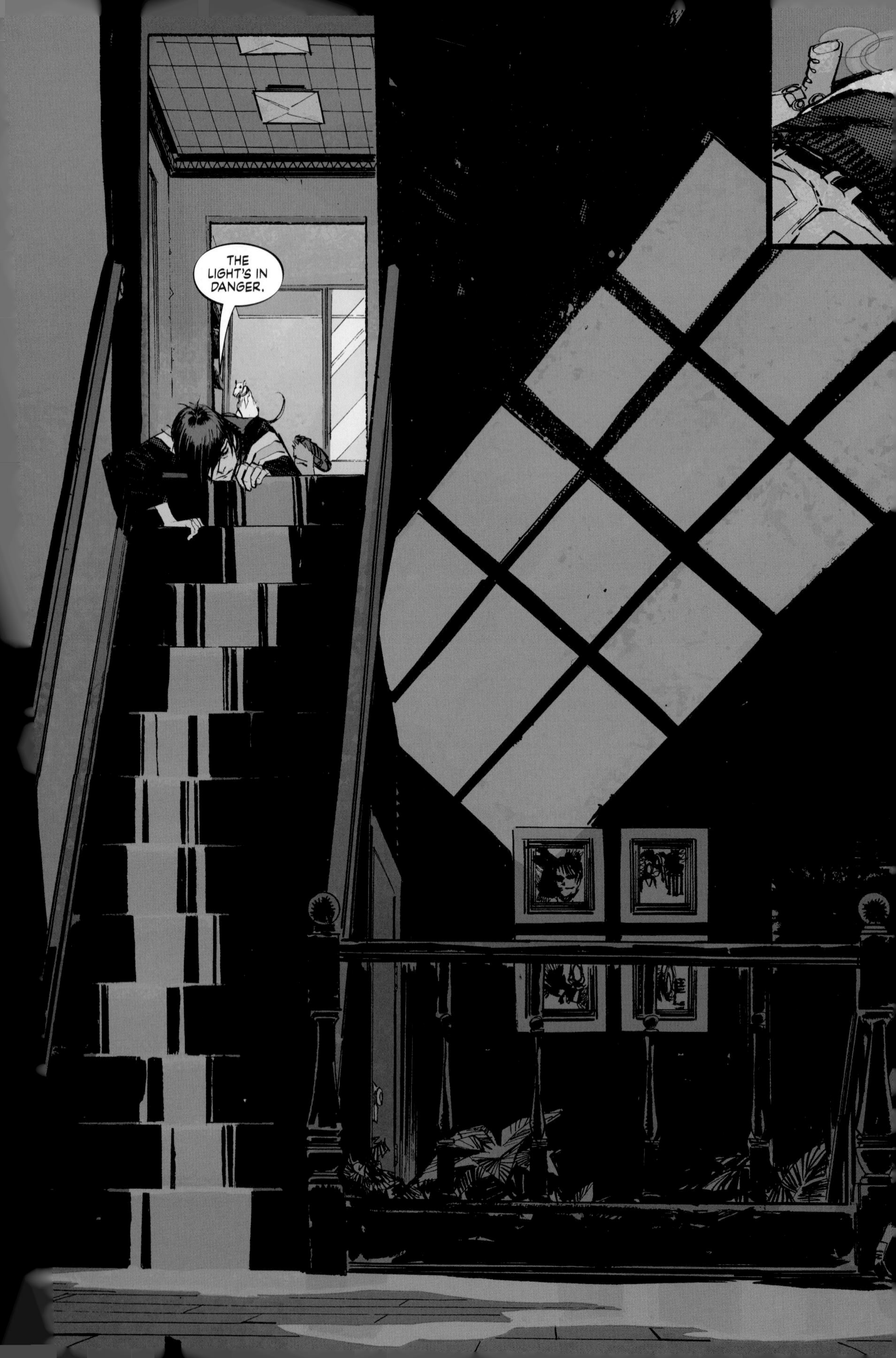
THE LIGHT'S IN DANGER.

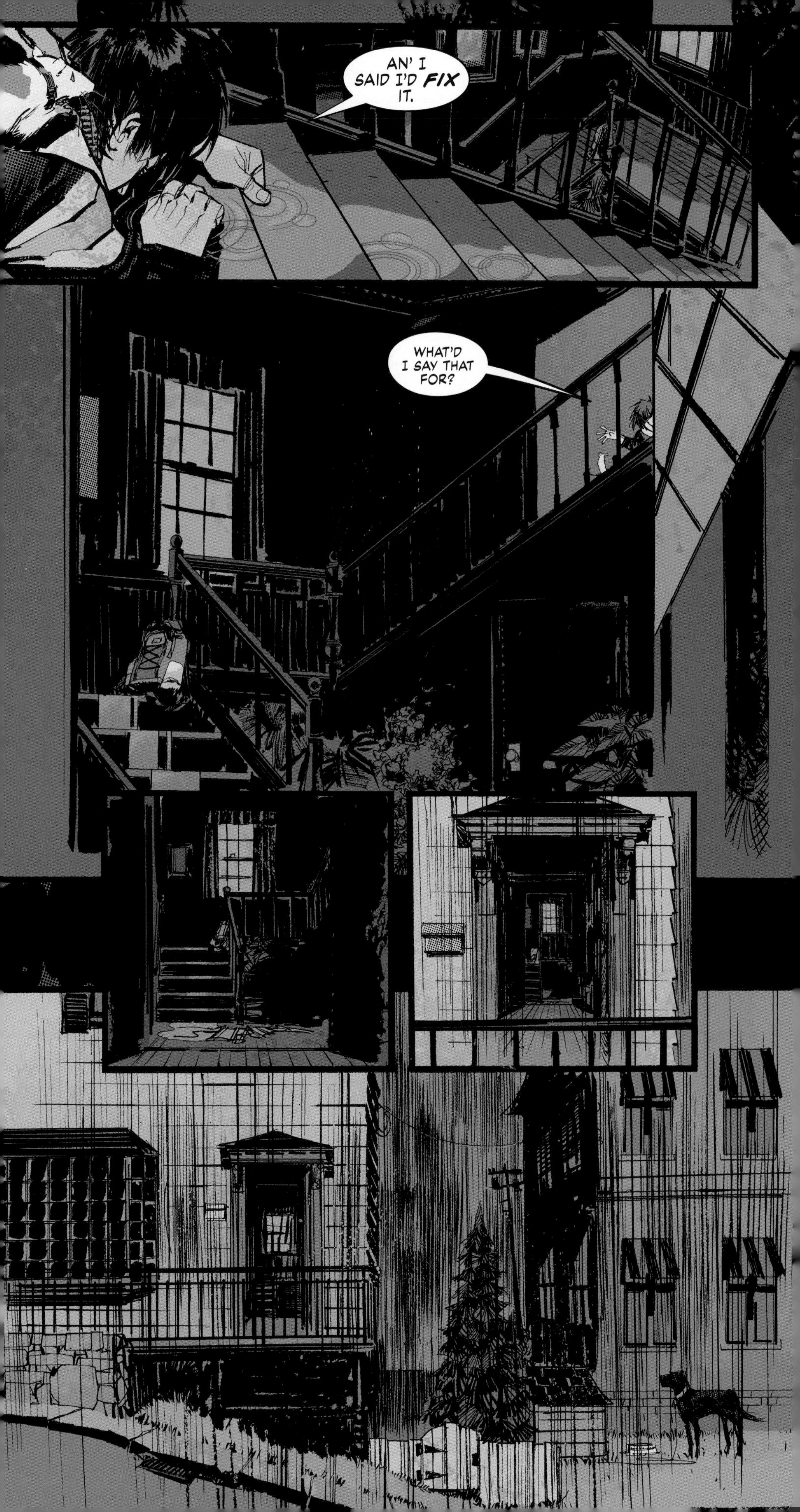
AN' I SAID I'D FIX IT.
WHAT'D I SAY THAT FOR?

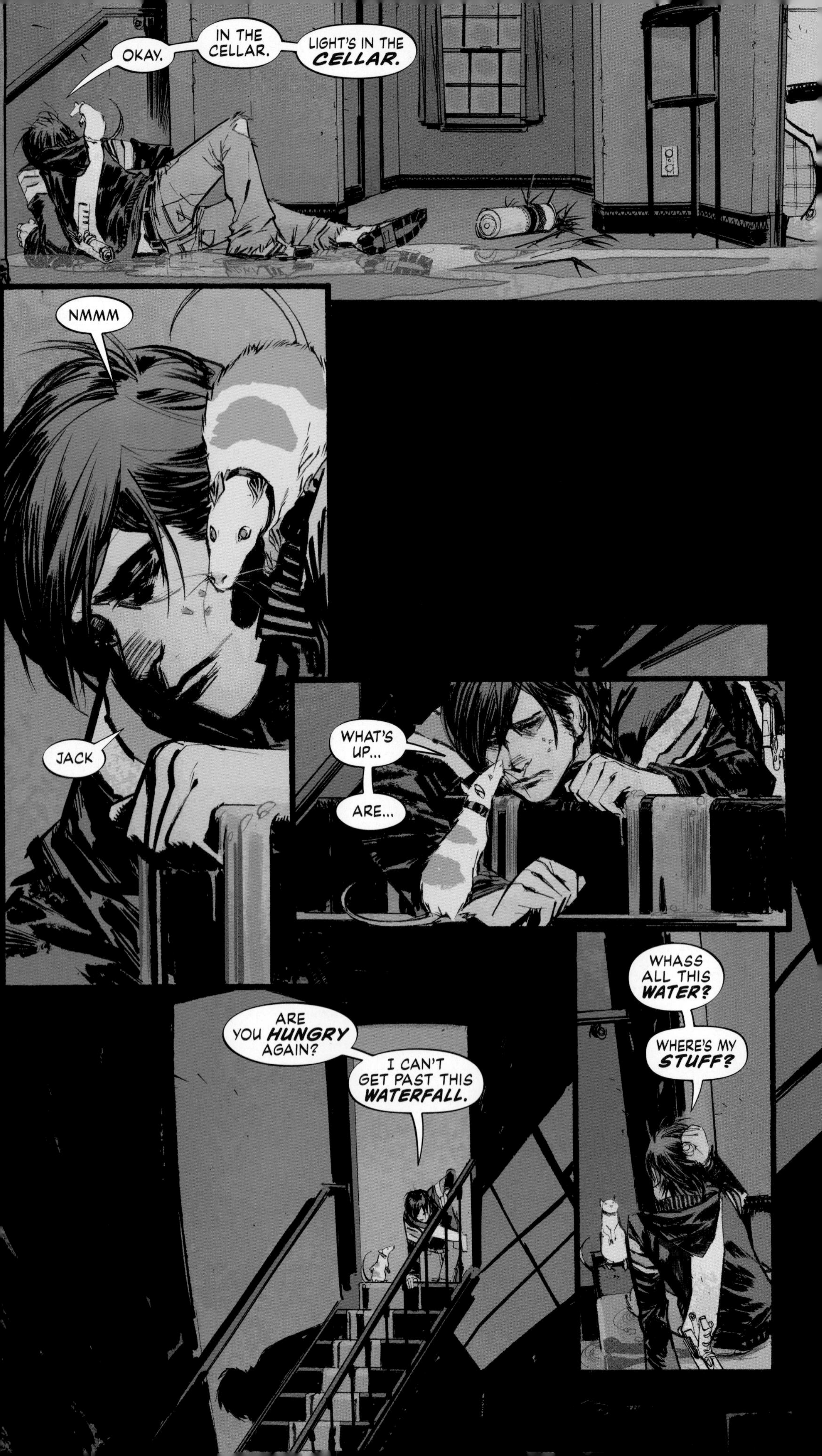

LIGHT'S IN THE CELLAR.
IN THE CELLAR.
OKAY.
NMMM
JACK
WHAT'S UP...
ARE...
WHASS ALL THIS WATER?
WHERE'S MY STUFF?
ARE YOU HUNGRY AGAIN?
I CAN'T GET PAST THIS WATERFALL.

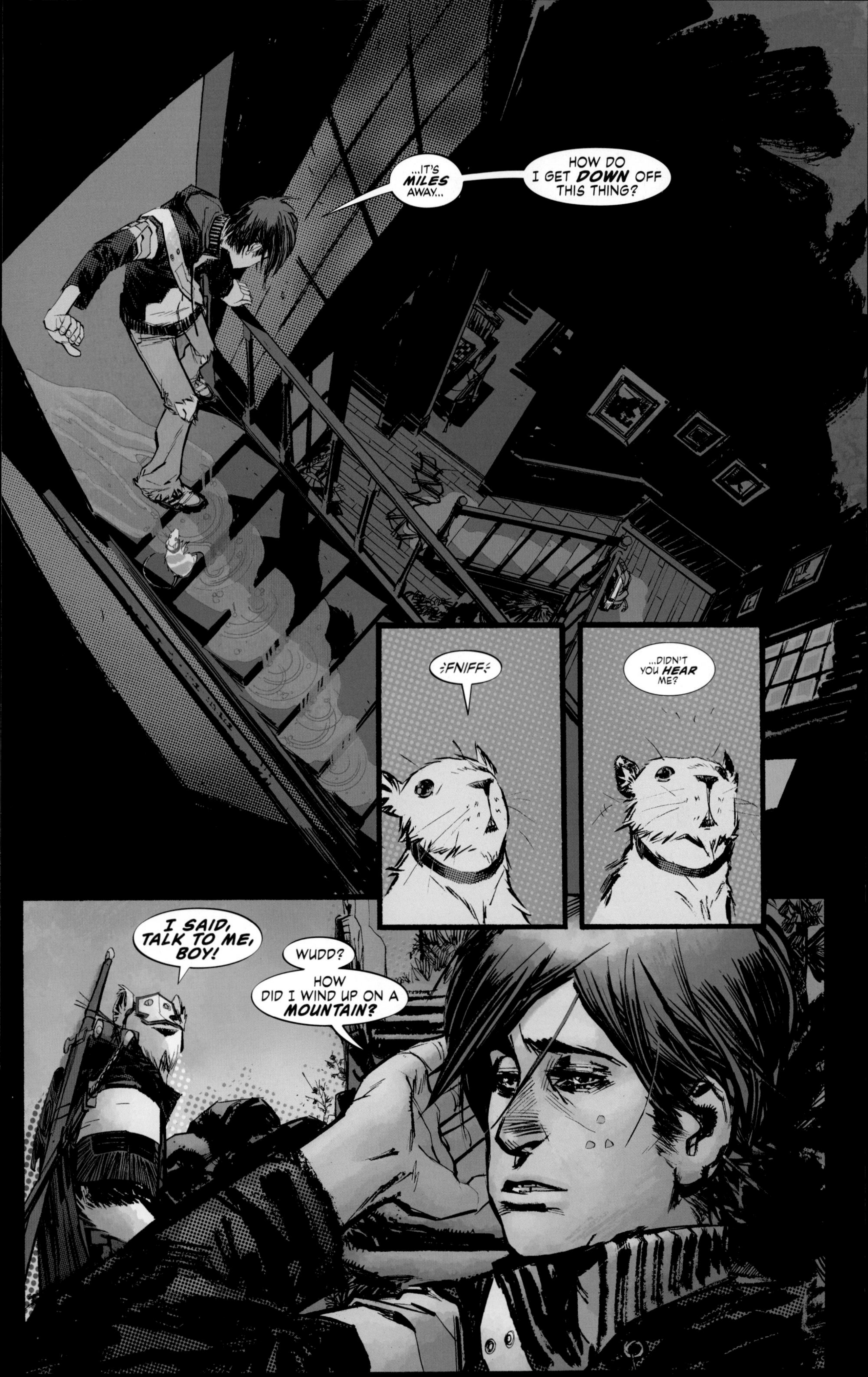

...IT'S MILES AWAY...
HOW DO I GET DOWN OFF THIS THING?
FNIFF
...DIDN'T YOU HEAR ME?
I SAID, TALK TO ME, BOY!
WUDD?
HOW DID I WIND UP ON A MOUNTAIN?

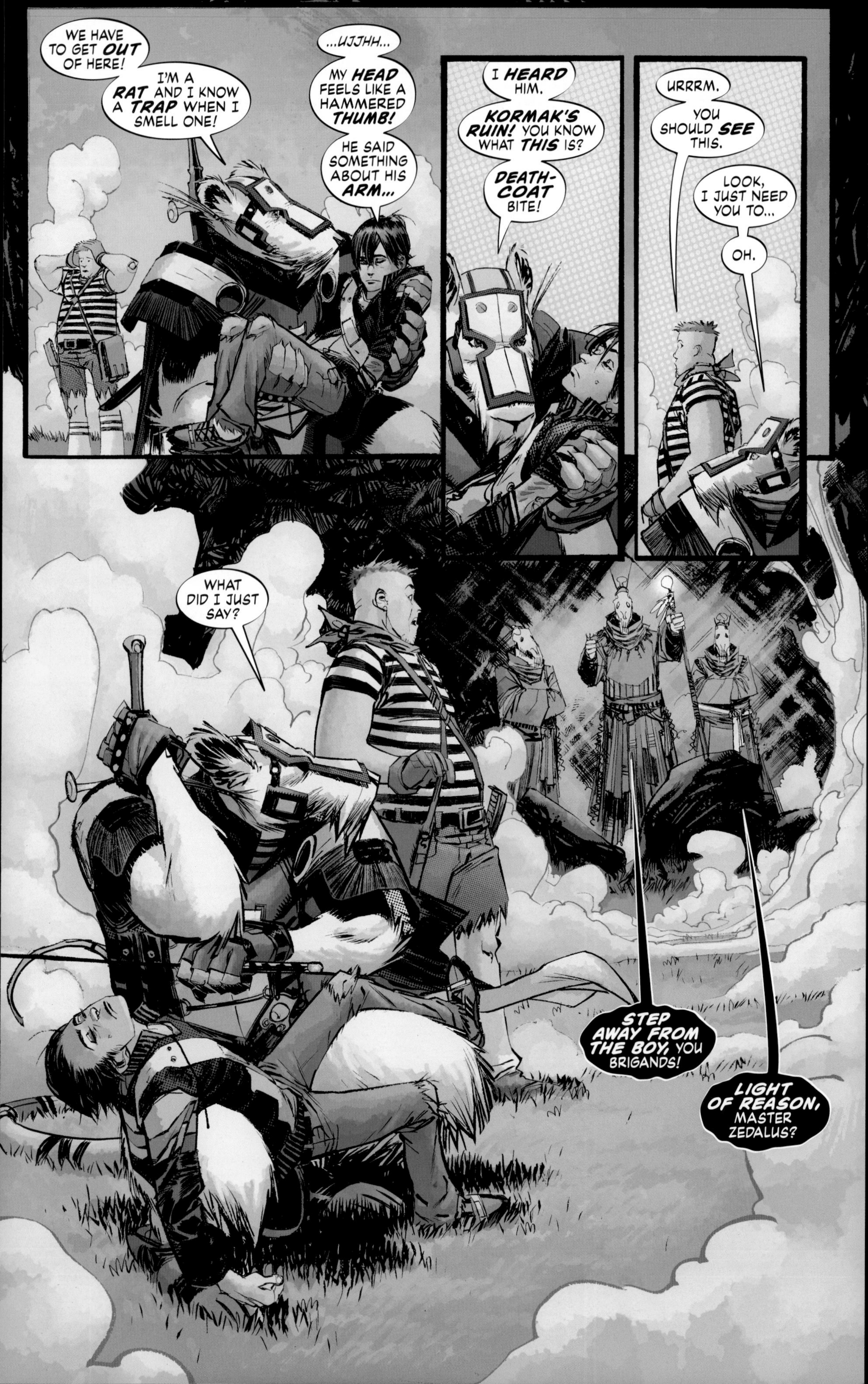
WE HAVE TO GET OUT OF HERE!
I'M A RAT AND I KNOW A TRAP WHEN I SMELL ONE!
...UJJHH...
MY HEAD FEELS LIKE A HAMMERED THUMB!
HE SAID SOMETHING ABOUT HIS ARM...
I HEARD HIM.
KORMAK'S RUIN! YOU KNOW WHAT THIS IS?
DEATH-COAT BITE!
URRRM.
YOU SHOULD SEE THIS.
LOOK, I JUST NEED YOU TO...
OH.
WHAT DID I JUST SAY?
STEP AWAY FROM THE BOY, YOU BRIGANDS!
LIGHT OF REASON, MASTER ZEDALUS?

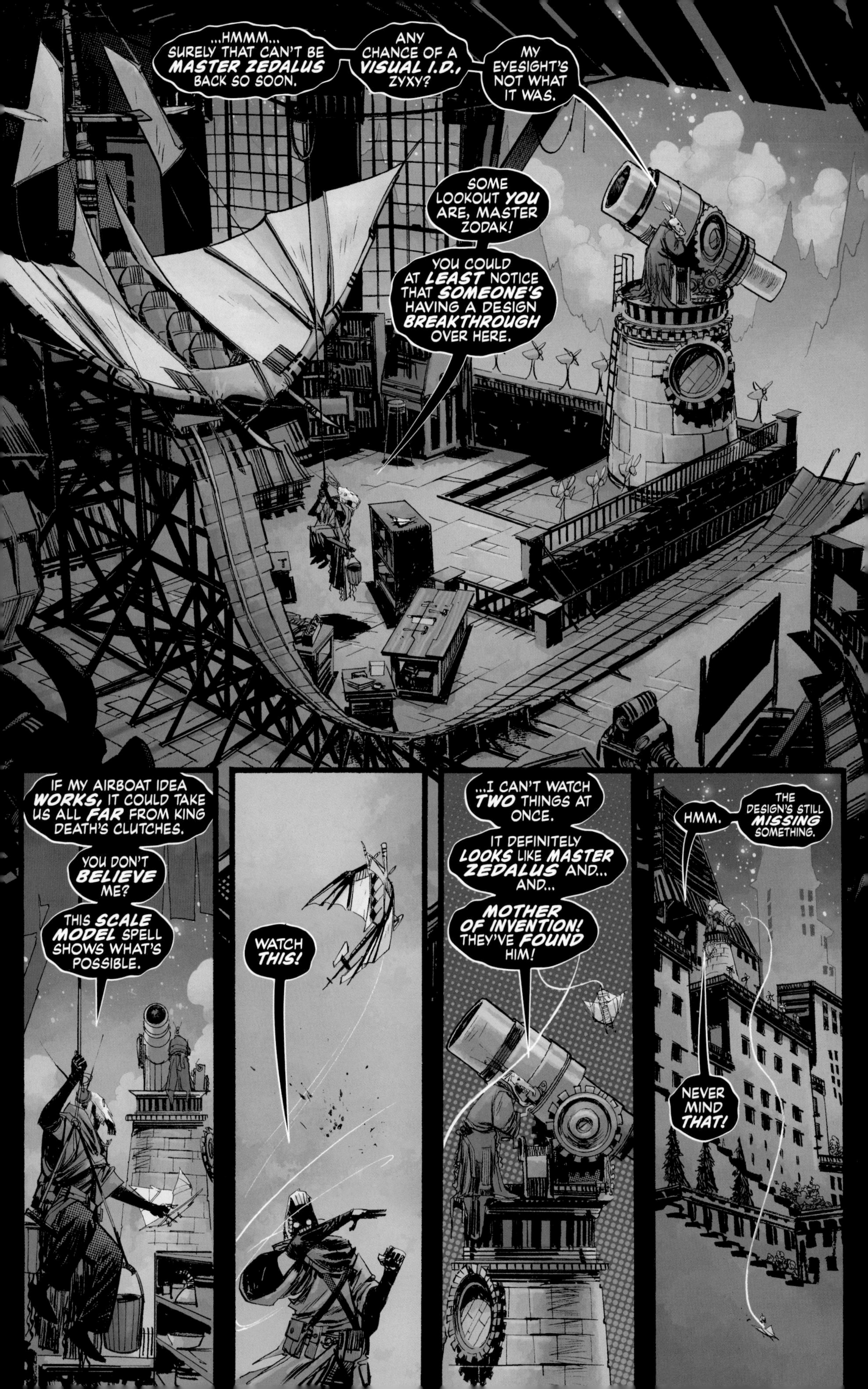
...HMMM... SURELY THAT CAN'T BE MASTER ZEDALUS BACK SO SOON.
ANY CHANCE OF A VISUAL I.D., ZYXY?
MY EYESIGHT'S NOT WHAT IT WAS.
SOME LOOKOUT YOU ARE, MASTER ZODAK!
YOU COULD AT LEAST NOTICE THAT SOMEONE'S HAVING A DESIGN BREAKTHROUGH OVER HERE.
IF MY AIRBOAT IDEA WORKS, IT COULD TAKE US ALL FAR FROM KING DEATH'S CLUTCHES.
YOU DON'T BELIEVE ME?
THIS SCALE MODEL SPELL SHOWS WHAT'S POSSIBLE.
WATCH THIS!
...I CAN'T WATCH TWO THINGS AT ONCE.
IT DEFINITELY LOOKS LIKE MASTER ZEDALUS AND... AND...
MOTHER OF INVENTION! THEY'VE FOUND HIM!
HMM.
THE DESIGN'S STILL MISSING SOMETHING.
NEVER MIND THAT!

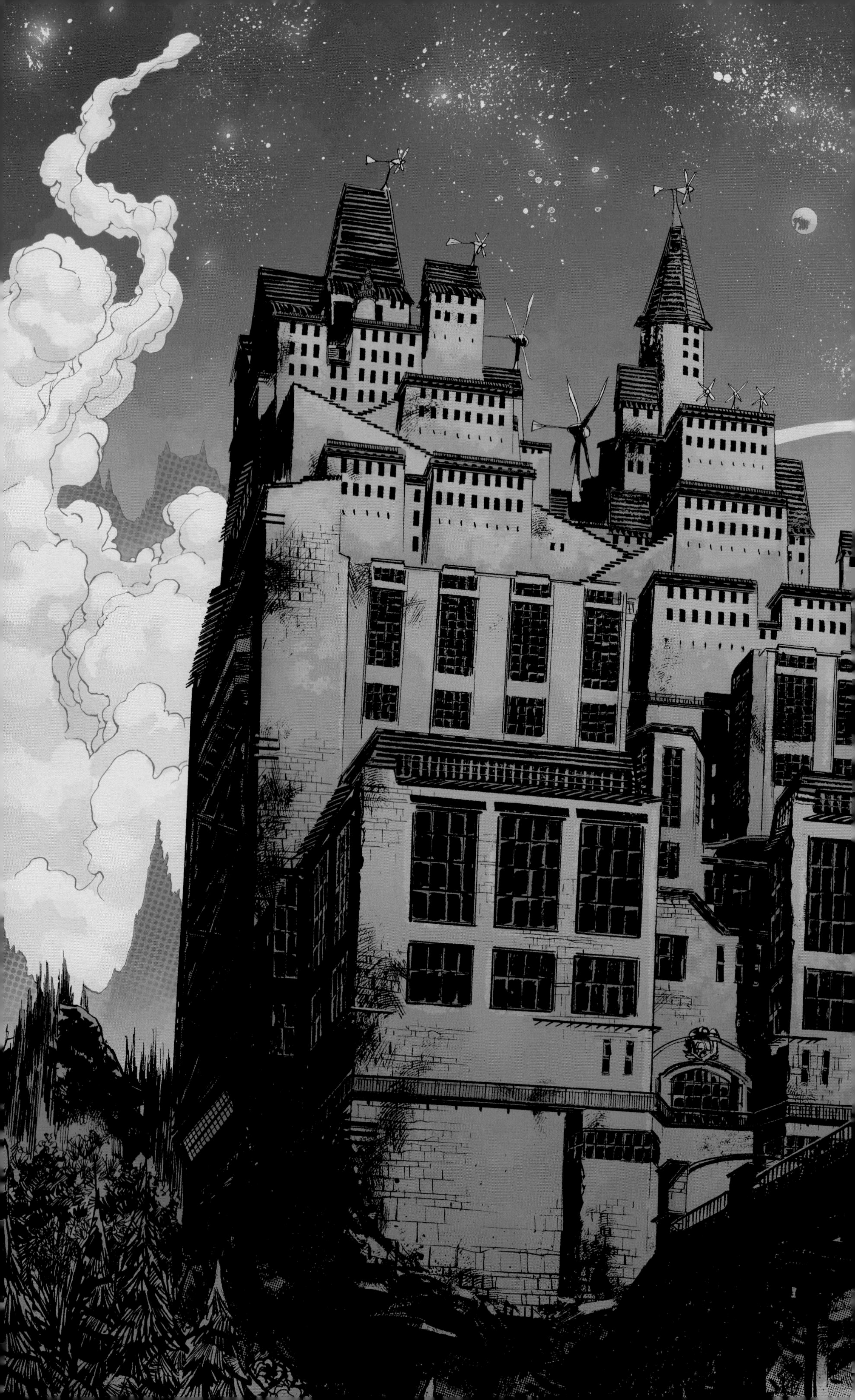

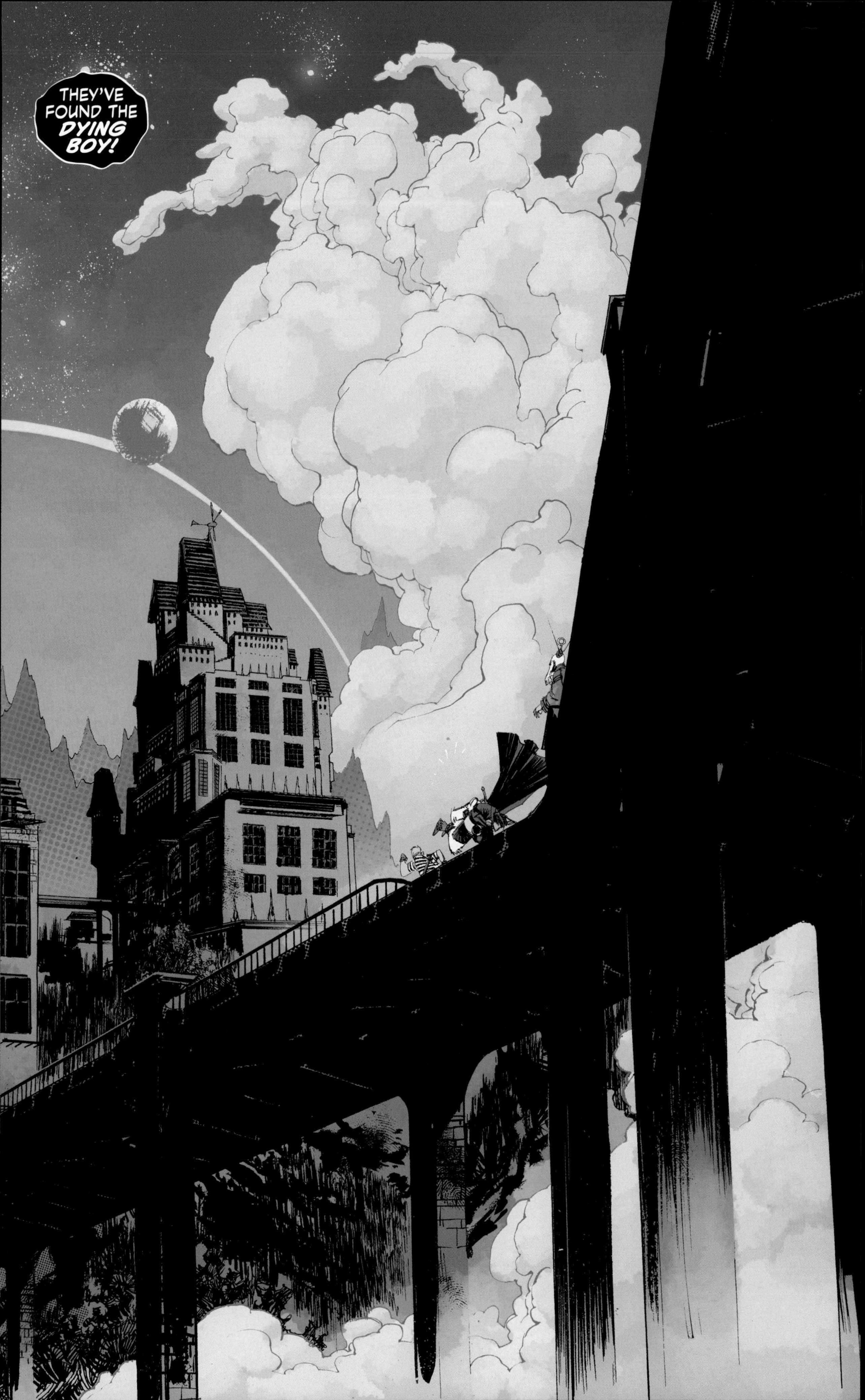
THEY'VE FOUND THE DYING BOY!

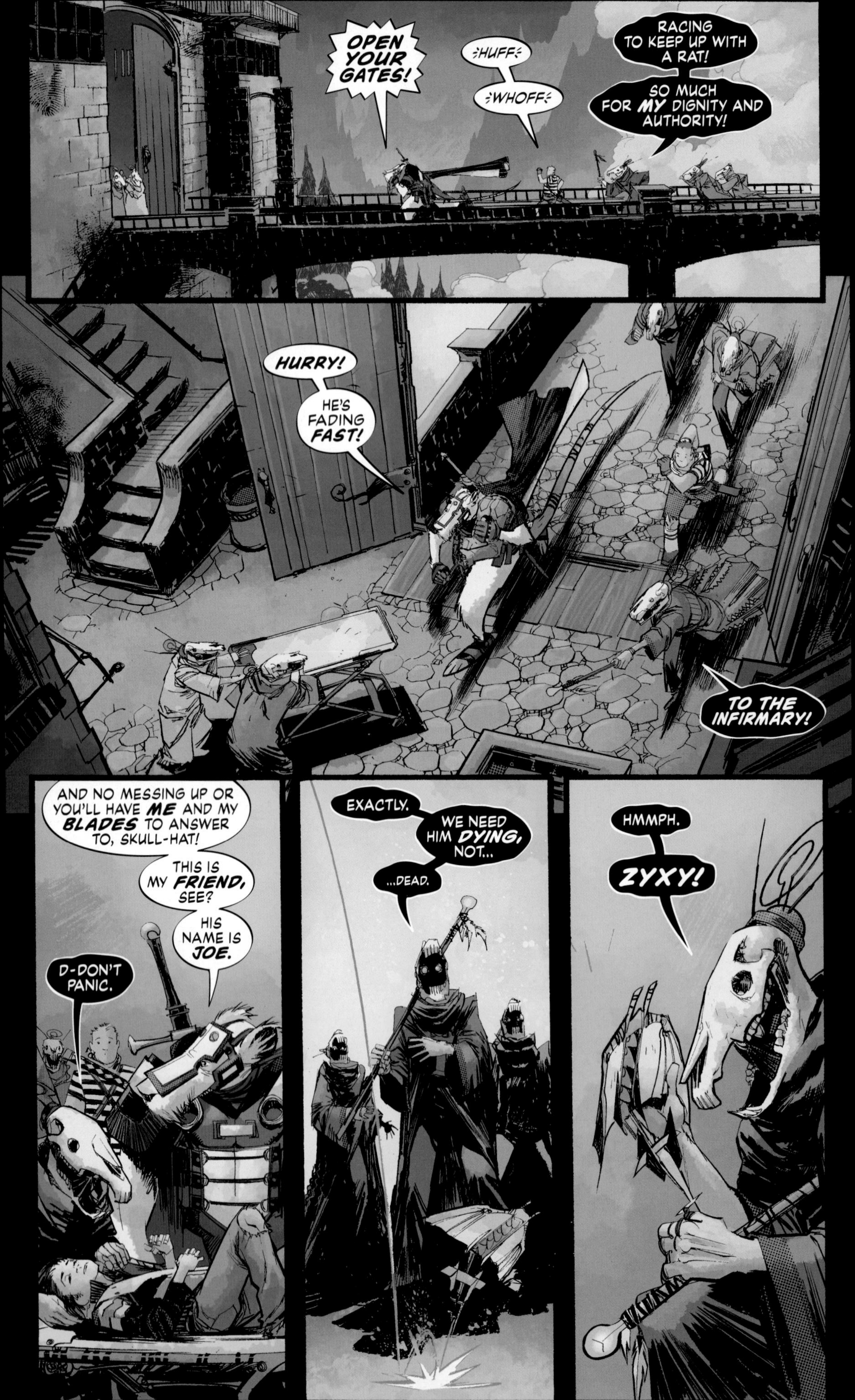

OPEN YOUR GATES!
HUFF
WHOFF
RACING TO KEEP UP WITH A RAT!
SO MUCH FOR MY DIGNITY AND AUTHORITY!
HURRY!
HE'S FADING FAST!
TO THE INFIRMARY!
AND NO MESSING UP OR YOU'LL HAVE ME AND MY BLADES TO ANSWER TO, SKULL-HAT!
THIS IS MY FRIEND, SEE?
HIS NAME IS JOE.
D-DON'T PANIC.
EXACTLY.
WE NEED HIM DYING, NOT...
...DEAD.
HMMPH.
ZYXY!

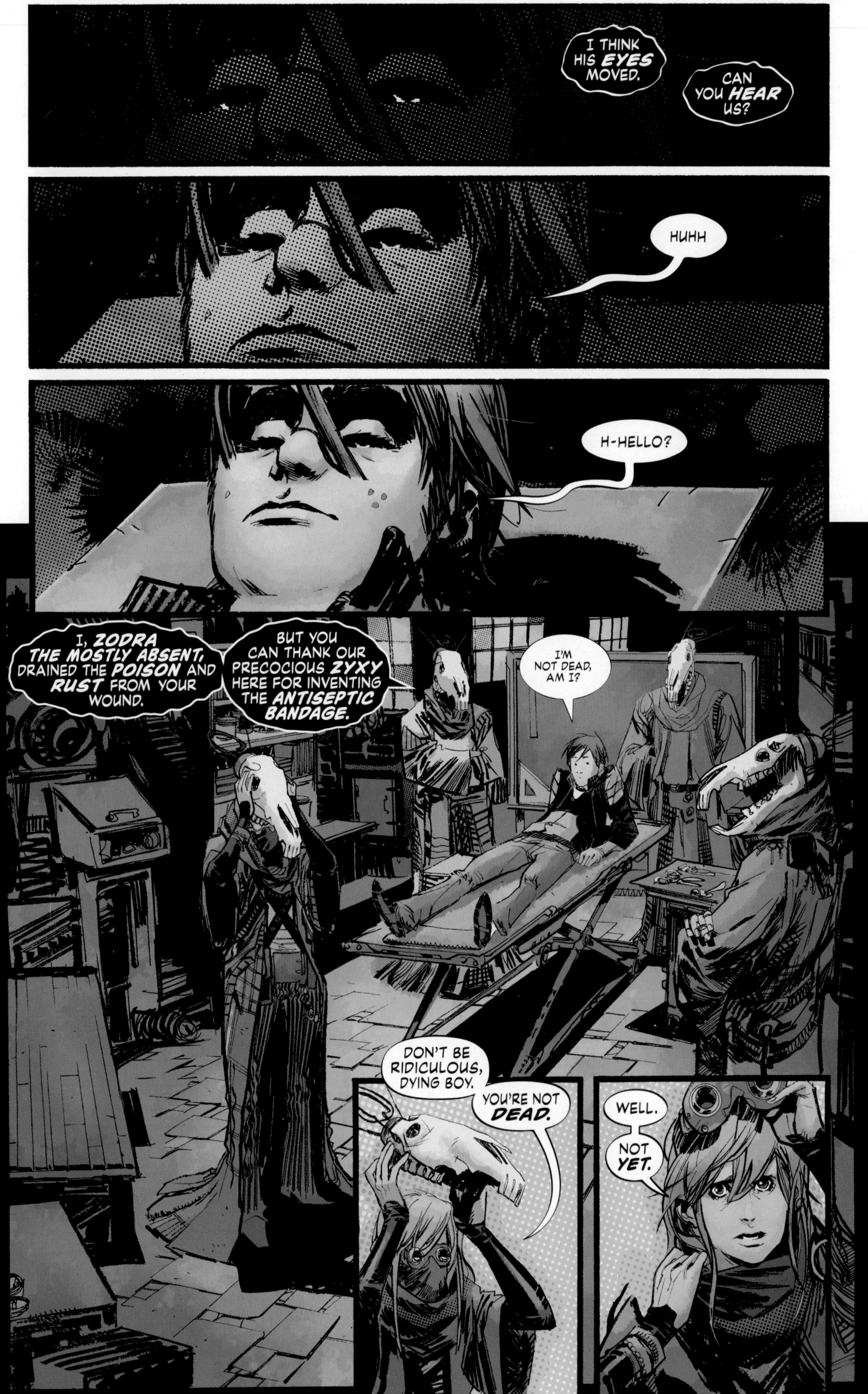

I THINK HIS EYES MOVED.
CAN YOU HEAR US?
HUHH
H-HELLO?
I, ZODRA THE MOSTLY ABSENT, DRAINED THE POISON AND RUST FROM YOUR WOUND.
BUT YOU CAN THANK OUR PRECOCIOUS ZYXY HERE FOR INVENTING THE ANTISEPTIC BANDAGE.
I'M NOT DEAD, AM I?
DON'T BE RIDICULOUS, DYING BOY.
YOU'RE NOT DEAD.
WELL.
NOT YET.

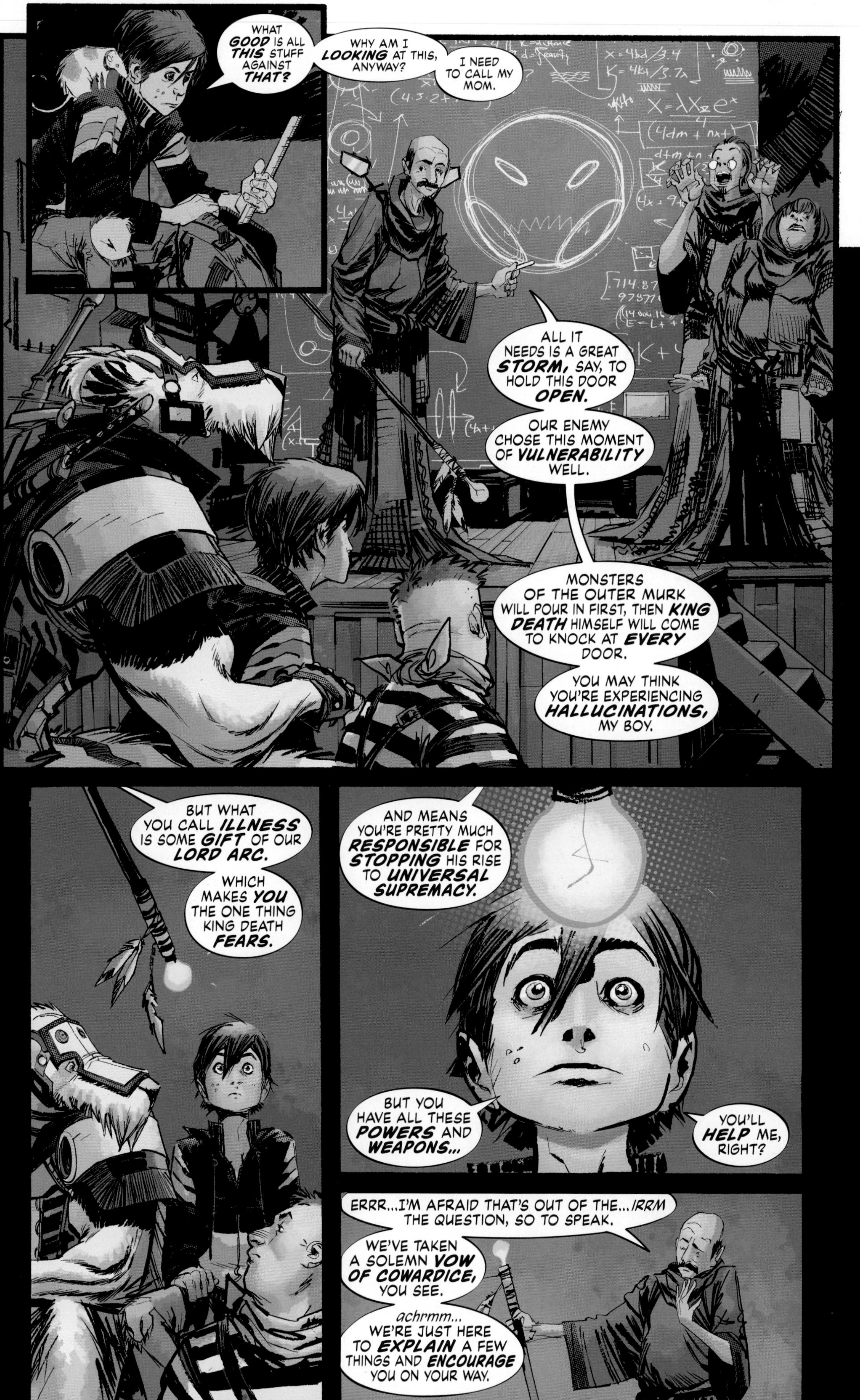
WHAT GOOD IS ALL THIS STUFF AGAINST THAT?
WHY AM I LOOKING AT THIS, ANYWAY?
I NEED TO CALL MY MOM.
ALL IT NEEDS IS A GREAT STORM, SAY, TO HOLD THIS DOOR OPEN.
OUR ENEMY CHOSE THIS MOMENT OF VULNERABILITY WELL.
MONSTERS OF THE OUTER MURK WILL POUR IN FIRST, THEN KING DEATH HIMSELF WILL COME TO KNOCK AT EVERY DOOR.
YOU MAY THINK YOU'RE EXPERIENCING HALLUCINATIONS, MY BOY.
BUT WHAT YOU CALL ILLNESS IS SOME GIFT OF OUR LORD ARC.
WHICH MAKES YOU THE ONE THING KING DEATH FEARS.
AND MEANS YOU'RE PRETTY MUCH RESPONSIBLE FOR STOPPING HIS RISE TO UNIVERSAL SUPREMACY.
BUT YOU HAVE ALL THESE POWERS AND WEAPONS...
YOU'LL HELP ME, RIGHT?
ERRR...I'M AFRAID THAT'S OUT OF THE...IRRM THE QUESTION, SO TO SPEAK.
WE'VE TAKEN A SOLEMN VOW OF COWARDICE, YOU SEE.
achrmm... WE'RE JUST HERE TO EXPLAIN A FEW THINGS AND ENCOURAGE YOU ON YOUR WAY.

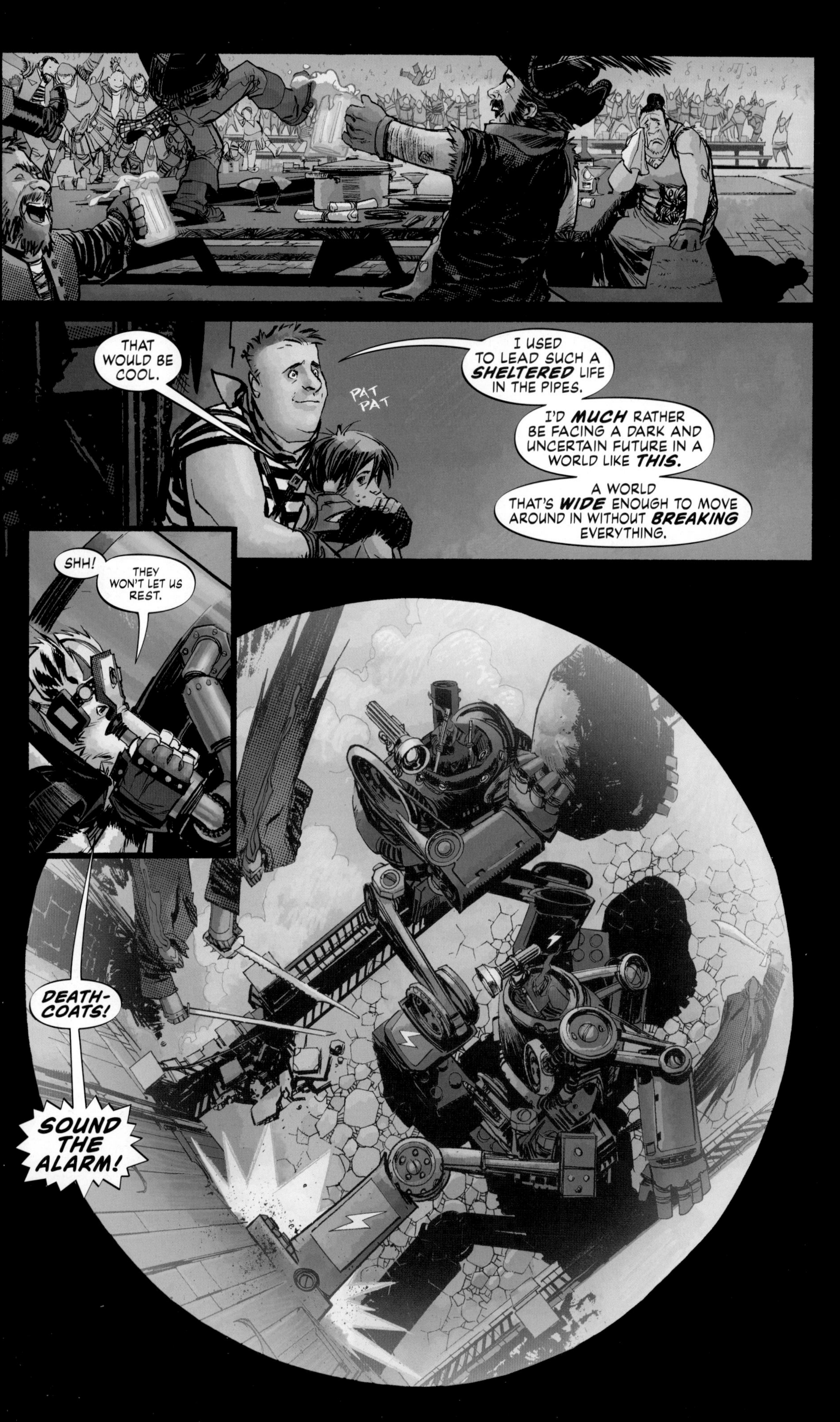

I USED TO LEAD SUCH A SHELTERED LIFE IN THE PIPES.
PAT PAT
I'D MUCH RATHER BE FACING A DARK AND UNCERTAIN FUTURE IN A WORLD LIKE THIS.
A WORLD THAT'S WIDE ENOUGH TO MOVE AROUND IN WITHOUT BREAKING EVERYTHING.
THAT WOULD BE COOL.
SHH!
THEY WON'T LET US REST.
DEATH-COATS!
SOUND THE ALARM!

WHAT WAS THAT *NOISE?*

YOU *KNOW* SOMETHING, DON'T YOU?

I KNOW THE BOY HAS SOME *POWER* OVER DEATH THAT THE *UNDER-KING* FEARS.

WHAT IF THERE *IS* NO *HEARTH,* NO *QUEEN BREE,* NO *SILVER LEGION?*

WHAT IF IT'S JUST *US* IN ALL THE UPPER KINGDOM, *ALONE* AGAINST *KING DEATH?*

MASTER, HE *NEEDS* OUR HELP.

*I* HAVEN'T.

UNTIL MY *APPRENTICE SPELL* TAKES FLIGHT, I'M STILL A *NOVICE...*

I CAN *LEAVE* IF I WANT TO.

SOME *INSTINCTUAL* UNDERSTANDING OF THE FATAL *COMPLEXITIES* OF THE HYPOGEAN *LABYRINTH.*

I KNOW WE HAVE TO STAY OUT OF THE WAY UNTIL THE *HEARTH* HAS SET THINGS TO RIGHTS...

*NON-INVOLVEMENT,* ZYXY!

WE'VE TAKEN *VOWS,* REMEMBER?

BUT YOUR *STUDIES...*THE LONG, LONELY *HOURS* SPENT READING MILDEWED, ANCIENT *OPERATORS' MANUALS...*

HOW CAN ANY QUEST COMPETE WITH--

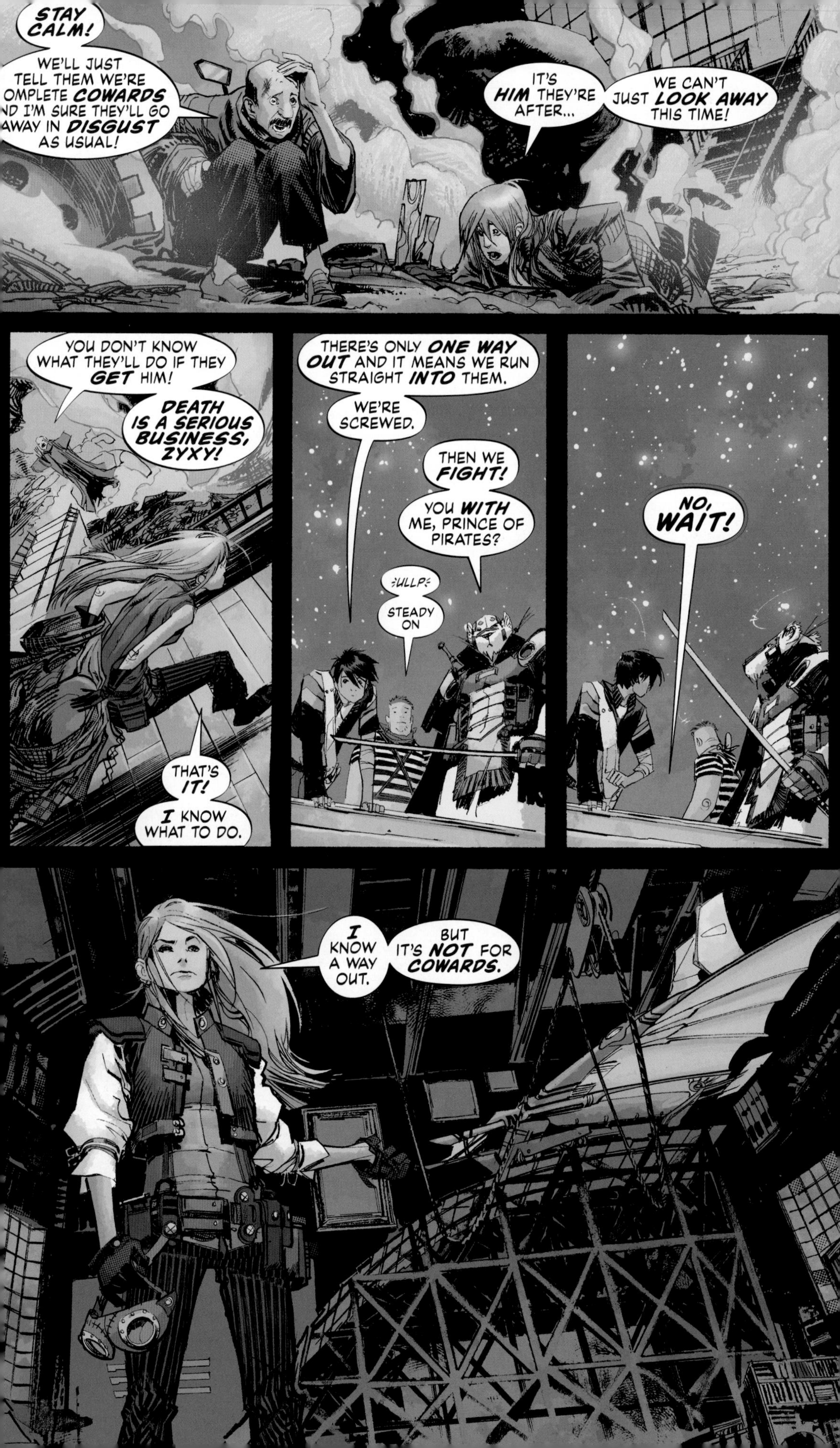

STAY CALM!
WE'LL JUST TELL THEM WE'RE OMPLETE COWARDS ND I'M SURE THEY'LL GO AWAY IN DISGUST AS USUAL!
IT'S HIM THEY'RE AFTER...
WE CAN'T JUST LOOK AWAY THIS TIME!
YOU DON'T KNOW WHAT THEY'LL DO IF THEY GET HIM!
DEATH IS A SERIOUS BUSINESS, ZYXY!
THAT'S IT!
I KNOW WHAT TO DO.
THERE'S ONLY ONE WAY OUT AND IT MEANS WE RUN STRAIGHT INTO THEM.
WE'RE SCREWED.
THEN WE FIGHT!
YOU WITH ME, PRINCE OF PIRATES?
ULLP
STEADY ON
NO, WAIT!
I KNOW A WAY OUT.
BUT IT'S NOT FOR COWARDS.

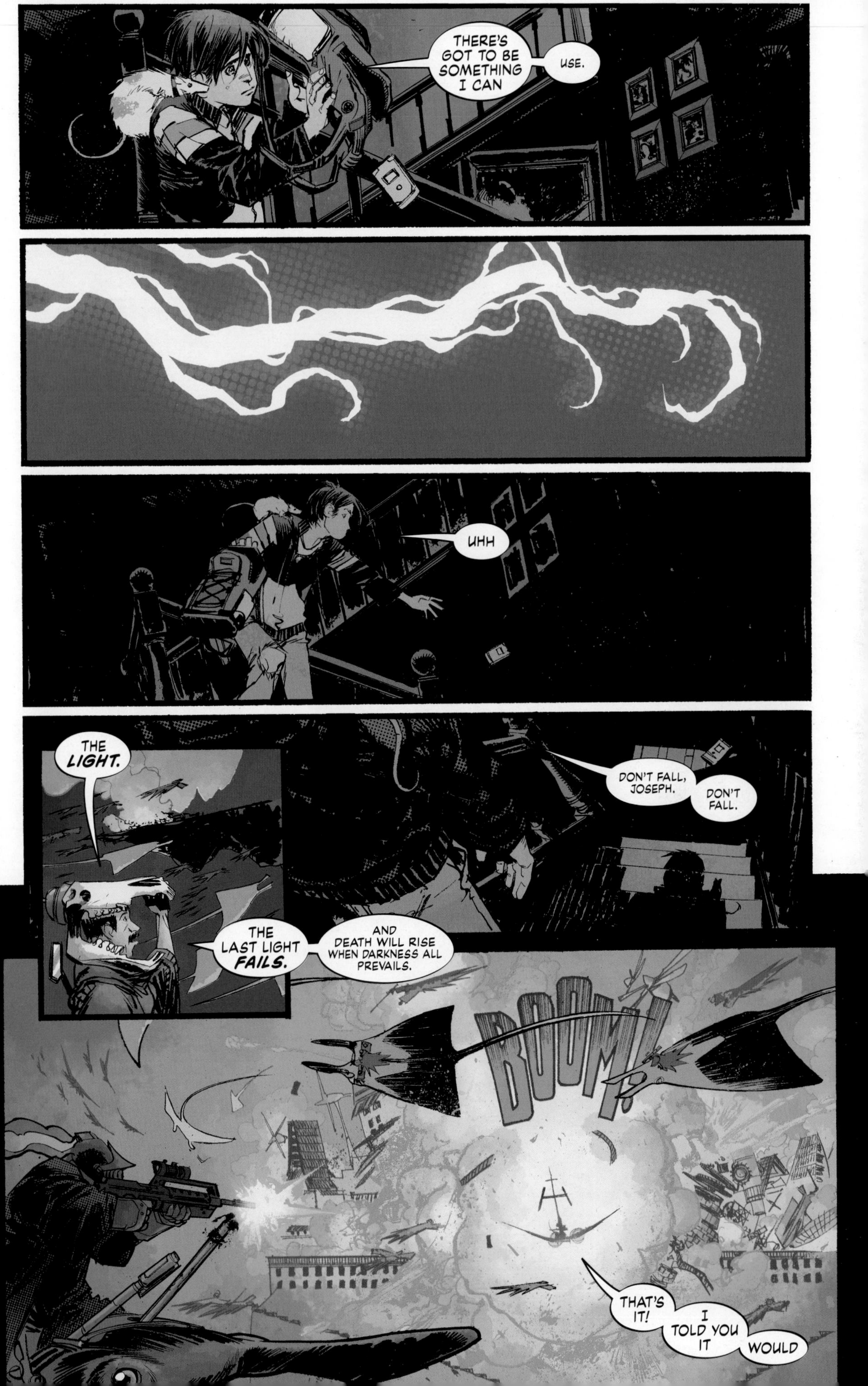

THERE'S GOT TO BE SOMETHING I CAN
USE.
UHH
THE *LIGHT*.
DON'T FALL, JOSEPH.
DON'T FALL.
THE LAST LIGHT *FAILS*.
AND DEATH WILL RISE WHEN DARKNESS ALL PREVAILS.
BOOM!
THAT'S IT!
I TOLD YOU IT
WOULD

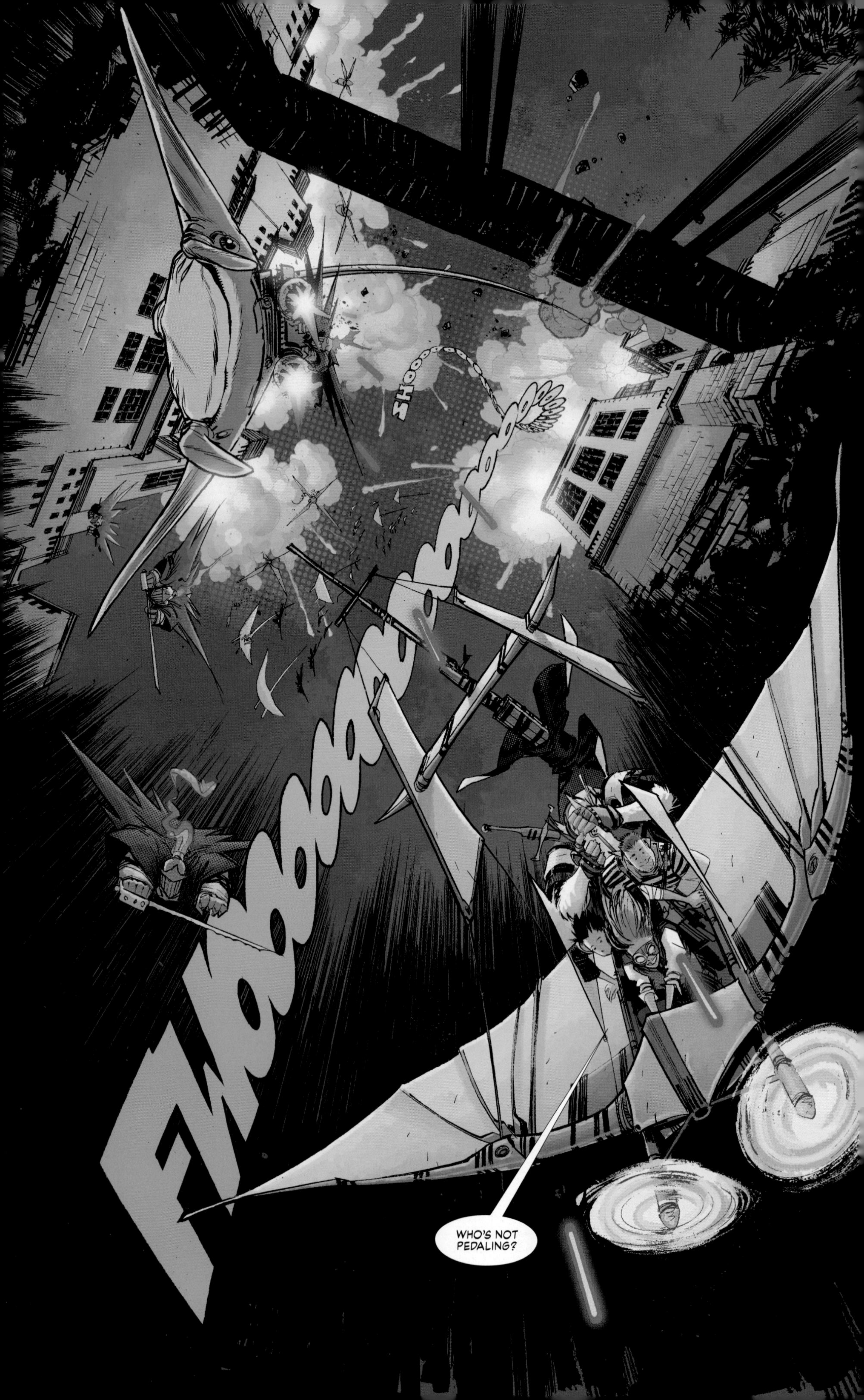
WHO'S NOT PEDALING?

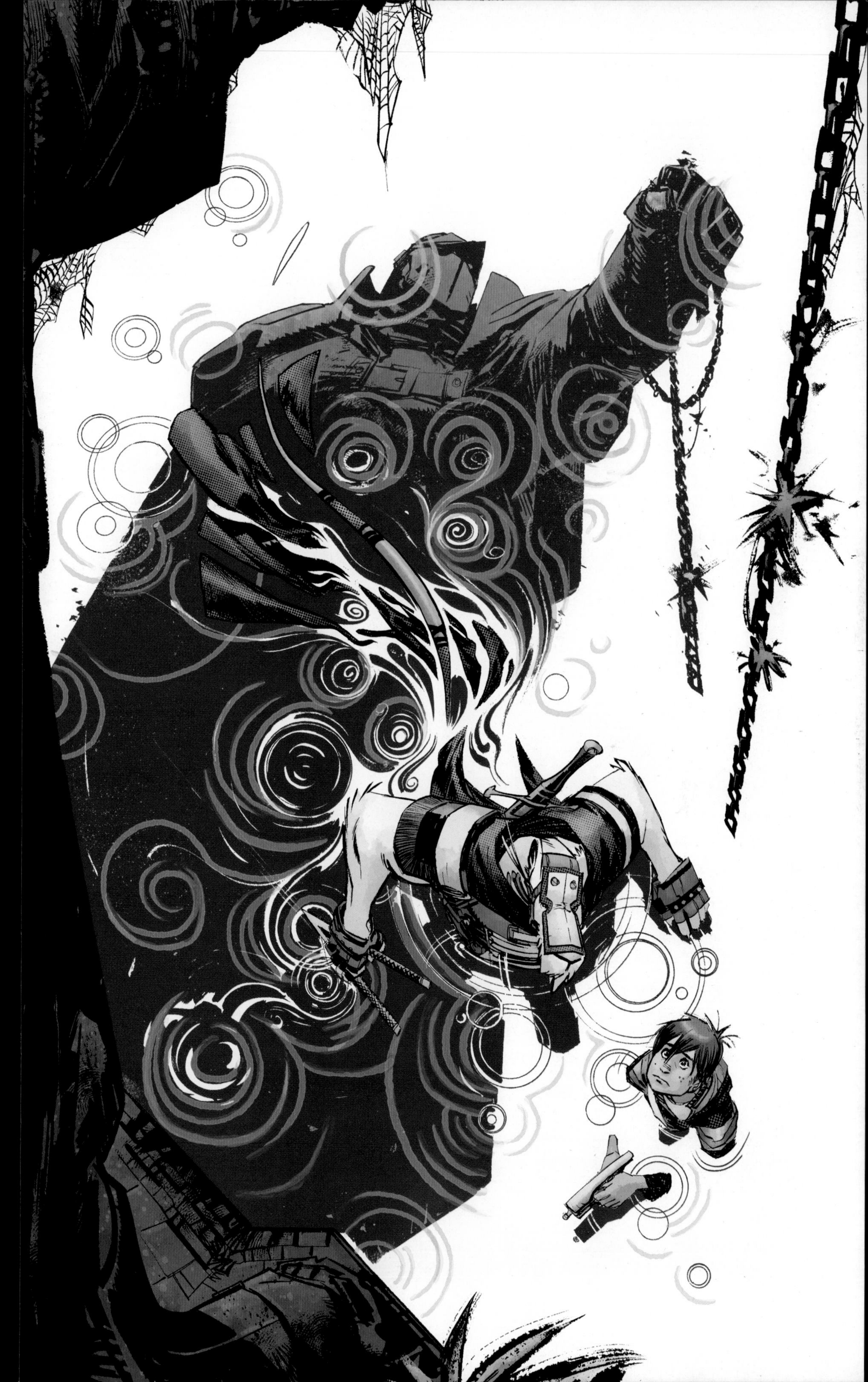

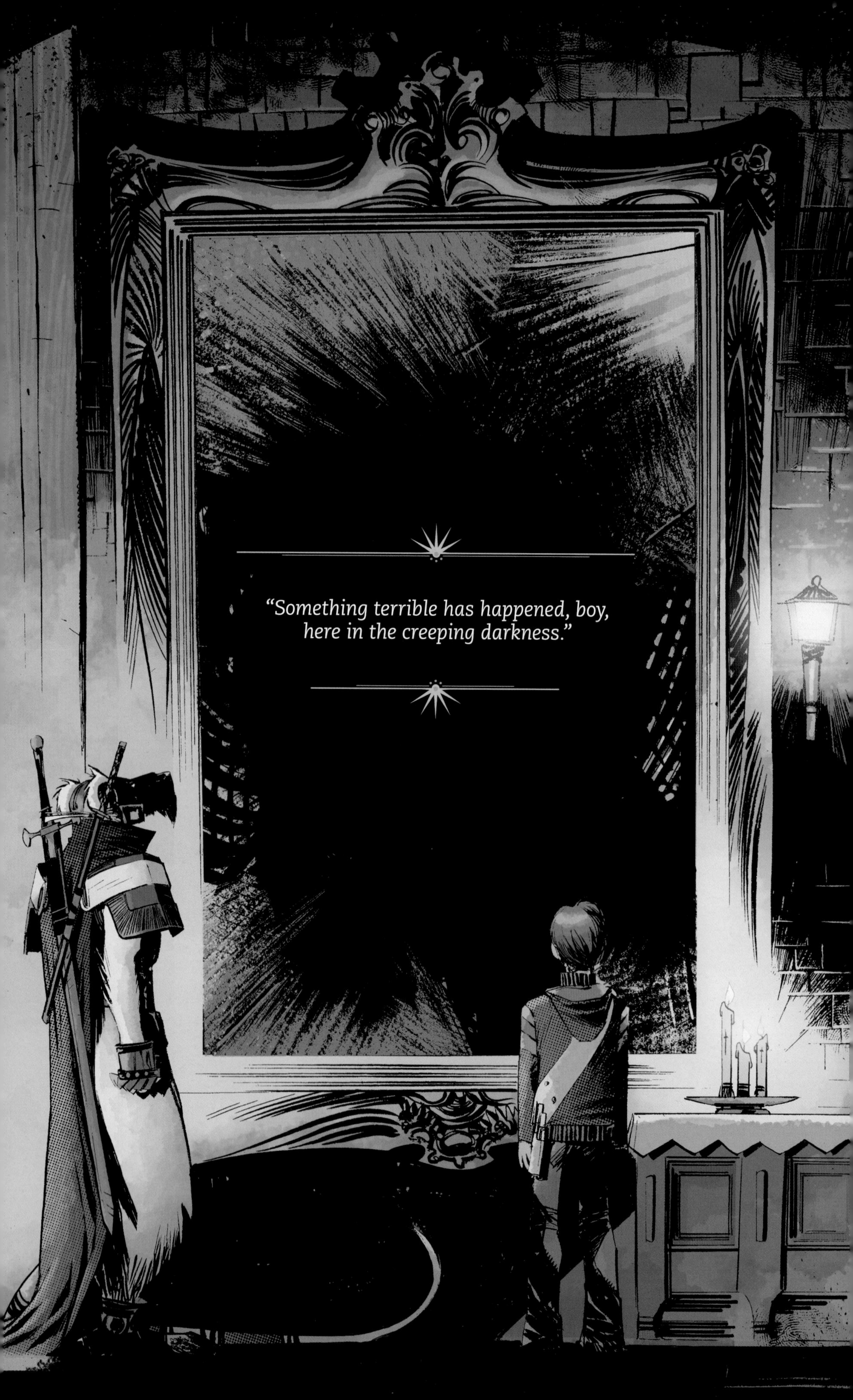
"Something terrible has happened, boy, here in the creeping darkness."

# chapter 5: from never to always

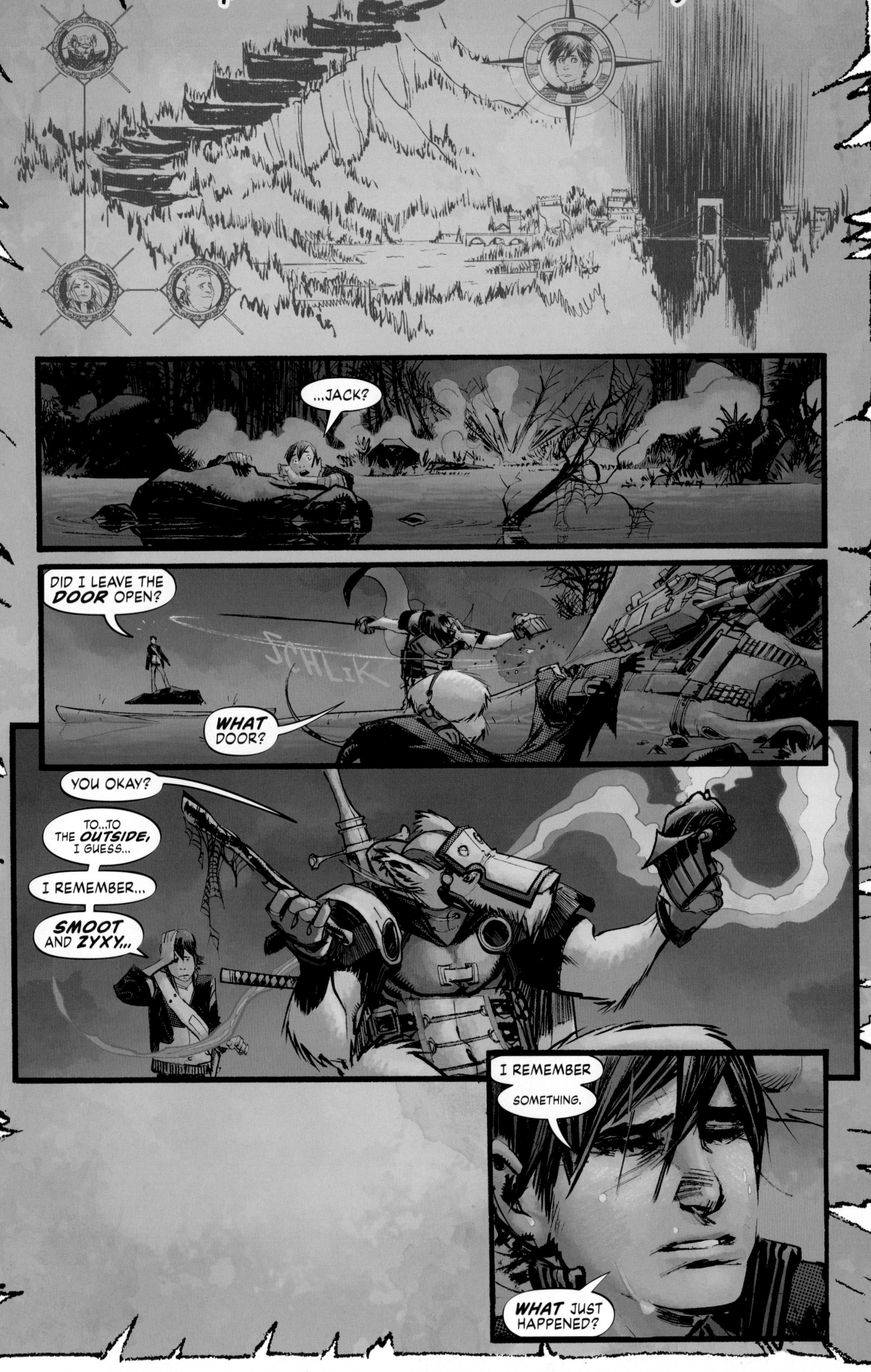
...JACK?
DID I LEAVE THE DOOR OPEN?
SCHLIK
WHAT DOOR?
YOU OKAY?
TO...TO THE OUTSIDE, I GUESS...
I REMEMBER...
SMOOT AND ZYXY...
I REMEMBER SOMETHING.
WHAT JUST HAPPENED?

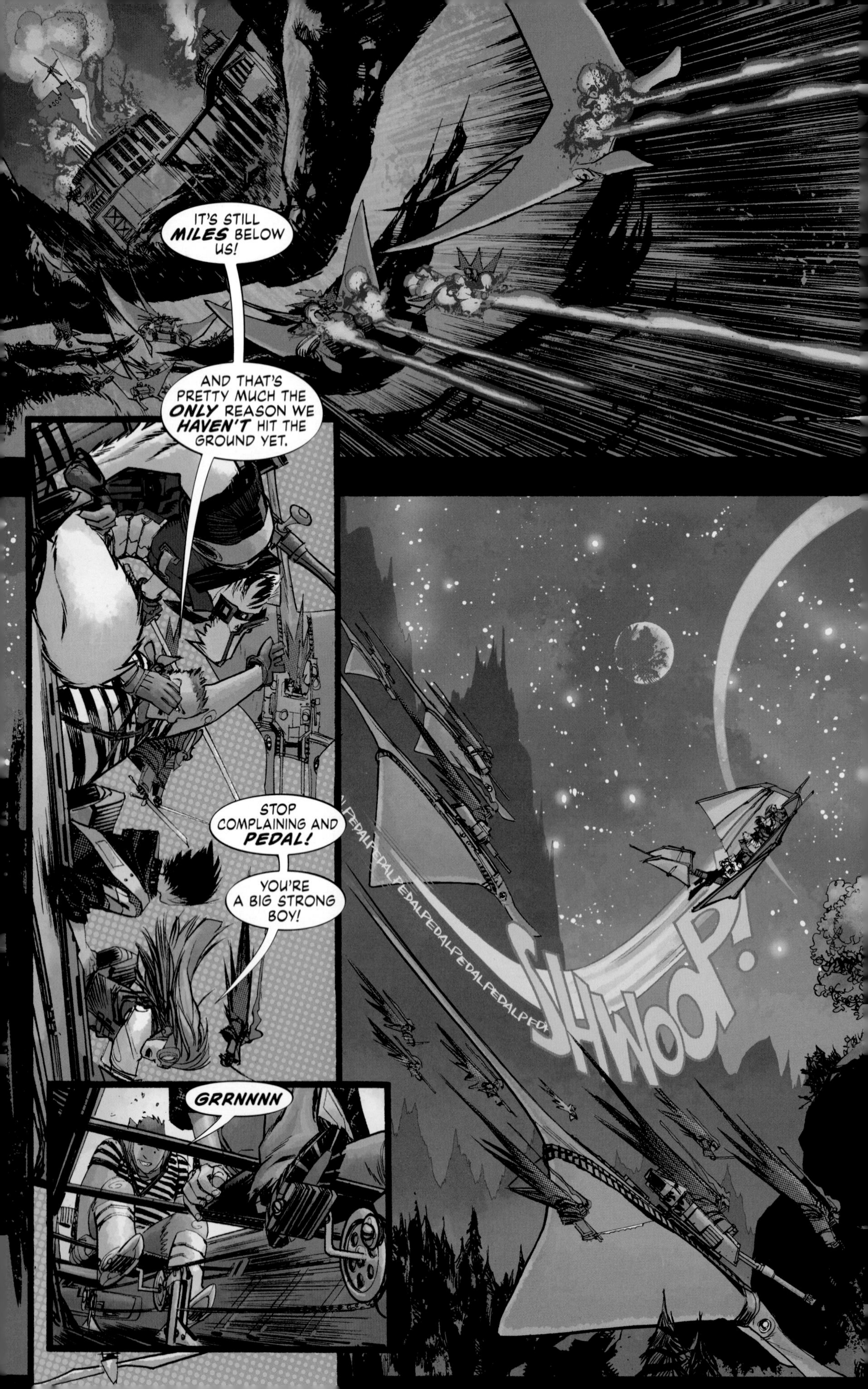
IT'S STILL MILES BELOW US!
AND THAT'S PRETTY MUCH THE ONLY REASON WE HAVEN'T HIT THE GROUND YET.
STOP COMPLAINING AND PEDAL!
YOU'RE A BIG STRONG BOY!
PEDALPEDALPEDALPEDALPEDALPEDALPEDAL
SHWOOP!
GRRNNNN

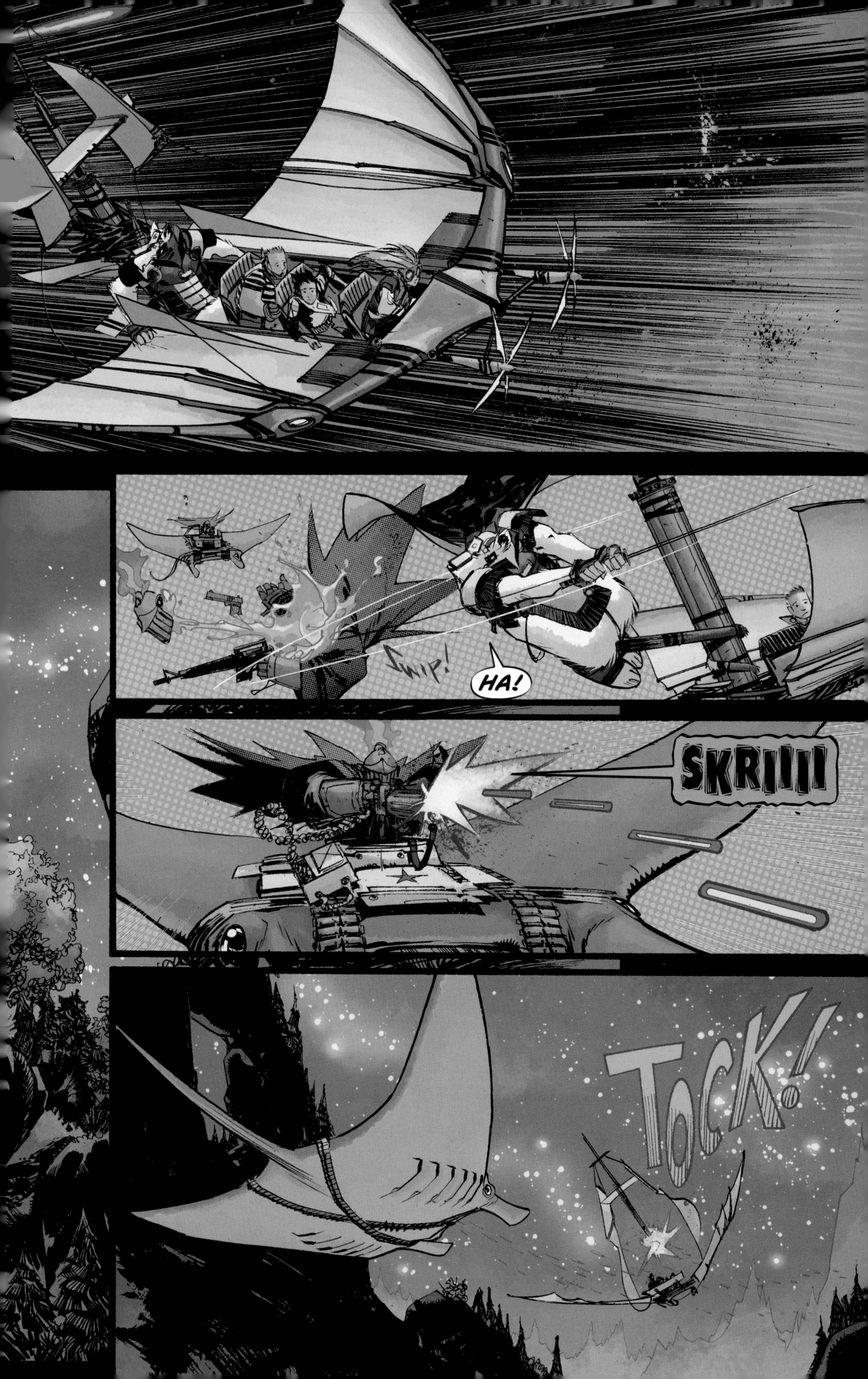
SWIP!
HA!
SKRIIII
TOCK!

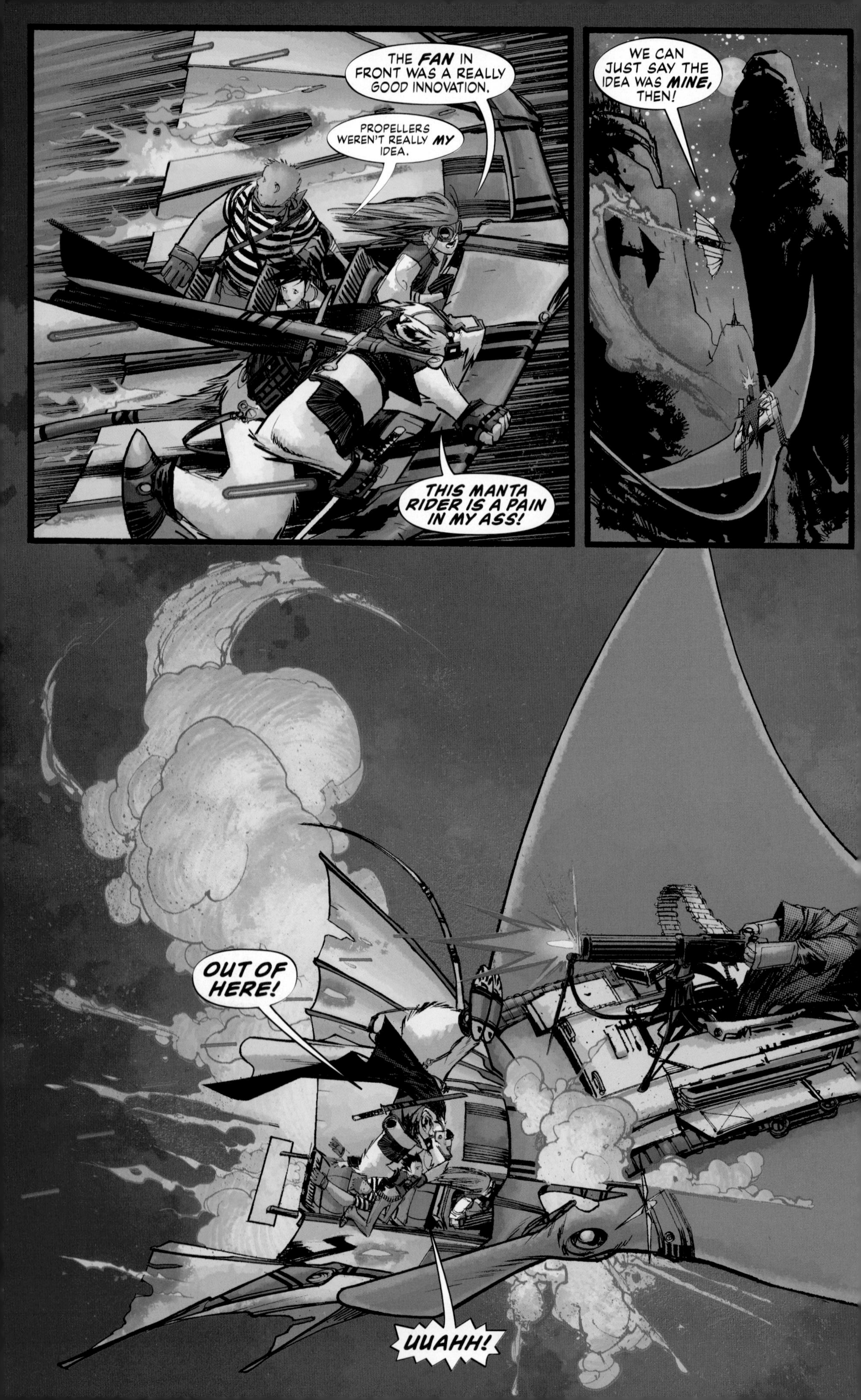
THE FAN IN FRONT WAS A REALLY GOOD INNOVATION.
PROPELLERS WEREN'T REALLY MY IDEA.
THIS MANTA RIDER IS A PAIN IN MY ASS!
WE CAN JUST SAY THE IDEA WAS MINE, THEN!
OUT OF HERE!
UUAHH!

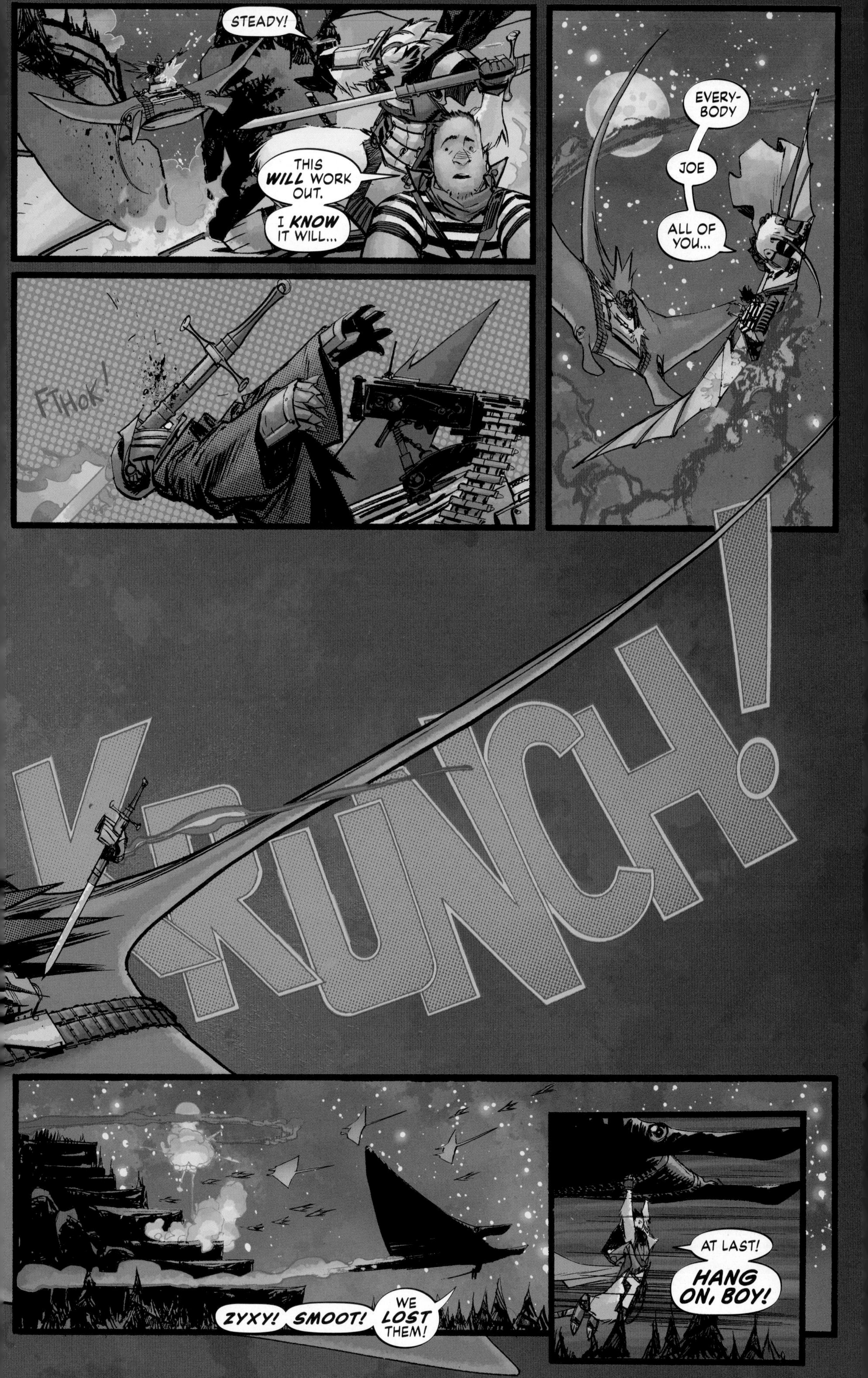
STEADY!
THIS WILL WORK OUT.
I KNOW IT WILL...
EVERY-BODY
JOE
ALL OF YOU...
FTHOK!
K-RUNCH!
ZYXY!
SMOOT!
WE LOST THEM!
AT LAST!
HANG ON, BOY!

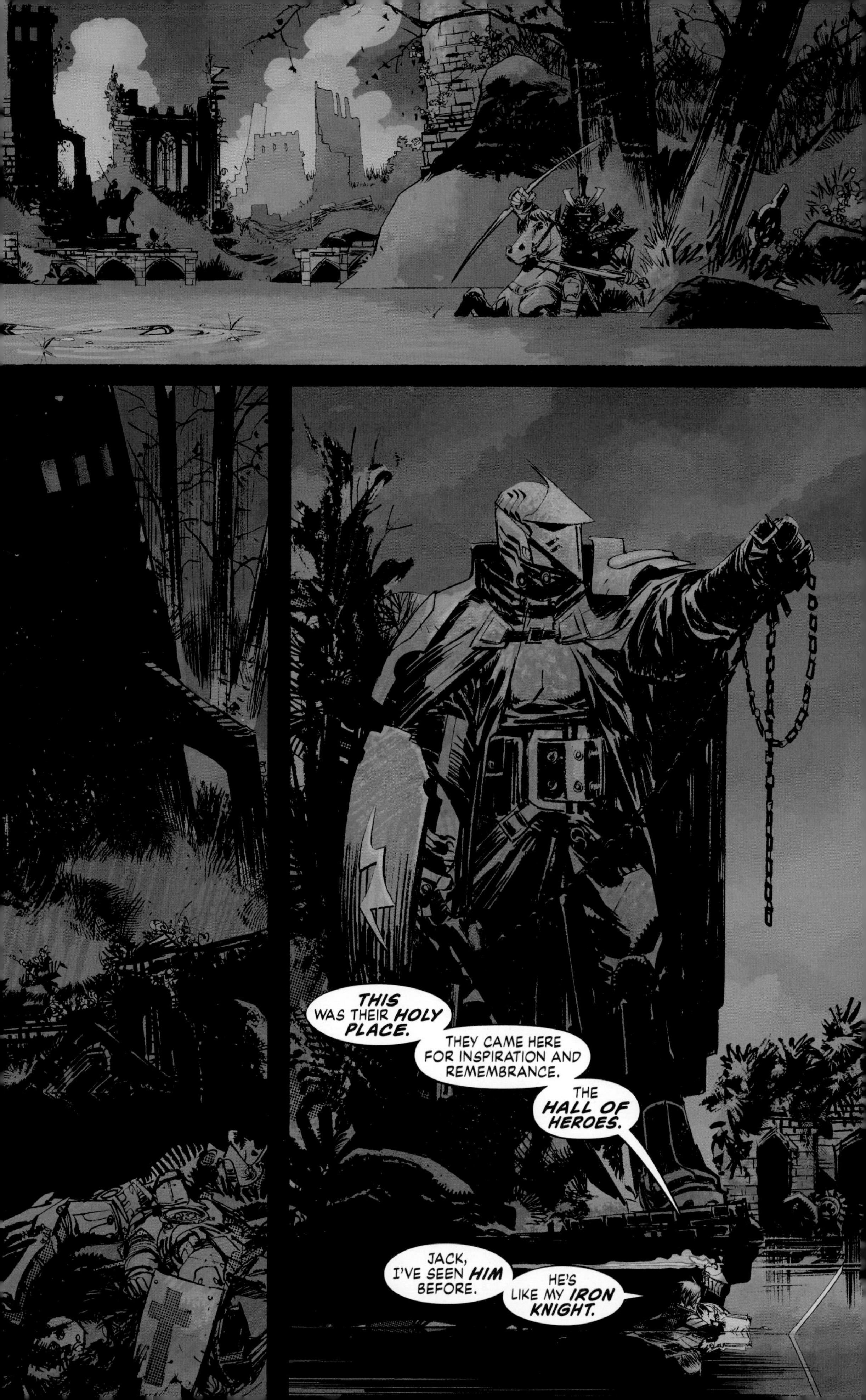
THIS WAS THEIR HOLY PLACE.
THEY CAME HERE FOR INSPIRATION AND REMEMBRANCE.
THE HALL OF HEROES.
JACK, I'VE SEEN HIM BEFORE.
HE'S LIKE MY IRON KNIGHT.

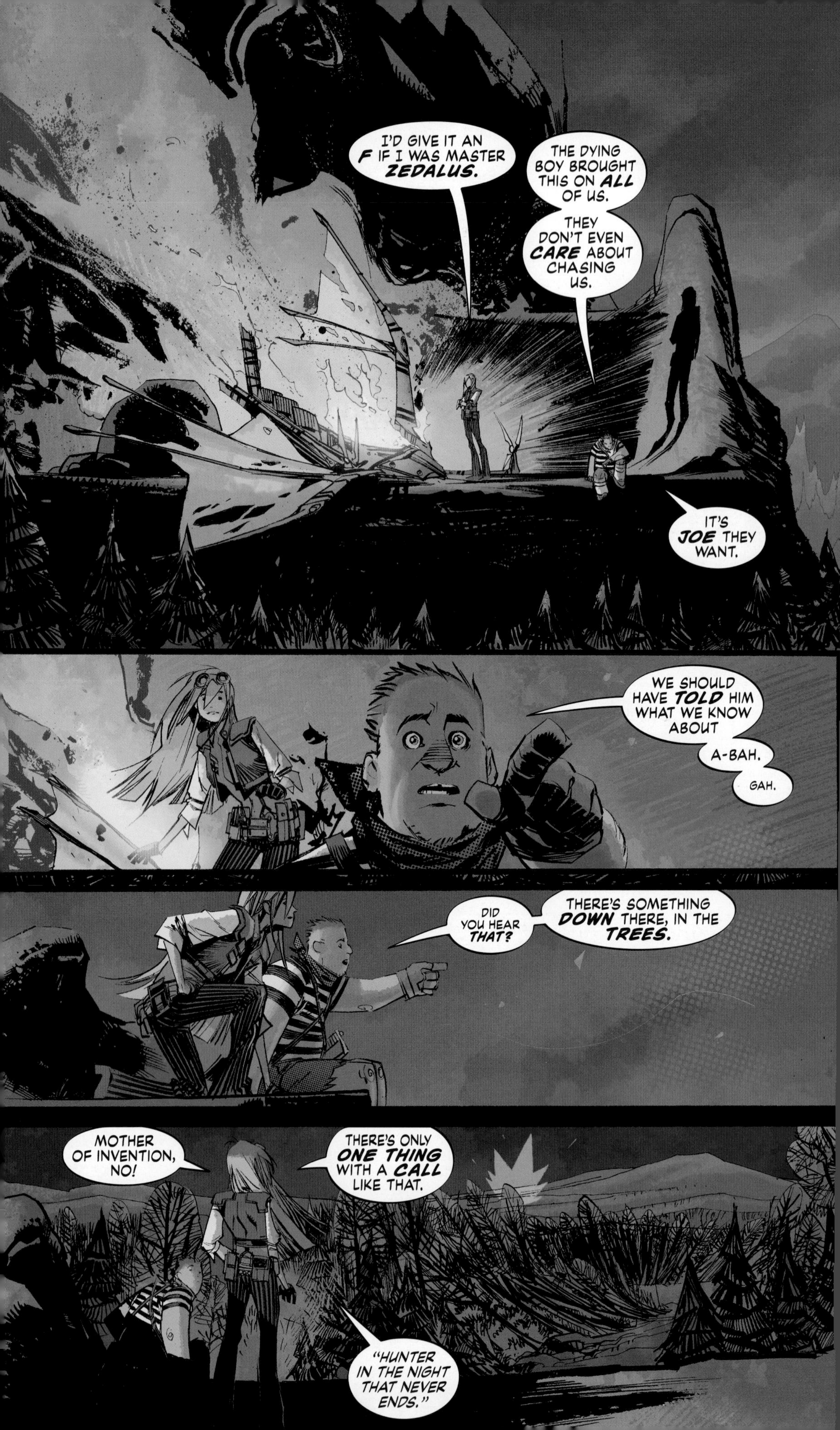
I'D GIVE IT AN F IF I WAS MASTER ZEDALUS.
THE DYING BOY BROUGHT THIS ON ALL OF US.
THEY DON'T EVEN CARE ABOUT CHASING US.
IT'S JOE THEY WANT.
WE SHOULD HAVE TOLD HIM WHAT WE KNOW ABOUT
A-BAH.
GAH.
DID YOU HEAR THAT?
THERE'S SOMETHING DOWN THERE, IN THE TREES.
MOTHER OF INVENTION, NO!
THERE'S ONLY ONE THING WITH A CALL LIKE THAT.
"HUNTER IN THE NIGHT THAT NEVER ENDS."

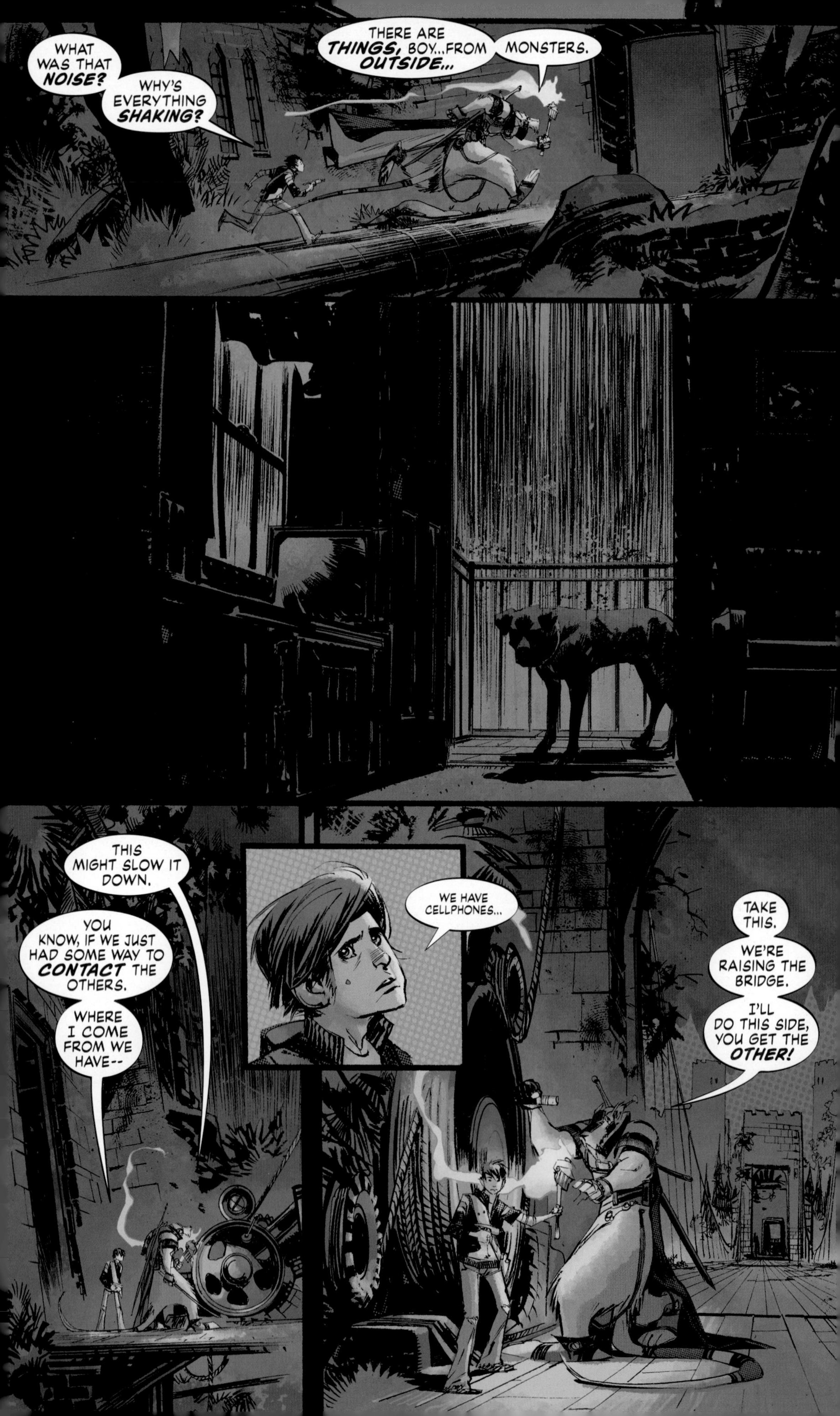
WHAT WAS THAT NOISE?
WHY'S EVERYTHING SHAKING?
THERE ARE THINGS, BOY...FROM OUTSIDE...
MONSTERS.
THIS MIGHT SLOW IT DOWN.
YOU KNOW, IF WE JUST HAD SOME WAY TO CONTACT THE OTHERS.
WHERE I COME FROM WE HAVE--
WE HAVE CELLPHONES...
TAKE THIS.
WE'RE RAISING THE BRIDGE.
I'LL DO THIS SIDE, YOU GET THE OTHER!

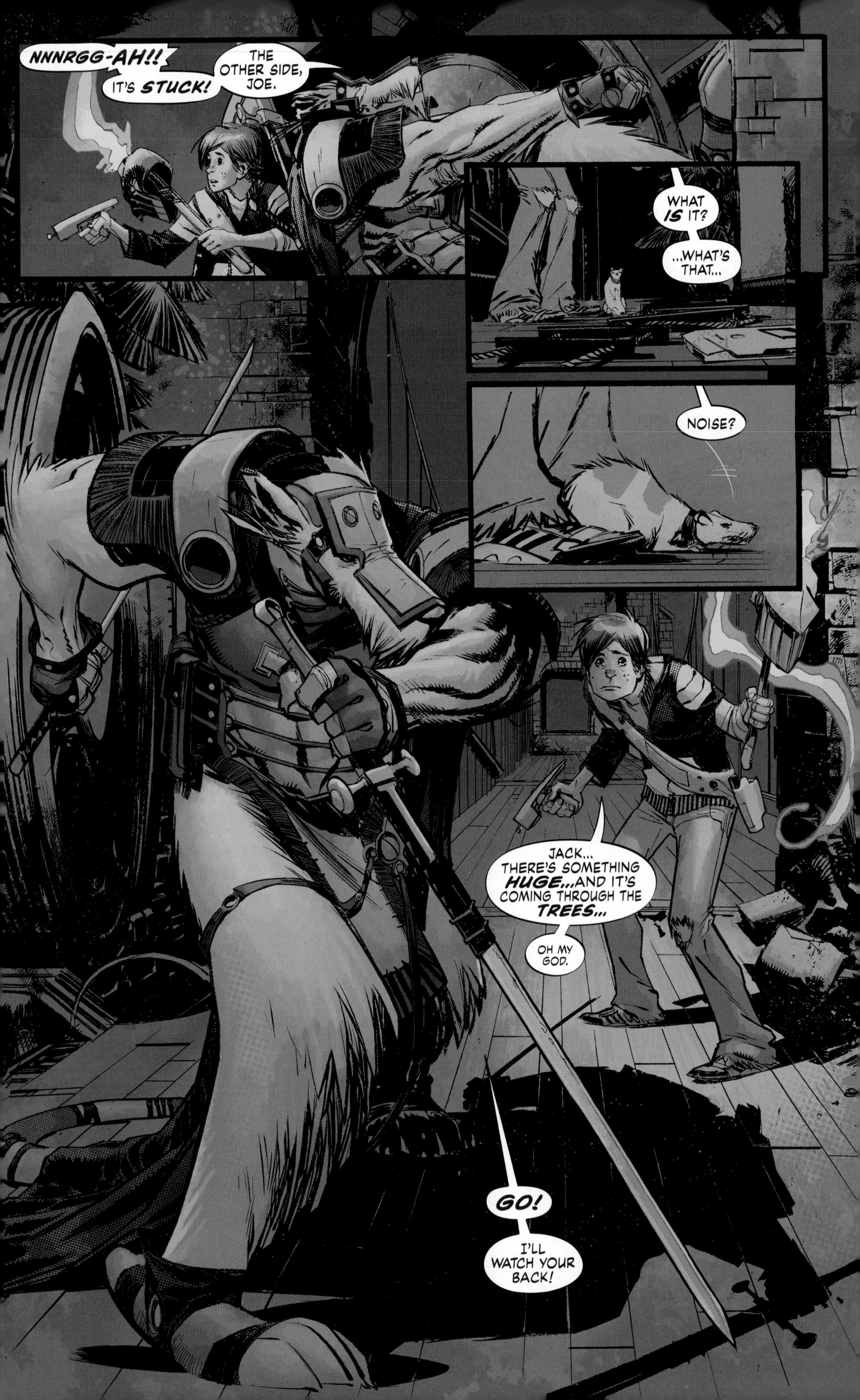
NNNRGG-AH!!
IT'S STUCK!
THE OTHER SIDE, JOE.
WHAT IS IT?
...WHAT'S THAT...
NOISE?
JACK... THERE'S SOMETHING HUGE...AND IT'S COMING THROUGH THE TREES...
OH MY GOD.
GO!
I'LL WATCH YOUR BACK!

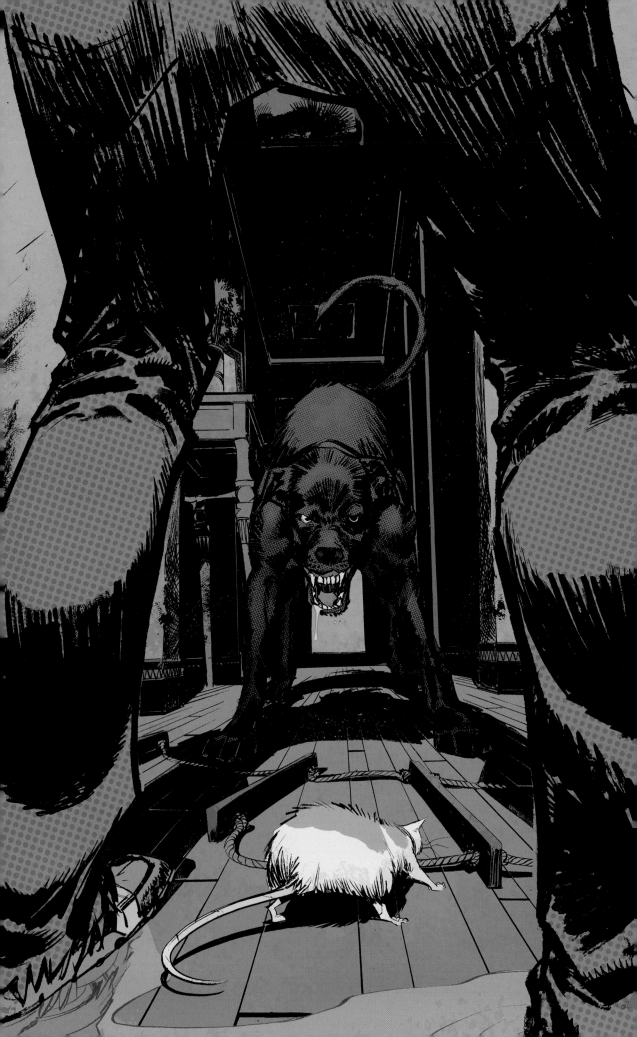

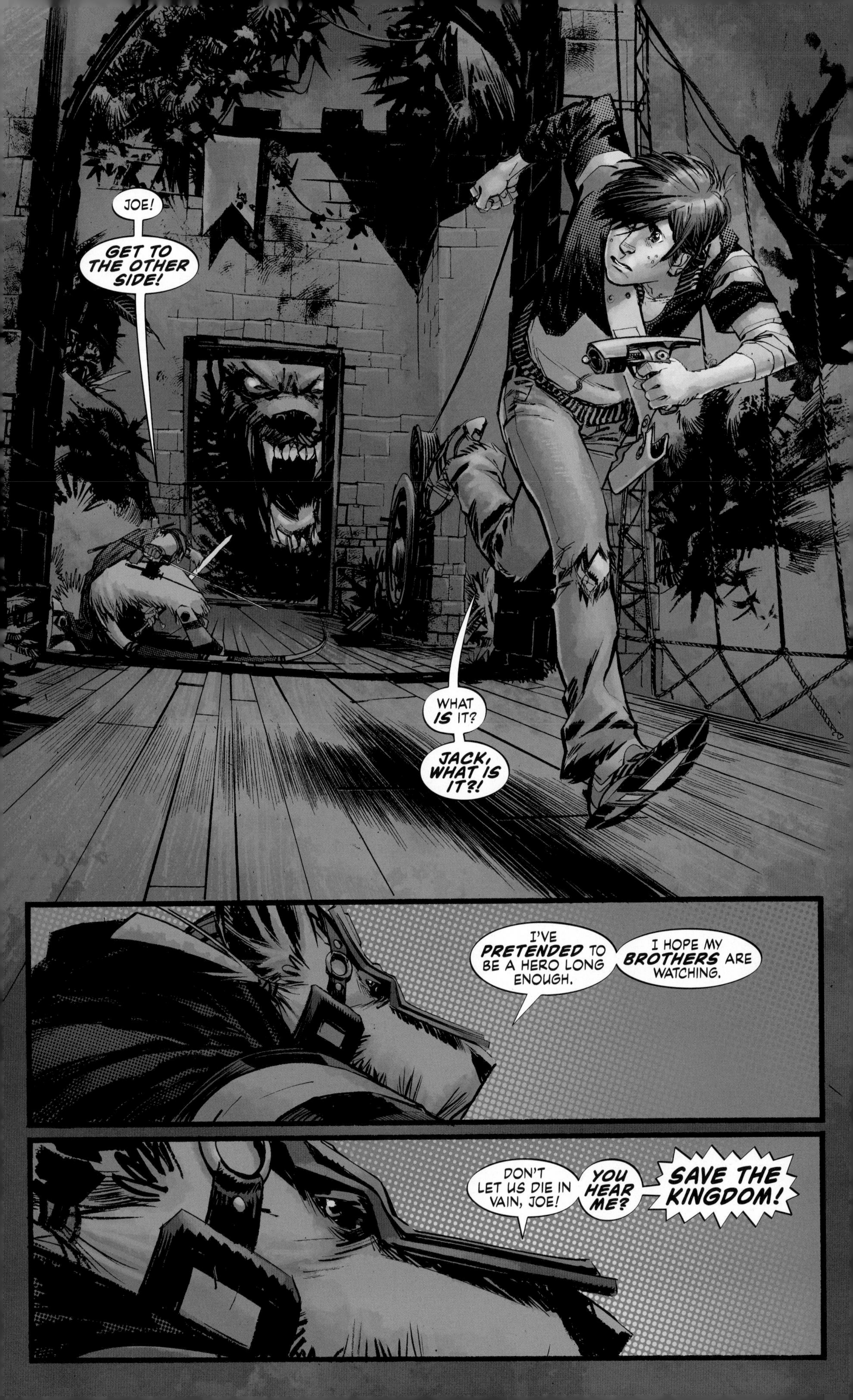
JOE!
GET TO THE OTHER SIDE!
WHAT IS IT?
JACK, WHAT IS IT?!
I'VE PRETENDED TO BE A HERO LONG ENOUGH.
I HOPE MY BROTHERS ARE WATCHING.
DON'T LET US DIE IN VAIN, JOE!
YOU HEAR ME?
SAVE THE KINGDOM!

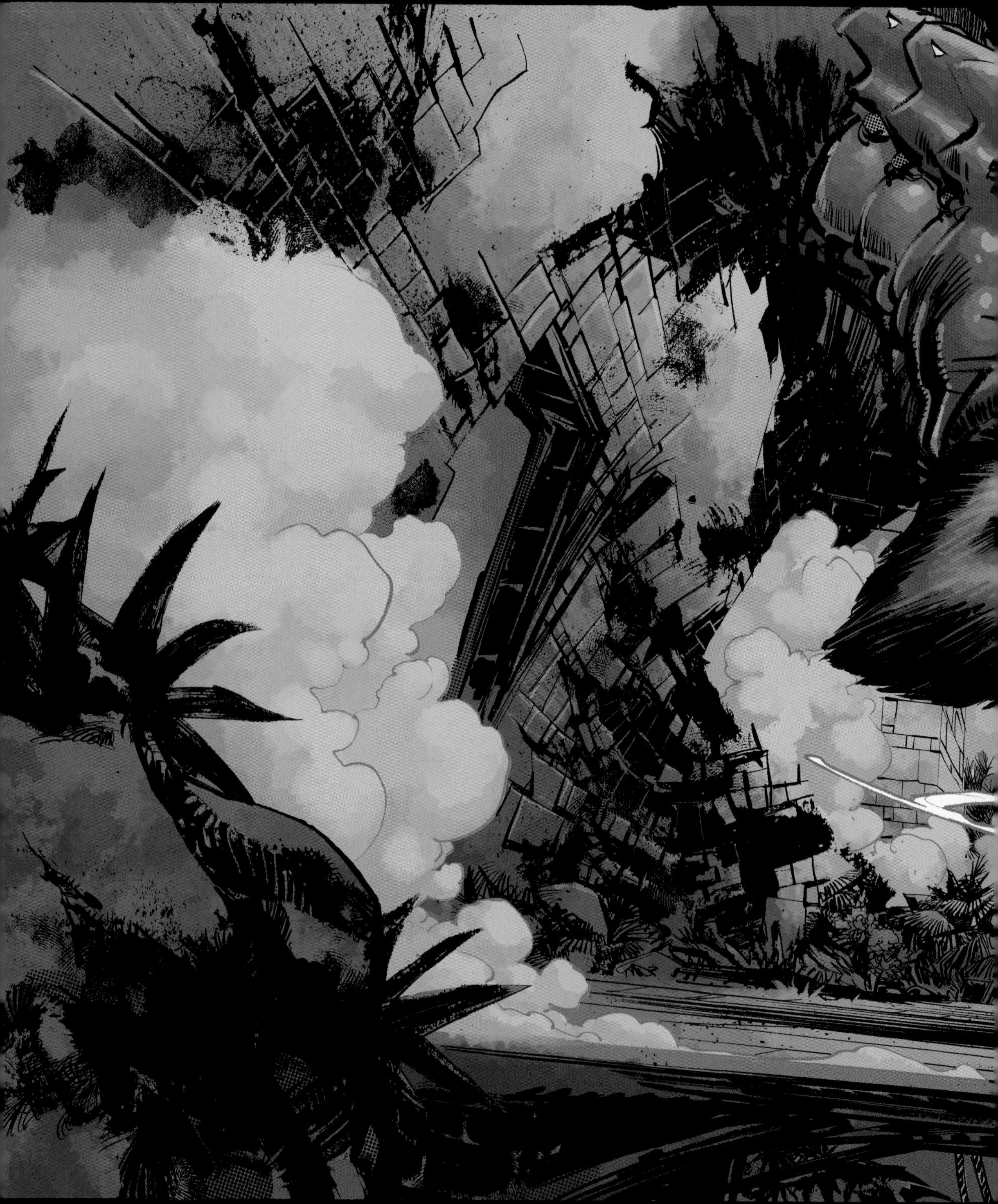

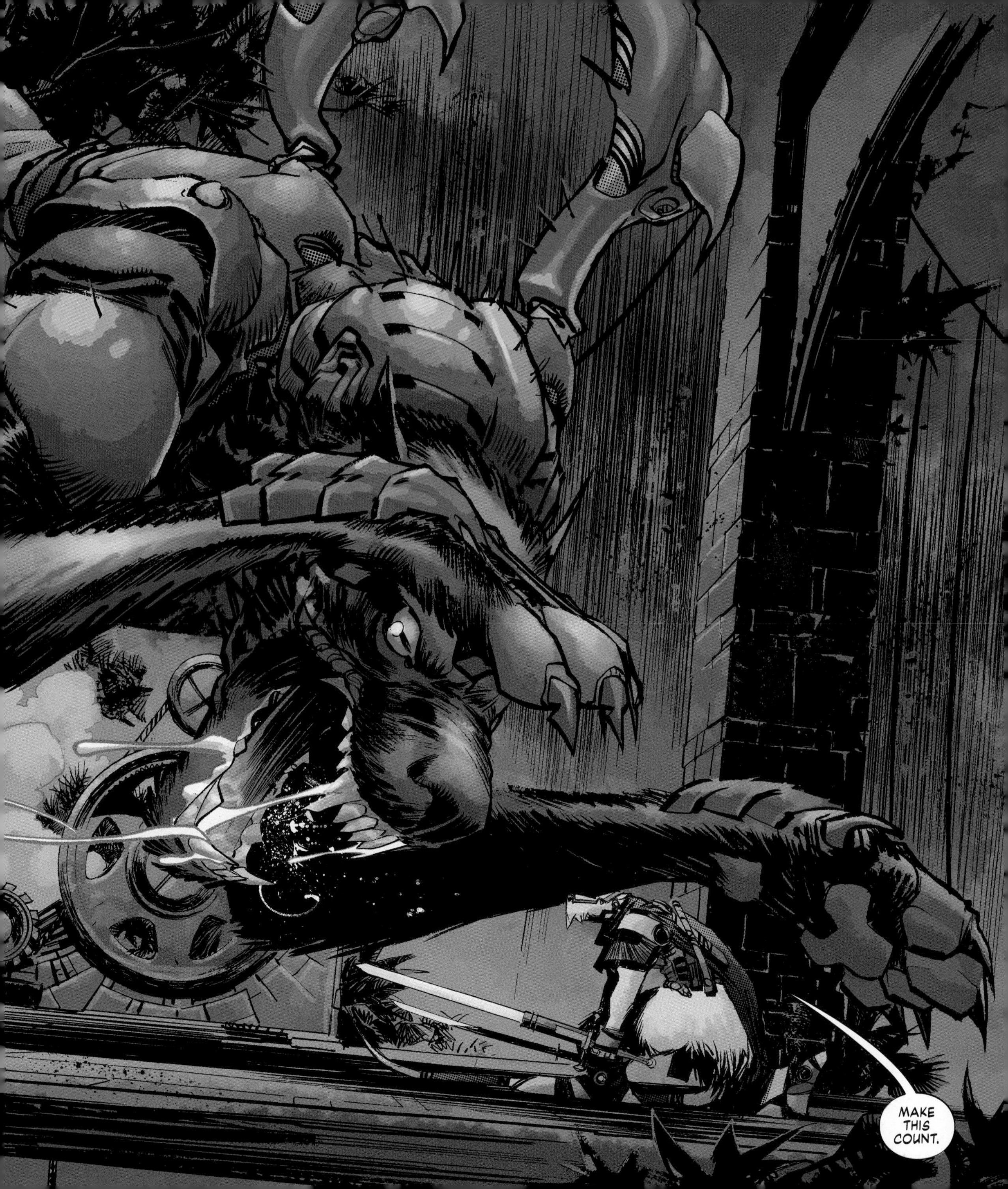
MAKE THIS COUNT.

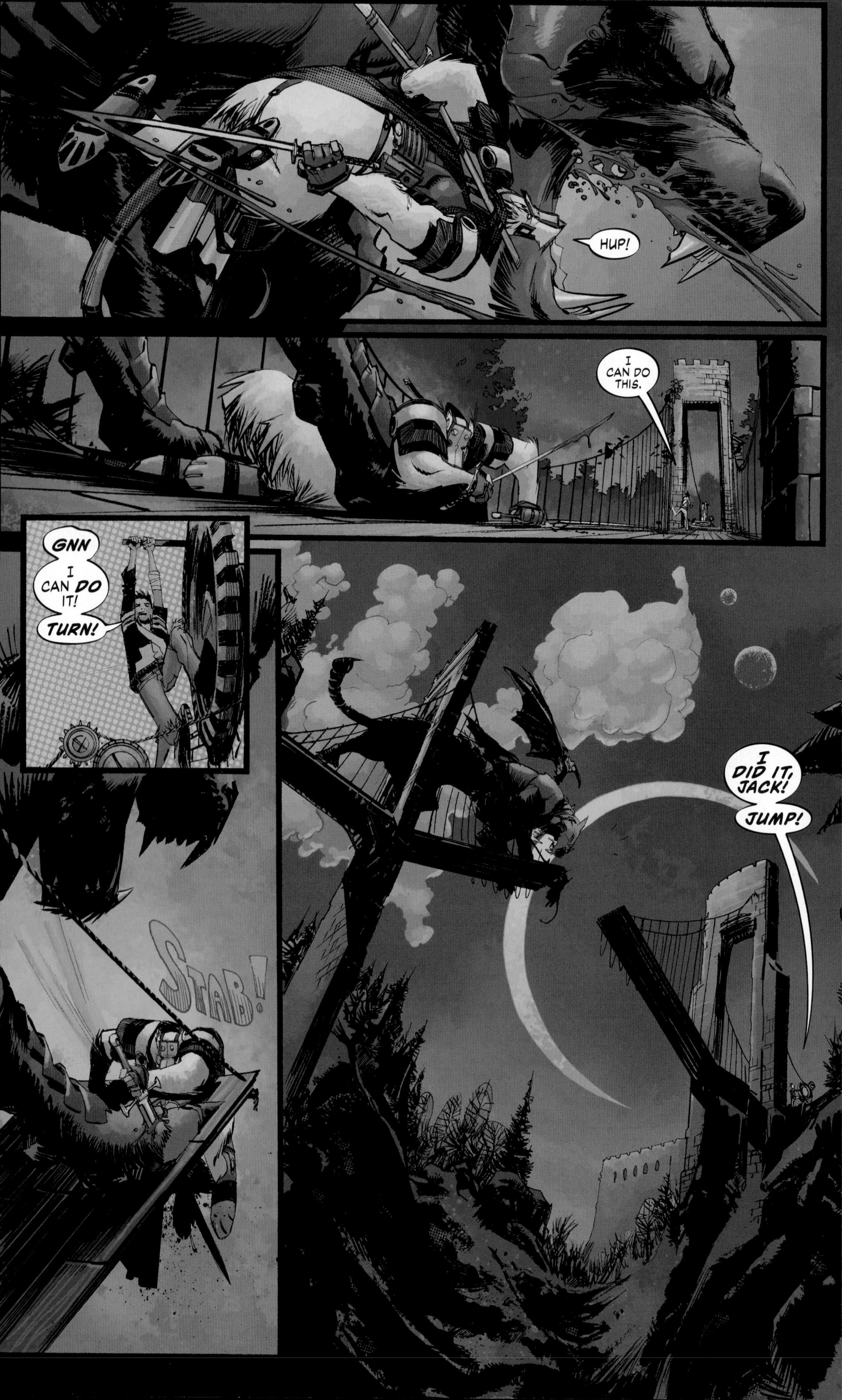
HUP!
I CAN DO THIS.
GNN
I CAN DO IT!
TURN!
STAB!
I DID IT, JACK!
JUMP!

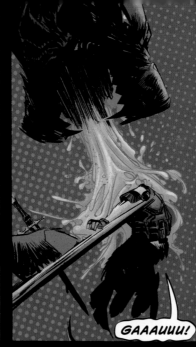

JUMP!

GAAAUUU!

YOU WON'T HAVE HIM. YOU'LL NEVER TAKE US ALL.

SHLUK!

HA!

JACK! NOW!!

LEAP!

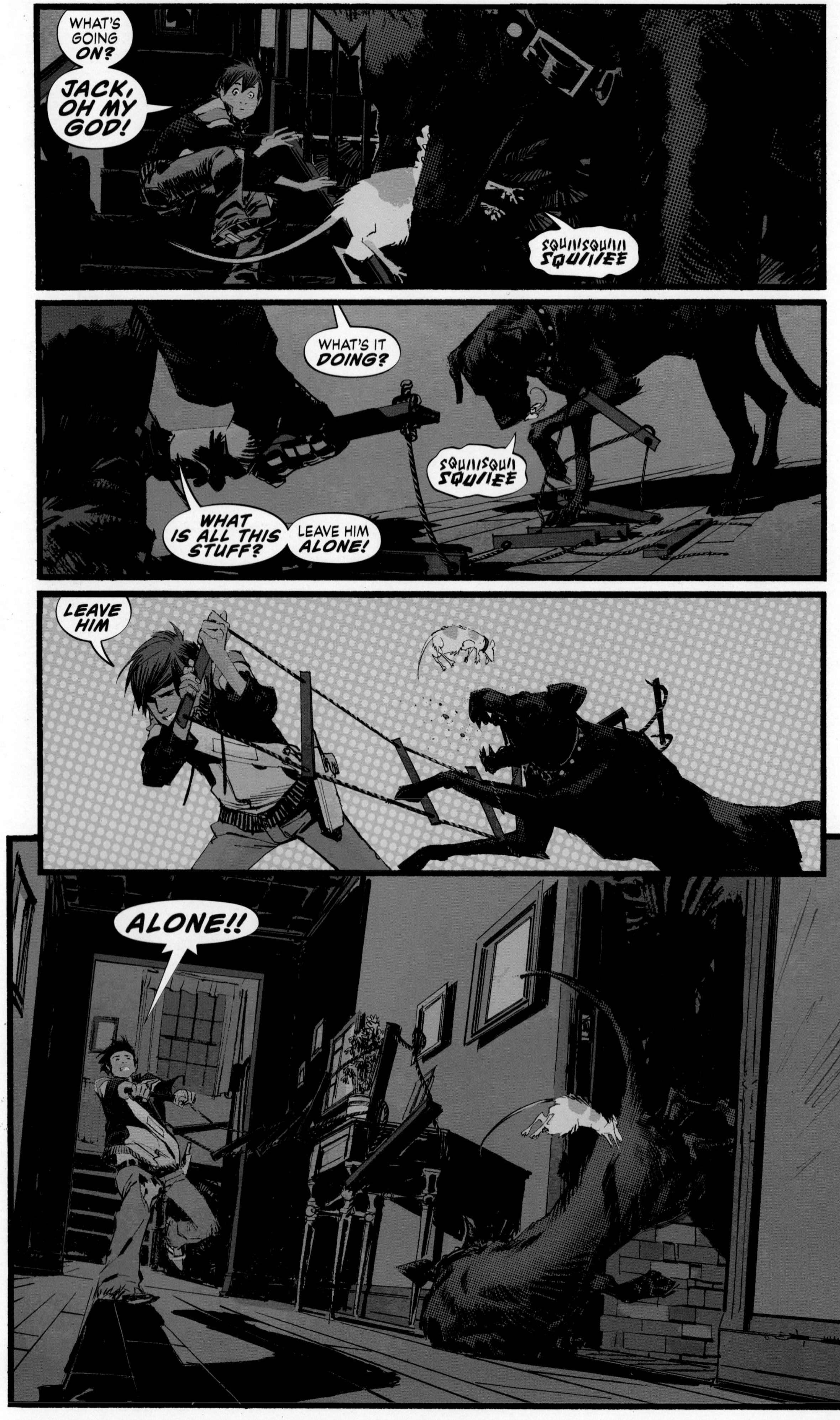
WHAT'S GOING ON?
JACK, OH MY GOD!
SQUIISQUII SQUIIEE
WHAT'S IT DOING?
SQUIISQUII SQUIIEE
WHAT IS ALL THIS STUFF?
LEAVE HIM ALONE!
LEAVE HIM
ALONE!!

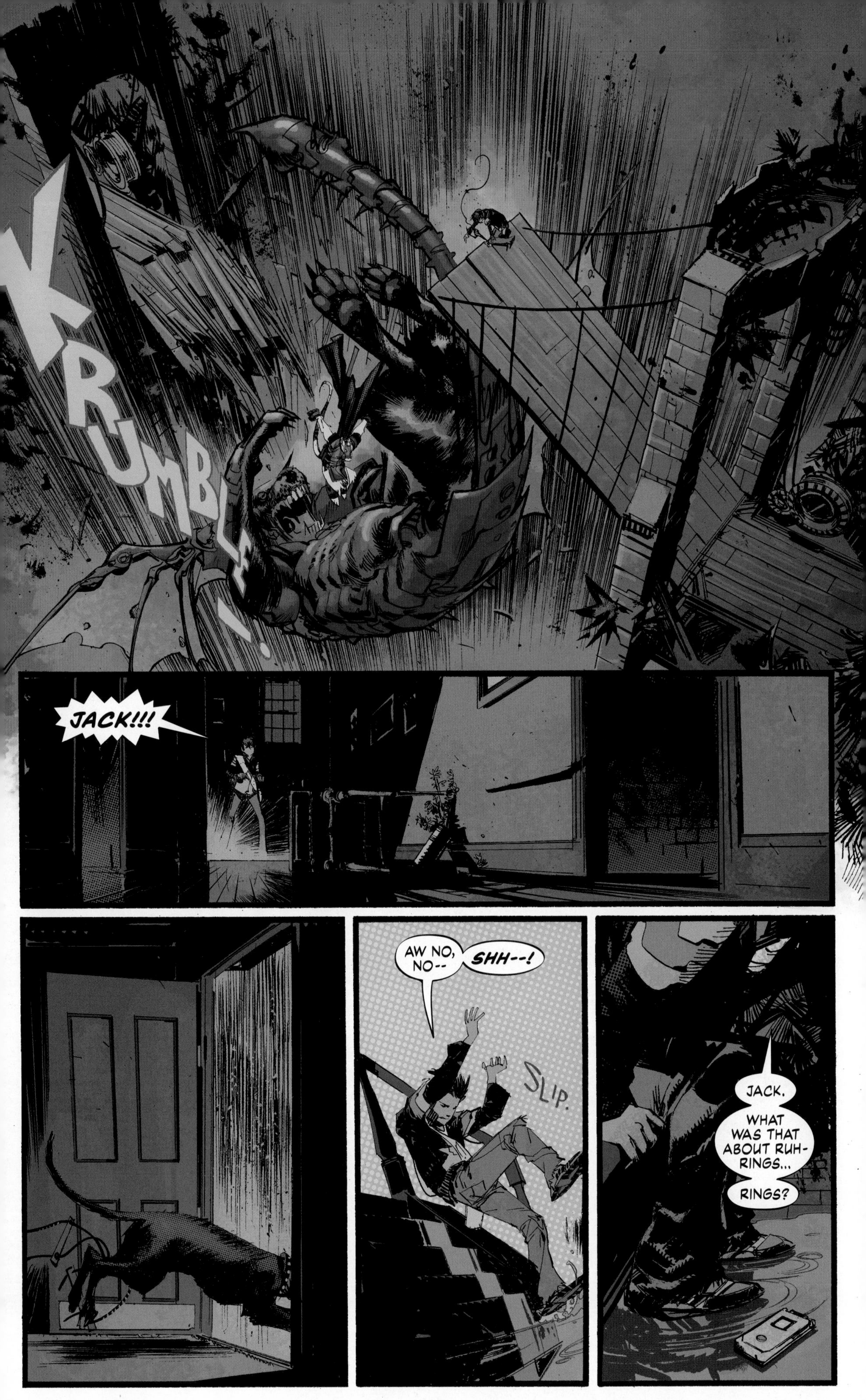
KRUMBLE!
JACK!!!
AW NO, NO--
SHH--!
SLIP.
JACK.
WHAT WAS THAT ABOUT RUH-RINGS...
RINGS?

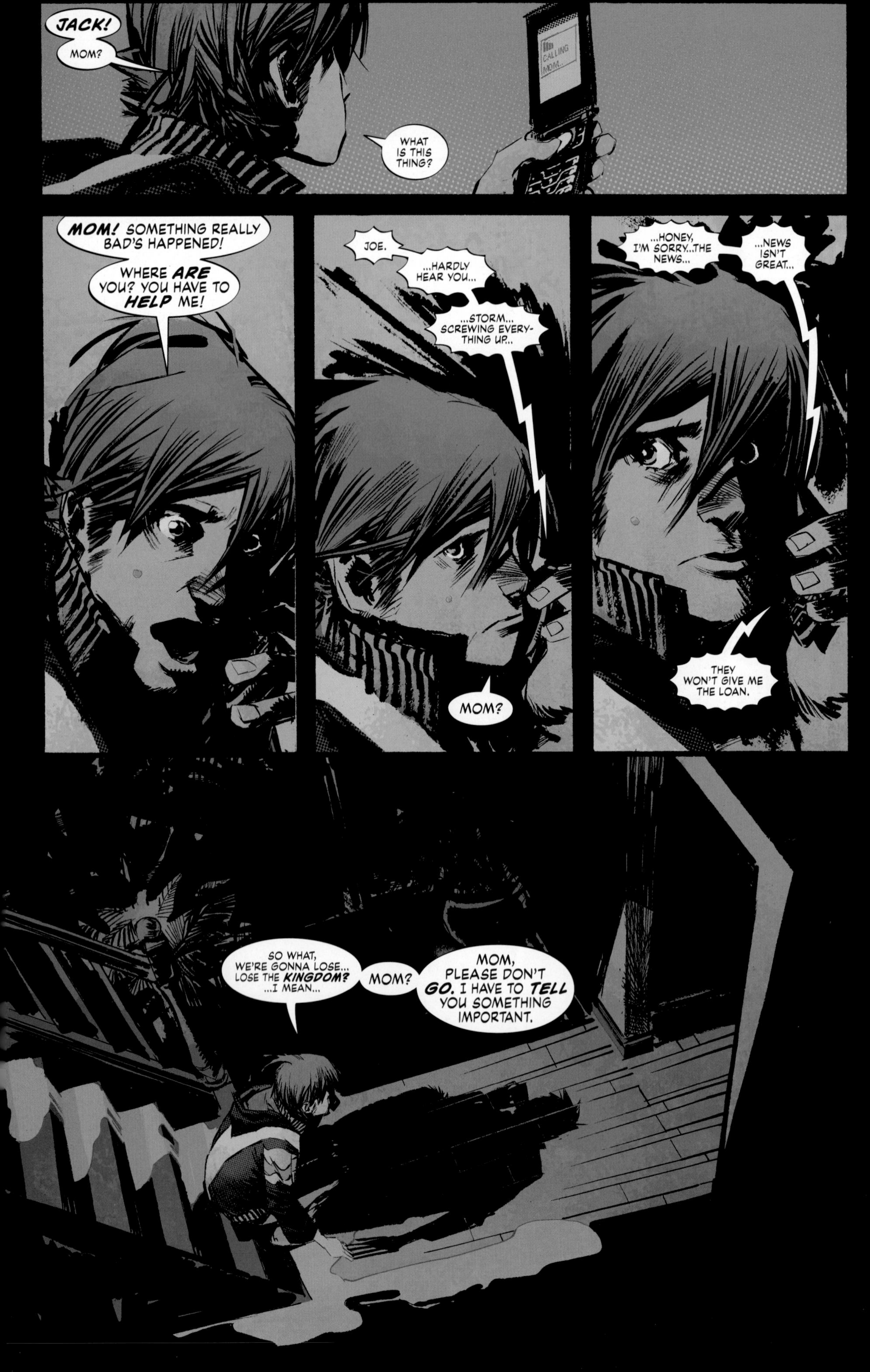
JACK!
MOM?
CALLING MOM...
WHAT IS THIS THING?
MOM! SOMETHING REALLY BAD'S HAPPENED!
WHERE ARE YOU? YOU HAVE TO HELP ME!
JOE.
...HARDLY HEAR YOU...
...STORM... SCREWING EVERY-THING UP...
MOM?
...HONEY, I'M SORRY...THE NEWS...
...NEWS ISN'T GREAT...
THEY WON'T GIVE ME THE LOAN.
SO WHAT, WE'RE GONNA LOSE... LOSE THE KINGDOM? ...I MEAN...
MOM?
MOM, PLEASE DON'T GO. I HAVE TO TELL YOU SOMETHING IMPORTANT.

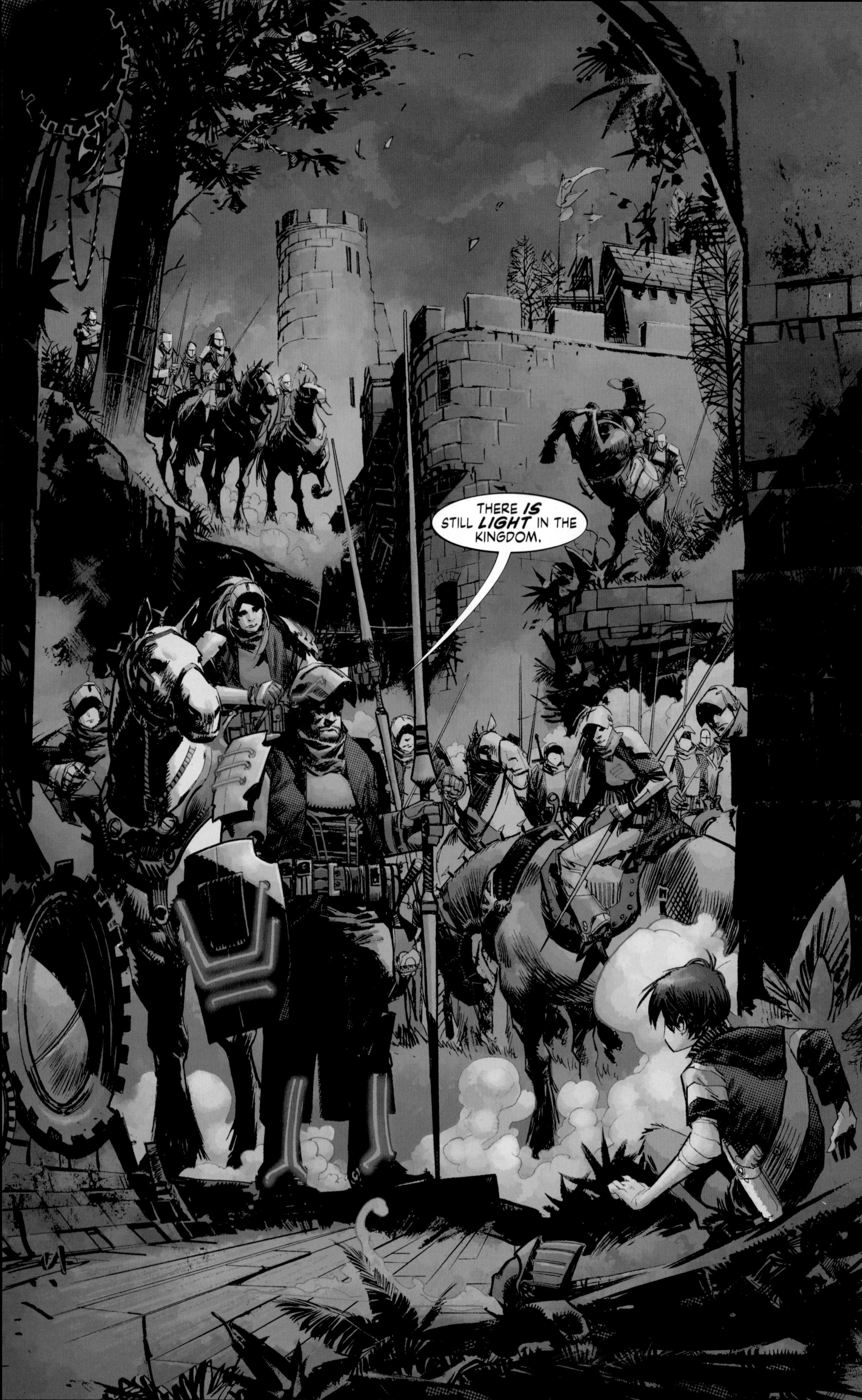
THERE IS STILL LIGHT IN THE KINGDOM.

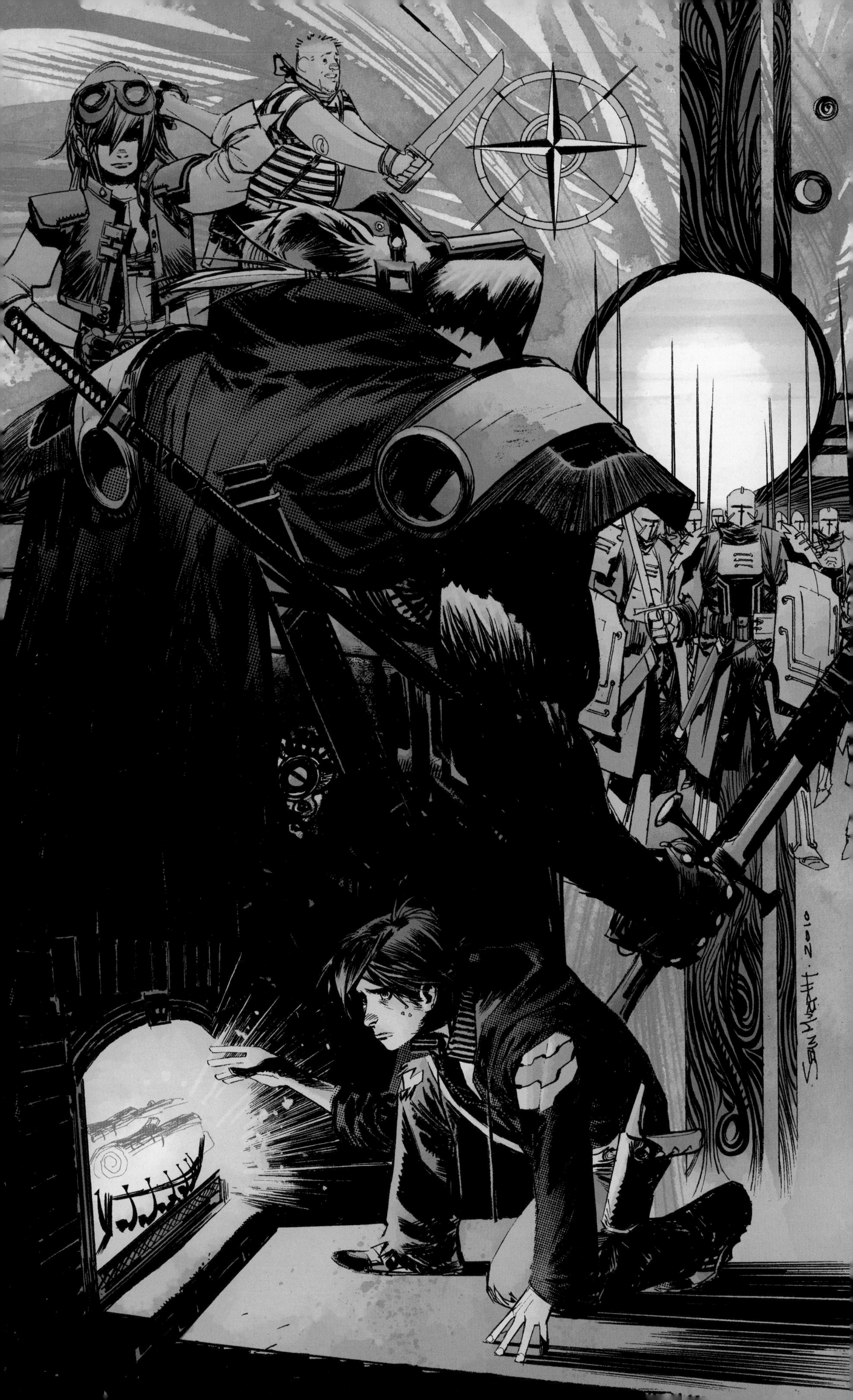

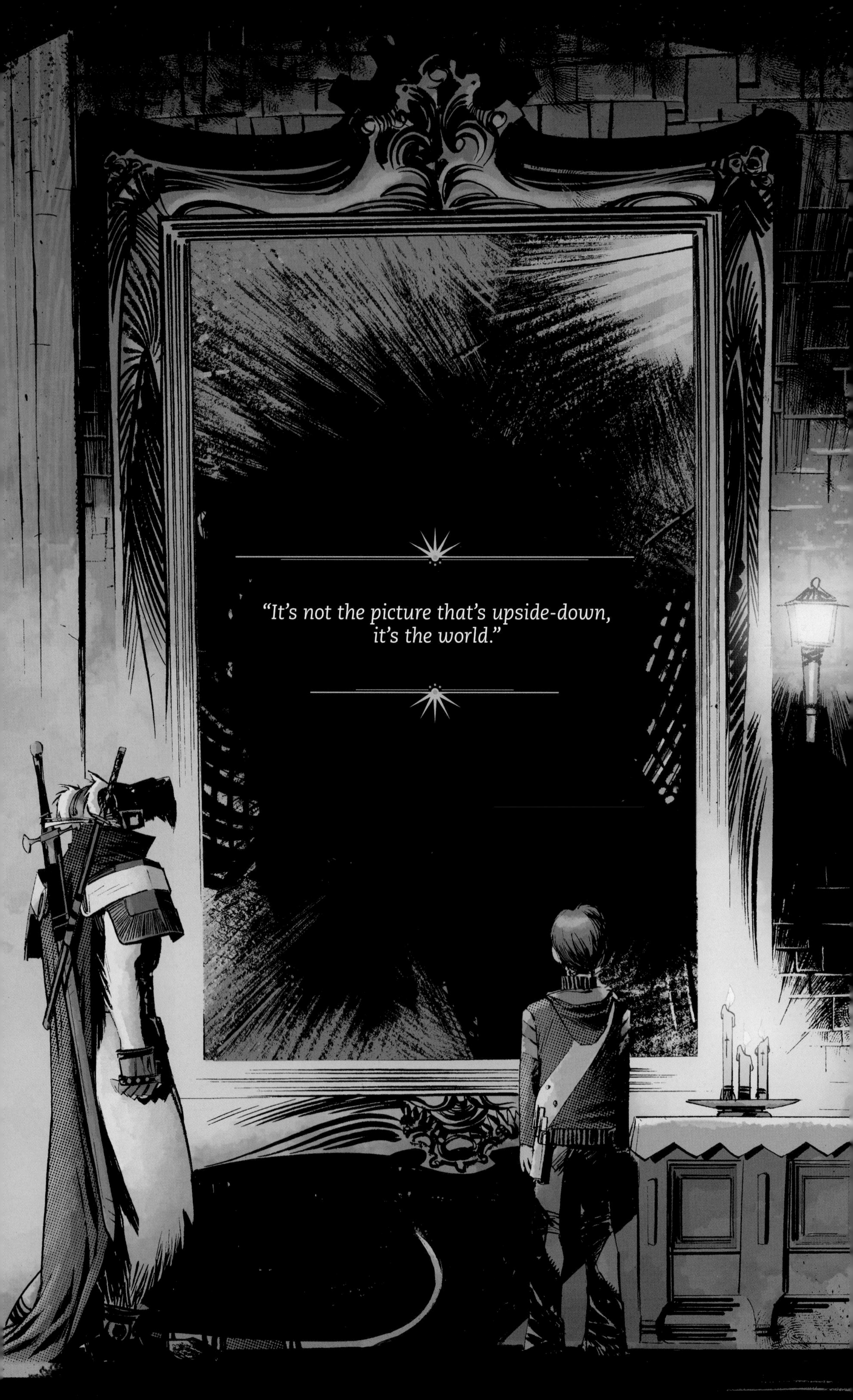
"It's not the picture that's upside-down,
it's the world."

# chapter 6: our lady in mourning

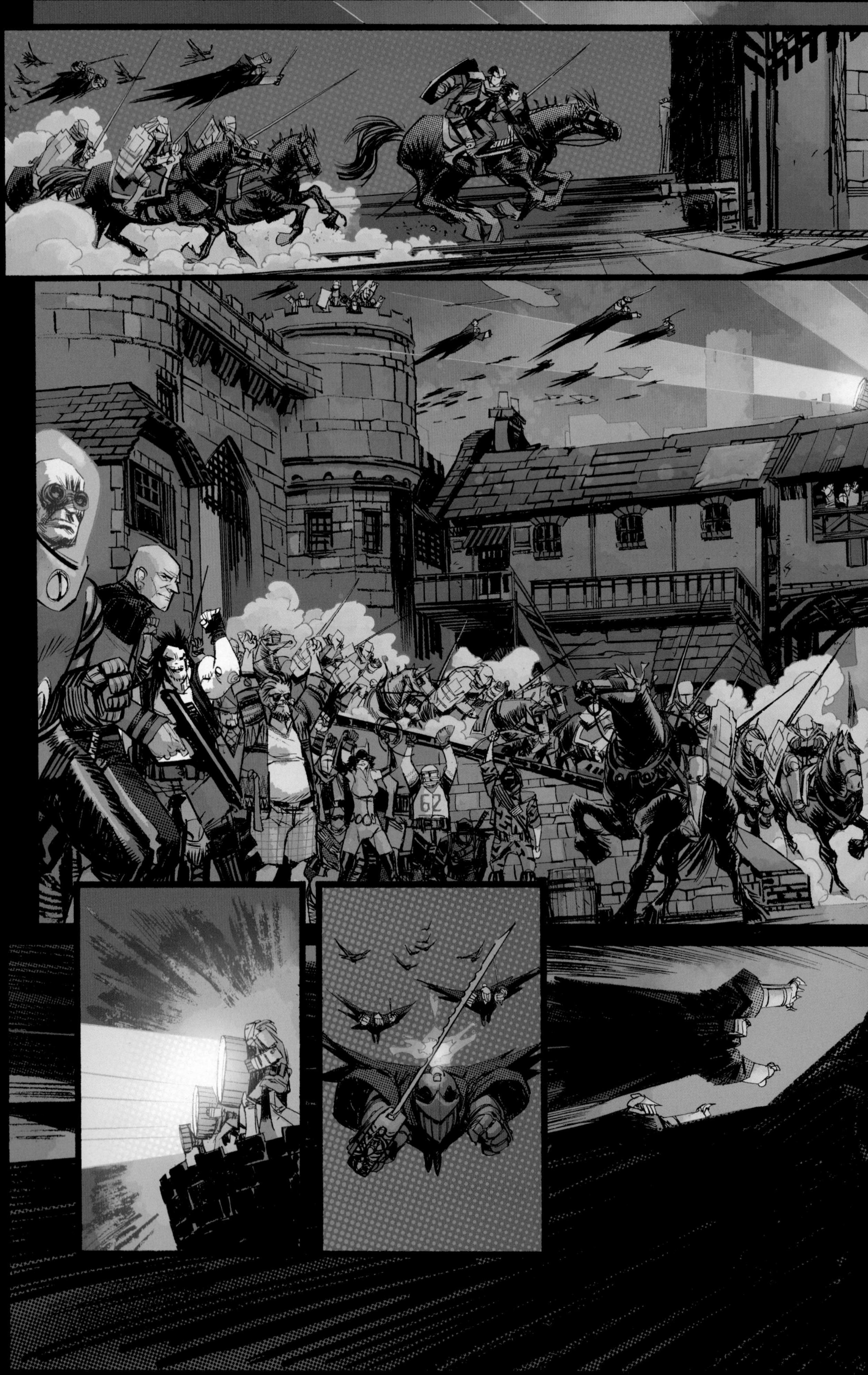

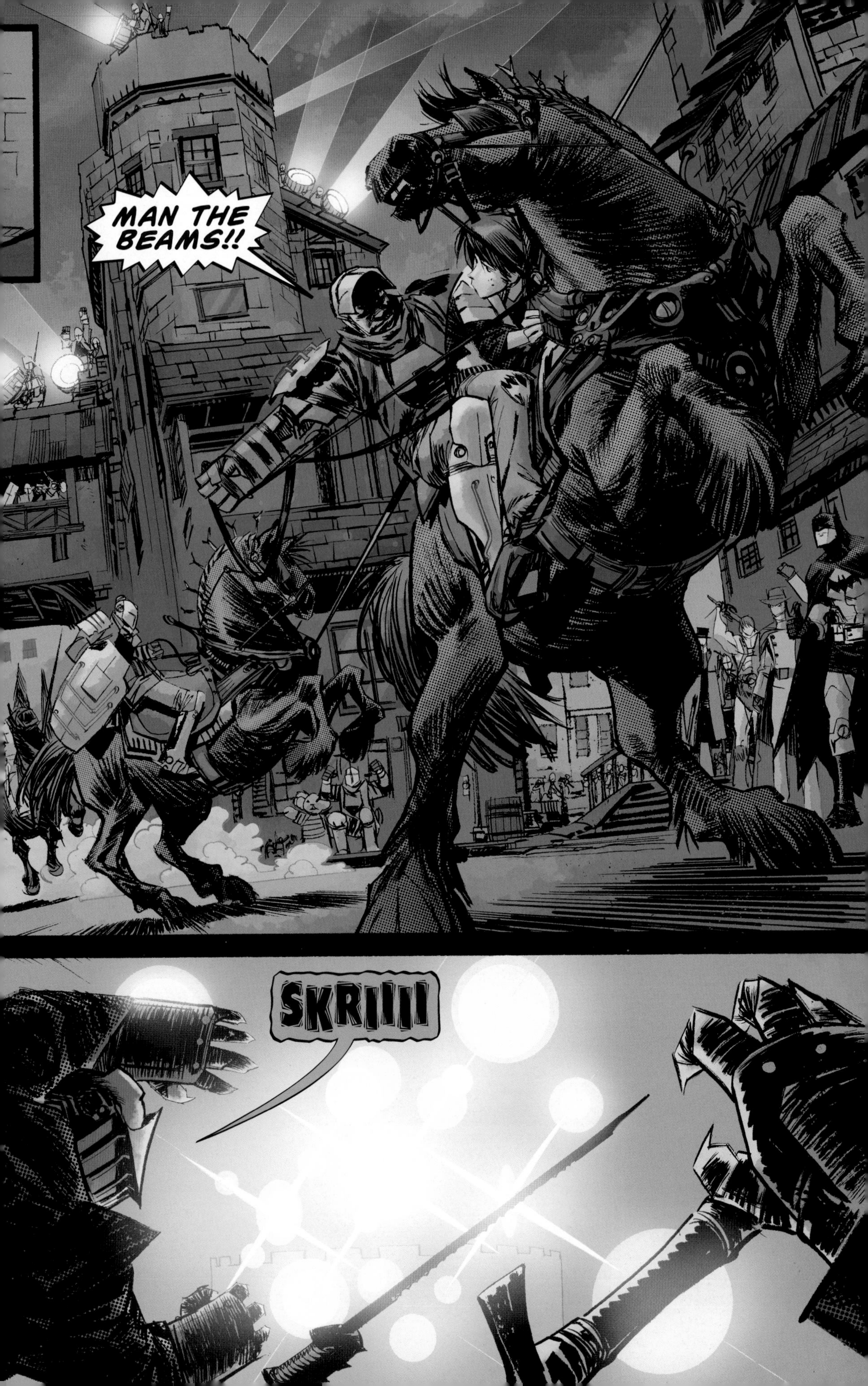
MAN THE BEAMS!!
SKRIIII

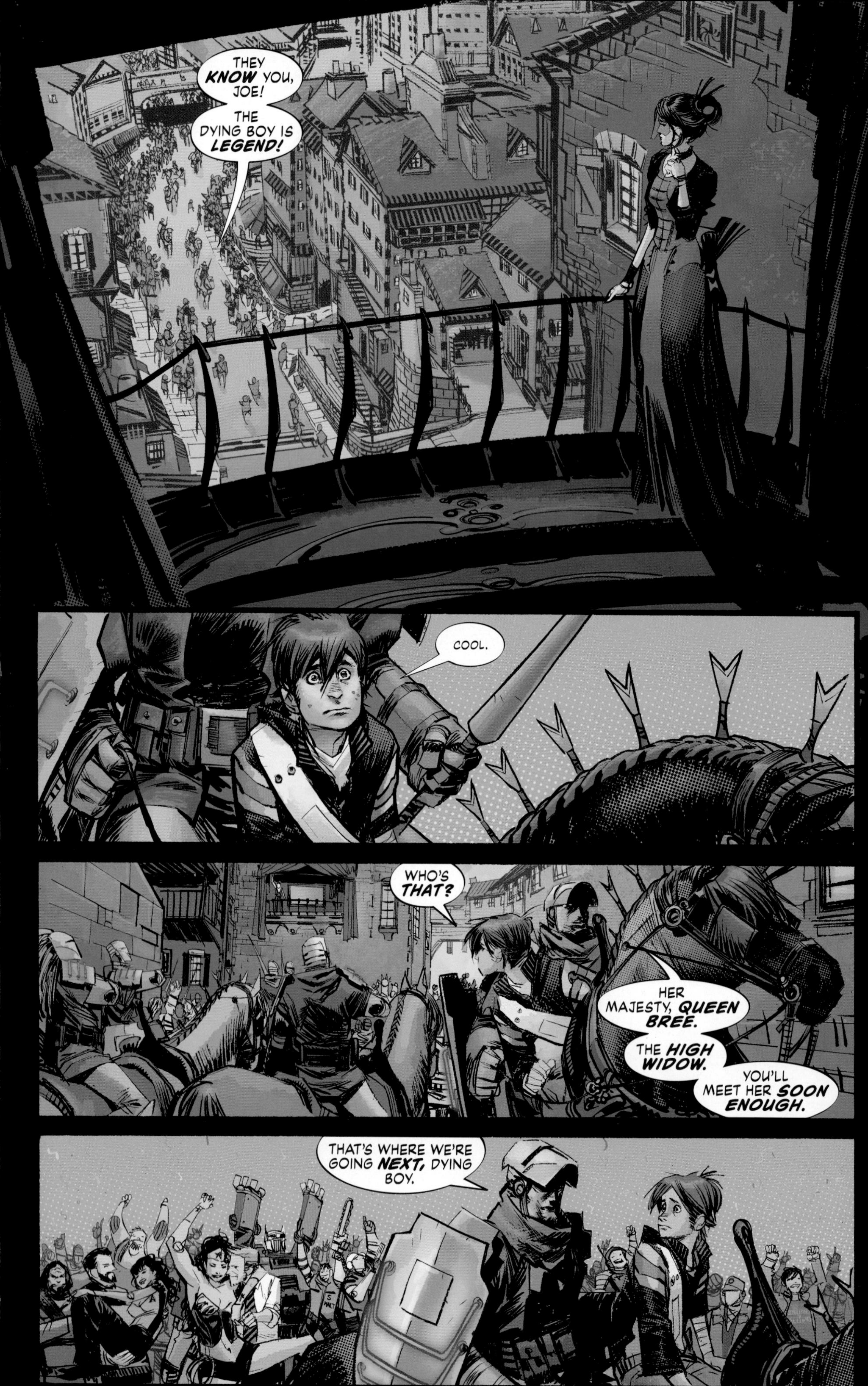
THEY **KNOW** YOU, JOE!
THE DYING BOY IS **LEGEND!**
COOL.
WHO'S **THAT?**
HER MAJESTY, **QUEEN BREE.**
THE **HIGH WIDOW.**
YOU'LL MEET HER **SOON ENOUGH.**
THAT'S WHERE WE'RE GOING **NEXT,** DYING BOY.

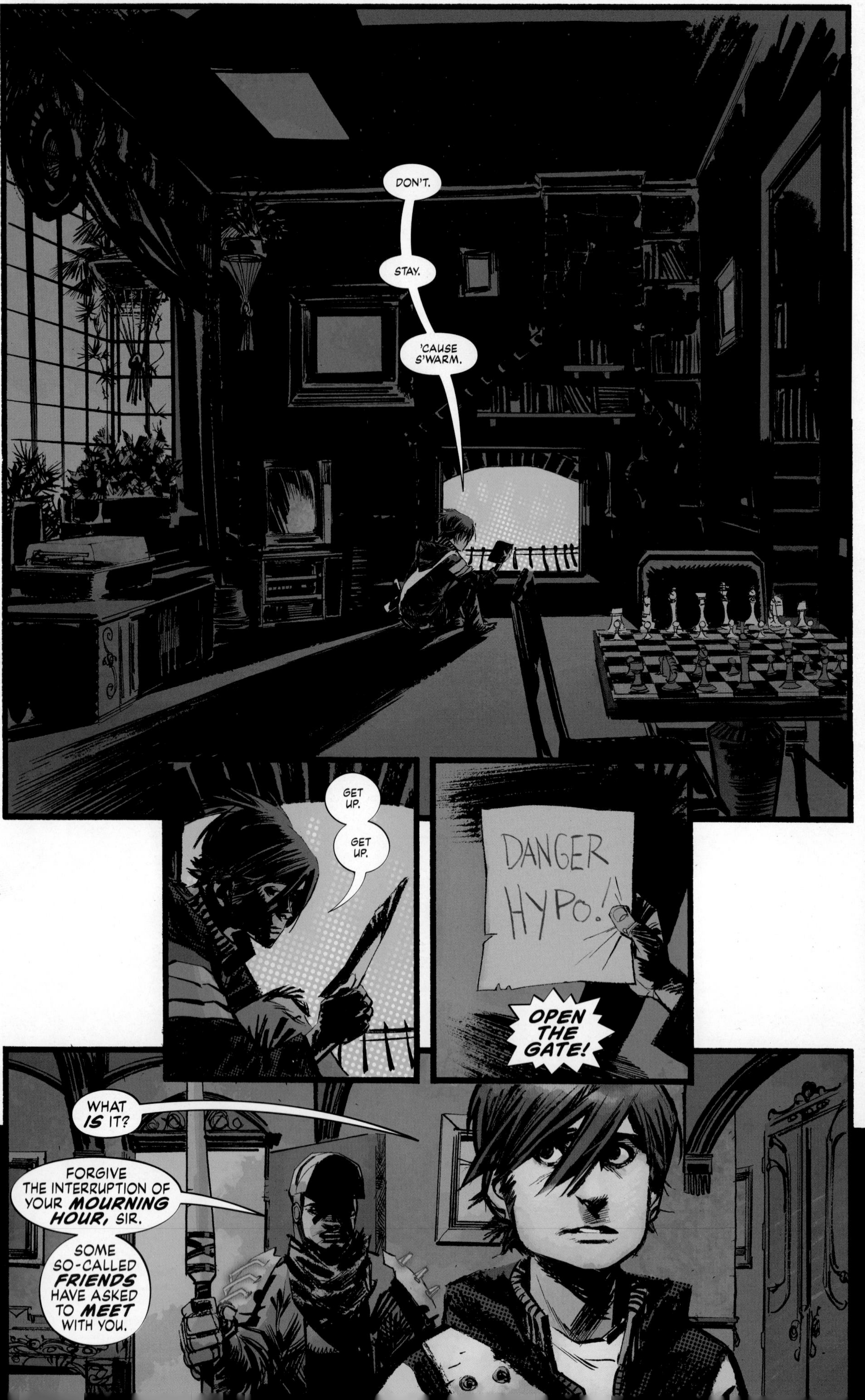
DON'T.
STAY.
'CAUSE S'WARM.
GET UP.
GET UP.
DANGER HYPO.!
OPEN THE GATE!
WHAT *IS* IT?
FORGIVE THE INTERRUPTION OF YOUR ***MOURNING HOUR,*** SIR.
SOME SO-CALLED ***FRIENDS*** HAVE ASKED TO ***MEET*** WITH YOU.

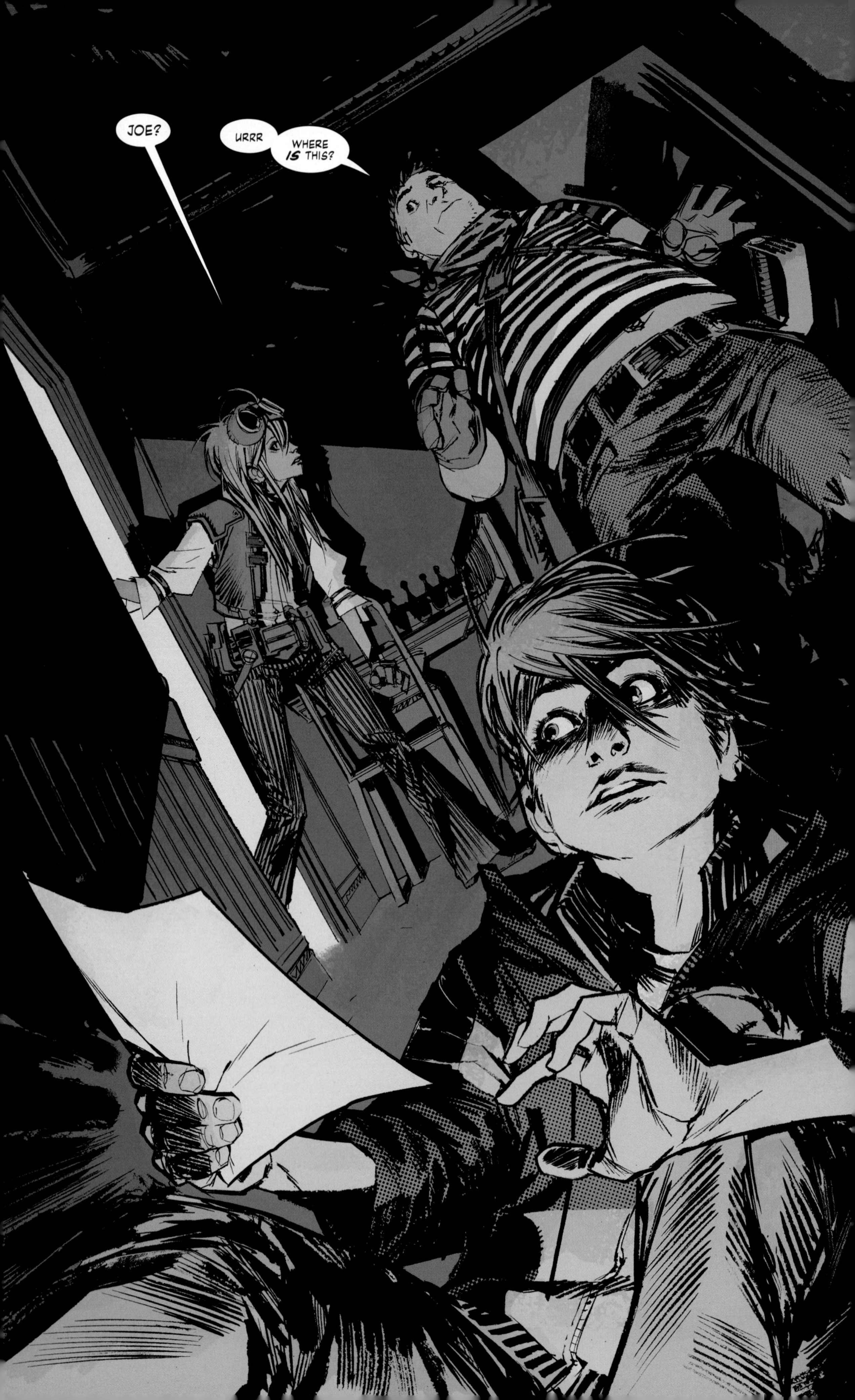
JOE?
URRR
WHERE *IS* THIS?

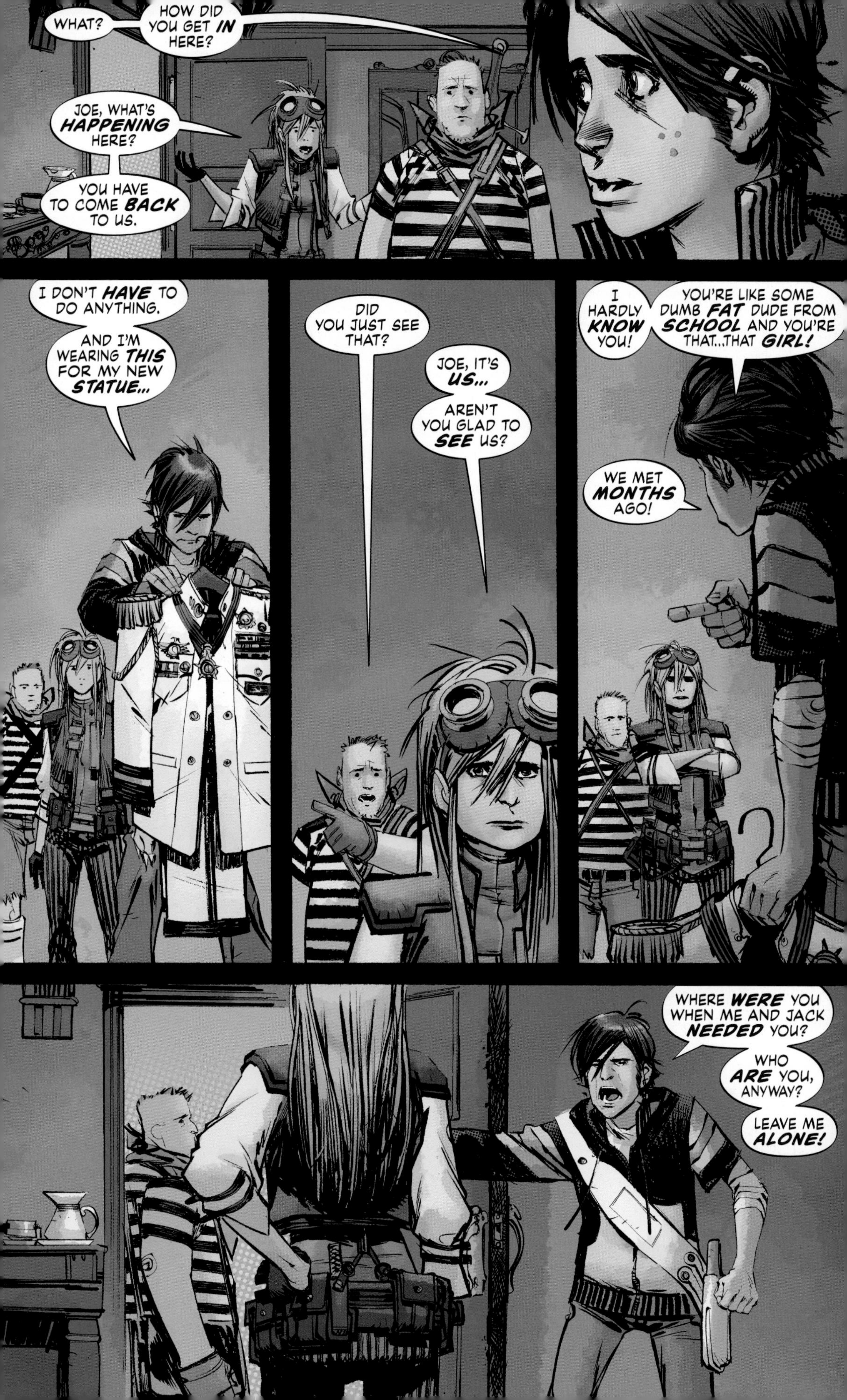
WHAT?
HOW DID YOU GET IN HERE?
JOE, WHAT'S HAPPENING HERE?
YOU HAVE TO COME BACK TO US.
I DON'T HAVE TO DO ANYTHING.
AND I'M WEARING THIS FOR MY NEW STATUE...
DID YOU JUST SEE THAT?
JOE, IT'S US...
AREN'T YOU GLAD TO SEE US?
I HARDLY KNOW YOU!
YOU'RE LIKE SOME DUMB FAT DUDE FROM SCHOOL AND YOU'RE THAT...THAT GIRL!
WE MET MONTHS AGO!
WHERE WERE YOU WHEN ME AND JACK NEEDED YOU?
WHO ARE YOU, ANYWAY?
LEAVE ME ALONE!

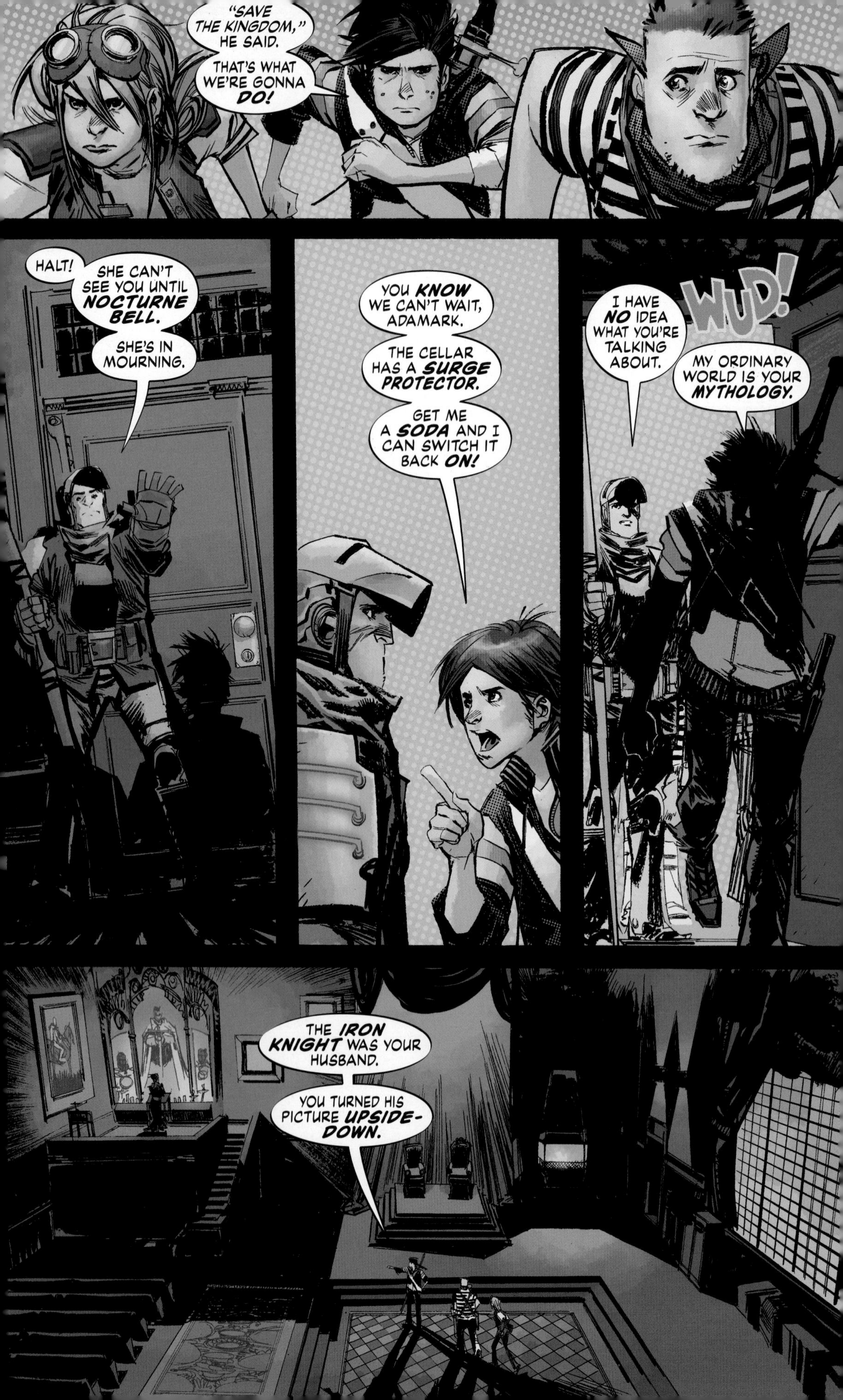
"SAVE THE KINGDOM," HE SAID.
THAT'S WHAT WE'RE GONNA DO!
HALT!
SHE CAN'T SEE YOU UNTIL NOCTURNE BELL.
SHE'S IN MOURNING.
YOU KNOW WE CAN'T WAIT, ADAMARK.
THE CELLAR HAS A SURGE PROTECTOR.
GET ME A SODA AND I CAN SWITCH IT BACK ON!
WUD!
I HAVE NO IDEA WHAT YOU'RE TALKING ABOUT.
MY ORDINARY WORLD IS YOUR MYTHOLOGY.
THE IRON KNIGHT WAS YOUR HUSBAND.
YOU TURNED HIS PICTURE UPSIDE-DOWN.

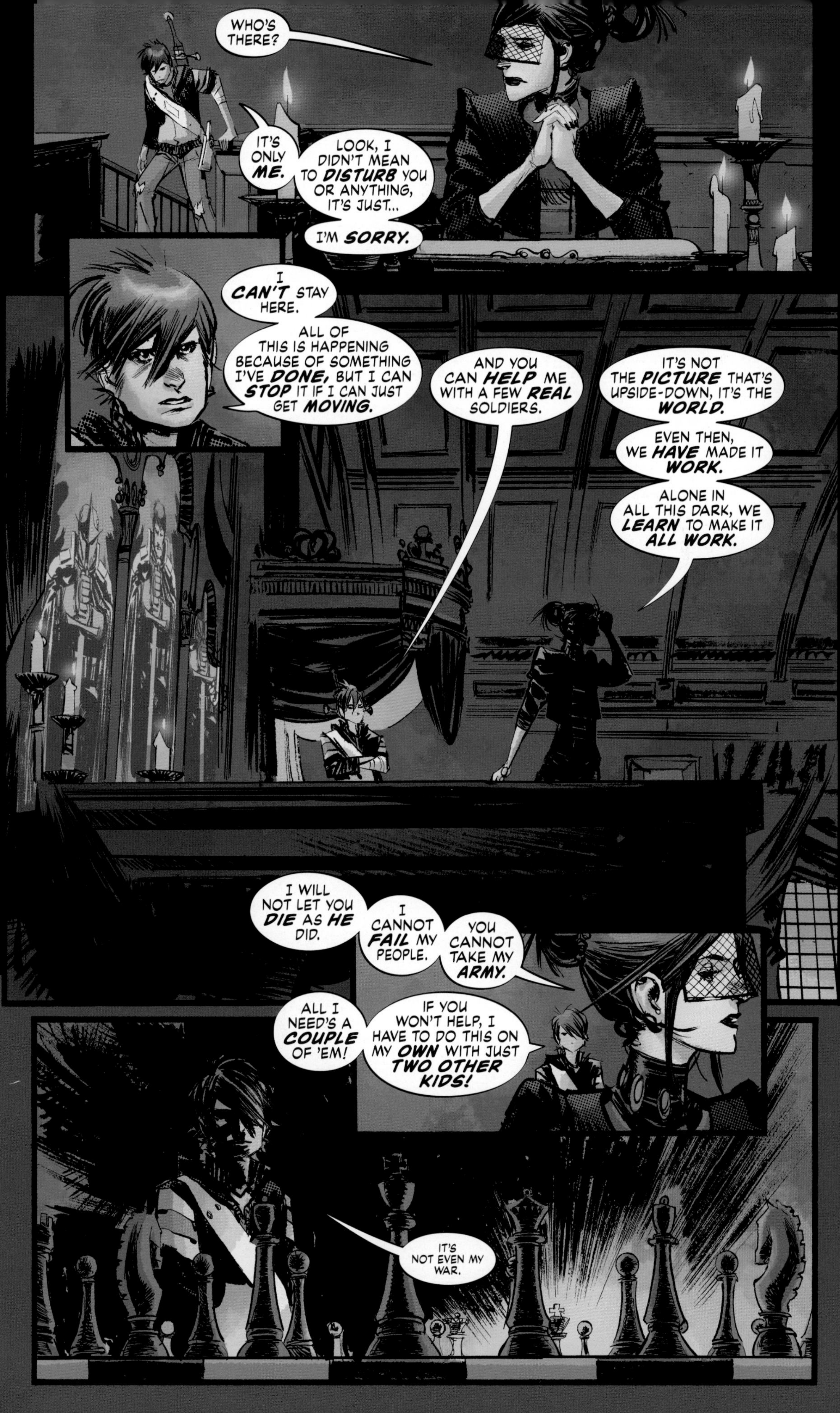
WHO'S THERE?
IT'S ONLY ME.
LOOK, I DIDN'T MEAN TO DISTURB YOU OR ANYTHING, IT'S JUST...
I'M SORRY.
I CAN'T STAY HERE.
ALL OF THIS IS HAPPENING BECAUSE OF SOMETHING I'VE DONE, BUT I CAN STOP IT IF I CAN JUST GET MOVING.
AND YOU CAN HELP ME WITH A FEW REAL SOLDIERS.
IT'S NOT THE PICTURE THAT'S UPSIDE-DOWN, IT'S THE WORLD.
EVEN THEN, WE HAVE MADE IT WORK.
ALONE IN ALL THIS DARK, WE LEARN TO MAKE IT ALL WORK.
I WILL NOT LET YOU DIE AS HE DID.
I CANNOT FAIL MY PEOPLE.
YOU CANNOT TAKE MY ARMY.
ALL I NEED'S A COUPLE OF 'EM!
IF YOU WON'T HELP, I HAVE TO DO THIS ON MY OWN WITH JUST TWO OTHER KIDS!
IT'S NOT EVEN MY WAR.

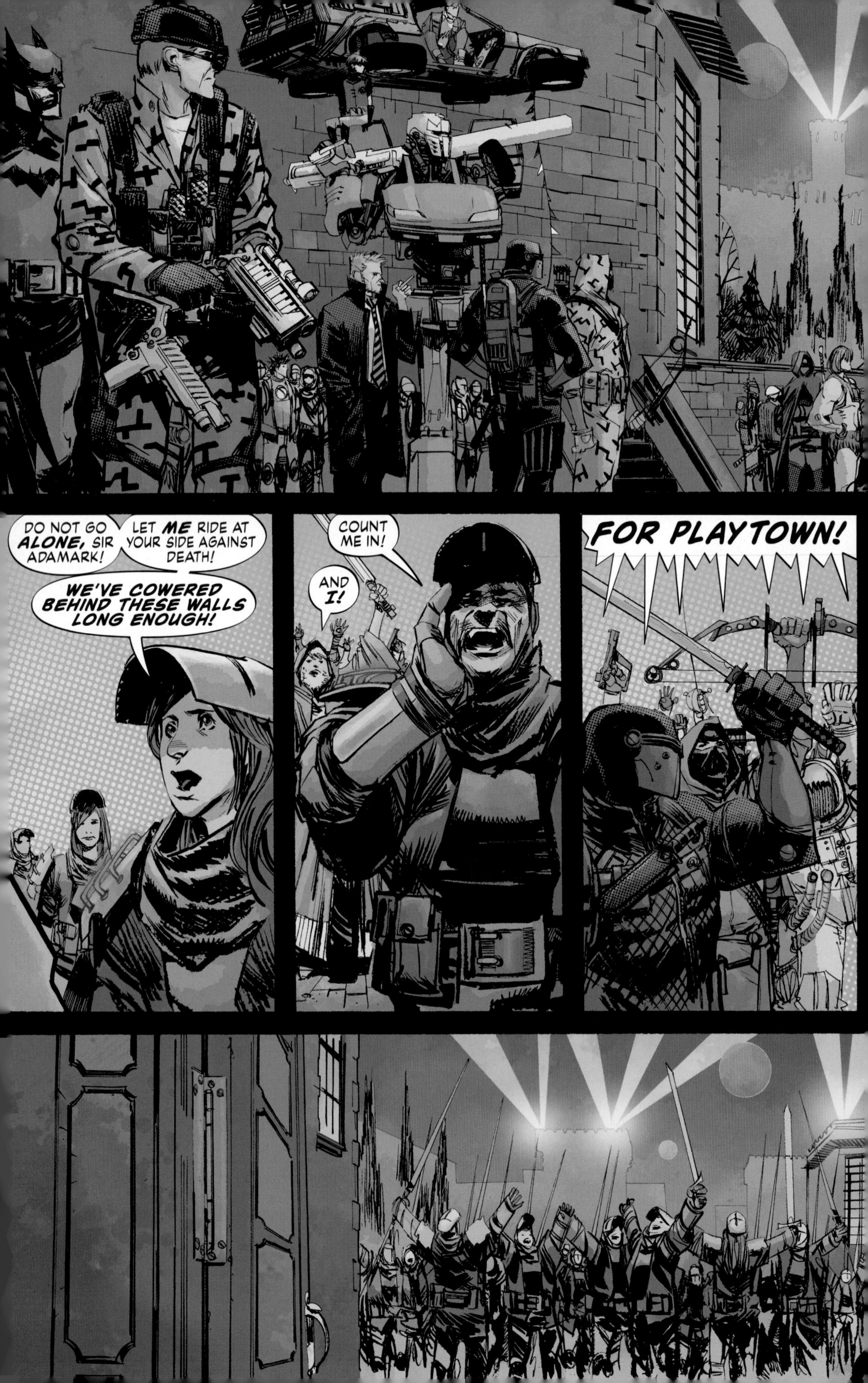

DO NOT GO ALONE, SIR ADAMARK!
LET ME RIDE AT YOUR SIDE AGAINST DEATH!
WE'VE COWERED BEHIND THESE WALLS LONG ENOUGH!
COUNT ME IN!
AND I!
FOR PLAYTOWN!

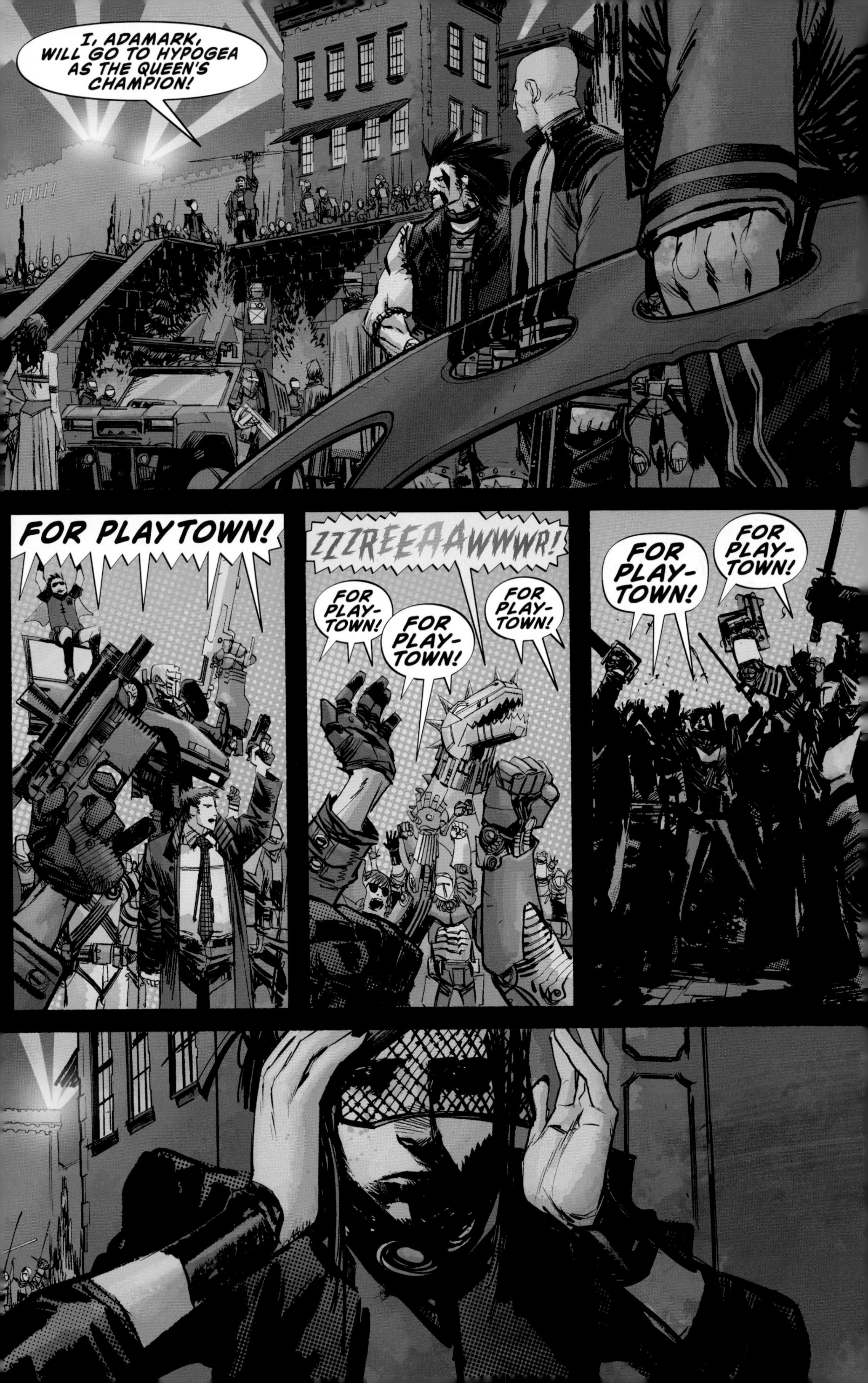
I, ADAMARK, WILL GO TO HYPOGEA AS THE QUEEN'S CHAMPION!
FOR PLAYTOWN!
ZZZREEEAAWWWR!
FOR PLAY-TOWN!
FOR PLAY-TOWN!
FOR PLAY-TOWN!
FOR PLAY-TOWN!
FOR PLAY-TOWN!

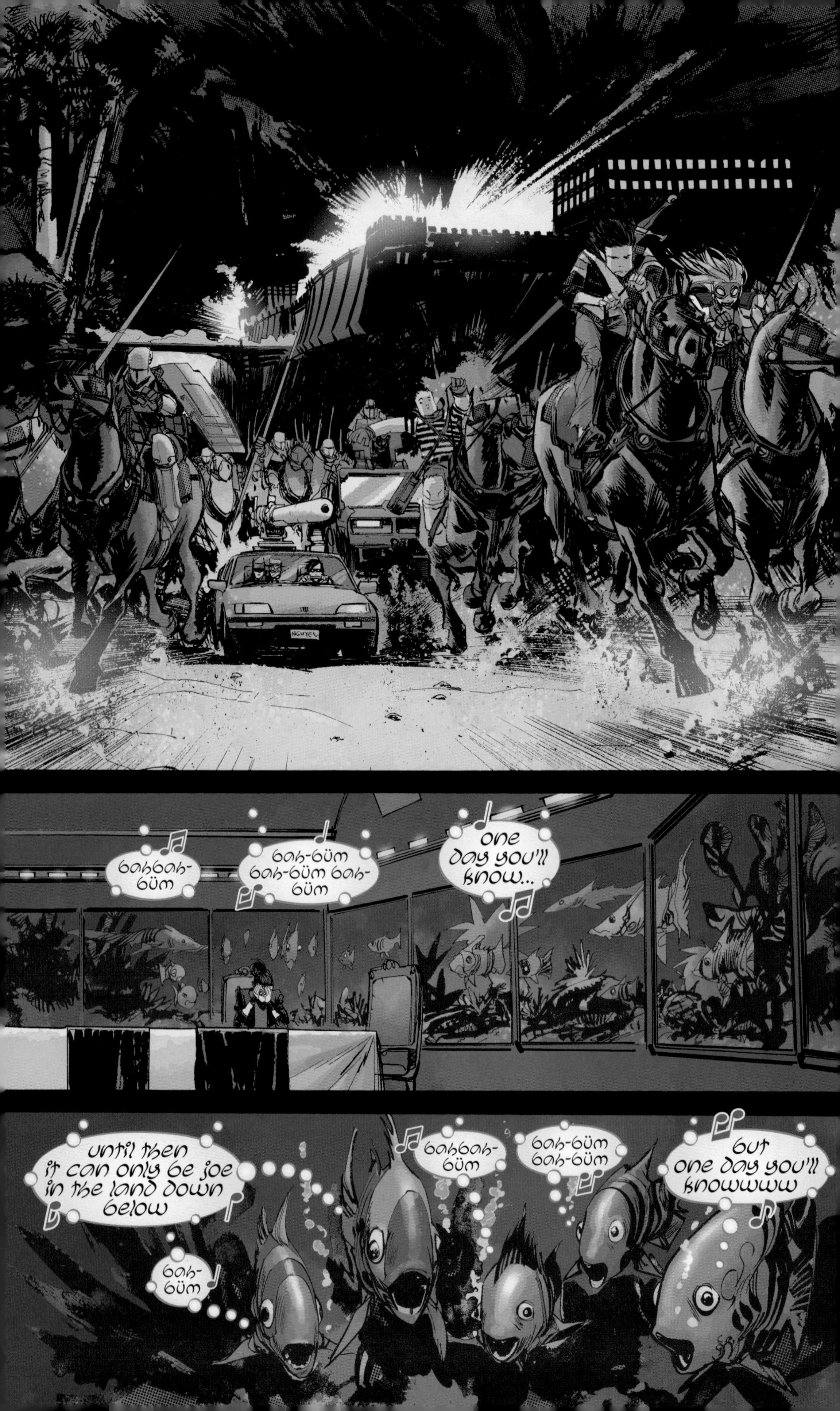
NGUYEN
bahbah-büm
bah-büm bah-büm bah-büm
one day you'll know...
until then it can only be joe in the land down below
bahbah-büm
bah-büm bah-büm
but one day you'll knowwww
bah-büm

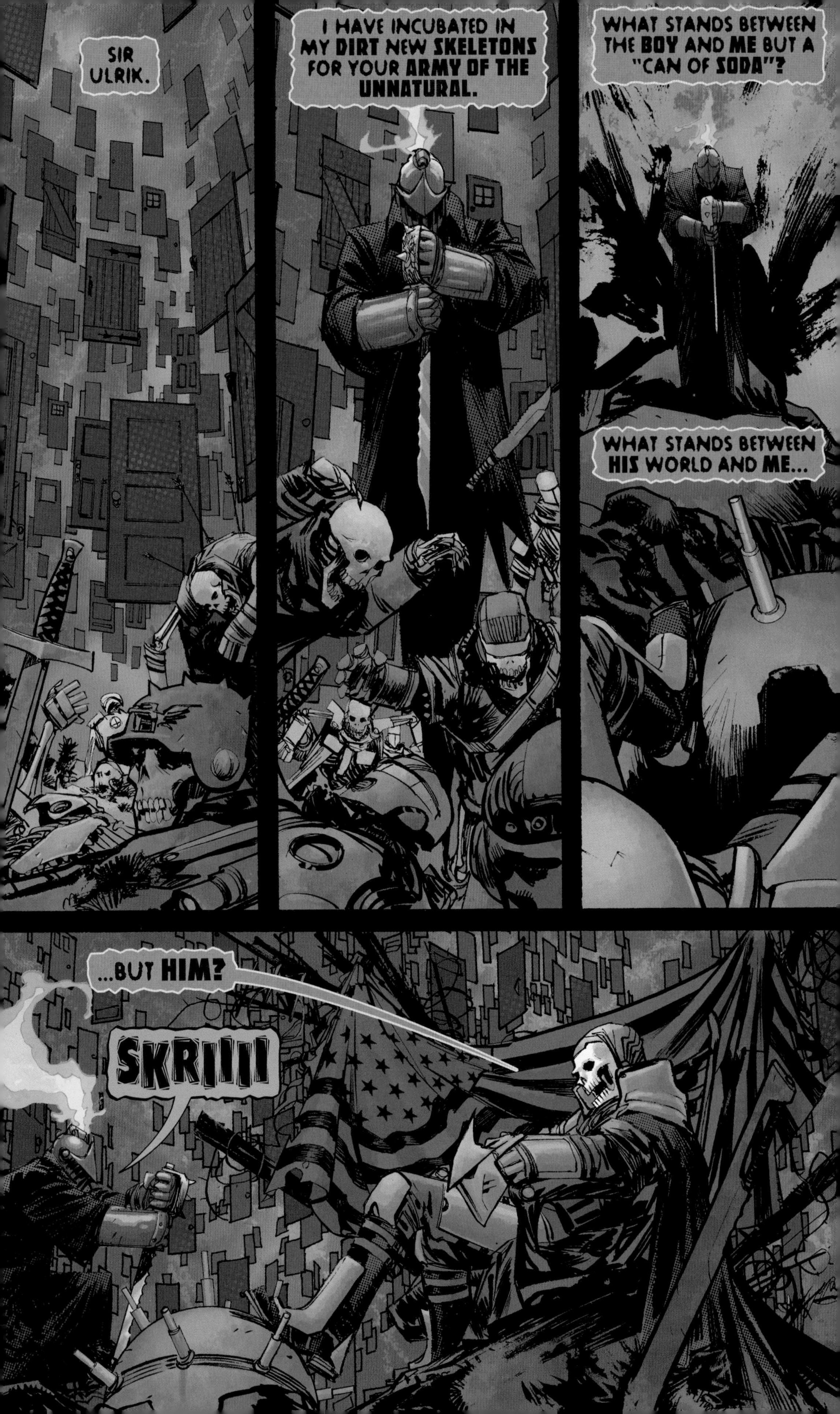
SIR ULRIK.
I HAVE INCUBATED IN MY DIRT NEW SKELETONS FOR YOUR ARMY OF THE UNNATURAL.
WHAT STANDS BETWEEN THE BOY AND ME BUT A "CAN OF SODA"?
WHAT STANDS BETWEEN HIS WORLD AND ME...
...BUT HIM?
SKRIIII

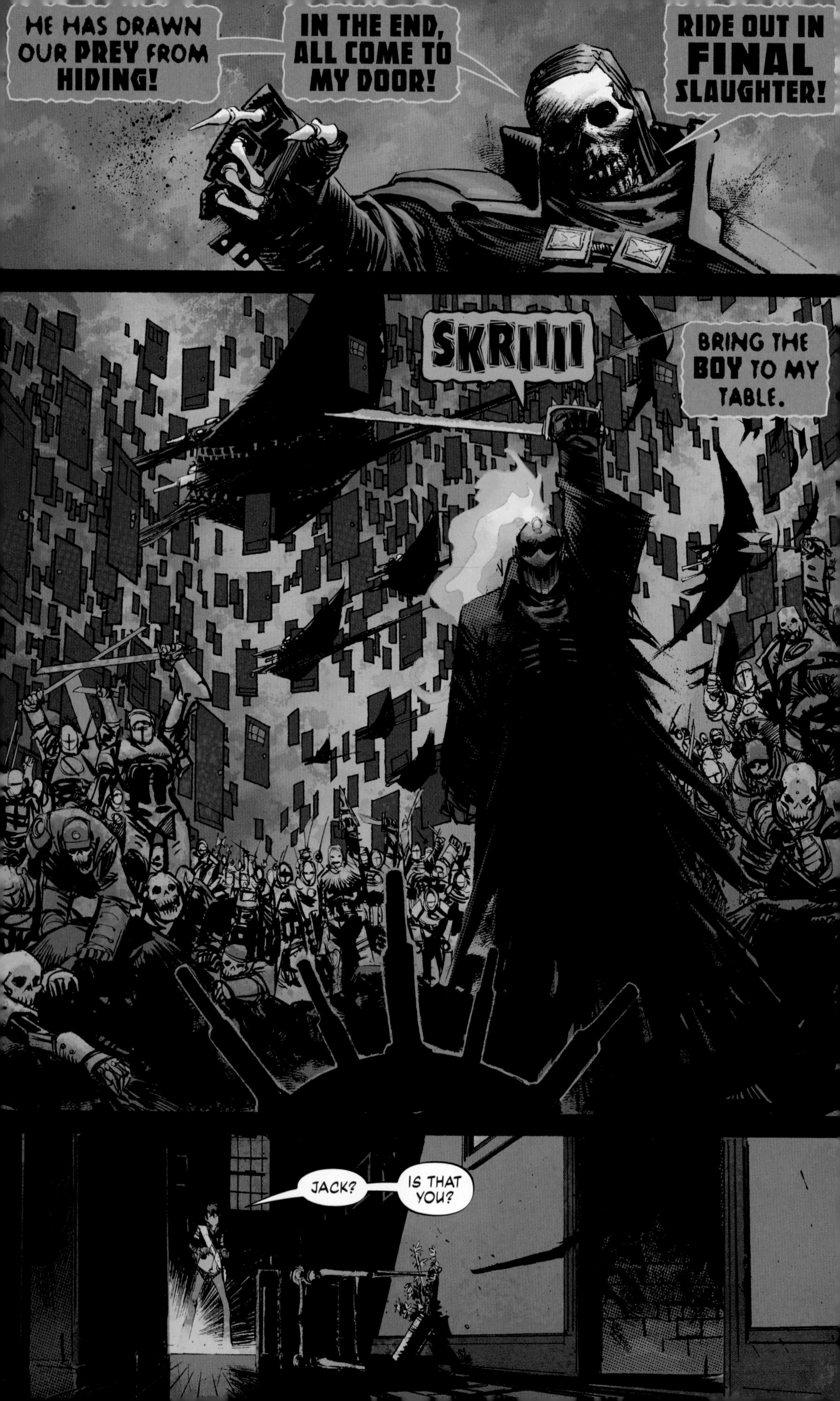
HE HAS DRAWN OUR PREY FROM HIDING!
IN THE END, ALL COME TO MY DOOR!
RIDE OUT IN FINAL SLAUGHTER!
SKRIIII
BRING THE BOY TO MY TABLE.
JACK?
IS THAT YOU?

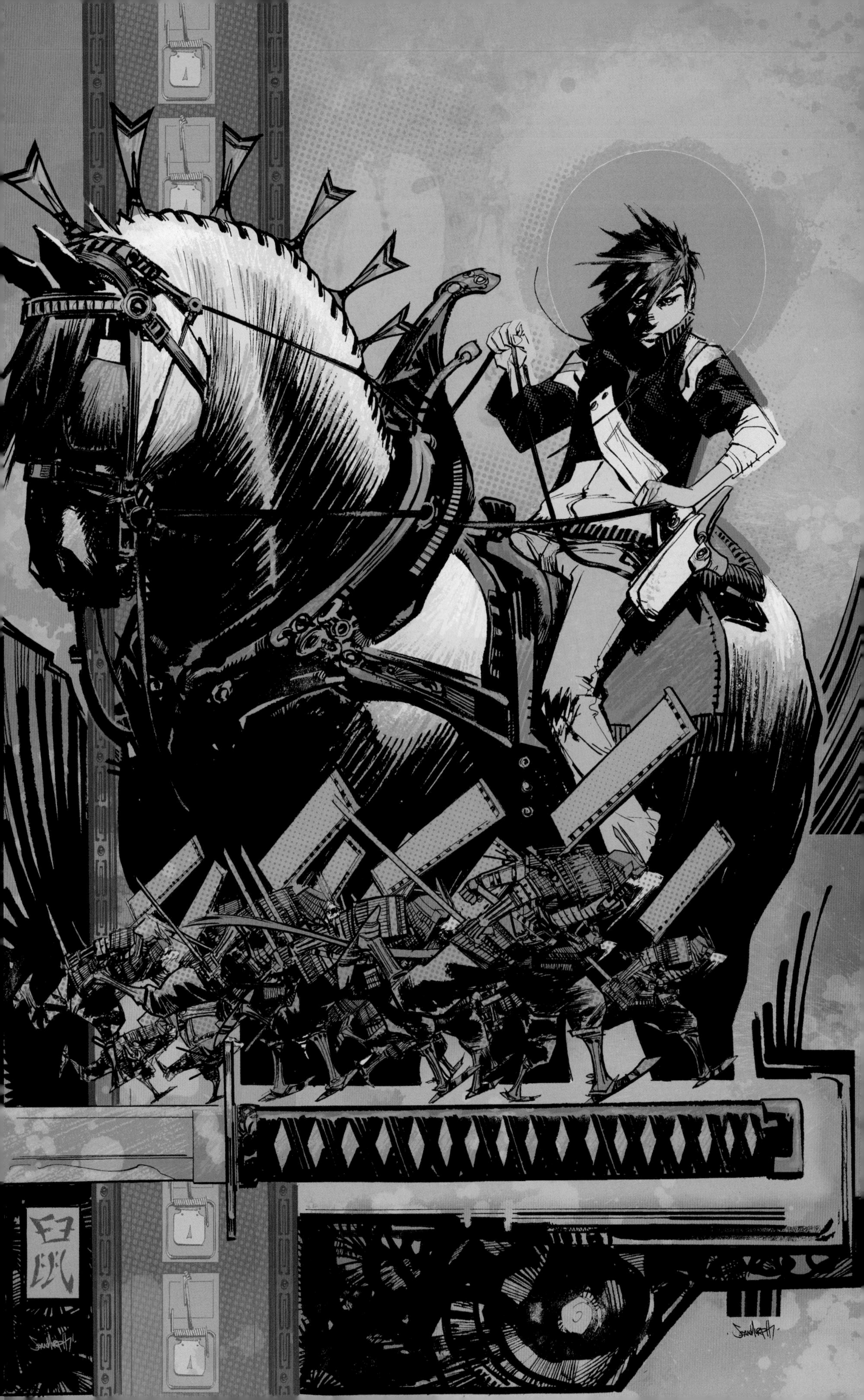

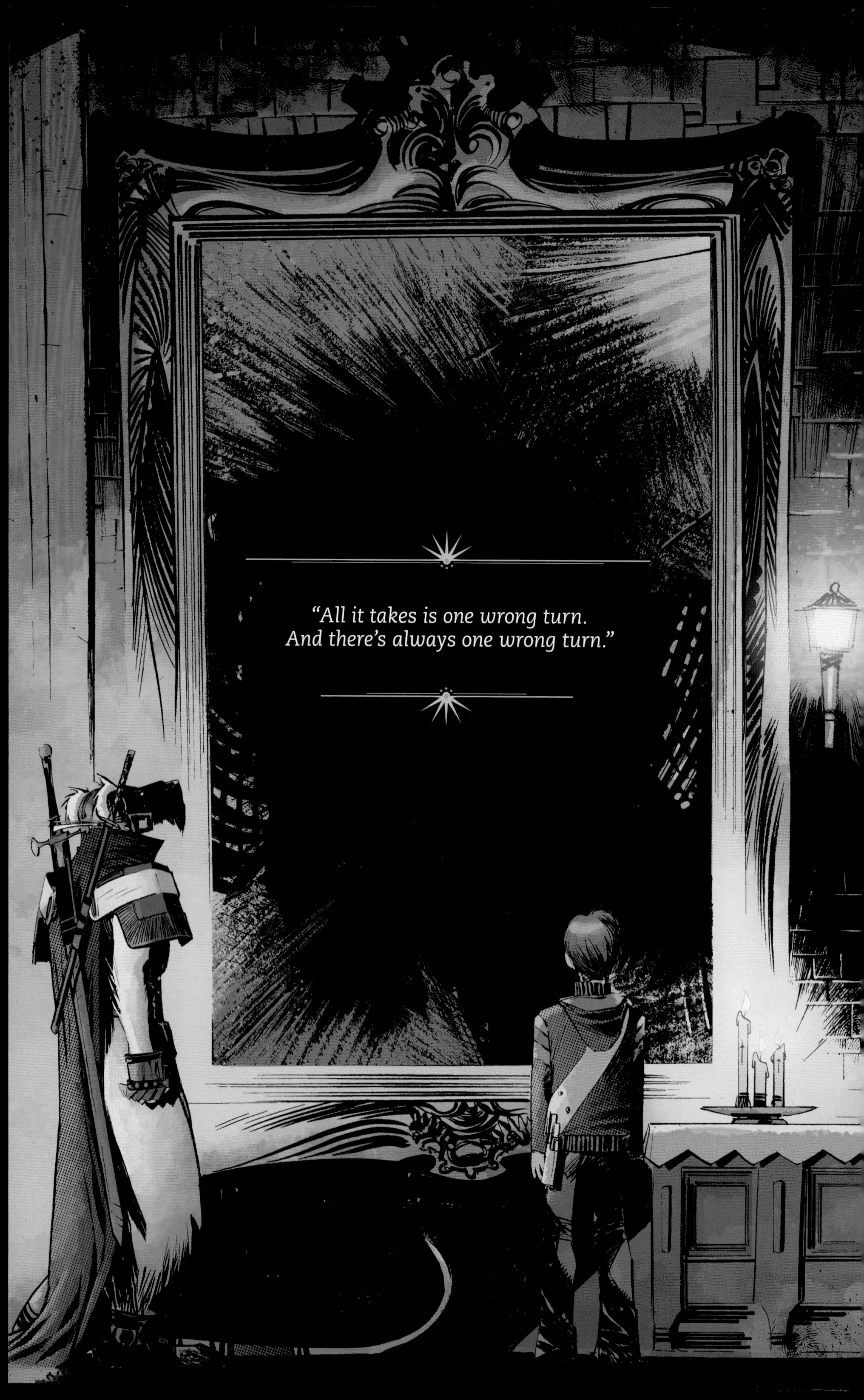
"All it takes is one wrong turn.
And there's always one wrong turn."

# chapter 7: labyrinth of the lost

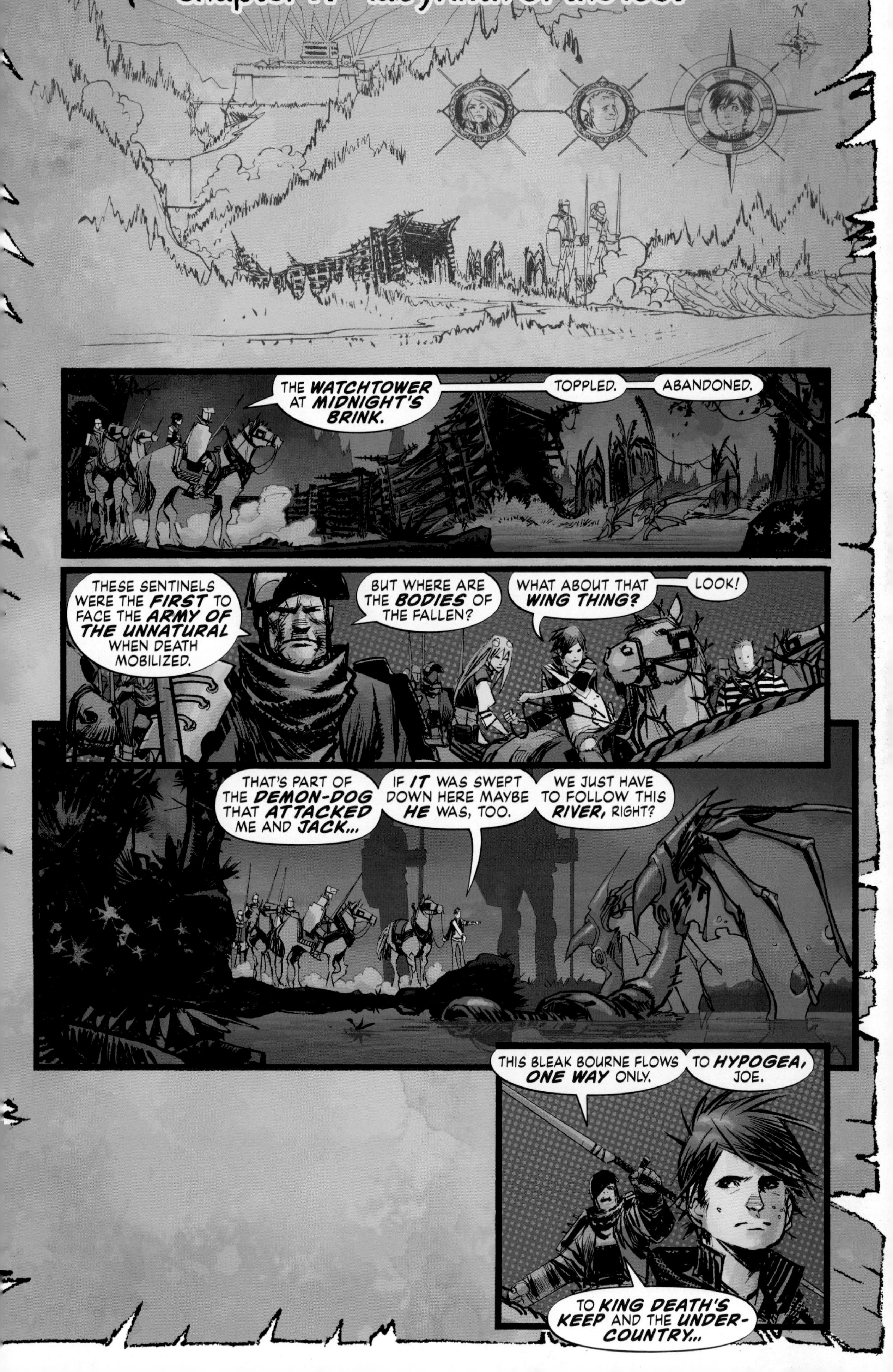

N
THE WATCHTOWER AT MIDNIGHT'S BRINK.
TOPPLED.
ABANDONED.
THESE SENTINELS WERE THE FIRST TO FACE THE ARMY OF THE UNNATURAL WHEN DEATH MOBILIZED.
BUT WHERE ARE THE BODIES OF THE FALLEN?
WHAT ABOUT THAT WING THING?
LOOK!
THAT'S PART OF THE DEMON-DOG THAT ATTACKED ME AND JACK...
IF IT WAS SWEPT DOWN HERE MAYBE HE WAS, TOO.
WE JUST HAVE TO FOLLOW THIS RIVER, RIGHT?
THIS BLEAK BOURNE FLOWS ONE WAY ONLY.
TO HYPOGEA, JOE.
TO KING DEATH'S KEEP AND THE UNDER-COUNTRY...

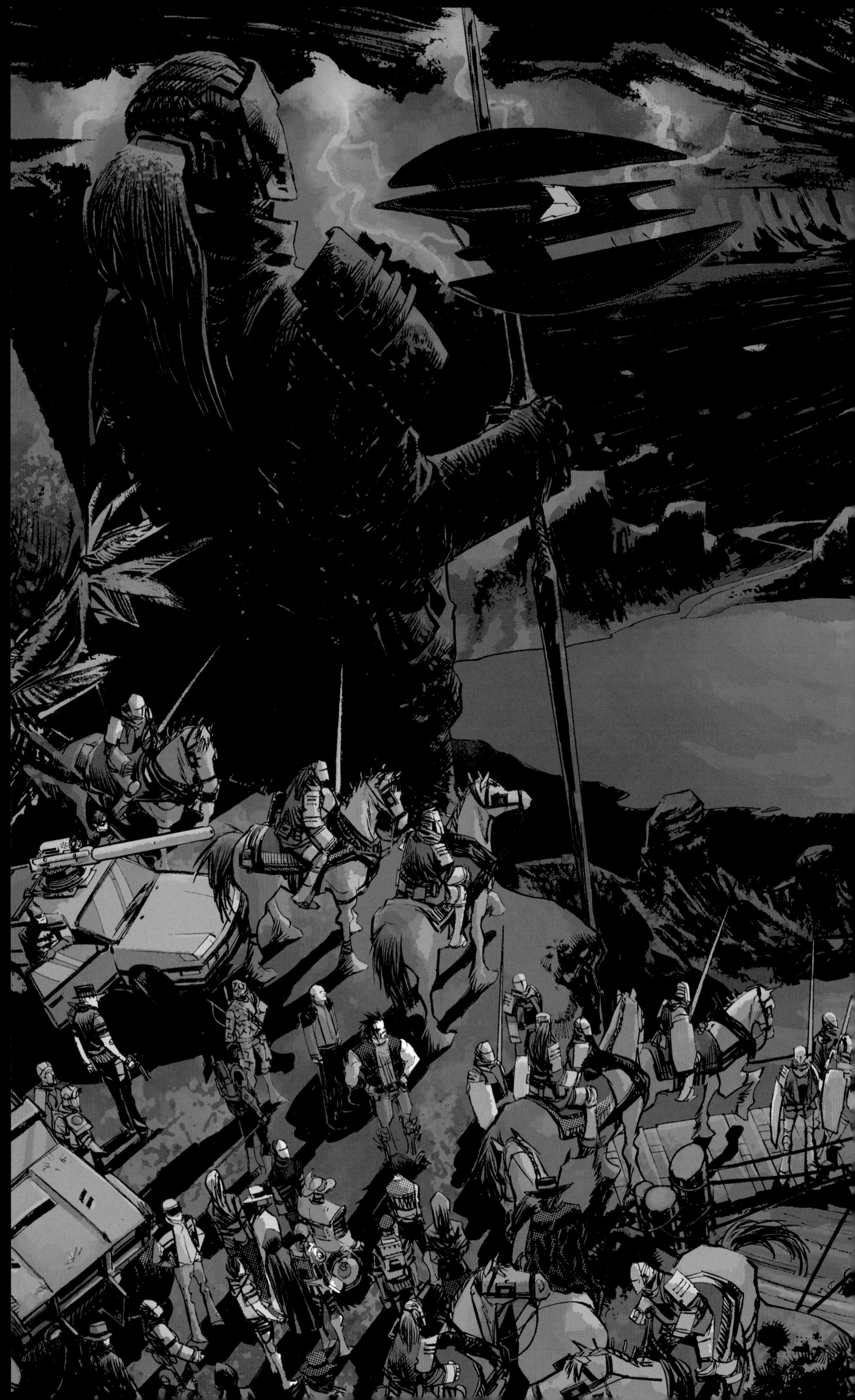

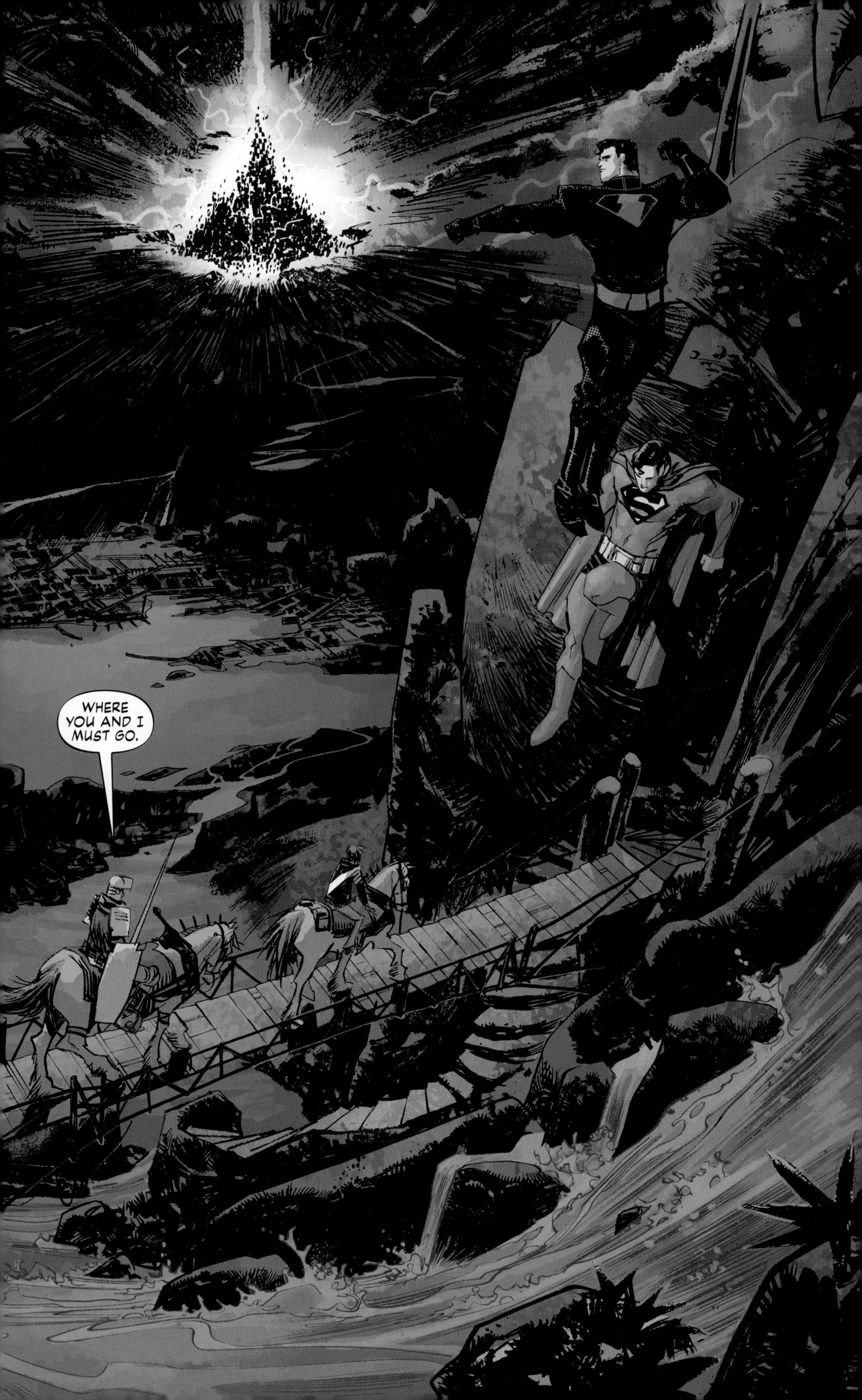
WHERE YOU AND I MUST GO.

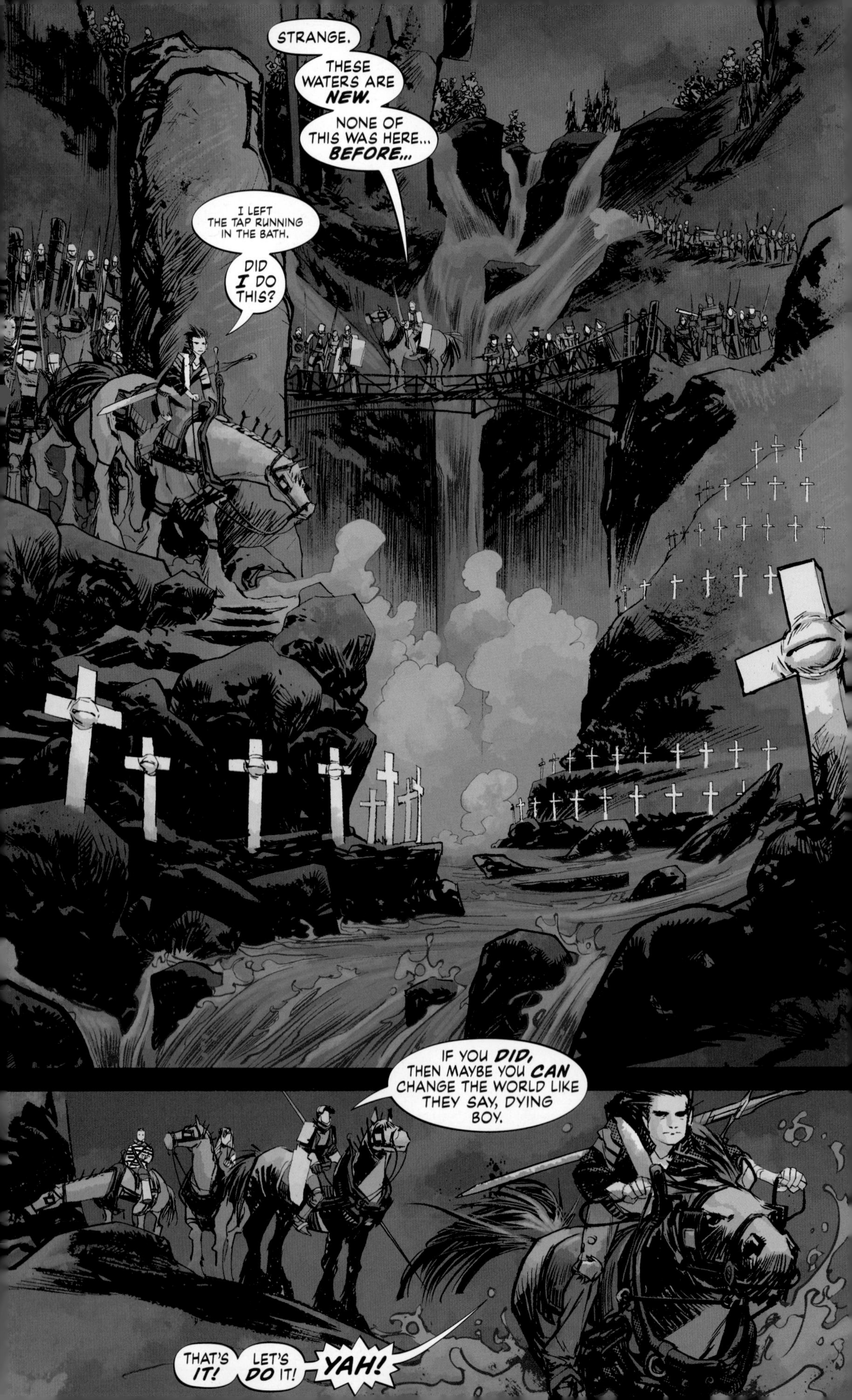
STRANGE.
THESE WATERS ARE NEW.
NONE OF THIS WAS HERE... BEFORE...
I LEFT THE TAP RUNNING IN THE BATH.
DID I DO THIS?
IF YOU DID, THEN MAYBE YOU CAN CHANGE THE WORLD LIKE THEY SAY, DYING BOY.
THAT'S IT!
LET'S DO IT!
YAH!

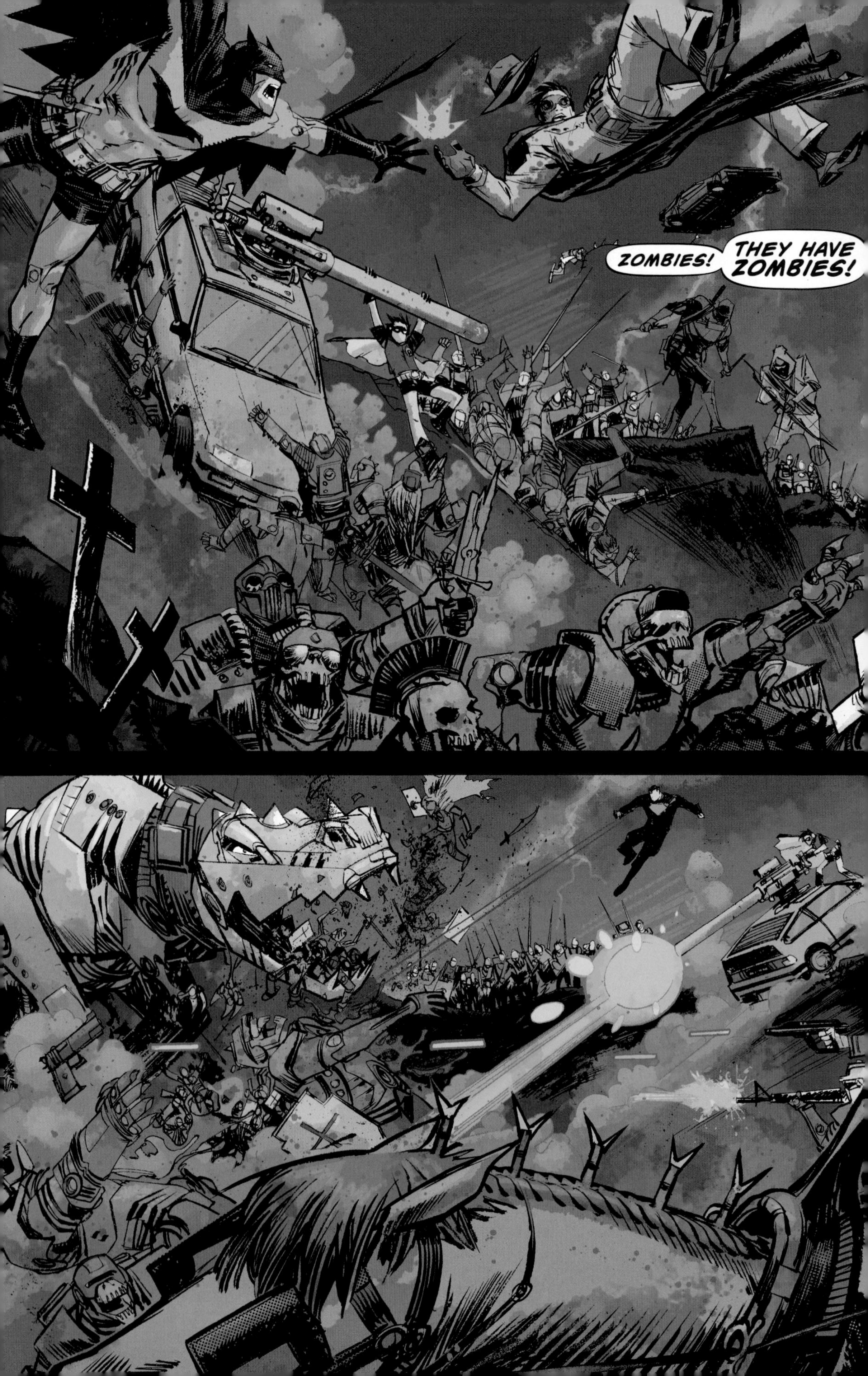
ZOMBIES!
THEY HAVE ZOMBIES!

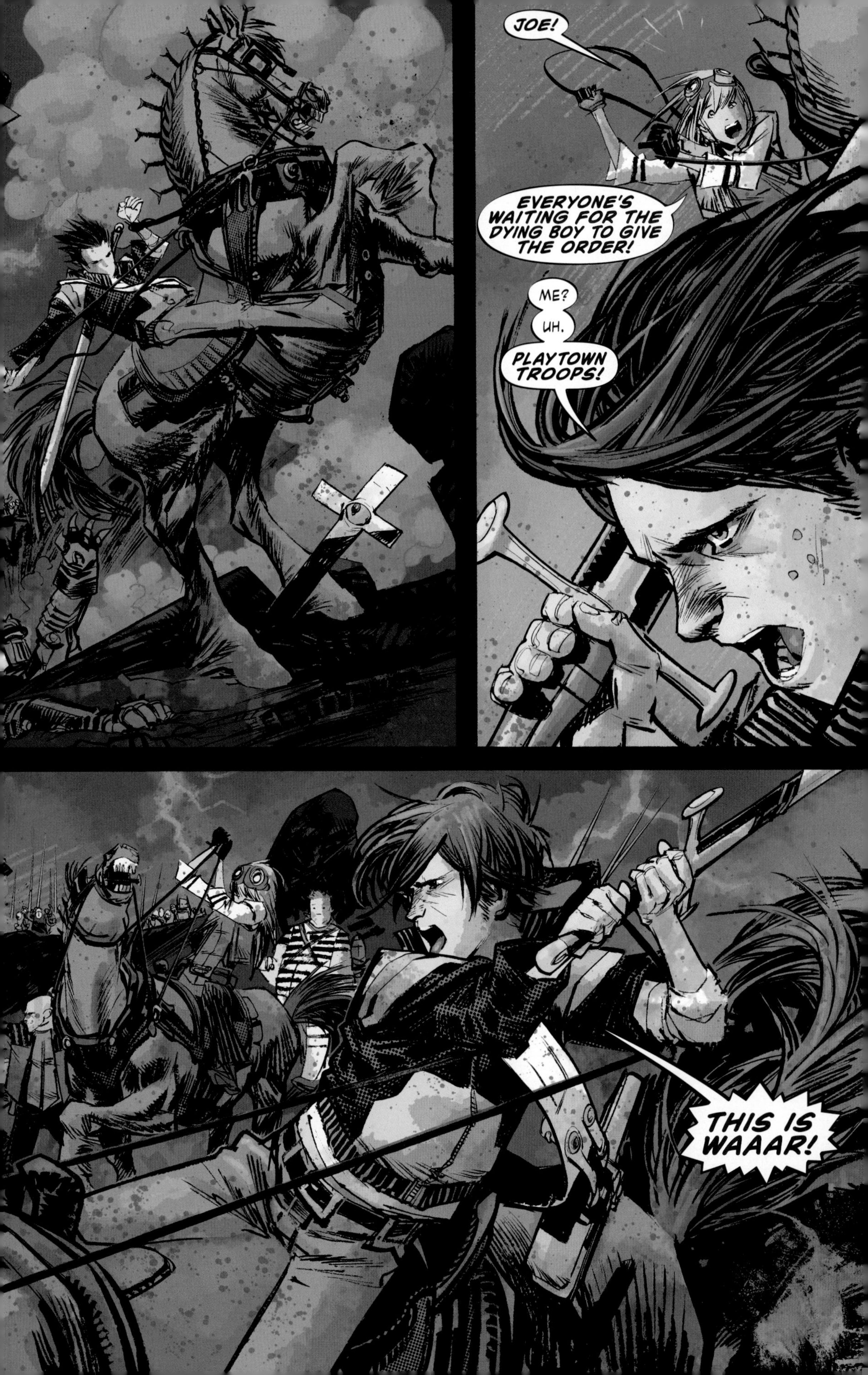
JOE!
EVERYONE'S WAITING FOR THE DYING BOY TO GIVE THE ORDER!
ME?
UH.
PLAYTOWN TROOPS!
THIS IS WAAAR!

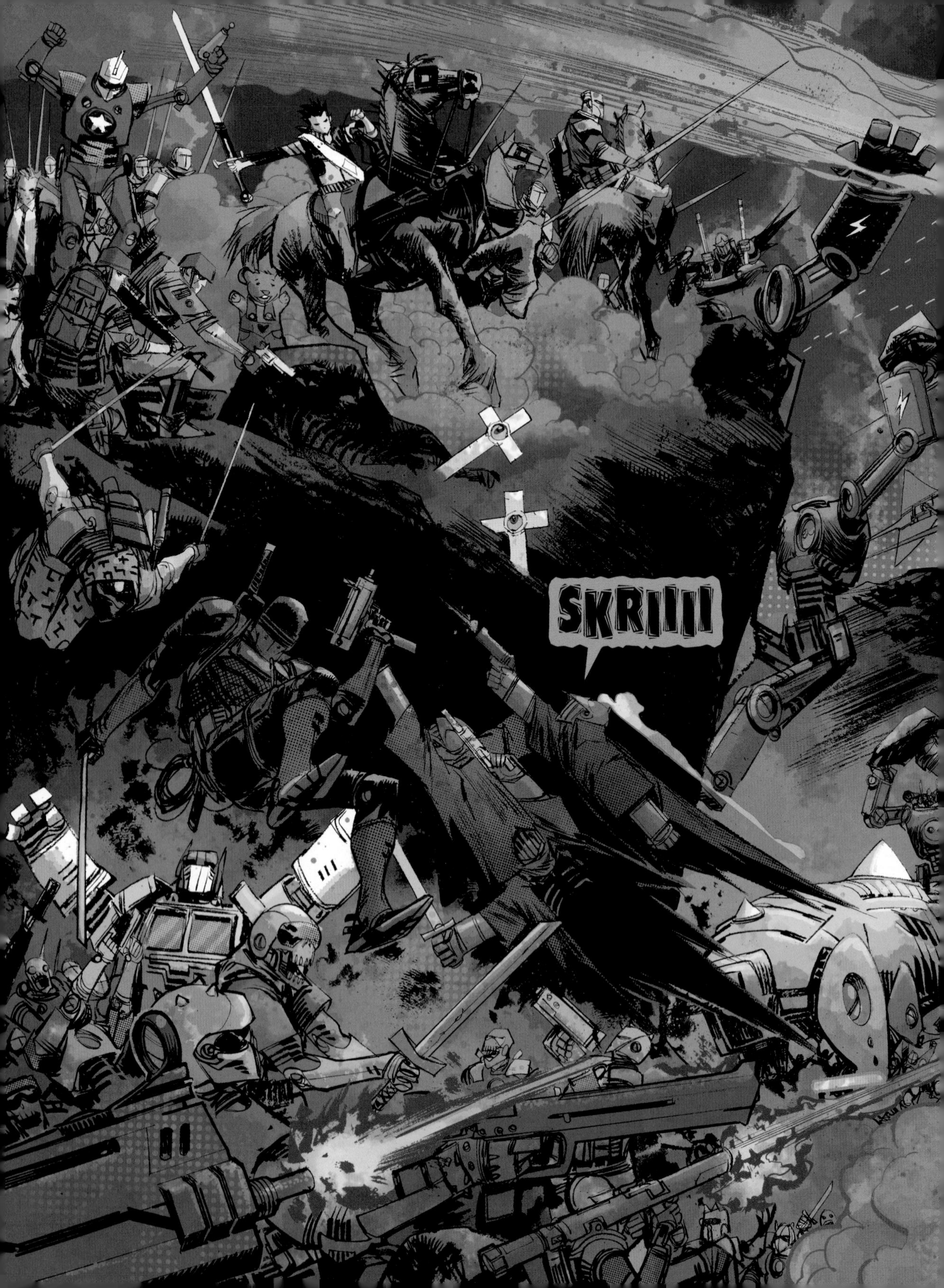
SKRIIII

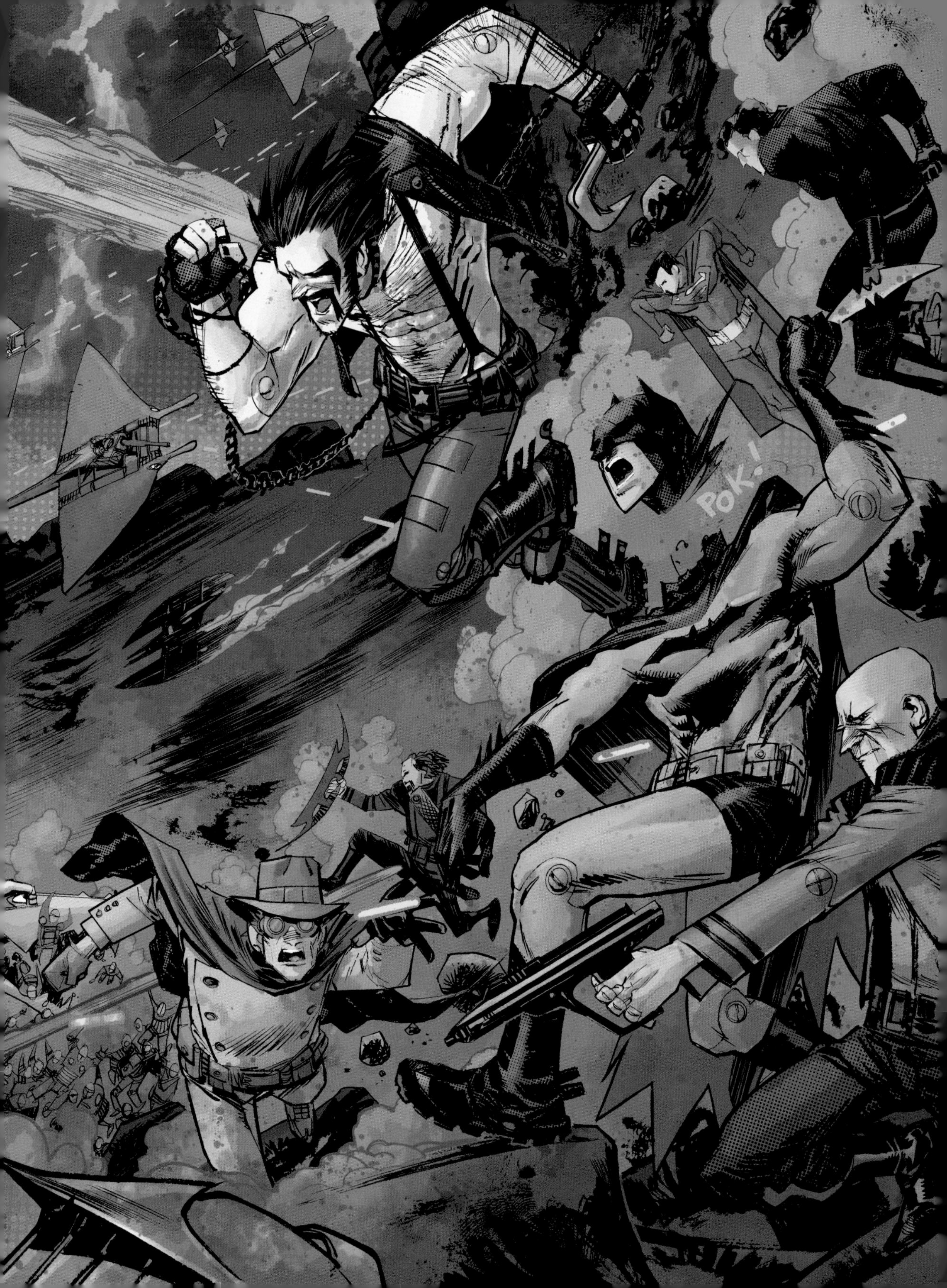
POK!

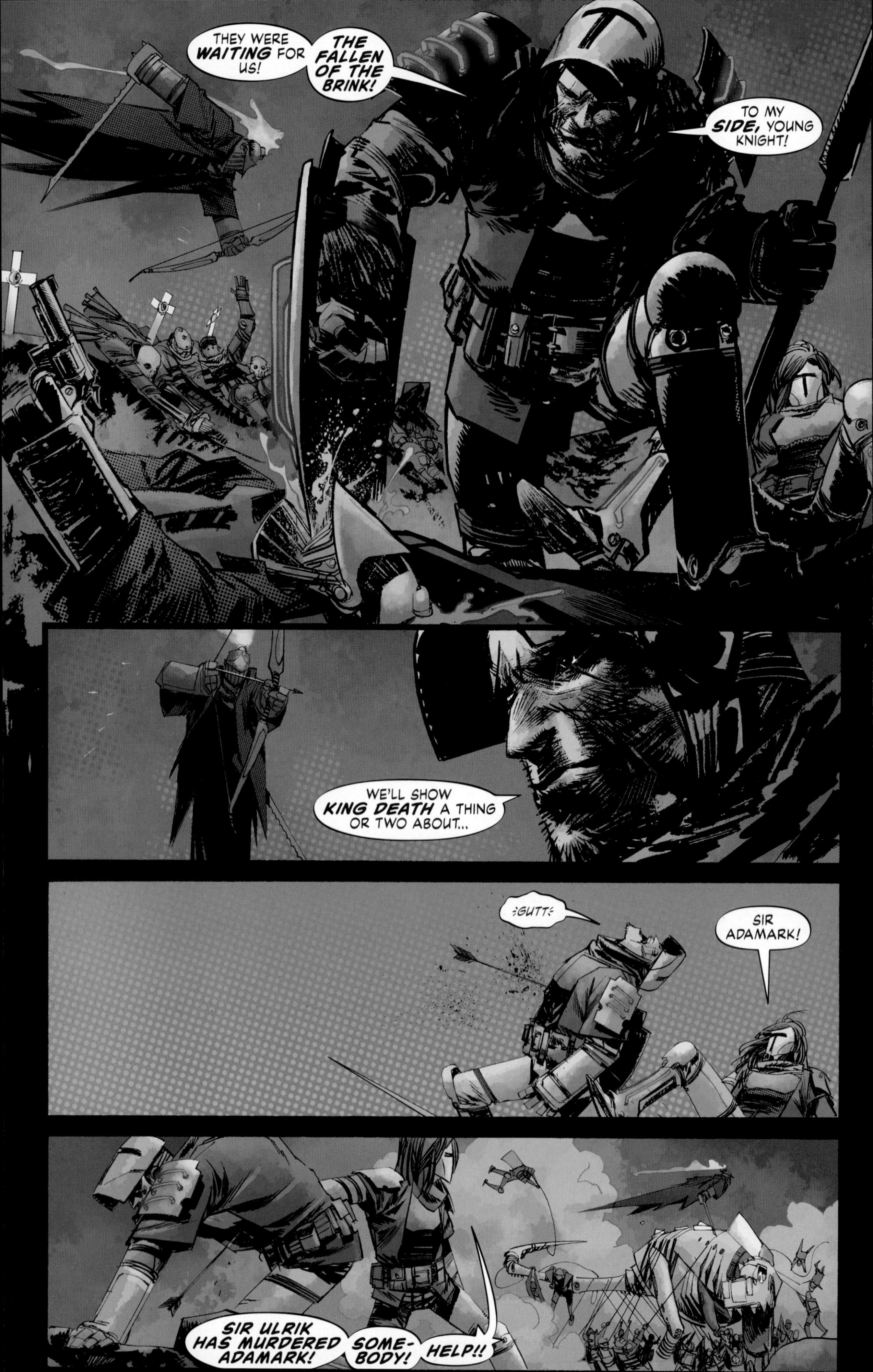
THEY WERE WAITING FOR US!
THE FALLEN OF THE BRINK!
TO MY SIDE, YOUNG KNIGHT!
WE'LL SHOW KING DEATH A THING OR TWO ABOUT...
GUTT
SIR ADAMARK!
SIR ULRIK HAS MURDERED ADAMARK!
SOME-BODY!
HELP!!

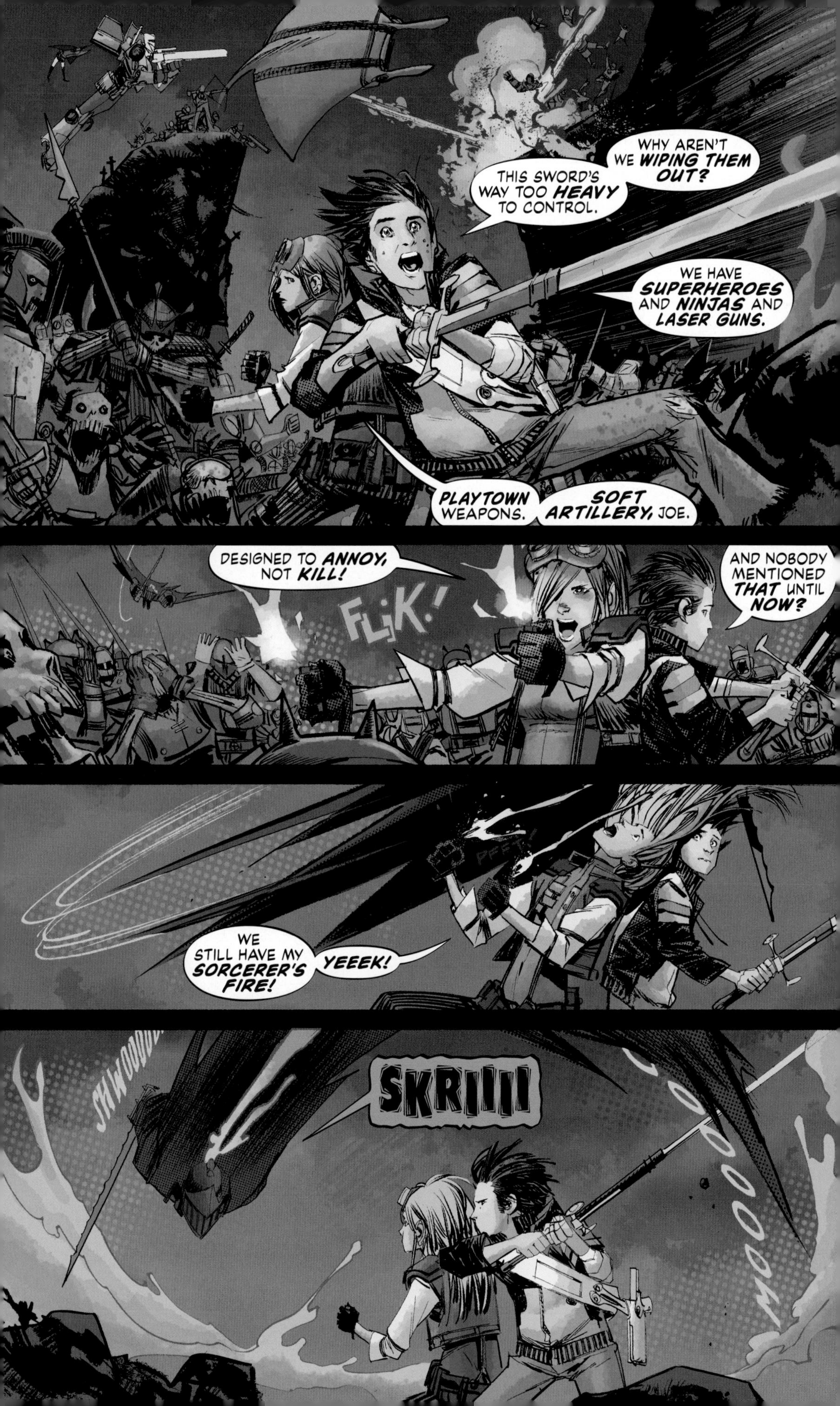

THIS SWORD'S WAY TOO **HEAVY** TO CONTROL.
WHY AREN'T WE **WIPING THEM OUT?**
WE HAVE **SUPERHEROES** AND **NINJAS** AND **LASER GUNS.**
**PLAYTOWN** WEAPONS.
**SOFT ARTILLERY,** JOE.
DESIGNED TO **ANNOY,** NOT **KILL!**
FLIK!
AND NOBODY MENTIONED **THAT** UNTIL **NOW?**
WE STILL HAVE MY **SORCERER'S FIRE!**
**YEEEK!**
SKRIIII

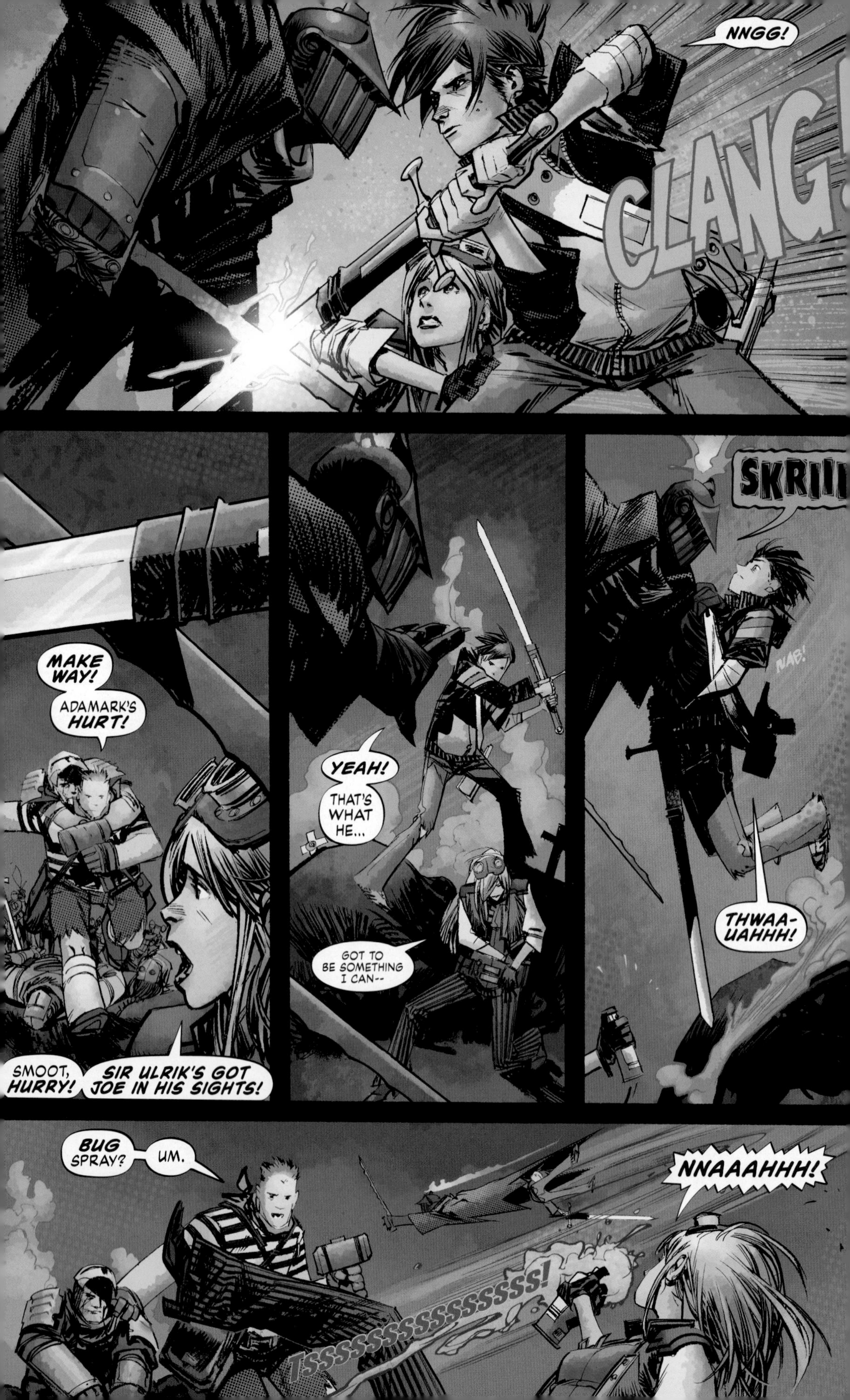
NNGG!
CLANG
MAKE WAY!
ADAMARK'S HURT!
SMOOT, HURRY!
SIR ULRIK'S GOT JOE IN HIS SIGHTS!
YEAH!
THAT'S WHAT HE...
GOT TO BE SOMETHING I CAN--
SKRIII
THWAA-UAHHH!
BUG SPRAY?
UM.
NNAAAHHH!
TSSSSSSSSSSSSSSSSS!

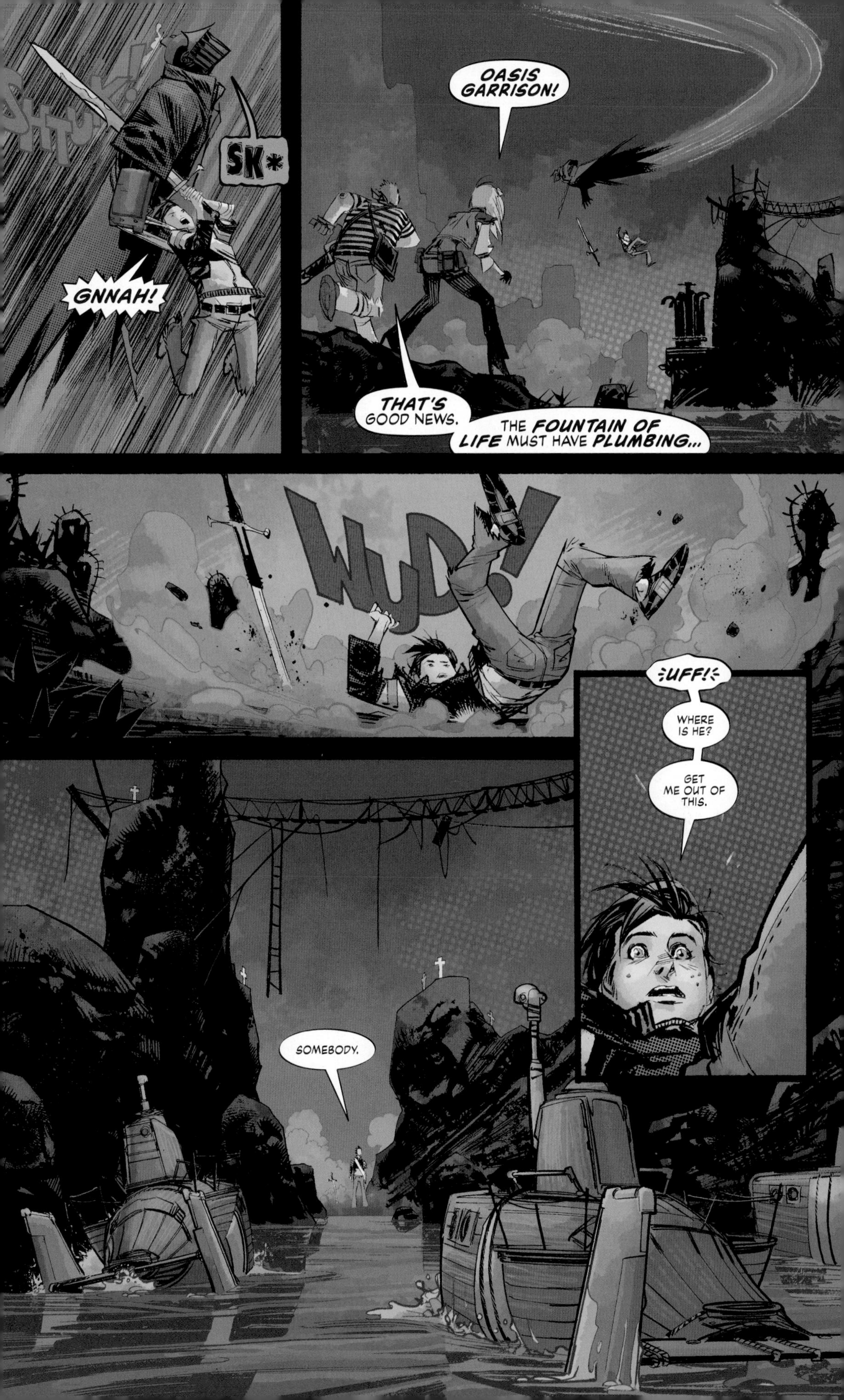
SHTUK!
SK*
GNNAH!
OASIS GARRISON!
THAT'S GOOD NEWS.
THE FOUNTAIN OF LIFE MUST HAVE PLUMBING...
WUD!
UFF!
WHERE IS HE?
GET ME OUT OF THIS.
SOMEBODY.

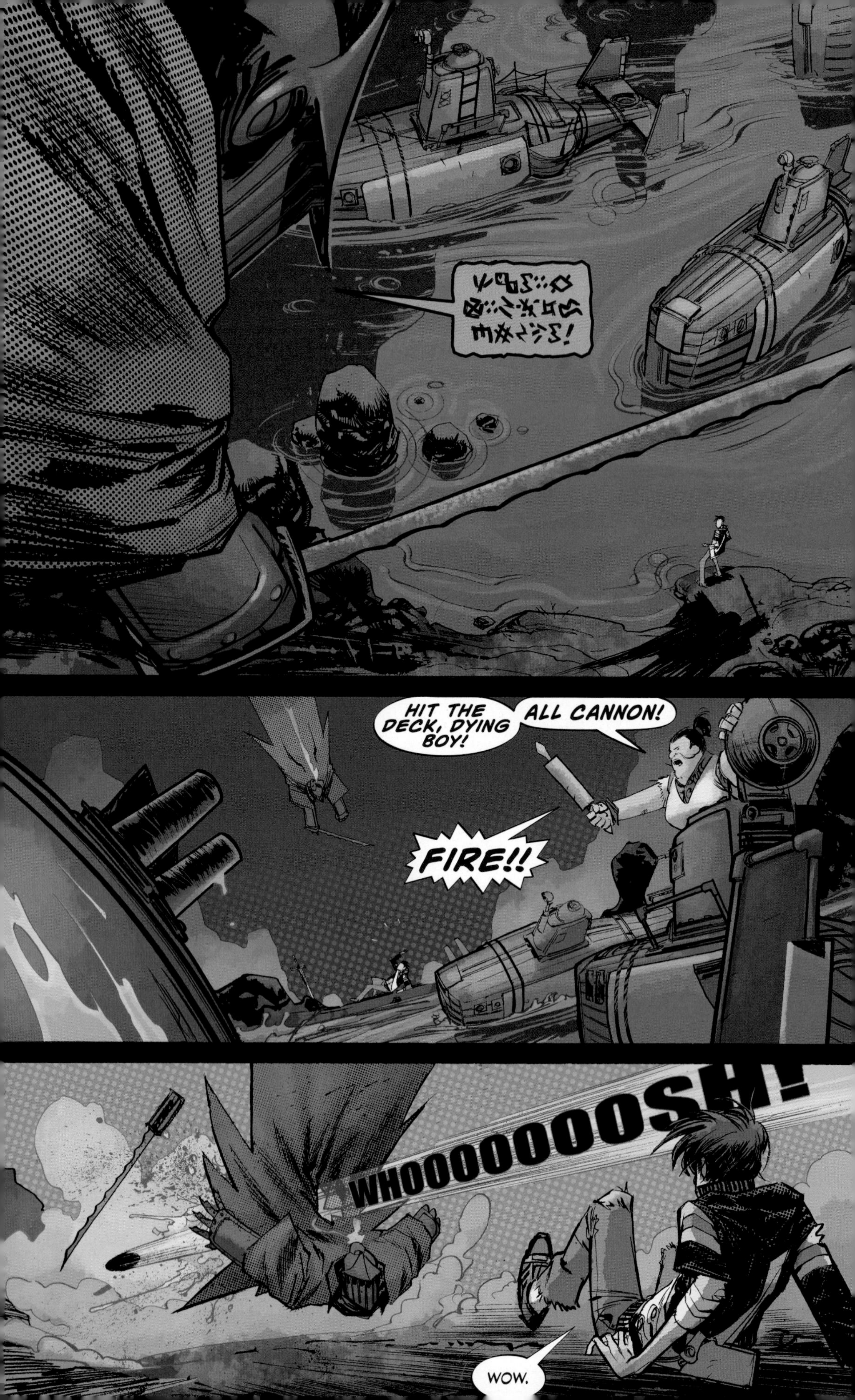
HIT THE DECK, DYING BOY!
ALL CANNON!
FIRE!!
WHOOOOOOOSH!
WOW.

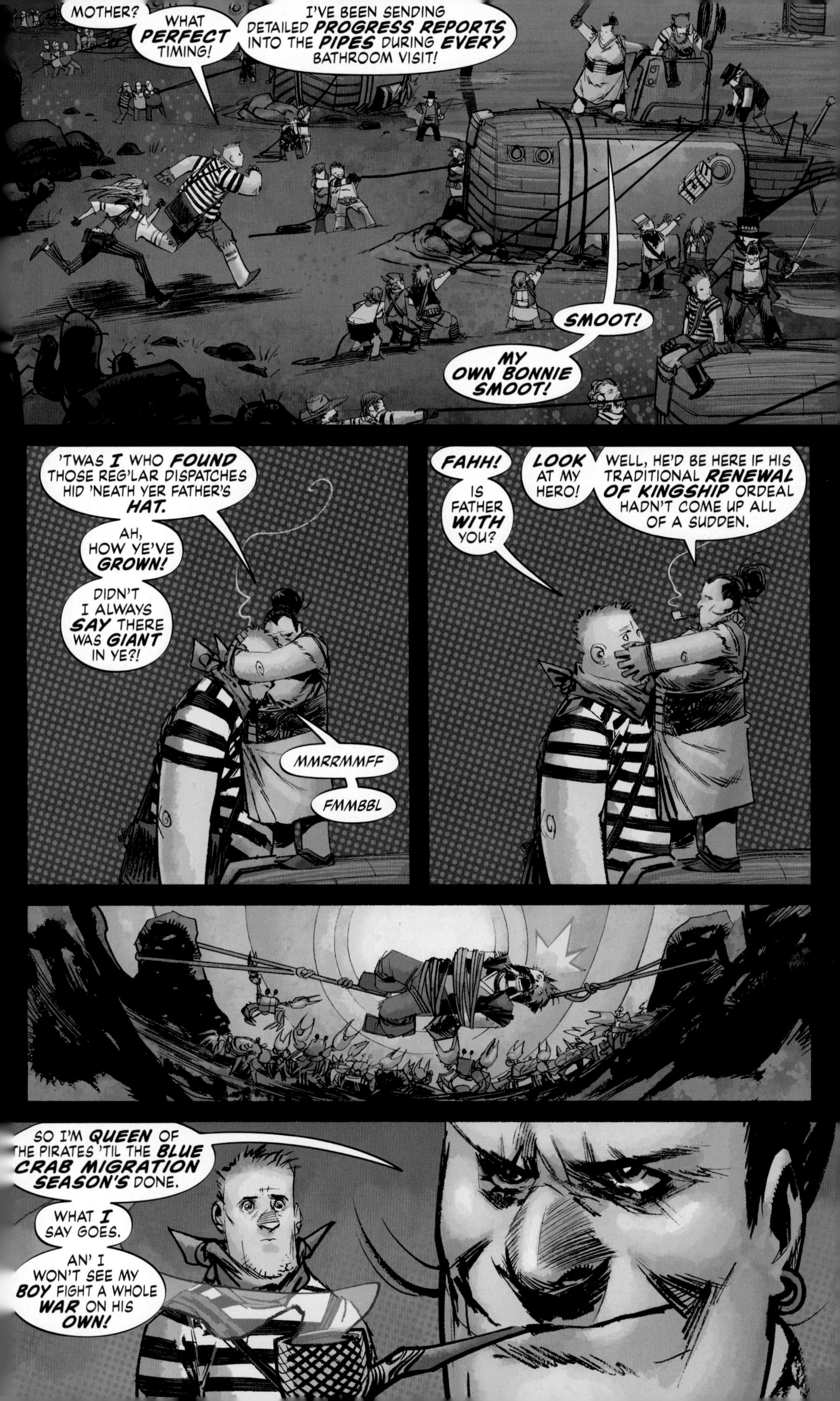
MOTHER?
WHAT PERFECT TIMING!
I'VE BEEN SENDING DETAILED PROGRESS REPORTS INTO THE PIPES DURING EVERY BATHROOM VISIT!
SMOOT!
MY OWN BONNIE SMOOT!
'TWAS I WHO FOUND THOSE REG'LAR DISPATCHES HID 'NEATH YER FATHER'S HAT.
AH, HOW YE'VE GROWN!
DIDN'T I ALWAYS SAY THERE WAS GIANT IN YE?!
MMRRMMFF
FMMBBL
FAHH!
IS FATHER WITH YOU?
LOOK AT MY HERO!
WELL, HE'D BE HERE IF HIS TRADITIONAL RENEWAL OF KINGSHIP ORDEAL HADN'T COME UP ALL OF A SUDDEN.
SO I'M QUEEN OF THE PIRATES 'TIL THE BLUE CRAB MIGRATION SEASON'S DONE.
WHAT I SAY GOES.
AN' I WON'T SEE MY BOY FIGHT A WHOLE WAR ON HIS OWN!

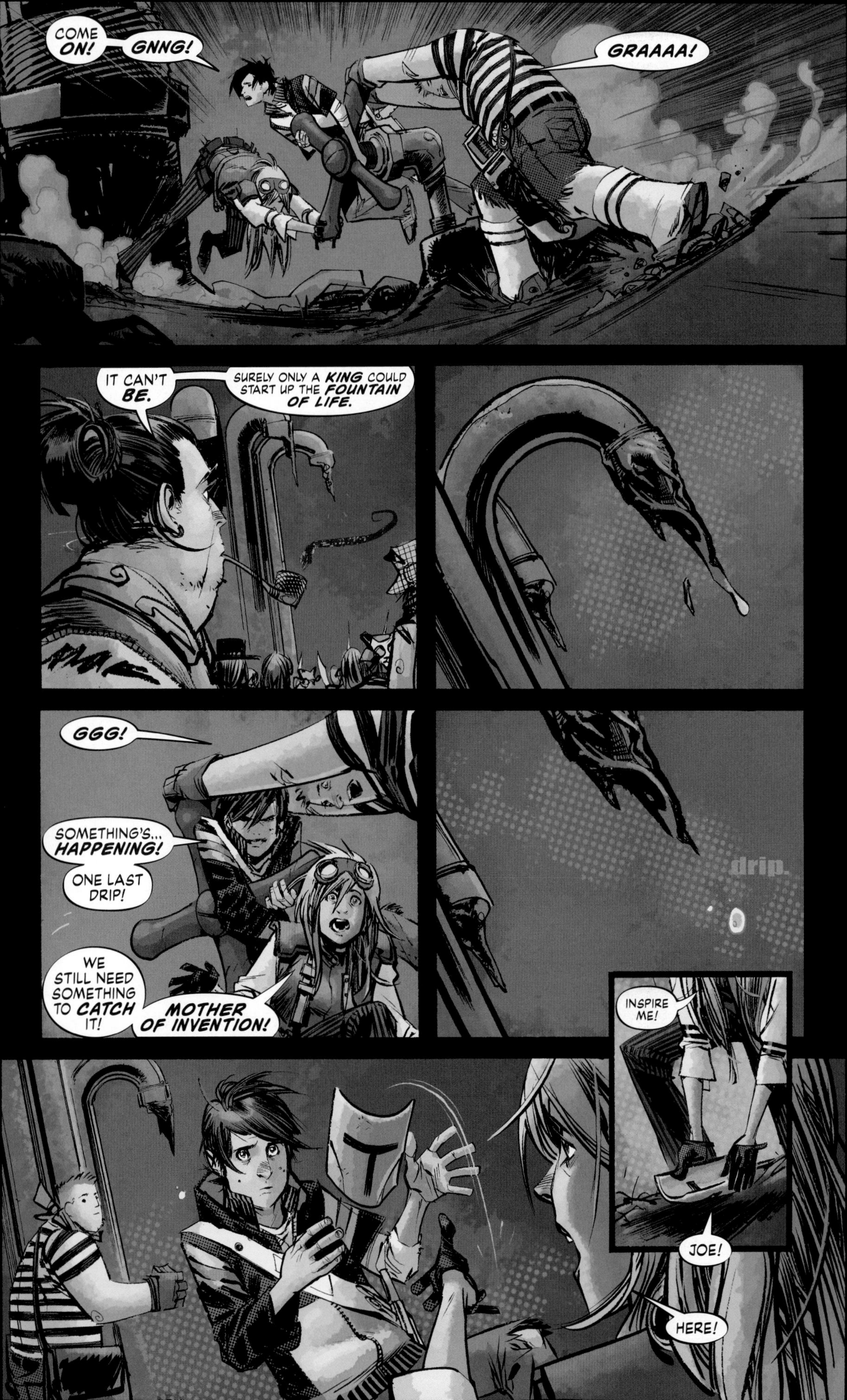
COME ON!
GNNG!
GRAAAA!
IT CAN'T BE.
SURELY ONLY A KING COULD START UP THE FOUNTAIN OF LIFE.
GGG!
SOMETHING'S... HAPPENING!
ONE LAST DRIP!
WE STILL NEED SOMETHING TO CATCH IT!
MOTHER OF INVENTION!
drip.
INSPIRE ME!
JOE!
HERE!

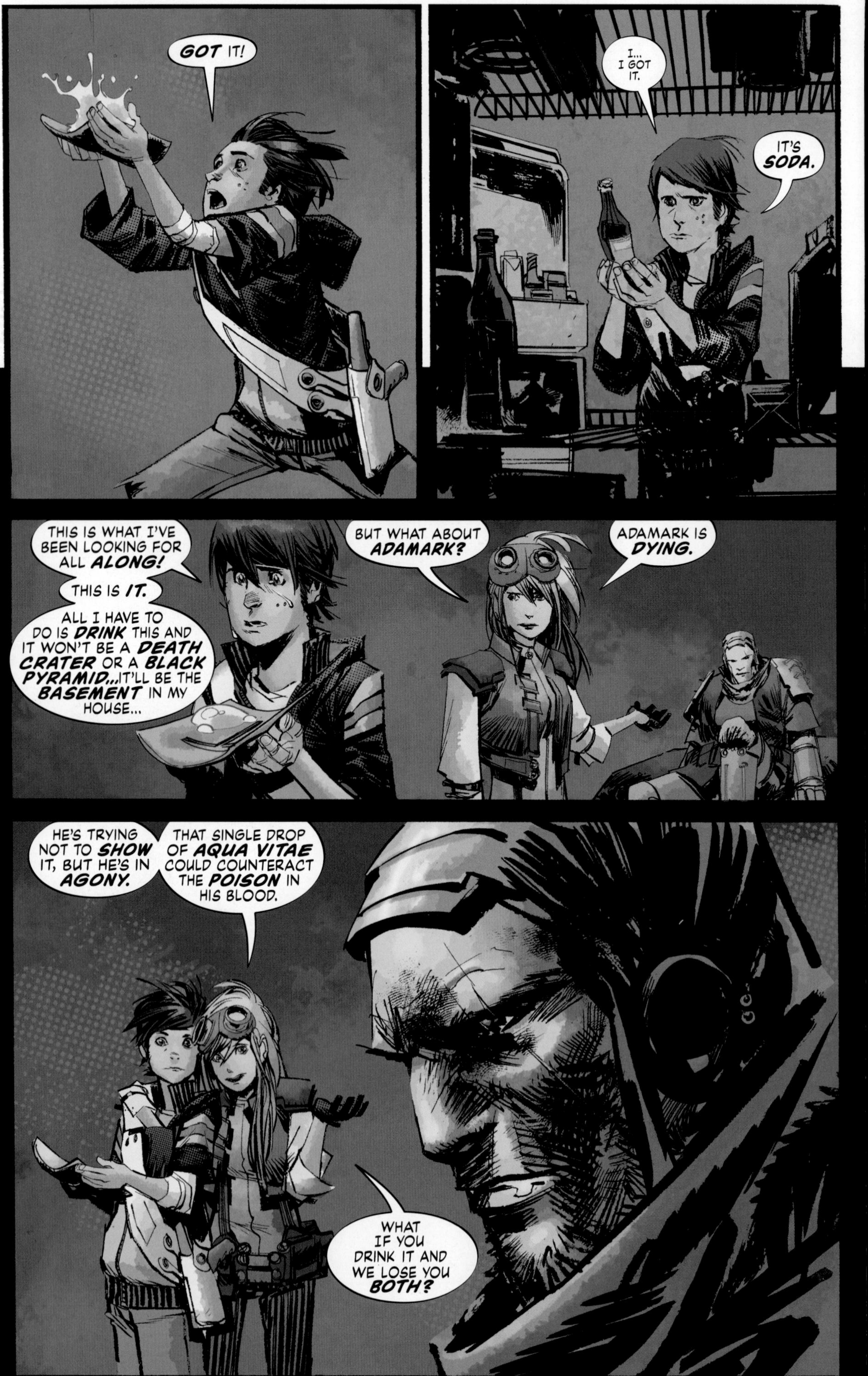
GOT IT!
I... I GOT IT.
IT'S SODA.
THIS IS WHAT I'VE BEEN LOOKING FOR ALL ALONG!
THIS IS IT.
ALL I HAVE TO DO IS DRINK THIS AND IT WON'T BE A DEATH CRATER OR A BLACK PYRAMID...IT'LL BE THE BASEMENT IN MY HOUSE...
BUT WHAT ABOUT ADAMARK?
ADAMARK IS DYING.
HE'S TRYING NOT TO SHOW IT, BUT HE'S IN AGONY.
THAT SINGLE DROP OF AQUA VITAE COULD COUNTERACT THE POISON IN HIS BLOOD.
WHAT IF YOU DRINK IT AND WE LOSE YOU BOTH?

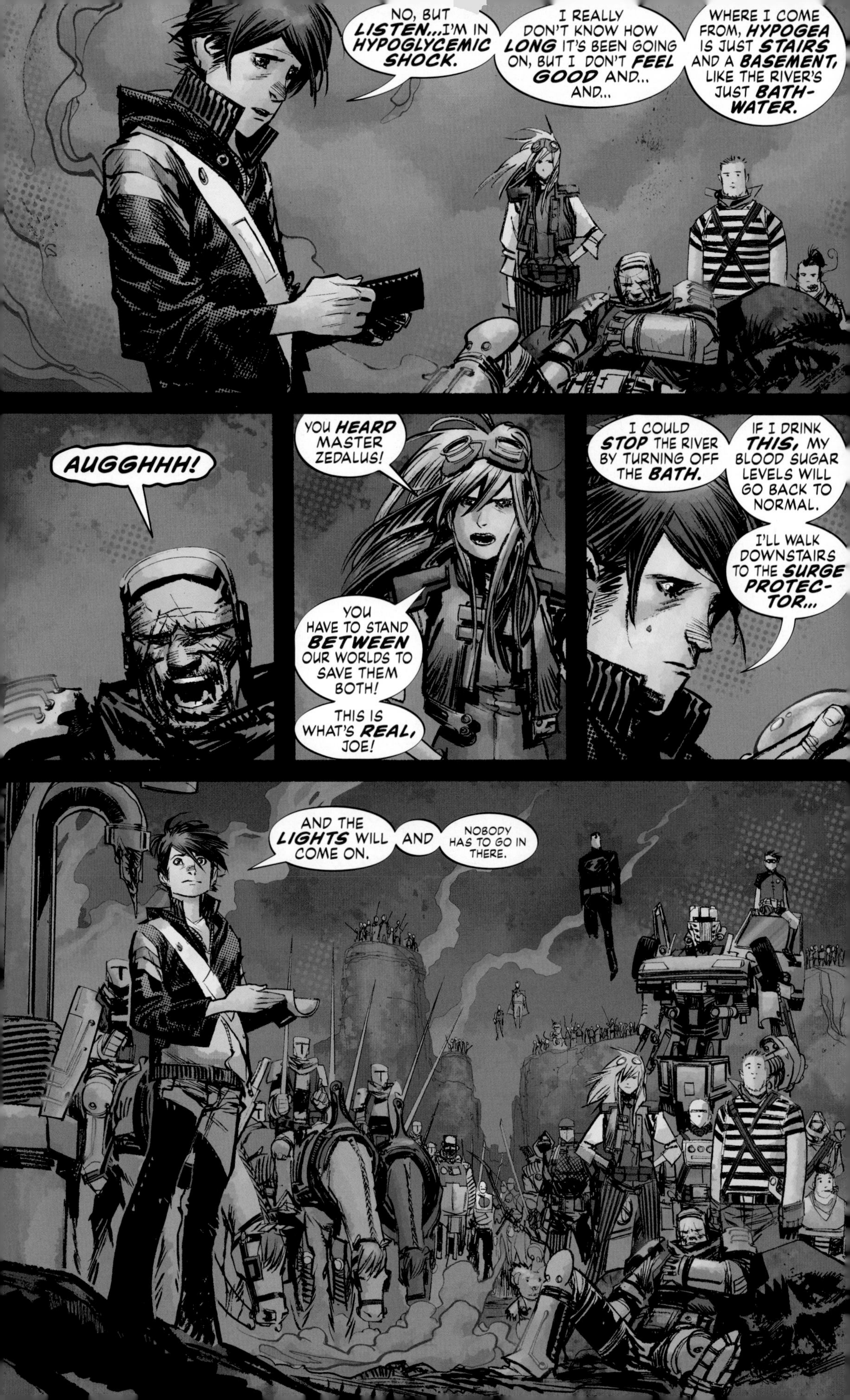

NO, BUT LISTEN...I'M IN HYPOGLYCEMIC SHOCK.
I REALLY DON'T KNOW HOW LONG IT'S BEEN GOING ON, BUT I DON'T FEEL GOOD AND... AND...
WHERE I COME FROM, HYPOGEA IS JUST STAIRS AND A BASEMENT, LIKE THE RIVER'S JUST BATH-WATER.
AUGGHHH!
YOU HEARD MASTER ZEDALUS!
YOU HAVE TO STAND BETWEEN OUR WORLDS TO SAVE THEM BOTH!
THIS IS WHAT'S REAL, JOE!
I COULD STOP THE RIVER BY TURNING OFF THE BATH.
IF I DRINK THIS, MY BLOOD SUGAR LEVELS WILL GO BACK TO NORMAL.
I'LL WALK DOWNSTAIRS TO THE SURGE PROTEC-TOR...
AND THE LIGHTS WILL COME ON.
AND
NOBODY HAS TO GO IN THERE.

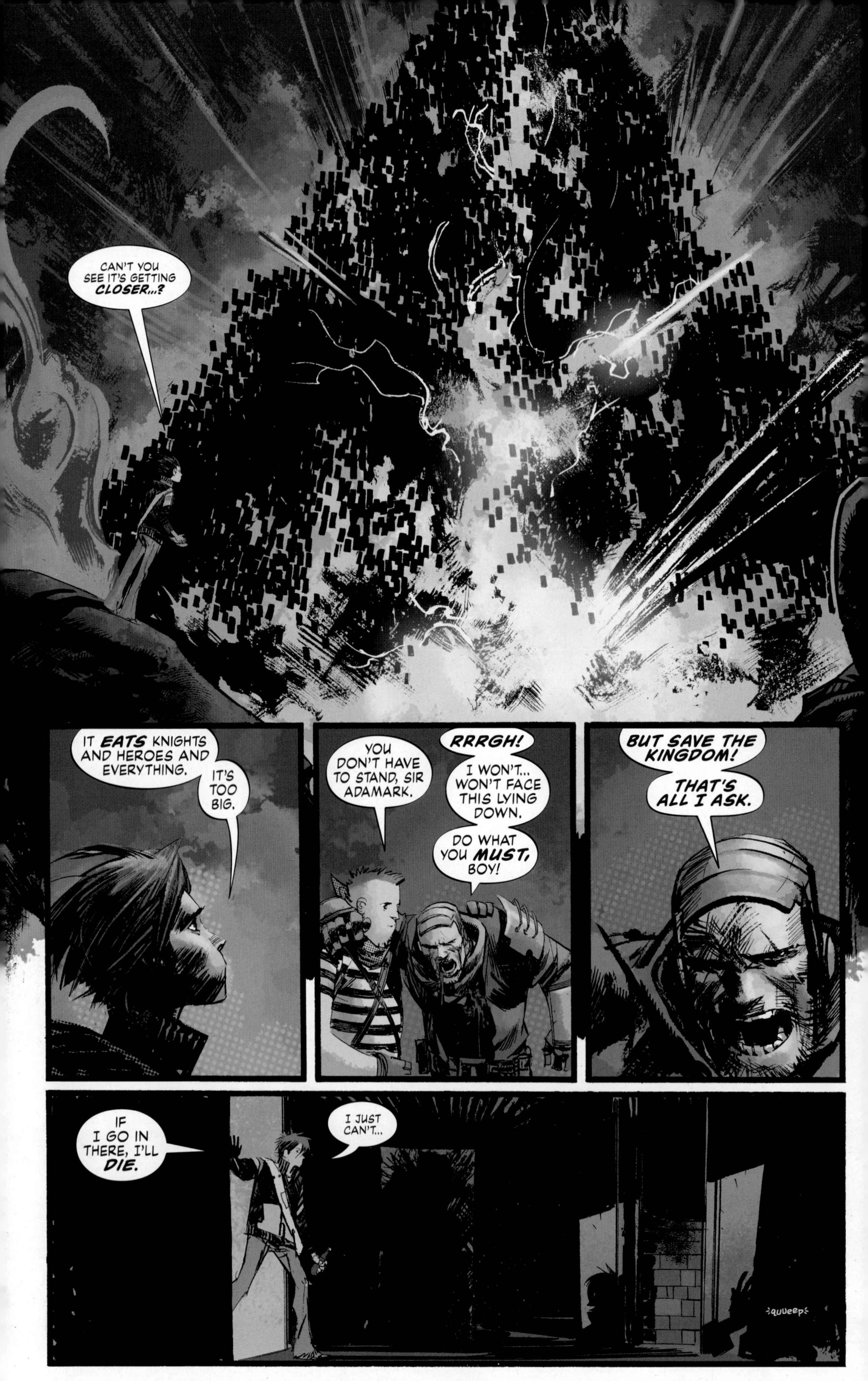
CAN'T YOU SEE IT'S GETTING CLOSER...?
IT EATS KNIGHTS AND HEROES AND EVERYTHING.
IT'S TOO BIG.
YOU DON'T HAVE TO STAND, SIR ADAMARK.
RRRGH!
I WON'T... WON'T FACE THIS LYING DOWN.
DO WHAT YOU MUST, BOY!
BUT SAVE THE KINGDOM!
THAT'S ALL I ASK.
IF I GO IN THERE, I'LL DIE.
I JUST CAN'T...
QUUEEP

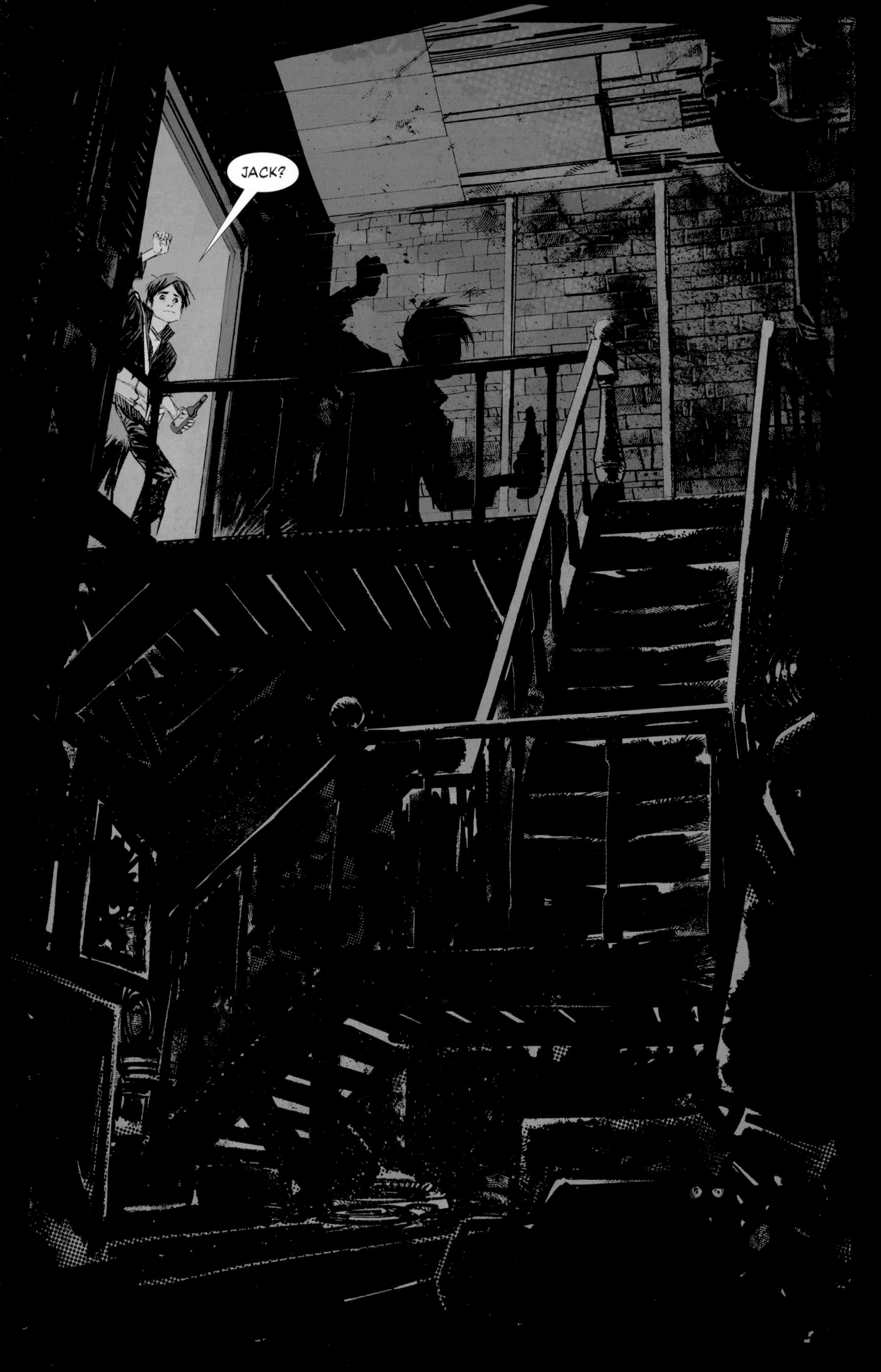
JACK?

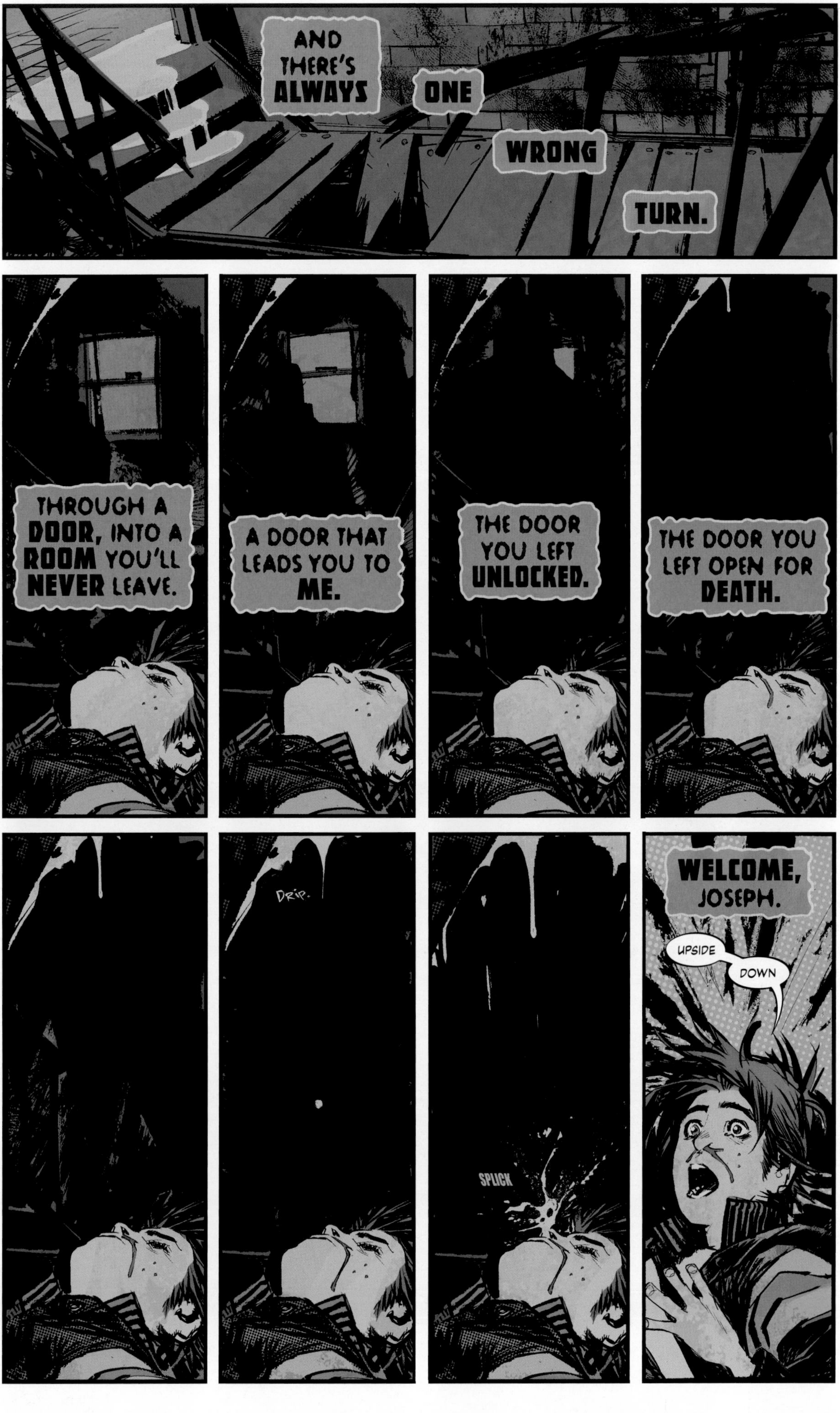
AND THERE'S ALWAYS
ONE
WRONG
TURN.
THROUGH A DOOR, INTO A ROOM YOU'LL NEVER LEAVE.
A DOOR THAT LEADS YOU TO ME.
THE DOOR YOU LEFT UNLOCKED.
THE DOOR YOU LEFT OPEN FOR DEATH.
DRIP.
SPLICK
WELCOME, JOSEPH.
UPSIDE
DOWN

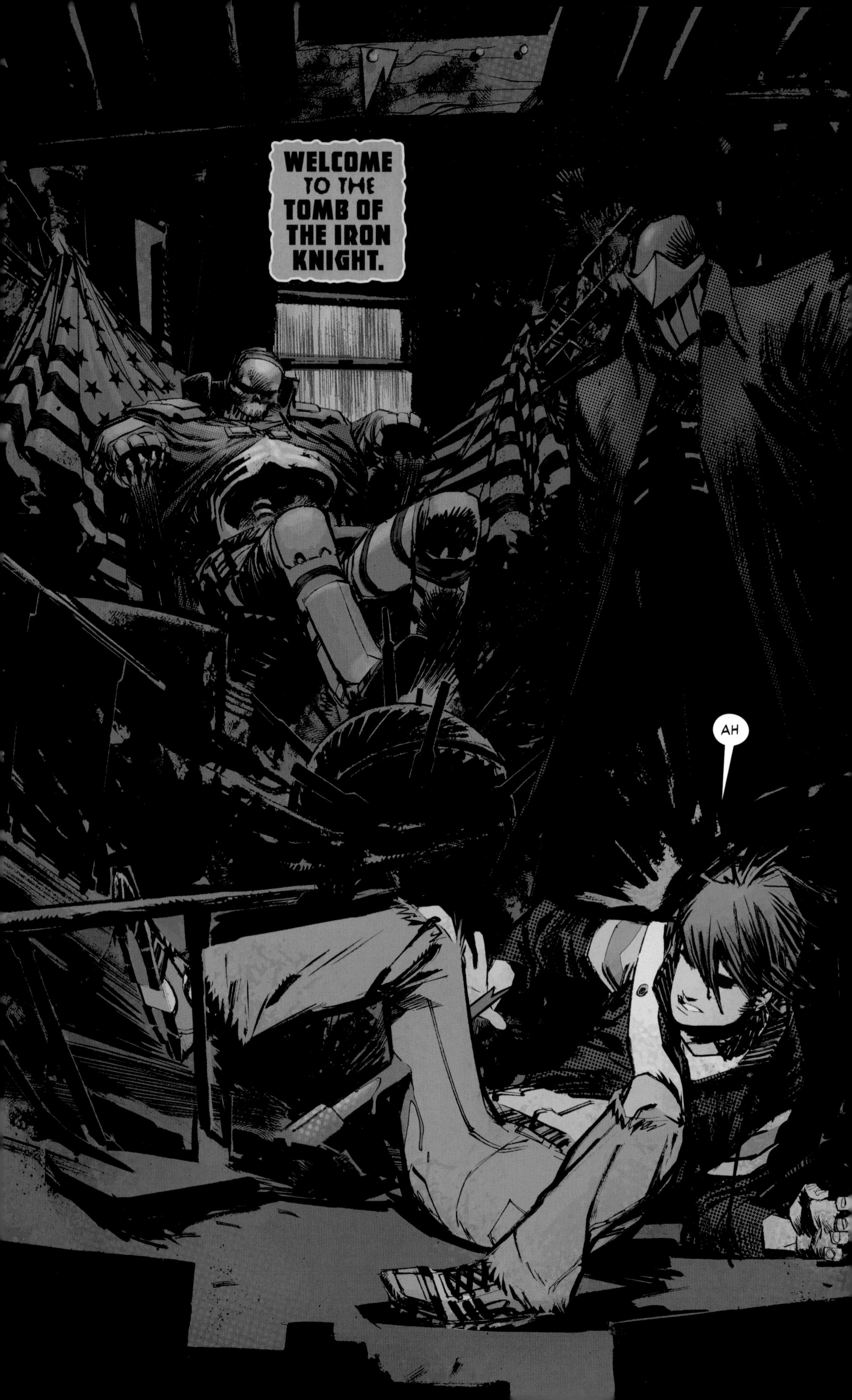
WELCOME TO THE TOMB OF THE IRON KNIGHT.
AH

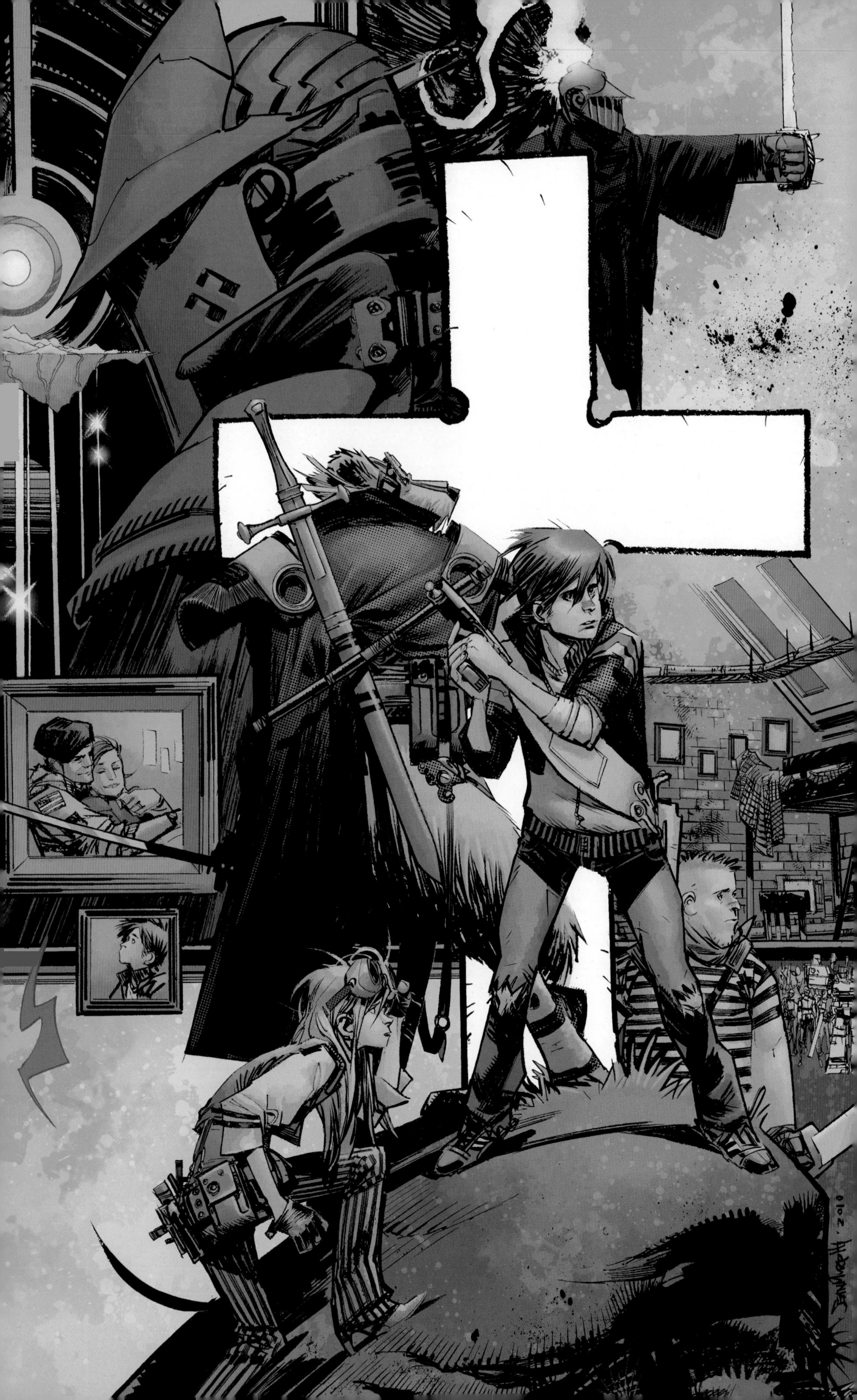

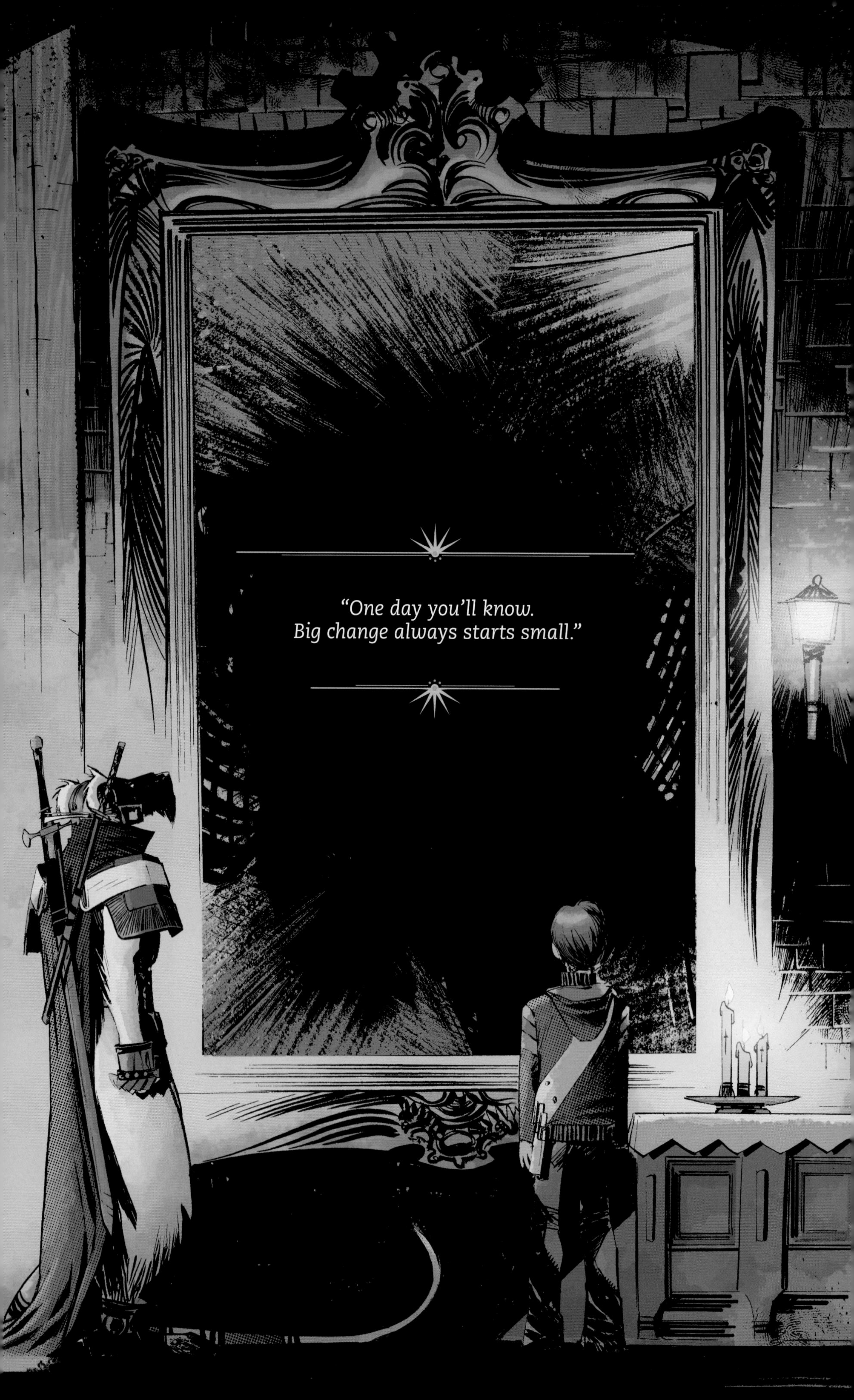
"One day you'll know.
Big change always starts small."

# chapter 8: tomb of the iron knight

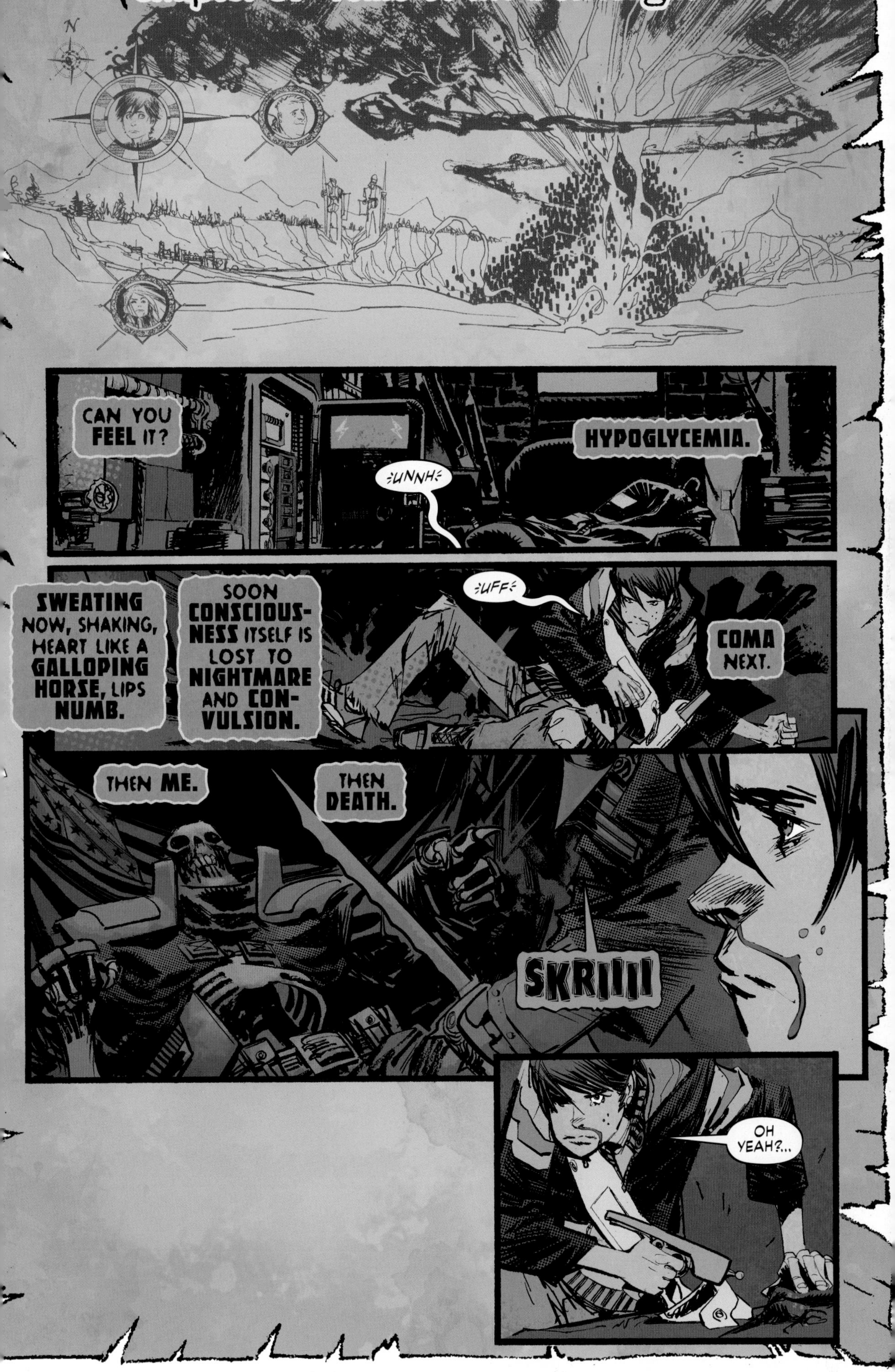
CAN YOU FEEL IT?
HYPOGLYCEMIA.
UNNH
SWEATING NOW, SHAKING, HEART LIKE A GALLOPING HORSE, LIPS NUMB.
SOON CONSCIOUSNESS ITSELF IS LOST TO NIGHTMARE AND CONVULSION.
UFF
COMA NEXT.
THEN ME.
THEN DEATH.
SKRIIIII
OH YEAH?...

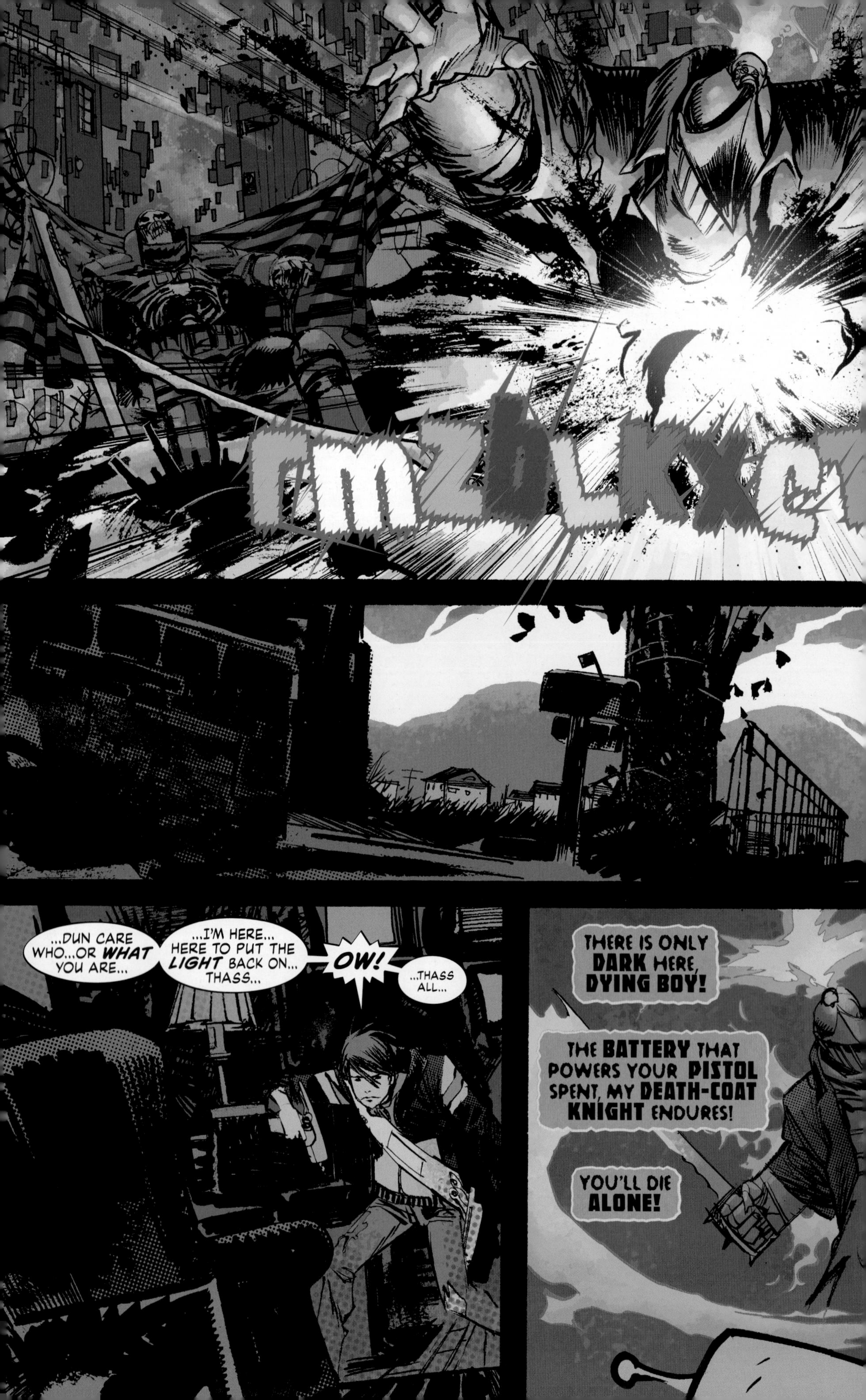

...DUN CARE WHO...OR WHAT YOU ARE...
...I'M HERE... HERE TO PUT THE LIGHT BACK ON... THASS...
OW!
...THASS ALL...
THERE IS ONLY DARK HERE, DYING BOY!
THE BATTERY THAT POWERS YOUR PISTOL SPENT, MY DEATH-COAT KNIGHT ENDURES!
YOU'LL DIE ALONE!

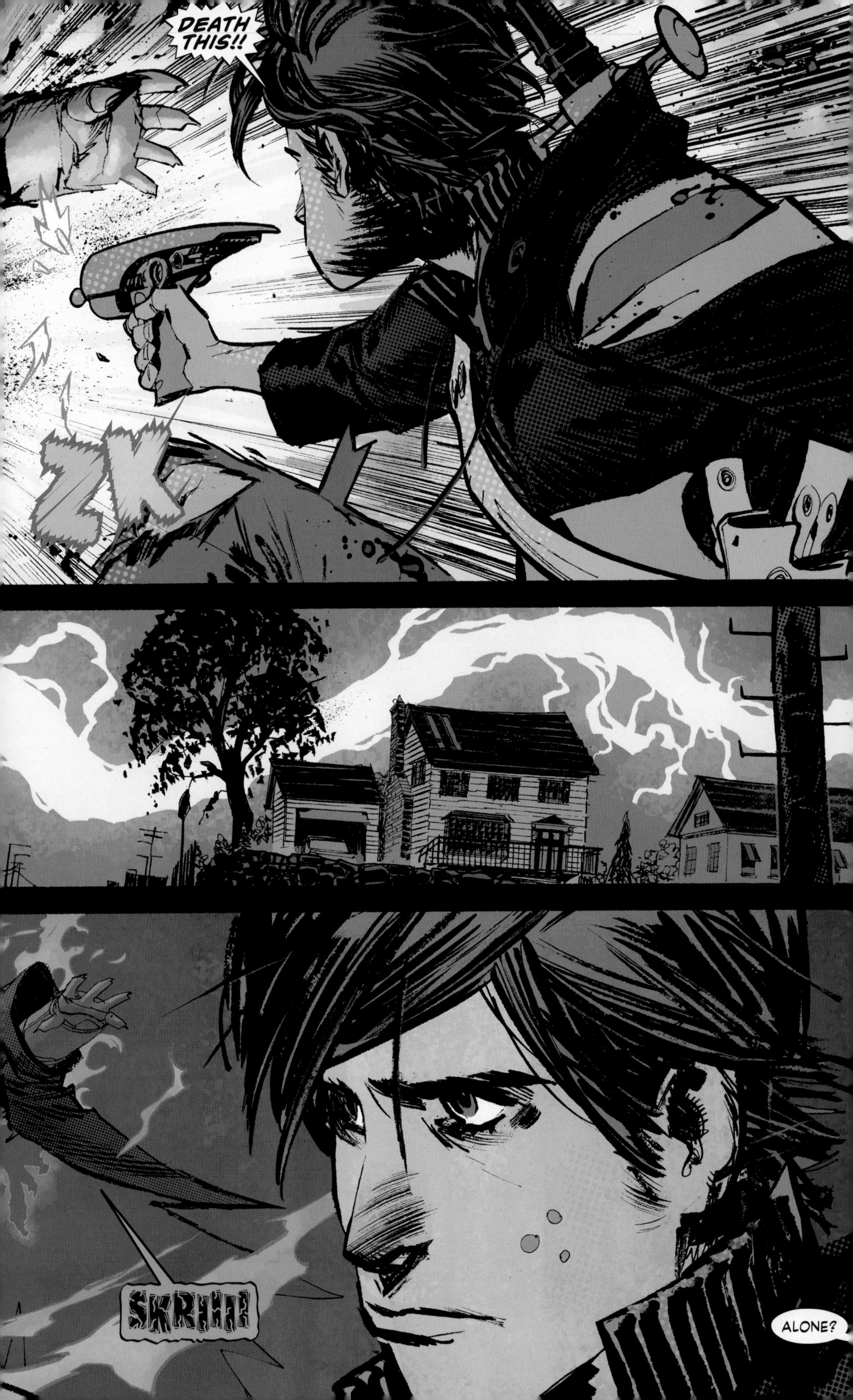
DEATH THIS!!
ZK
SKRIII!
ALONE?

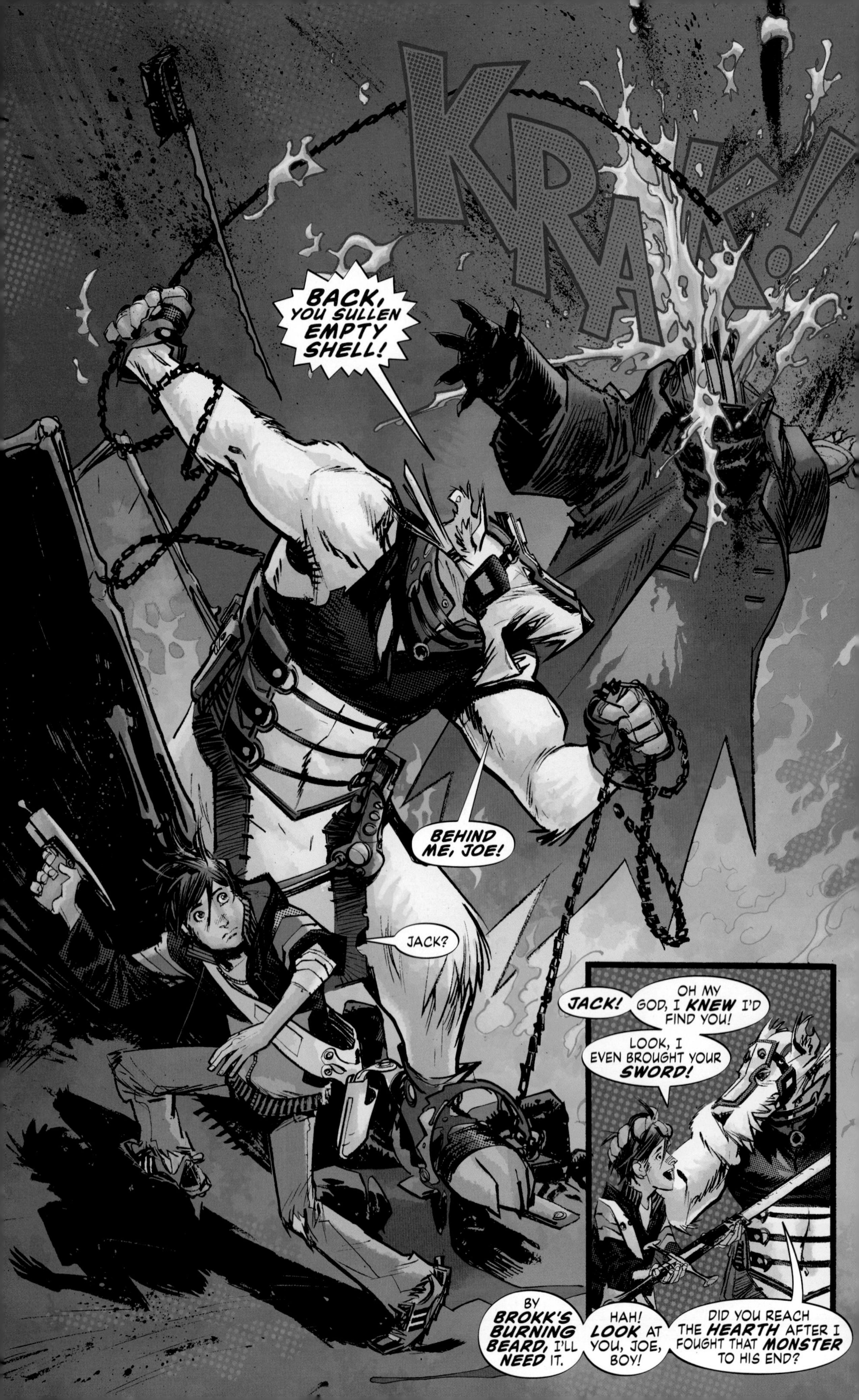
KRAKK!!
BACK, YOU SULLEN EMPTY SHELL!
BEHIND ME, JOE!
JACK?
JACK!
OH MY GOD, I KNEW I'D FIND YOU!
LOOK, I EVEN BROUGHT YOUR SWORD!
DID YOU REACH THE HEARTH AFTER I FOUGHT THAT MONSTER TO HIS END?
HAH! LOOK AT YOU, JOE, BOY!
BY BROKK'S BURNING BEARD, I'LL NEED IT.

...**BYRINTH** THING, FIGHTING FOR US.

I **KNEW** I HEARD YOUR VOICE.

HELP ME OUT OF THIS **TRAP.**

THEY... GNNNGH... THEY ONLY KEPT ME ALIVE WHILE THEY WAITED FOR **YOU.**

GNN!

YOUR WOUNDS AFFORD YOU **NO RELEASE** FROM SERVICE, PROUD SIR ULRIK.

SKK-SKKK-SKK

RISE **AGAIN,** MY LORD OF SUFFERING.

THE HOUR IS COME WHEN OF THE WORLD A GRAVEYARD I MUST MAKE!

**GAHHH!**

**GOT** IT!

AH, YOUR POOR LEG'S ALL **MANGLED.**

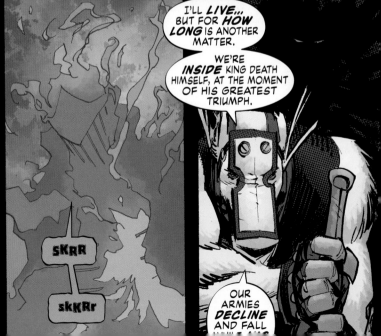

I'LL **LIVE...** BUT FOR **HOW LONG** IS ANOTHER MATTER.

WE'RE **INSIDE** KING DEATH HIMSELF, AT THE MOMENT OF HIS GREATEST TRIUMPH.

SKRR

skKRr

OUR ARMIES **DECLINE** AND FALL

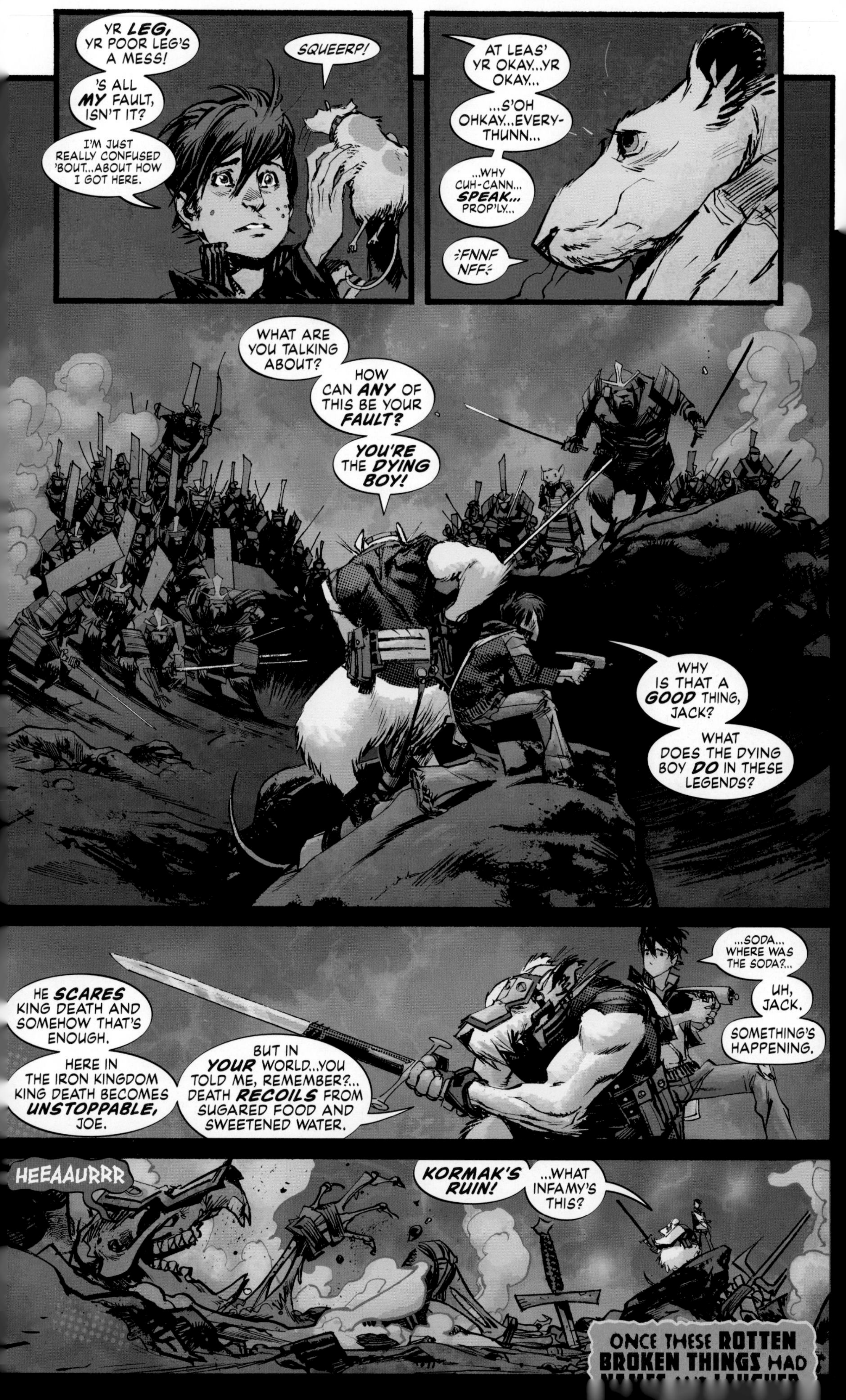
YR LEG, YR POOR LEG'S A MESS!
'S ALL MY FAULT, ISN'T IT?
I'M JUST REALLY CONFUSED 'BOUT...ABOUT HOW I GOT HERE.
SQUEERP!
AT LEAS' YR OKAY...YR OKAY...
...S'OH OHKAY...EVERY-THUNN...
...WHY CUH-CANN... SPEAK... PROP'LY...
FNNF NFF
WHAT ARE YOU TALKING ABOUT?
HOW CAN ANY OF THIS BE YOUR FAULT?
YOU'RE THE DYING BOY!
WHY IS THAT A GOOD THING, JACK?
WHAT DOES THE DYING BOY DO IN THESE LEGENDS?
HE SCARES KING DEATH AND SOMEHOW THAT'S ENOUGH.
HERE IN THE IRON KINGDOM KING DEATH BECOMES UNSTOPPABLE, JOE.
BUT IN YOUR WORLD...YOU TOLD ME, REMEMBER?... DEATH RECOILS FROM SUGARED FOOD AND SWEETENED WATER.
...SODA... WHERE WAS THE SODA?...
UH, JACK.
SOMETHING'S HAPPENING.
HEEAAURRR
KORMAK'S RUIN!
...WHAT INFAMY'S THIS?
ONCE THESE ROTTEN BROKEN THINGS HAD

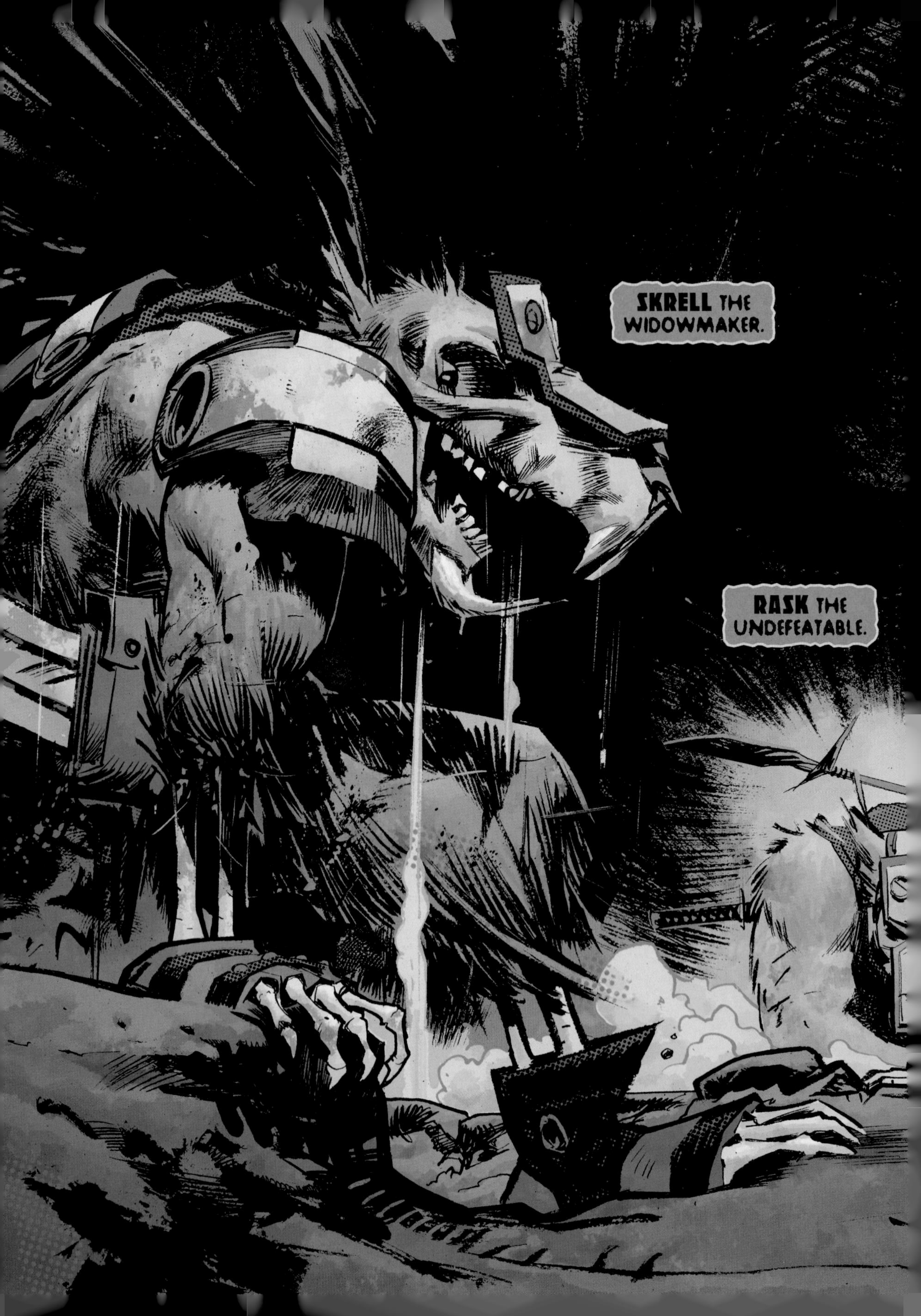
SKRELL THE WIDOWMAKER.
RASK THE UNDEFEATABLE.

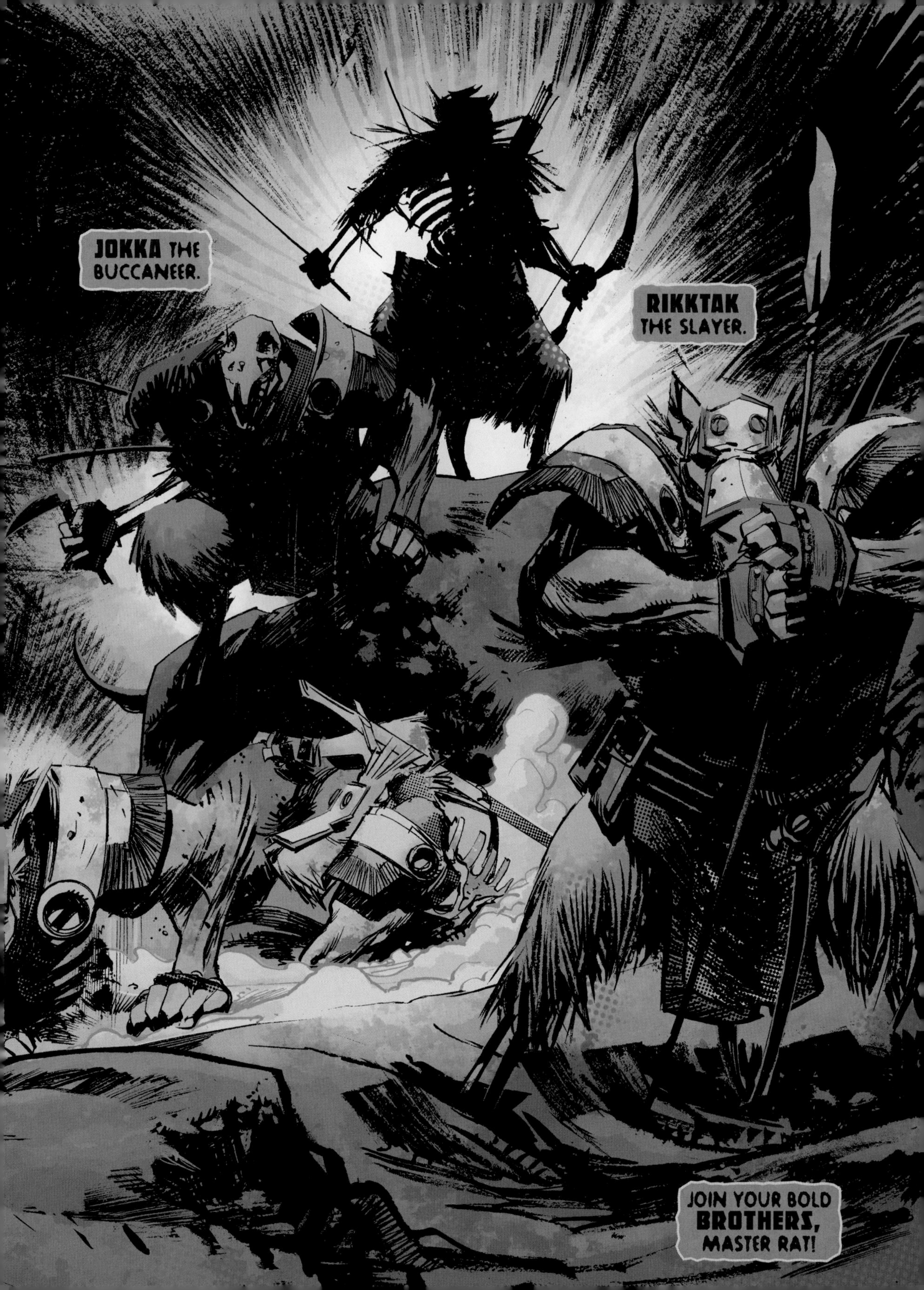
JOKKA THE BUCCANEER.
RIKKTAK THE SLAYER.
JOIN YOUR BOLD BROTHERS, MASTER RAT!

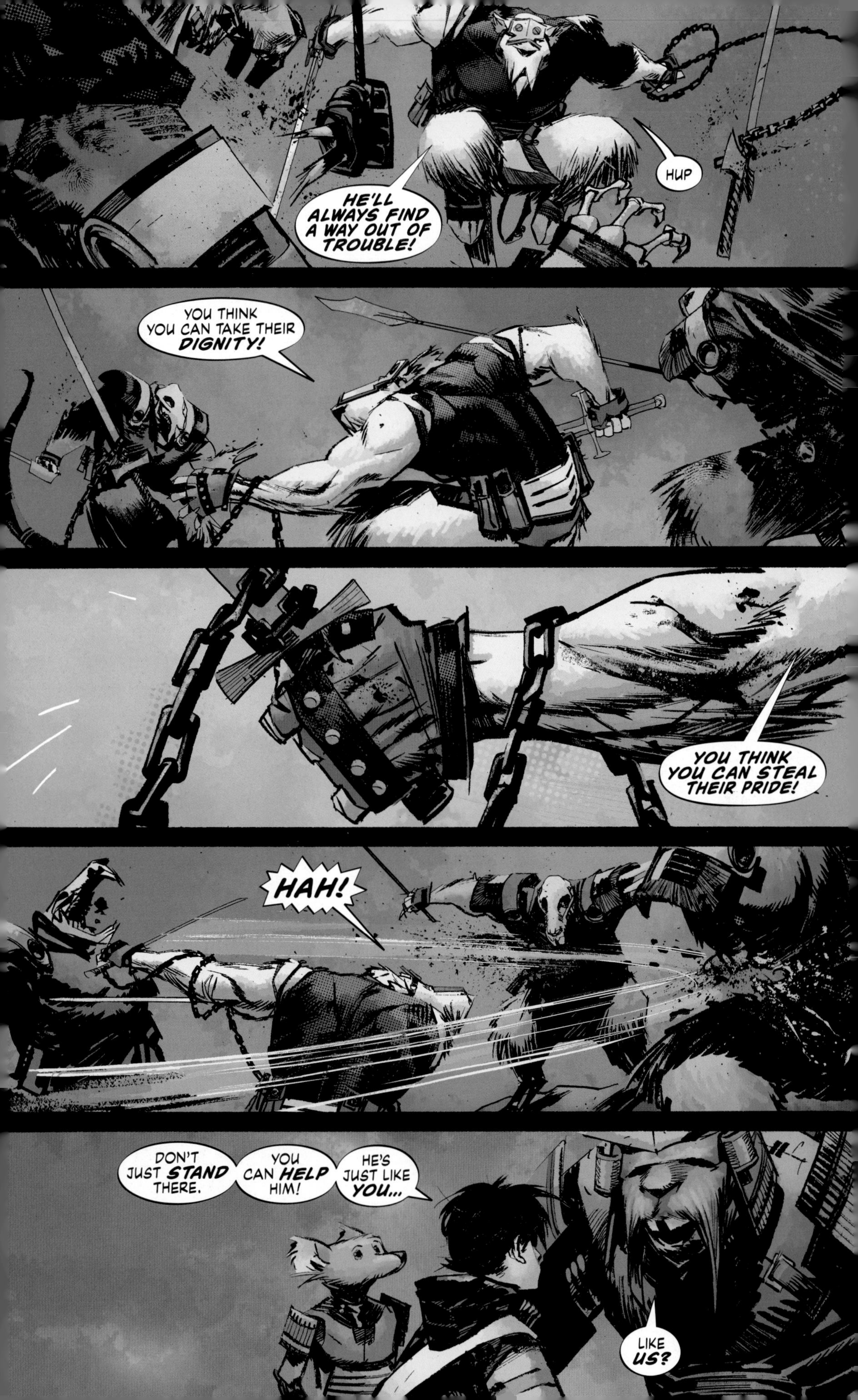
HUP
HE'LL ALWAYS FIND A WAY OUT OF TROUBLE!
YOU THINK YOU CAN TAKE THEIR DIGNITY!
YOU THINK YOU CAN STEAL THEIR PRIDE!
HAH!
DON'T JUST STAND THERE.
YOU CAN HELP HIM!
HE'S JUST LIKE YOU...
LIKE US?

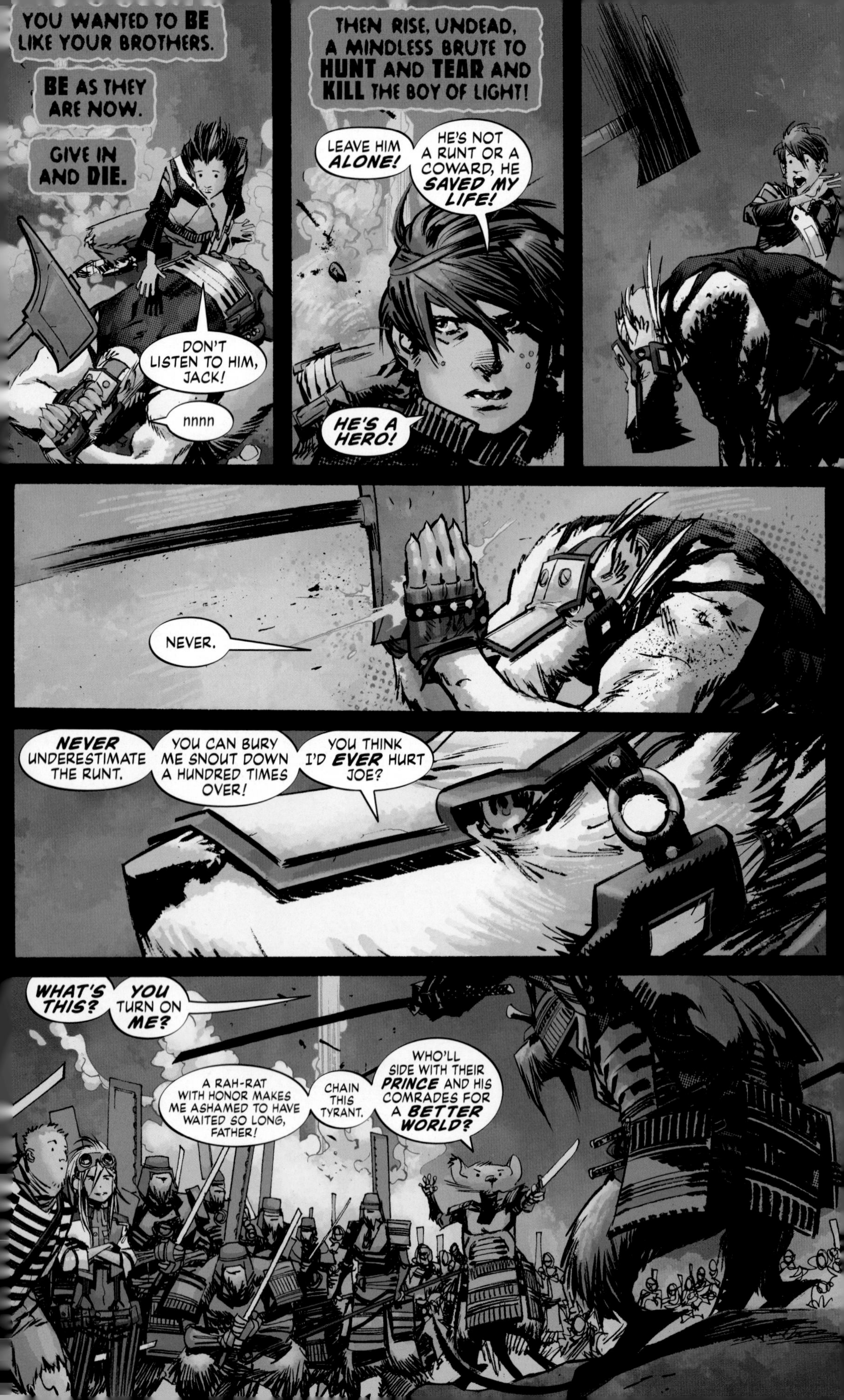
YOU WANTED TO BE LIKE YOUR BROTHERS.
BE AS THEY ARE NOW.
GIVE IN AND DIE.
DON'T LISTEN TO HIM, JACK!
nnnn
THEN RISE, UNDEAD, A MINDLESS BRUTE TO HUNT AND TEAR AND KILL THE BOY OF LIGHT!
LEAVE HIM ALONE!
HE'S NOT A RUNT OR A COWARD, HE SAVED MY LIFE!
HE'S A HERO!
NEVER.
NEVER UNDERESTIMATE THE RUNT.
YOU CAN BURY ME SNOUT DOWN A HUNDRED TIMES OVER!
YOU THINK I'D EVER HURT JOE?
WHAT'S THIS?
YOU TURN ON ME?
A RAH-RAT WITH HONOR MAKES ME ASHAMED TO HAVE WAITED SO LONG, FATHER!
CHAIN THIS TYRANT.
WHO'LL SIDE WITH THEIR PRINCE AND HIS COMRADES FOR A BETTER WORLD?

RAARGH!

REVOLUTION!

HAK!

YOU'LL ALL *REGRET* THIS!

YOU *FOLLOWED* ME? YOU'RE *CRAZY!*

HOW IS THAT *POSSIBLE?*

YOU DROPPED *THIS.*

TOK!

WHICH IS *ONLY* THE LOST MAP OF *HYPOGEA.*

THE TREASURE YOU FORGOT TO *MENTION* YOU WERE *CARRYING* ALL THIS TIME.

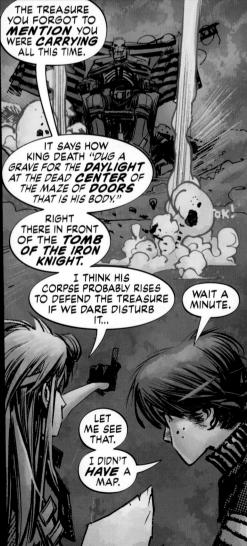

IT SAYS HOW KING DEATH "DUG A GRAVE FOR THE *DAYLIGHT* AT THE DEAD *CENTER* OF THE *MAZE OF DOORS* THAT IS HIS BODY."

RIGHT THERE IN FRONT OF THE *TOMB OF THE IRON KNIGHT.*

I THINK HIS CORPSE PROBABLY RISES TO DEFEND THE TREASURE IF WE DARE DISTURB IT...

TOK!

WAIT A MINUTE.

LET ME SEE THAT.

I DIDN'T *HAVE* A MAP.

WAIT!

LEAVE THAT *BE!*

SMOOT, BE CAREFUL!

JOE WAS ⸗UNNGH⸗ *RIGHT* AFTER ALL.

ONLY A GIANT PRINCE COULD OPEN

*THIS!*

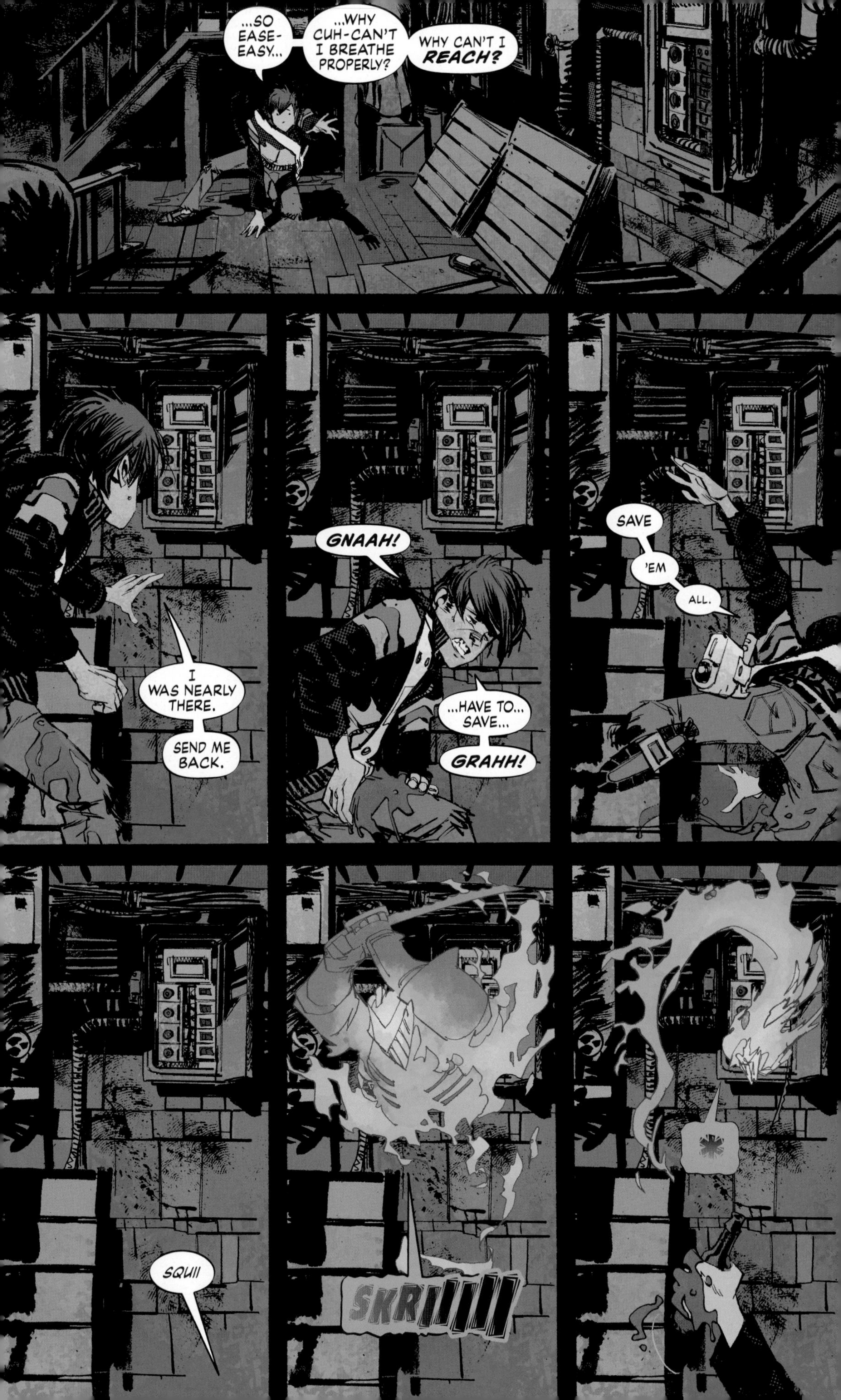
...SO EASE-EASY...
...WHY CUH-CAN'T I BREATHE PROPERLY?
WHY CAN'T I *REACH?*
I WAS NEARLY THERE.
SEND ME BACK.
*GNAAH!*
...HAVE TO... SAVE...
*GRAHH!*
SAVE
'EM
ALL.
SQUII
SKRIIIIII

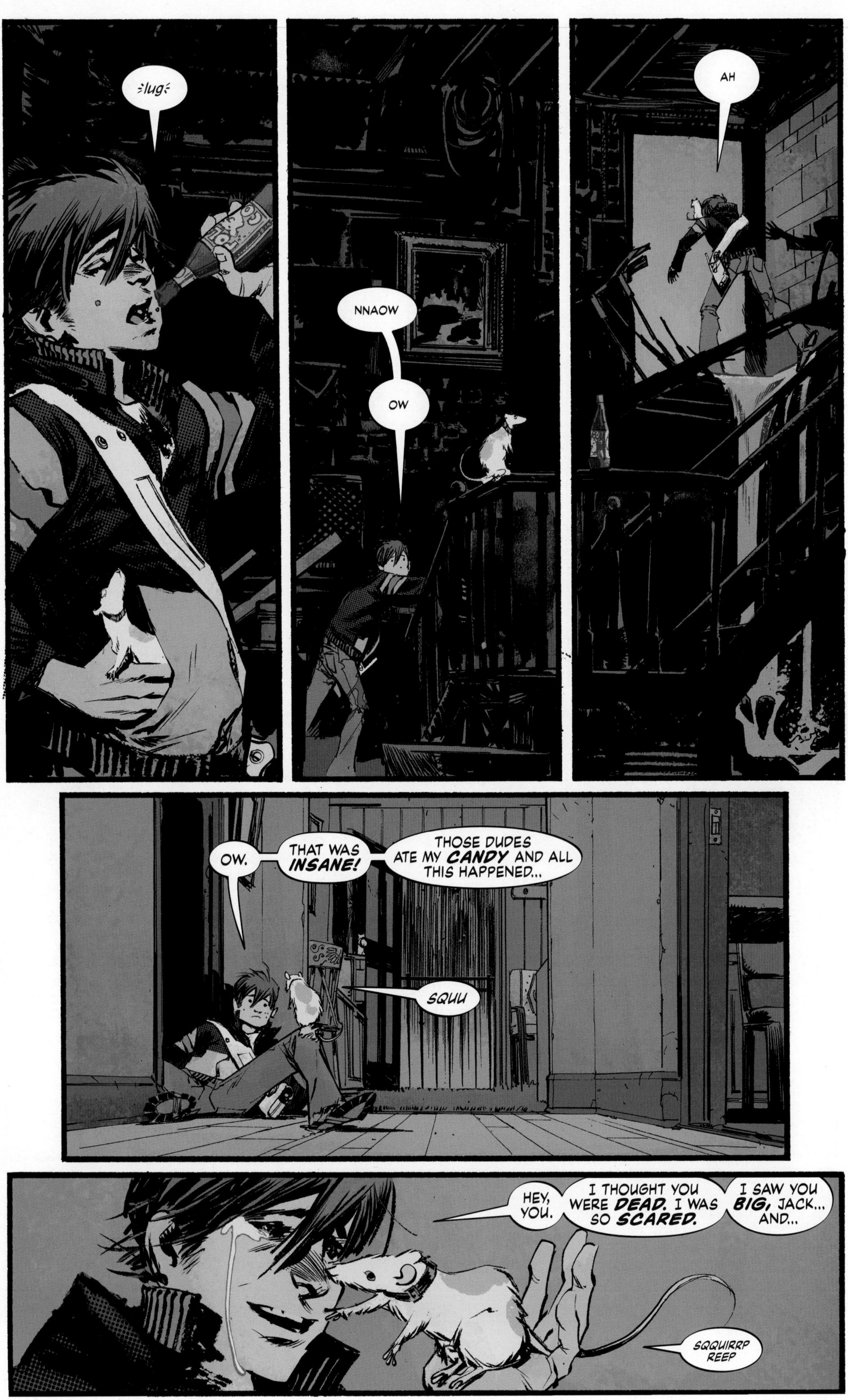

lug
NNAOW
OW
AH
OW.
THAT WAS INSANE!
THOSE DUDES ATE MY CANDY AND ALL THIS HAPPENED...
SQUU
HEY, YOU.
I THOUGHT YOU WERE DEAD. I WAS SO SCARED.
I SAW YOU BIG, JACK... AND...
SQQUIRRP REEP

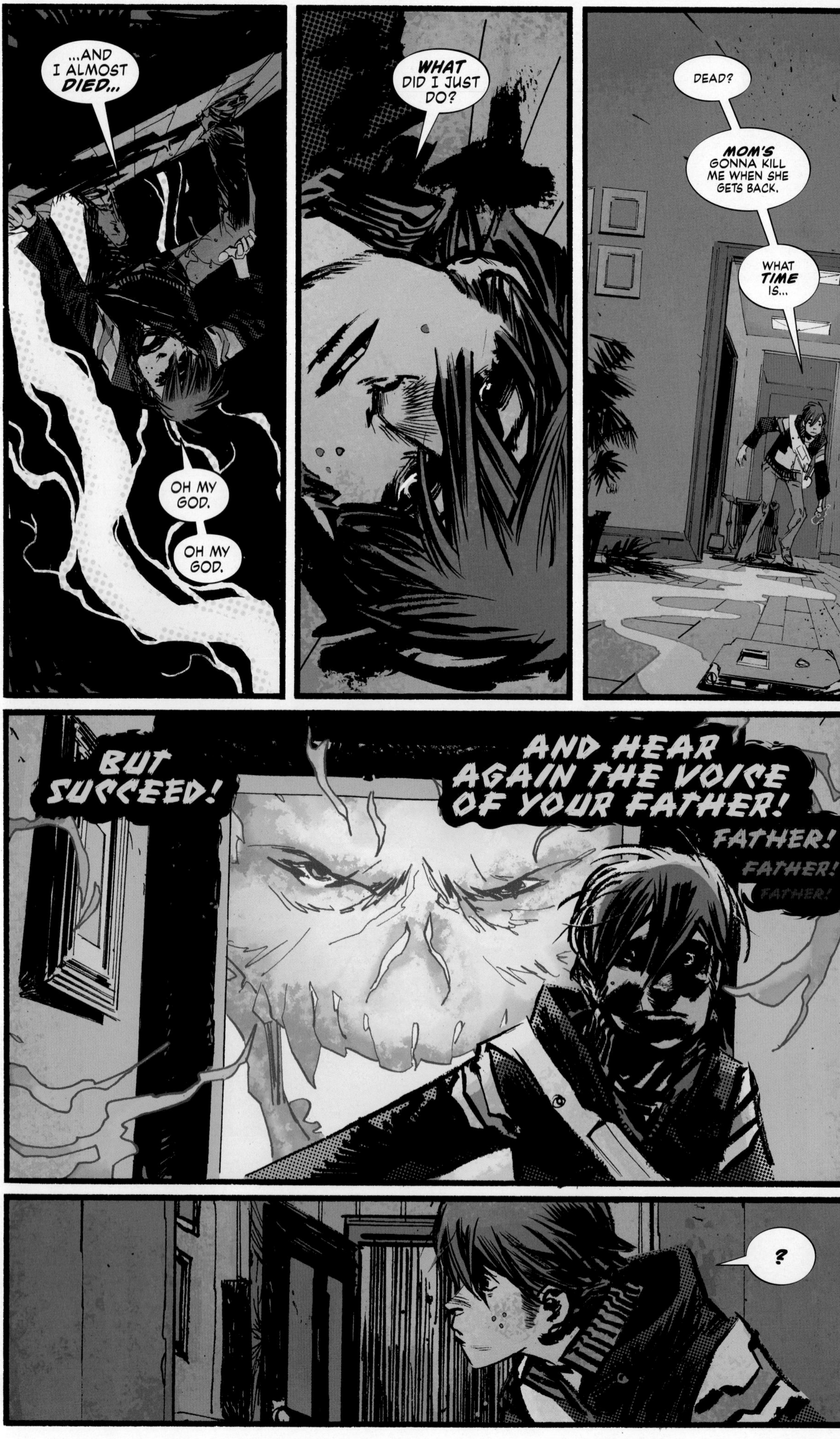
...AND I ALMOST DIED...
OH MY GOD.
OH MY GOD.
WHAT DID I JUST DO?
DEAD?
MOM'S GONNA KILL ME WHEN SHE GETS BACK.
WHAT TIME IS...
BUT SUCCEED!
AND HEAR AGAIN THE VOICE OF YOUR FATHER!
FATHER!
FATHER!
FATHER!
?

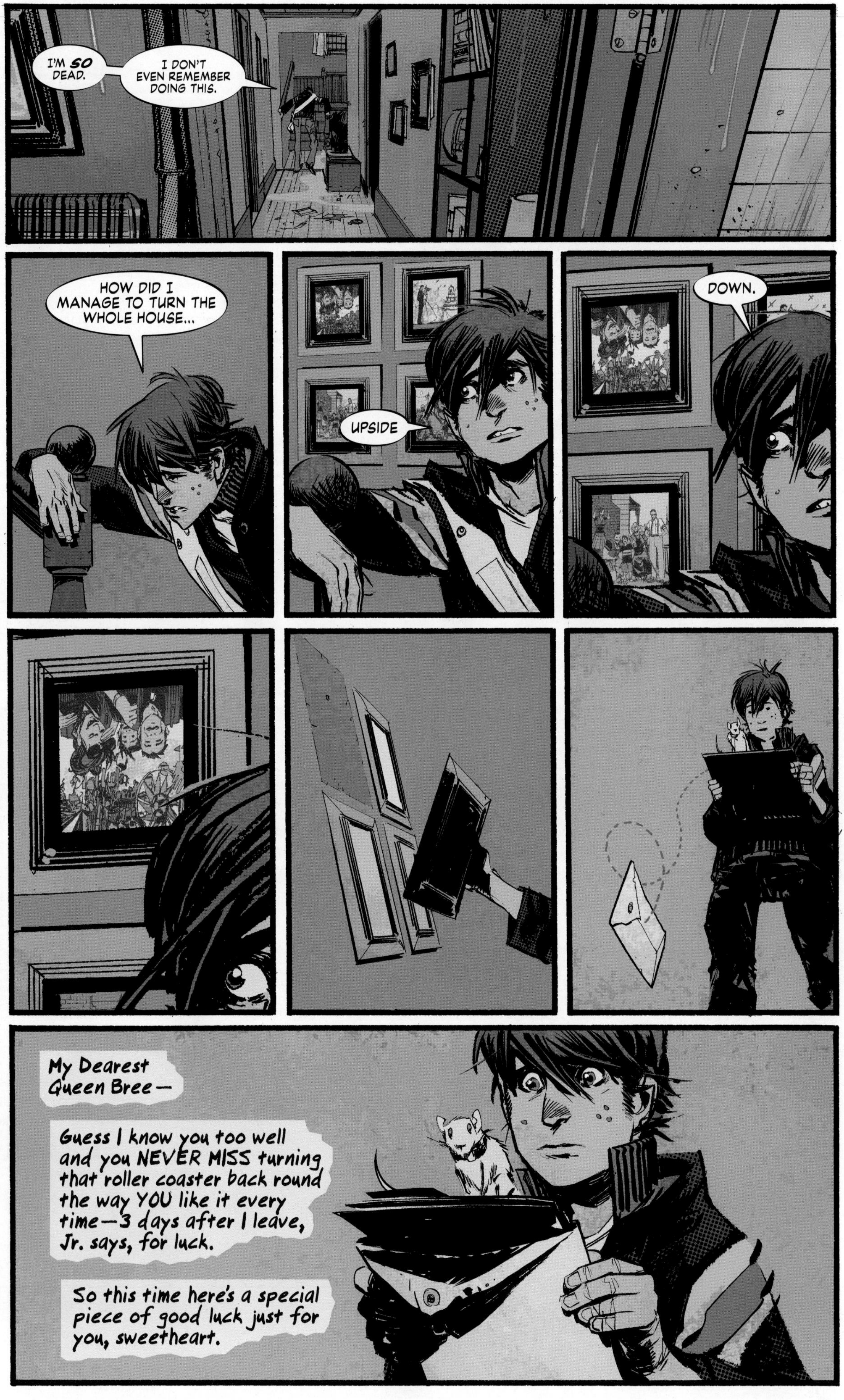

I'M SO DEAD.
I DON'T EVEN REMEMBER DOING THIS.
HOW DID I MANAGE TO TURN THE WHOLE HOUSE...
UPSIDE
DOWN.
My Dearest Queen Bree—
Guess I know you too well and you NEVER MISS turning that roller coaster back round the way YOU like it every time—3 days after I leave, Jr. says, for luck.
So this time here's a special piece of good luck just for you, sweetheart.

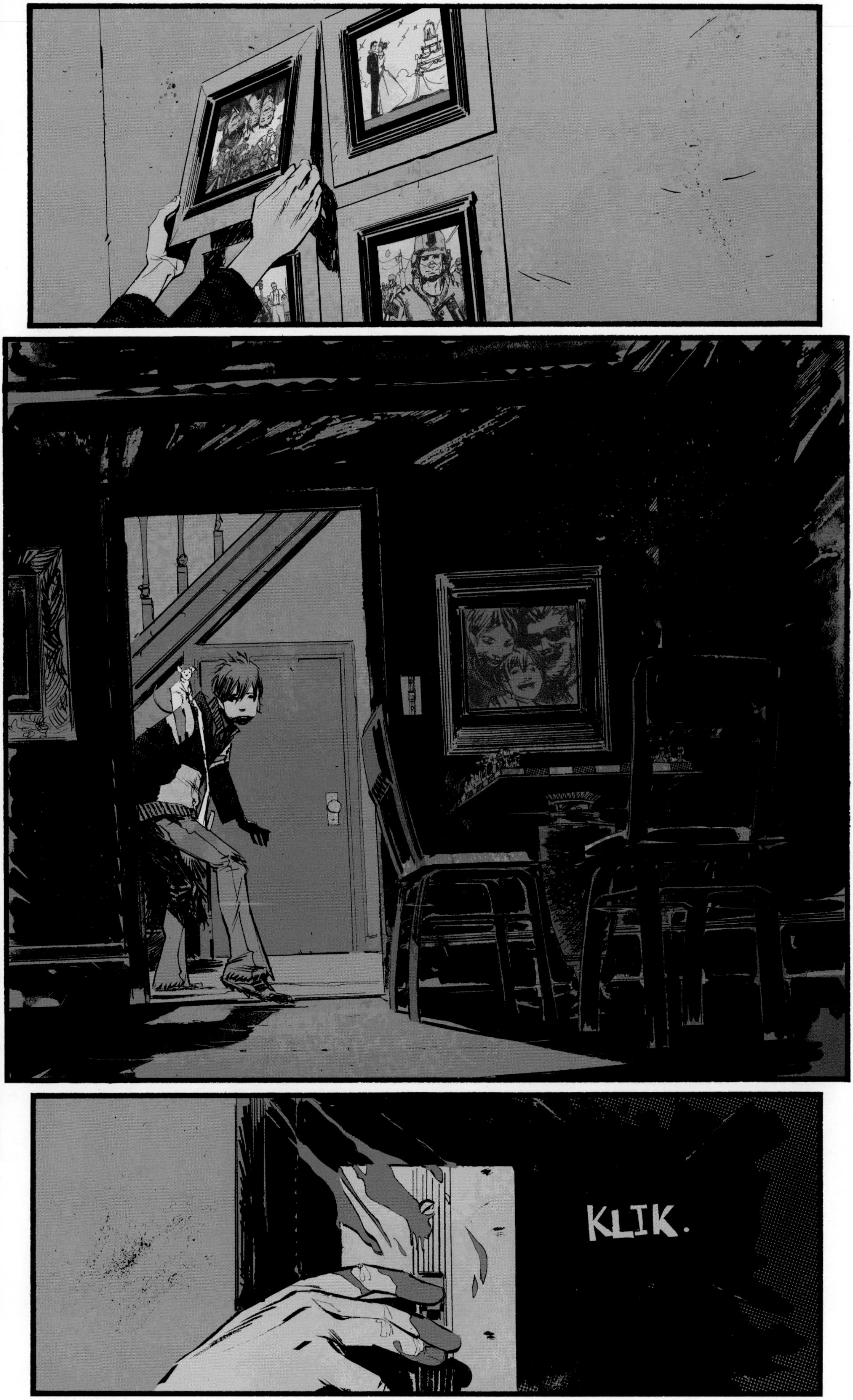
KLIK.

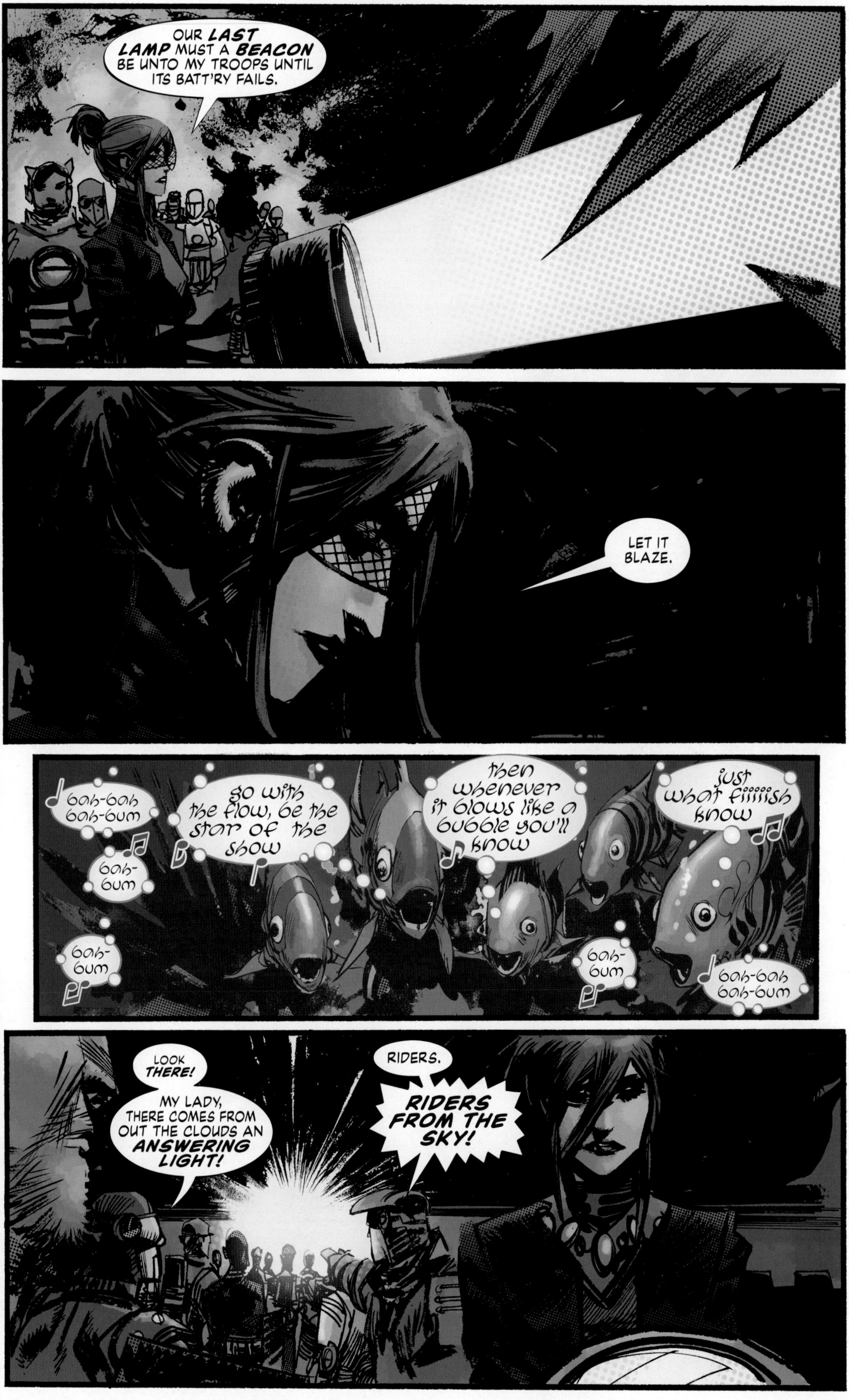
OUR LAST LAMP MUST A BEACON BE UNTO MY TROOPS UNTIL ITS BATT'RY FAILS.
LET IT BLAZE.
bah-bah bah-bum
bah-bum
bah-bum
go with the flow, be the star of the show
then whenever it blows like a bubble you'll know
just what fiiiiish know
bah-bum
bah-bah bah-bum
LOOK THERE!
MY LADY, THERE COMES FROM OUT THE CLOUDS AN ANSWERING LIGHT!
RIDERS.
RIDERS FROM THE SKY!

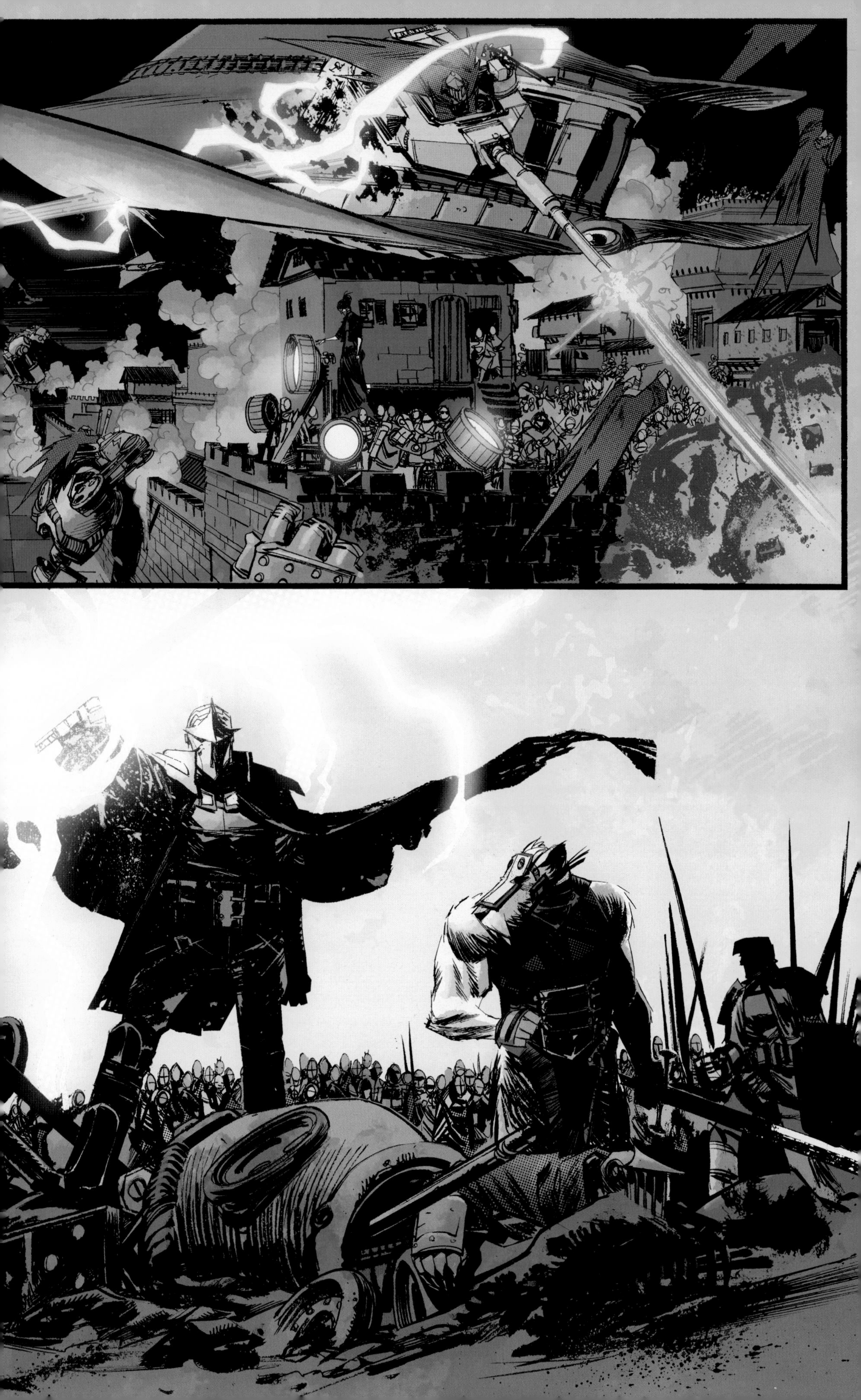

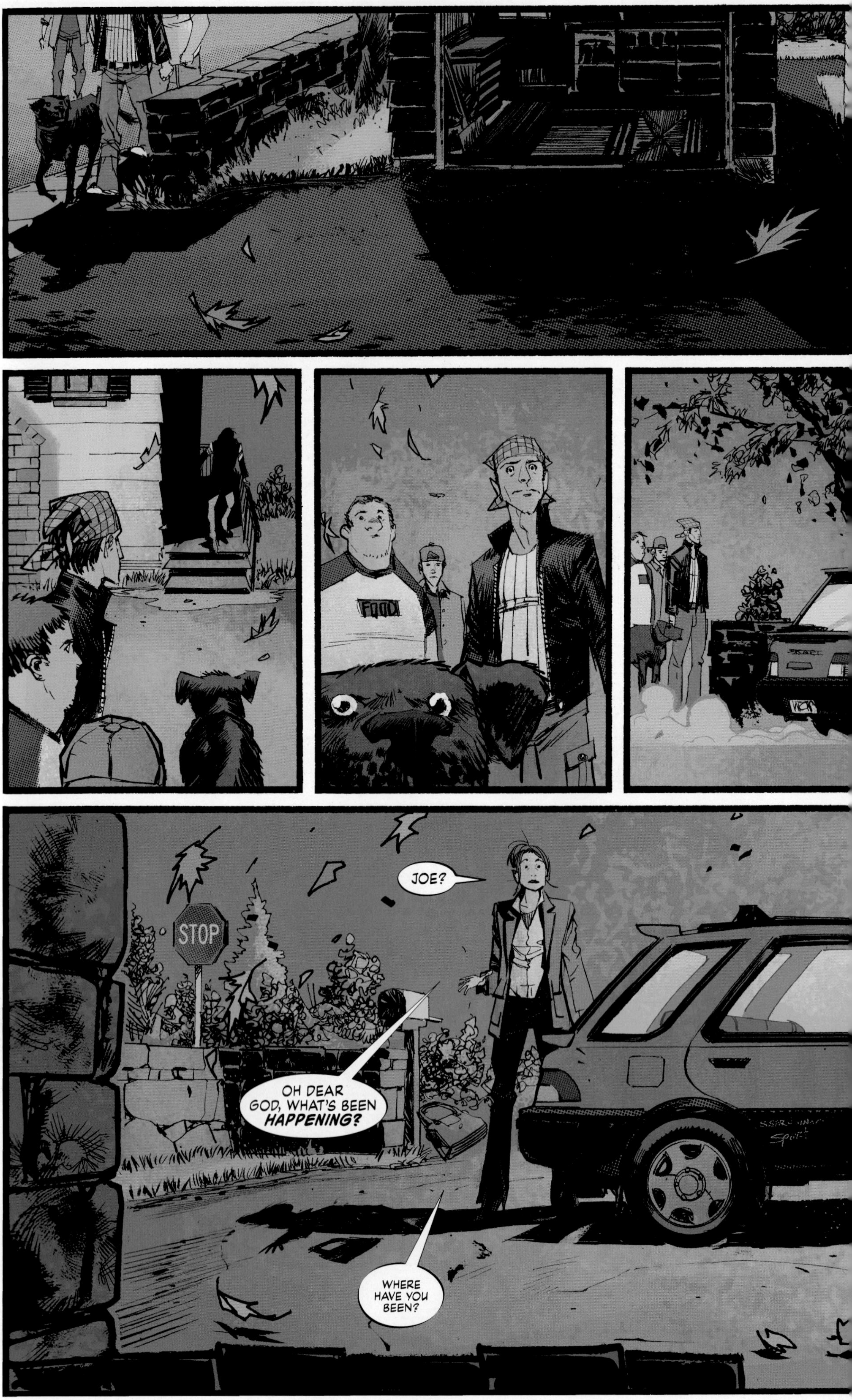
FOOD
STOP
JOE?
OH DEAR GOD, WHAT'S BEEN HAPPENING?
WHERE HAVE YOU BEEN?

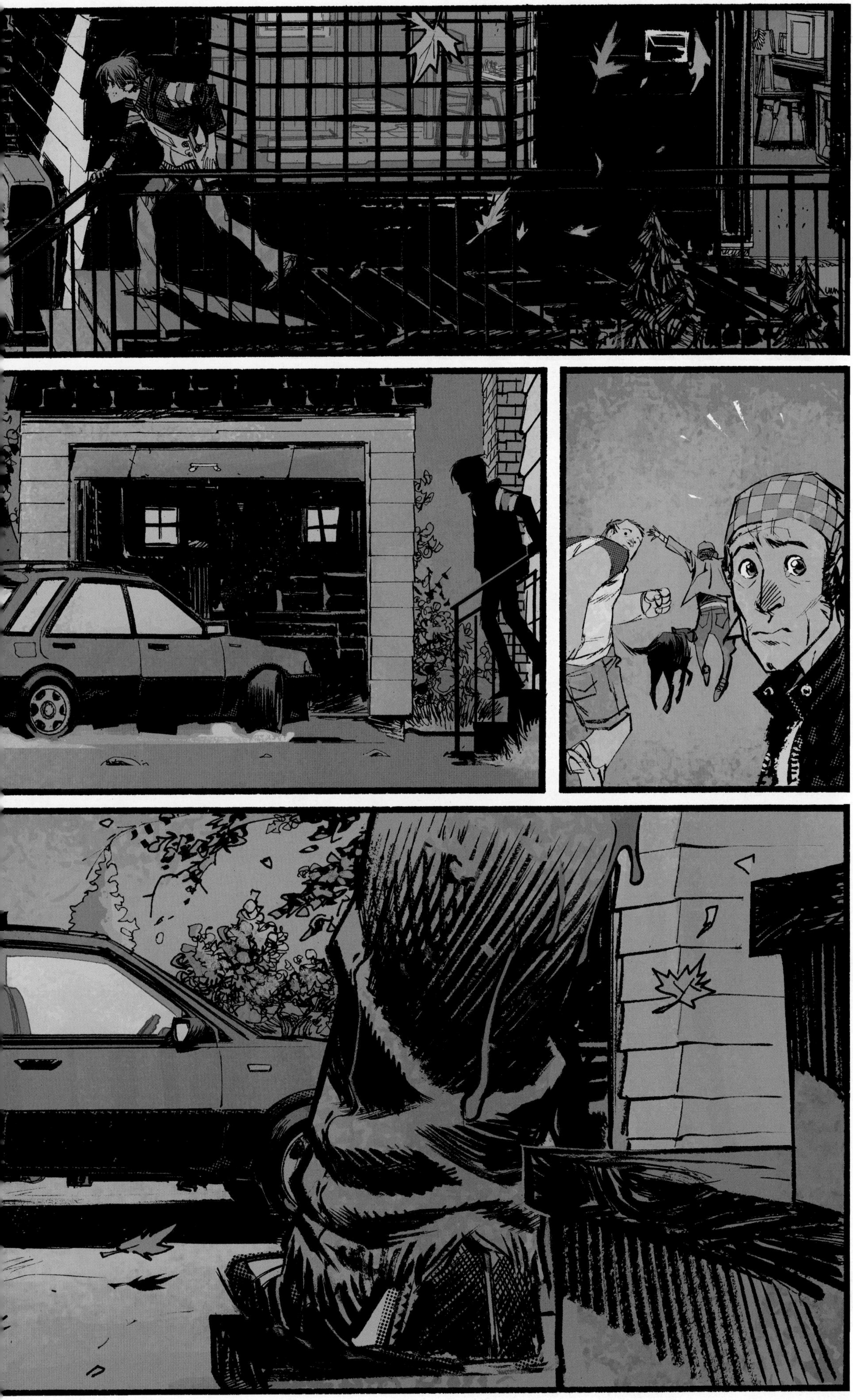

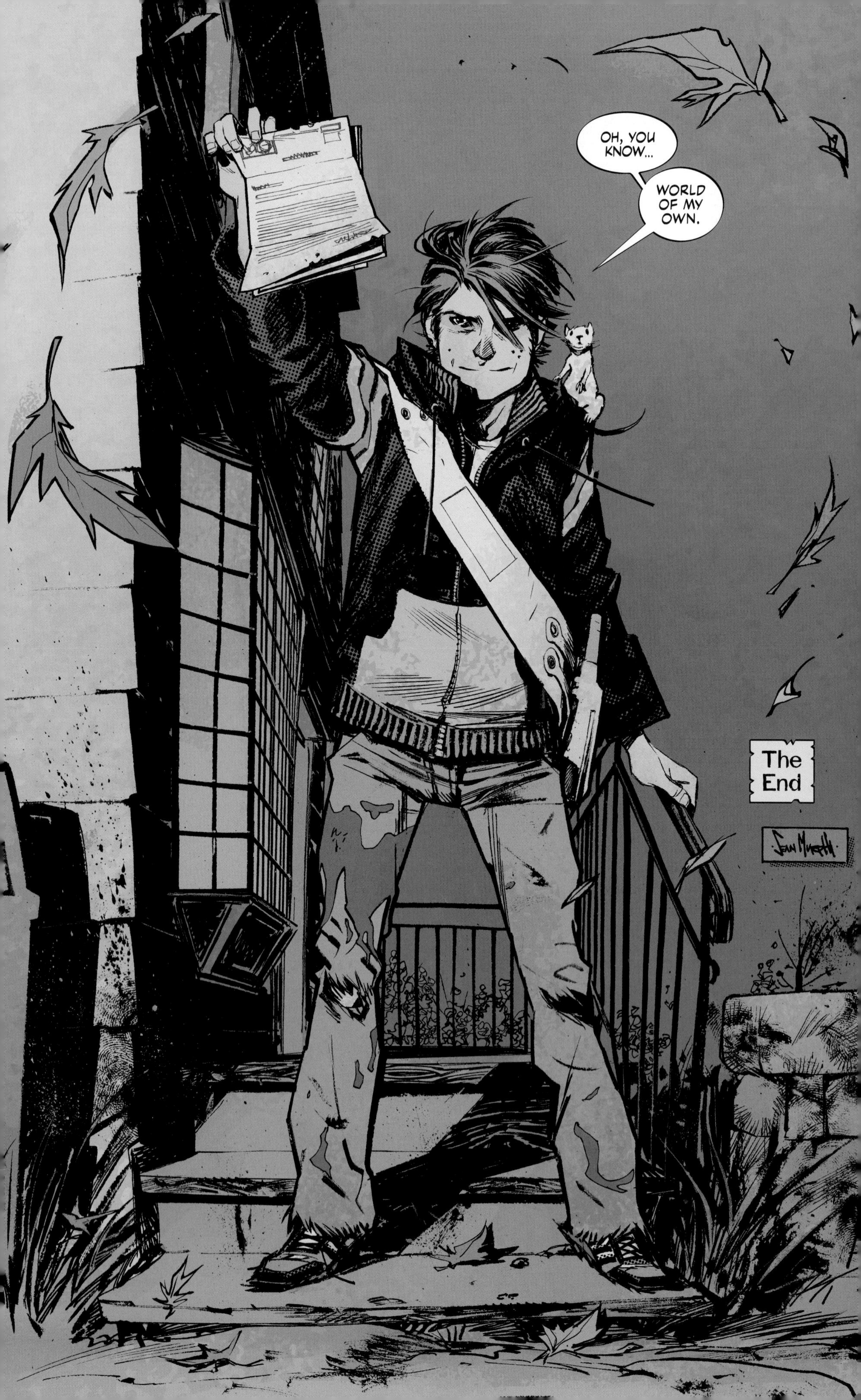
OH, YOU KNOW...
WORLD OF MY OWN.
The End

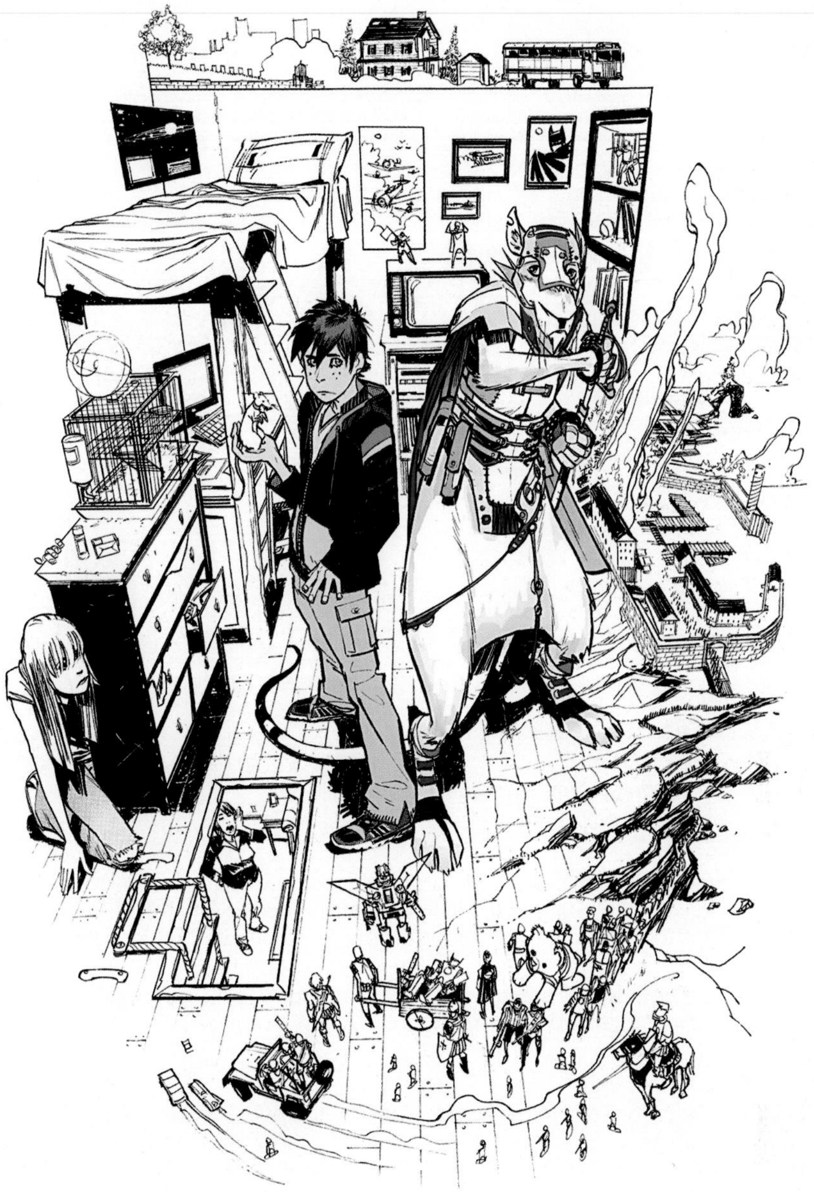

# FROM HYPOGLYCEMIC TO HYPOGEA

## *Drawing up the Iron Kingdom*

*with* GRANT MORRISON *and* SEAN MURPHY

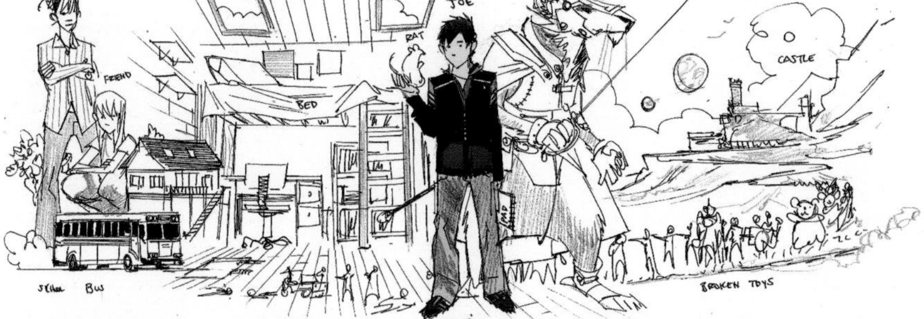
MOM
SKYLIGHTS
RAT WARRIOR
JOE
RAT
FRIEND
BED
CASTLE
SCHOOL BUS
TOYS
PILLS
BROKEN TOYS

*Initial sketch and final art for a promotional image by Sean Murphy displayed at the 2009 Comic-Con International in San Diego.*

# The House & The World

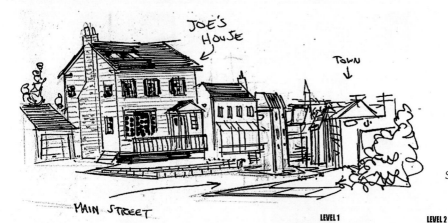

*Sean Murphy's design and floor plan for Joe's house.*

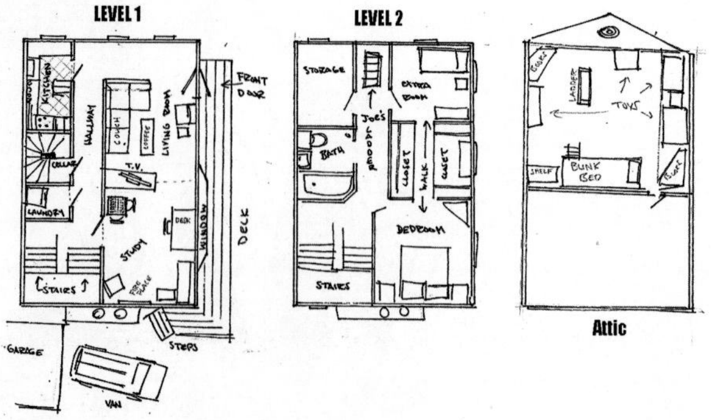

LEVEL 1  LEVEL 2  Attic

## JOE THE BARBARIAN  issue 1

### PAGE 15

**Frame 1**  Close up on Jack gnawing the bars of his cage.

**Frame 2**  Close up on Joe's sweating face — eyes look down now.

    *Joe:*    JACK?

    *Joe:*    WHAT WAS THAT?

**Frame 3**  Joe POV — looking down the length of the bed — the duvet is bunched up like hills in a miniature landscape. In the lightning glare beyond, we see toys on the shelf at the far wall, casting wild shadows. Above them a star chart is pinned to the wall. Next to them, on the left, there's a peg with a couple of Joe's jackets hung there.

    *Joe:*    DID SOMEBODY SAY SOMETHING.

    *Joe:*    MOM?

    *Joe:*    WHAT TIME IS IT?

**Frame 4**  Go closer into the folds that rise like hills around us now, growing in scale and wrapping around us in 360° surround sound. The glow from beyond is like fire... the star chart become part of a night sky. Phosgene spots on Joe's retinae, still bright in the darkness after the lightning flash struck tiny flares of the reflective surfaces of the polished toys on the shelf, remain as points of light in the sky, constellations in the shape of the toys — the Car, the Soldier, the X-Box. The Tie-Fighter, etc.

### PAGE 16

**Frame 1**  Full-page pic as Joe goes into a hallucinatory state. He's standing in mid-distance, facing away from us on a winding road that descends through the jumbled duvet cover, which has now become a looming landscape of embroidered hills that rise on either side... dust bunnies — like tumbleweeds as big as sheep but made of stray threads and fluff — blow across the road in a little flock, fleeing from something.

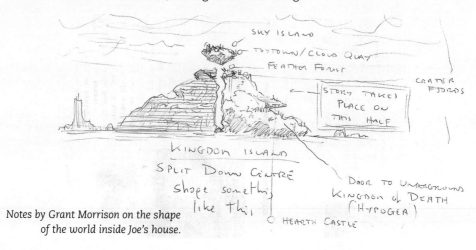

*Notes by Grant Morrison on the shape of the world inside Joe's house.*

BEACH
Bridge
forest
It's a HUGE ISLAND. as big as a COUNTRY
Feathers Forest
Sort of natural 'bowl' at the top with fjords
Island geography is arranged on a series of plateaux like the storeys of the house

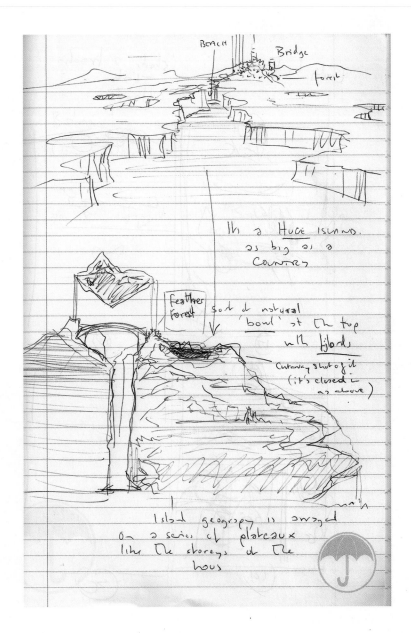

**JOE THE BARBARIAN** *issue 2*

**PAGE 1** The first-page panel arrangement is the same as in issue 1 — and we'll keep it consistent throughout the series so that the chapter titles and credits are always in the same place. So, as before, we have four panels in the centre of the page with one smaller one in the lower right corner next to the credits. These panels are inserts on 'white page' behind.

This time, drawings appear on the background white in this first panel — a MAP begins to be sketched out. It's like one of those Tolkien maps at the back of fantasy books and we see a new section of it in the first panel of every issue.

Here, we can see the FLOATING ISLAND in the top left and a little dotted trail leading down from the hills to TOYTOWN — which is arranged around the harbour area of CLOUD QUAY where huge sky-faring vessels shaped like cumulonimbus clouds are docked. From Cloud Quay, the dotted trail plummets DOWN to the much bigger island of the KINGDOM and a place called FEATHER FOREST next to BACKBONE BRIDGE (the island continent of the Kingdom is split mysteriously in two — like a giant human brain with its two hemispheres).

Our story takes place on one half of the island, leaving the other for any future sequels. The two halves of the Kingdom were once united by an incredible Kingdom Brunel-meets-Gaudi span called Backbone Bridge, which has been broken since the terrible Battle of Backbone Bridge generations ago.

# Character Designs

This helmet and this suit.

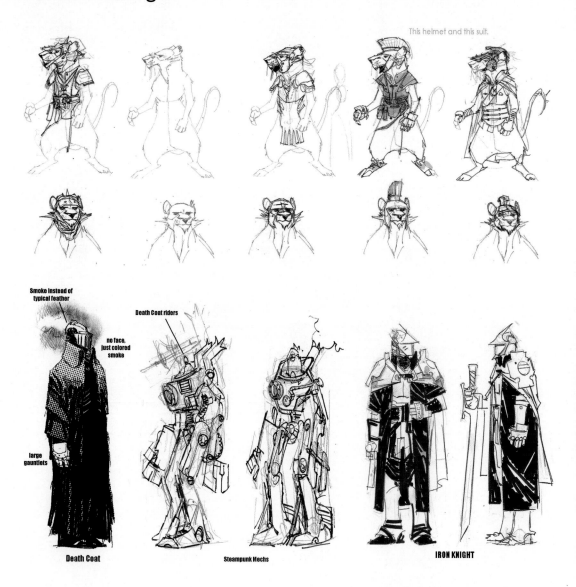

Smoke instead of typical feather

no face, just colored smoke

large gauntlets

**Death Coat**

Death Coat riders

**Steampunk Mechs**

**IRON KNIGHT**

Joe the Babaia

Plumes like flame (green/blue)

THEY LOOK LIKE CANDLES FLOATING ON RAGGED COAT TAILS...

(GLIMPSE OF SKELETAL RIBS -XRAY THRU COAT?) SOMETHING ALONG THESE LINES

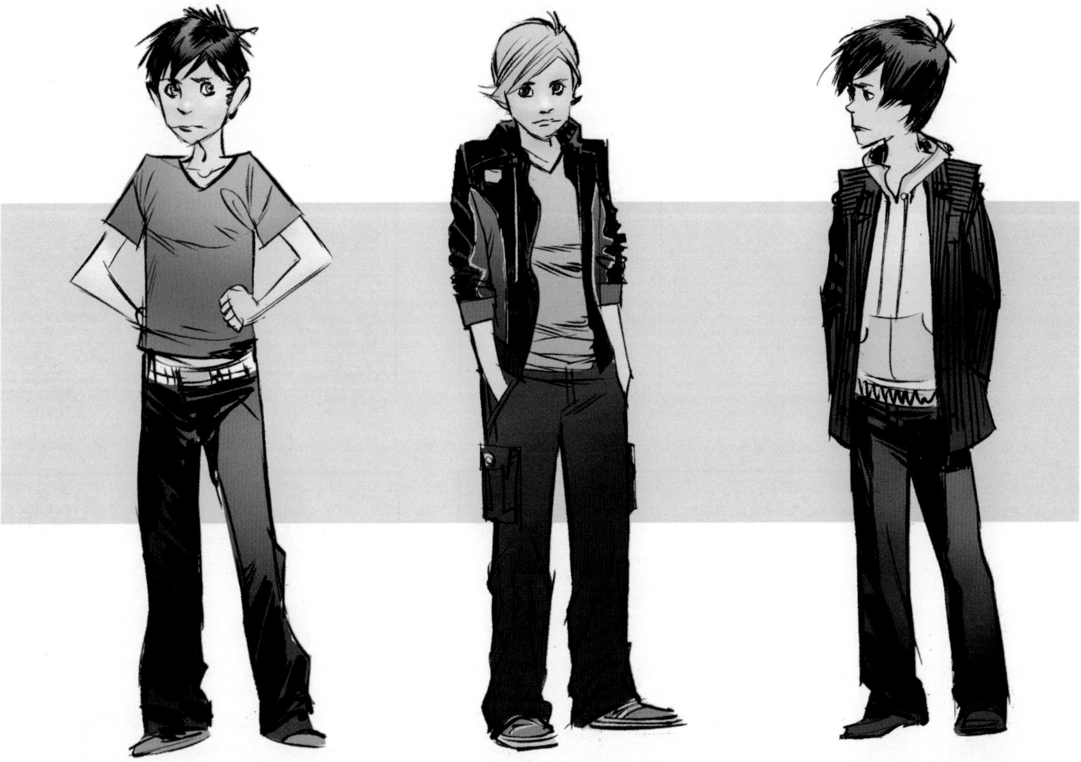

My favorite. If Joe is an introvert then I'm in favor of his hair covering his face a bit. And pale skin reflects someone whose mother is protective and doesn't want him playing outside. Fragile.

Too Harry Potter? Does Joe go to a private school or a public?

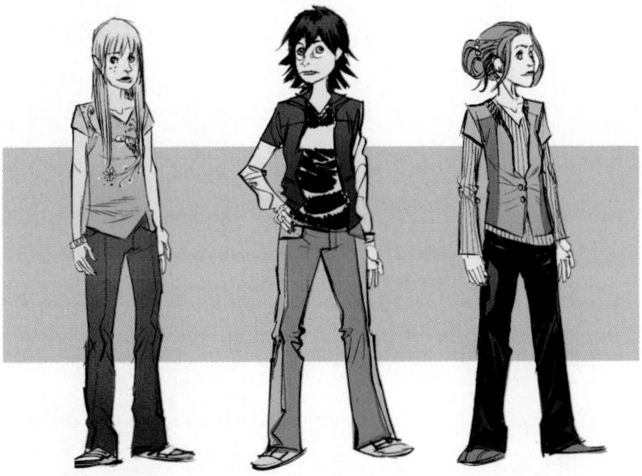

My favorite. Something about the blonde hair feels right. Maybe because Joe's world is so dark that she provides some light.

Young Poison Ivy? Haha.

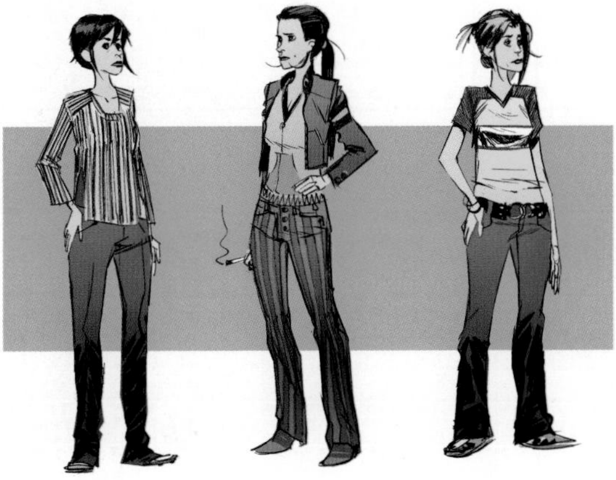

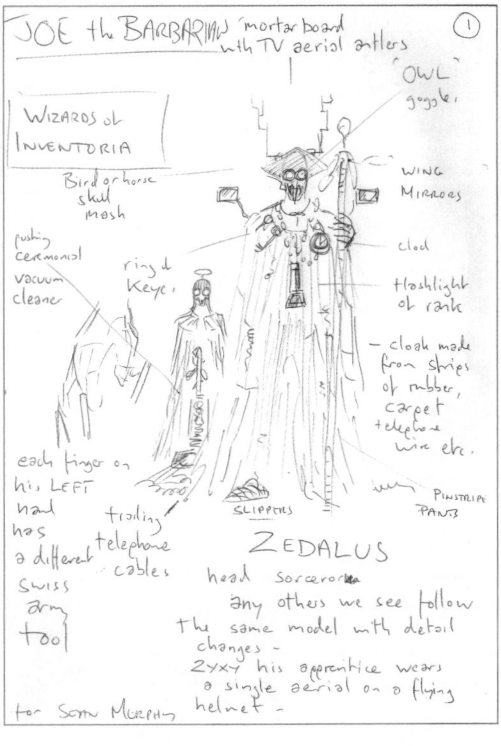

JOE the BARBARIAN
1
mortar board with TV aerial antlers
WIZARDS of INVENTORIA
"OWL" goggles
Bird or horse skull mask
WING MIRRORS
pushing ceremonial vacuum cleaner
ring of keys
clock
flashlight of rank
- cloak made from strips of rubber, carpet telephone wire etc.
each finger on his LEFT hand has a different Swiss army tool
trailing telephone cables
SLIPPERS
PINSTRIPE PANTS
ZEDALUS
head sorceror
any others we see follow the same model with detail changes -
ZYXY his apprentice wears a single aerial on a flying helmet -
for Sean Murphy

# Thumbnails

*Sean Murphy's complete layouts for issue #5.*

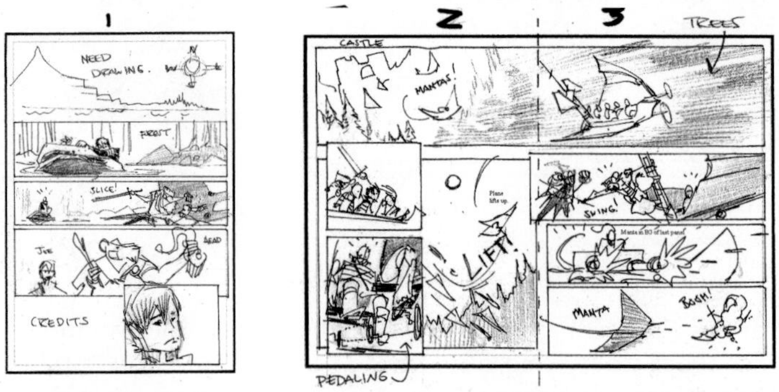

1
NEED DRAWING.
CREDITS
2
3
CASTLE
MANTAS!
TREES
LIFT!
SWING!
MANTA
BOSH!
PEDALING


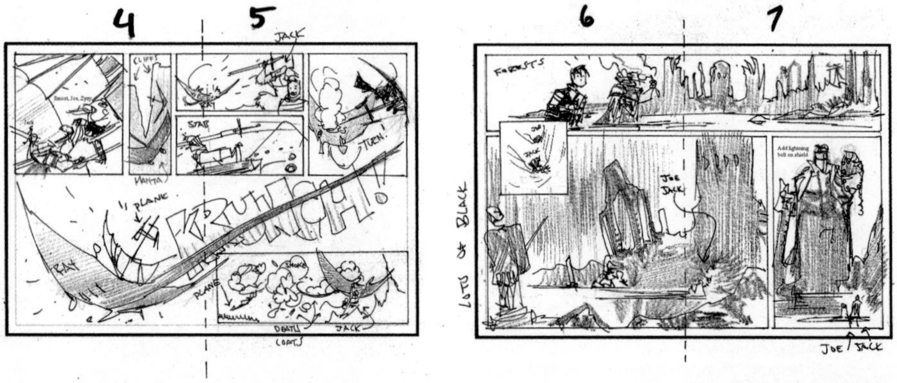

4
5
JACK
CLIFFS
STAB
TURN.
PLANE
KRUNCH!
DEATH COATS
6
7
FORESTS
LOTS OF BLACK
JOE JACK
Add lightning bolt on shield


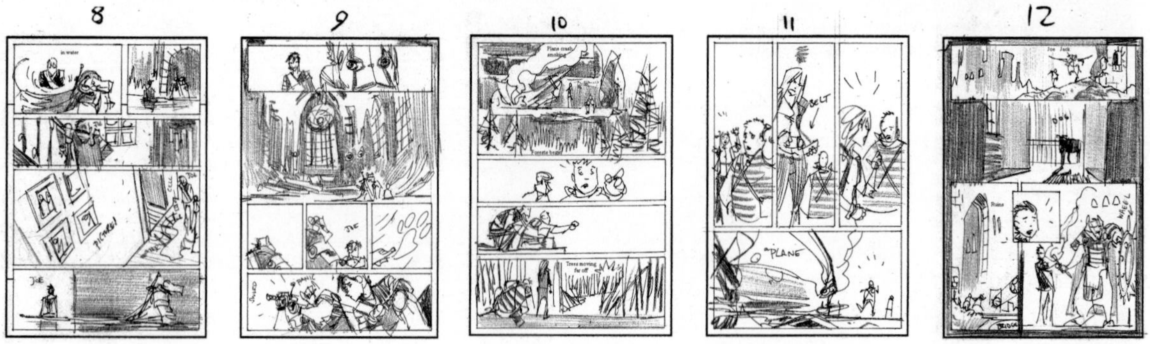

8
in water
PICTURE!
JOE
9
JOE
10
Plane crash smoking
Trees moving far off
11
BELT
PLANE
12
Joe Jack
Ruins


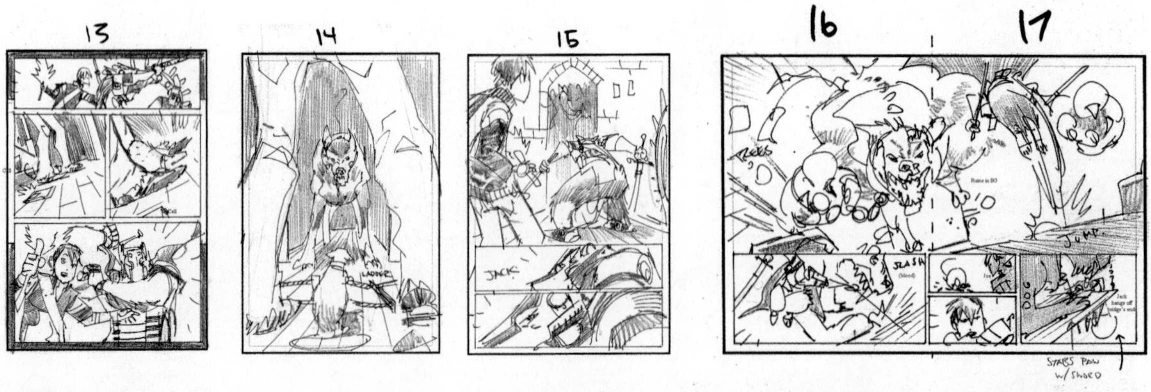

13
14
LADDER
15
JACK
16
17
TREES
Ruins in BG
SLASH
(blood)
JUMP
Jack hangs off bridge's end
STABS PAW W/SWORD


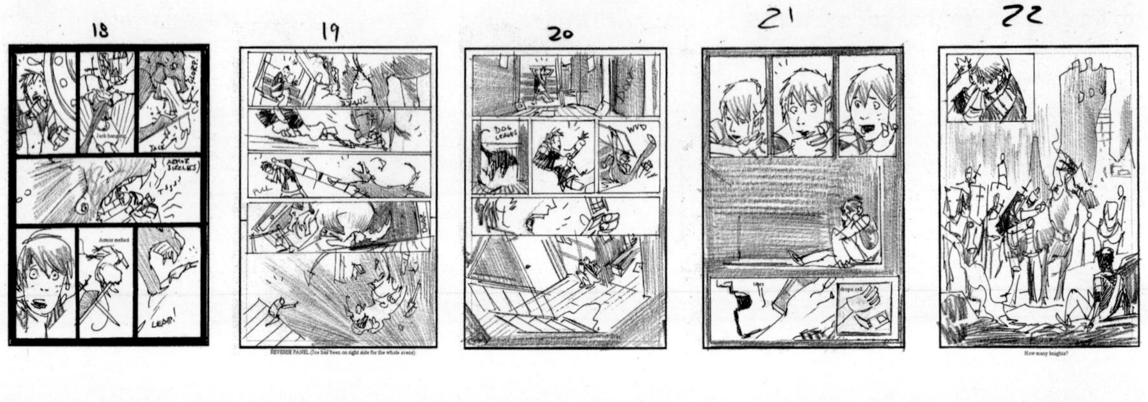

18
Jack hanging
Armor melted
LEAP!
19
REVERSE PANEL (Joe has been on right side for the whole scene)
20
DOG LEAVES
21
drops cell
22
How many knights?

# Storytelling Breakdown

*by Sean Murphy*

Grant's original script for issue #1 called for a silent sequence of Joe walking through his empty house. Because the details of the house were such an important part of the story, Grant wanted to be sure that the layout and room designs were clearly presented to the reader. Once Joe started hallucinating, each room design would present certain landscape elements for Joe to experience on his journey through each issue. Because the scene was running silent, I wanted to be sure that the art was interesting enough to hold the scene alone. Originally I thought that readers would think this sequence was boring, but to my surprise these pages turned out to be the ones applauded most by critics. Here are a few notes to help explain what I did and why.

• • • • •

**1.** The decor of the house wasn't specified, so I was able to run with a lot of ideas of my own that I hadn't seen done in comics before. The first choice I made was to decorate the house with bad '70s and '80s decor, something that I thought would really stand out to readers — especially those who were my age and had the unfortunate experience of growing up with horrible things like plaid couches, shag carpeting and hideous Navajo-style chairs.

**2.** The layout for panel one I kept very simple. I didn't want the reader to feel like anything too unusual was happening yet. As the panels progressed, however, I wanted to shift the camera to different angles to give readers a sense of eeriness. By putting the camera on the ceiling in panel two, I felt it helped disrupt the sense of balance in panel one. I chose to not show Joe's face because I feel that a character is in more danger when he's not noticing his surroundings.

**3.** I love pushing the blacks as much as I can, so a shot from the shadowy basement was a must. (While I didn't envision JOE as a dark book, I think it eventually turned into one because of how much I was playing with blacks.) This also allowed me to frame Joe as he looks warily toward the shadowy basement. If you aren't aware that something eerie is happening yet, this is the panel that makes it clearest.

**4.** A nice fish-eye effect really helped this shot. There are a hundred different ways to draw someone walking down a hallway where the reader will get bored. I was aiming to find the angles that got the reader interested in a scene that normally would have been dull. My goal was to have people thinking, "This is just a stupid scene of a kid walking through his house! So why can't I stop staring at these panels?"

**1.** Grant was clear about the photographs on the wall and about the staircase. I'm not sure if the script called for plants at the bottom of the stairs, but he eventually incorporated them into the series. I often felt that Grant was holding back on writing the script until he saw what I ended up drawing, then in each new script he would work around the details I'd added to the previous one. It was sort of like an improv performance: each artist working off what the other one did.

**2.** Again, this panel offered the chance to draw a lot of black — although I probably should have been more careful about the black at the bottom of the panel and how it blends in the with bleed panel underneath it.

**3.** This might be one of my favorite shots from the book. I decided to make the staircase twist around because it was more interesting — in reality, I doubt that a massive staircase like this would ever be built into such a small house, but in a comic book it makes for a great shot (even if an architect would shake his head).

**4.** I love tiny panels with small actions happening. Grant wanted to make it clear that Joe had dropped his bag. I believe that this was scripted as a four-panel page, to which I added a fifth panel specifically to show Joe dropping the bag. I hear that not only do most artists never add panels, but some of them even reduce the number of panels from what is listed in the script — something I would never do. I ended up adding panels every few pages to the entire script because I wanted the storytelling to be very clear. In a book where a lot of things are happening (toys coming to life, fantasy worlds, hallucinations, etc.), I was afraid that readers might get confused — so I made a point of trying to be as clear as possible with the art.

**5.** The best way to draw a chess board is from the side. That way you don't have to draw each annoying little piece in perspective.

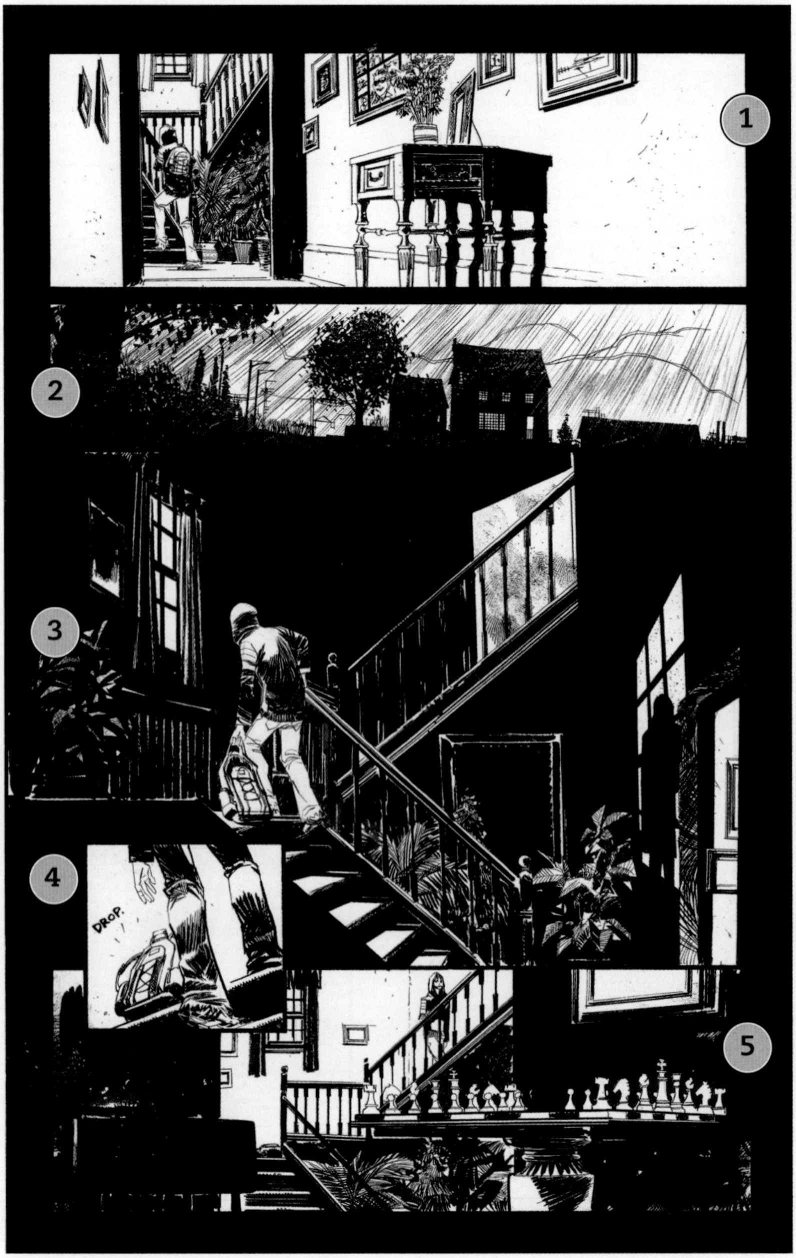

1
2
3
4
DROP.
5

When I sit down to lay out a story, my biggest concern is always clarity. I would rather have something be boring and clear than exciting and confusing. (The goal, of course, is to have it be clear and exciting.) A shot drawn in one-point perspective is usually clear, but it can also be boring. For this page I went with three one-point drawings, which is unusual for me. The reason I chanced it was because of all the details that I knew were going into the page. Even though Grant suggested things like soldiers, teddy bears and blocks, I couldn't resist drawing more specific toys from the '70s and '80s — stuff that I used to play with. Not only did this make the toys more interesting to draw, but it also became a selling point for a lot of readers. To this day, JOE THE BARBARIAN is described as "that book where the kid's toys all come to life." If I had gone with generic toys, I'm pretty sure the book would be tagged differently.

**1.** We start with a risky one-point perspective drawing. It's super symmetrical — another layout choice that can bite you in the ass — but because there are other panels helping to frame the shot, I'm more likely to get away with it.

**2.** Overlapping panels are tricky because if you overuse them they disrupt the storytelling. On Joe I tried to use them sparingly and with purpose. Because I wanted to draw attention to the bathroom (something clearly written into the script), I have panel two floating below the bathroom door so readers won't miss it. This panel also counts as one of those mini "one-action" panels that I love so much.

**3.** I'm not going to lie — this is the room I always wanted as a kid. I pretty much just glanced at the script and thought, "I don't even need to read this because I know exactly the type of room Joe should have!"

**4.** This shot was tough to figure out. The script called for a crow and I assumed it would take on some significance later on. But it never did. I think Grant threw in the crow just to mess with me. It did end up creating a very nice shot, though.

**1.** Any awesome bedroom of the '80s has to have a bunk bed. I picture Joe sitting up there on a rainy day, playing old-school video games with his pet rat scurrying off to the side.

**2.** I love drawing rain. I hate when artists leave rain to the colorist. For this shot I referenced the way Bill Watterson did rain in Calvin and Hobbes. With all the spotted blacks and rain textures, this panel ended up being a home run — and believe me, I'm not very secure in my work. Usually I dislike what I draw and lose sleep over it. So when something comes out okay at the end of the day, I'm thrilled because I know I'll sleep well. Drawing loose is fun, but because you're shooting from the hip with messy inks you're bound to screw up or get something you didn't plan on.

**3.** After the work that went into these pages, I felt a lot like Joe in this panel: I wanted to take a nap. This was actually a snap to draw because, in my mind, I was on top of that bunk bed and looking through the rainy skylight. Even now it's making me feel a bit drowsy. I can actually hear the rain.

**4.** I draw for black and white, so it's hard for me to leave anything for the colorist. Here I've left the job of color-holding that lightning bolt to the great Dave Stewart. Dave deserves a special shout-out for this entire scene. I don't usually give him a lot of color notes, but I loaded him up for this sequence. He probably thought I'd lost my mind when I started sending him horrible, yellowed pictures of broken-down '70s decor.